If These T-Shirts Could Talk…

50 years of GLBTQ+ Pride in Albuquerque

(1976-2026)

Dr. PJ Sedillo

New Mexico Highlands University

A Bright Child Books LLC Publication

Edited by Adam C. Laningham

This book is dedicated to all of those who have given their lives to supporting Pride in Albuquerque and to those 25 brave individuals who stepped up to start this movement. May this book record our historical, tireless, and countless efforts of volunteerism with the formation, creation, and continual growth of Albuquerque Pride, one of the largest GLBTQ+ Prides in the Southwest and New Mexico.

"Through our collective solidarity, all is possible."

The original book *Solidarity Through Pride (1976-2016) 40 Years* won best book 2018 in NM/Arizona with the sole purpose to continue honoring the legacy and history of Pride in the dessert known as Albuquerque Pride. Albuquerque Pride's first march was held in 1976 which is six years after the first Pride March held in New York. This is a remarkable feat for this little "beacon" of a city who had a Pride March to honor the Stonewall Riots. This sequel highlights 50 years of artifacts showcased at the Albuquerque Pride Pridefest which have included past official t-shirts. The oldest t-shirt is from 1981. Through extensive research no t-shirts were made prior to that year. Therefore, this book is intended to showcase those t-shirts and have them proclaim... PRIDE!

Forward

A book entitled *Solidarity Through Pride; 40 Years of GLBT Pride in Albuquerque (1976-2016)* published in 2017 by ABQ Press was written by Dr. PJ Sedillo. This book would go on to win best book from the New Mexico-Arizona Book Awards. The book was created to highlight over 350 panels which displayed Albuquerque Pride's memorabilia, documents, and artifacts. The book is now out of print. This new book was written with the sole purpose of continuing honoring the legacy and history, thus, highlighting 50 years of Pride in the desert known as Albuquerque Pride. Albuquerque Pride's first march was held in 1976, which is six years after the first Pride March held in New York. This is a remarkable feat for this little "beacon" of a city who presented a Pride March to honor the Stonewall Riots. Notably, this occurred before many larger cities in America. The number of 4'x 6'panels began to exceed 350. They highlighted past Prides in Albuquerque, which has made it difficult to showcase all of them each year. Notably, the Albuquerque Pride Board of Directors has approved unanimously to have the archives curated at a local university for future researchers to have access to this valuable archival history.

Since 2019 (except 2020 during the Pandemic), the only artifacts that have been showcased at the Albuquerque Pride Pridefest have been the past official t-shirts. The oldest T-shirt is from 1981. Through extensive research there were no t-Shirts made prior to that year. Therefore, this book is intended to highlight those t-shirts and have them proclaim, *If These T-Shirts Could Talk…50 of GLBTQ+ Pride in Albuquerque 1976-2026.*

ALBUQUERQUE (1976-2026)

TABLE OF CONTENTS

Chapter 1

Catalyst for the 1st Pride March in Albuquerque

What is the history and catalyst behind the many Pride Celebrations held throughout the world? Parades, picnics, marches, rallies all honor the Stonewall Riots, an event that took place in New York fifty-six years ago. The original Stonewall Inn was a Gay bar which catered to an assortment of patrons. It was popular at the time with the most ostracized people in the Gay community: transvestites, transgender people, effeminate young men, hustlers, and homeless youth. The Stonewall Riots were a series of spontaneous, violent demonstrations against a police raid that took place in the early morning hours of June 28, 1969, at the Stonewall Inn raids Greenwich Village neighborhood of New York City. The riots are frequently cited as the first instance in American history when people in the homosexual community fought back against a government-sponsored system that persecuted sexual minorities. The Stonewall Riots have become the defining event that marked the start of the Gay Rights Movement in the United States and around the world.

Questions have been posed about why this event became the defining moment in the Gay Rights Movement. What led to that night of riots? The individuals who were there at the riots have stated that there were no gay organizations in existence and that the apparent cause of the demonstration was unplanned and spontaneous. Fictitiously, historical recounts have cited Judy Garland's funeral services, which were on the same day, as the cause of the Stonewall Riots; however, there has been limited evidence or no substantial confirmation to support this as the possible cause.

What was happening in 1969? Gay Americans in the 1950's and 1960's faced many troubles and difficulties. Very few people had the courage to come out of the closet because of the social taboo. In many states, being who they are, was illegal, and there were consequences if one was found out. A person could be fired from his or her job, be labeled as mentally unstable, ridiculed and scorned, lose family and friends or in some cases even be murdered. People suspicious of a person's lifestyle could go to the law and have the person arrested. If one was Gay, he or she kept it "top secret". This was a time when most of the society did not know or even use the word Gay to describe homosexuals as well as other labels such as lesbian, bisexual and transgender. This also included the many letters that followed the acronym GLBT which did not exist. Segments of society did not want these individuals to exist as well. This was a time when the word gay (sometimes used derogatory) was transformed into a label for homosexuals to claim for a common solidarity, and for some years before the wide use of the word lesbian they were noted as Gay women.

It is important to note that many organizations prior to the 1980's utilized the acronym GLB, then changed to GLBT in the 1990's to include the transgender community and then altered to LGBT (starting with the letter L placed first and then the letter G second). This change occurred in the 1990's to support the women's movement and the immense efforts of the lesbian community during the AIDS crisis. Therefore, organizations prior to the 1980's have continued to utilize the acronym GLBT. The acronym has now become an extensive acronym. Therefore, as a survivor from the AIDs epidemic I identify sometimes by honoring referencing the acronym GLBT by honoring this owned heritage which allows me to refer and use this throughout this book.

As this book was being written the current acronym was LGBTQQI2SAA (Lesbian, Gay, Bisexual, Transgender, Queer, Questioning, Intersex, Two-Spirit, Asexual, Ally).

Gays who were living in the United States during this time had experienced very few establishments and businesses that welcomed them. Those who stood in the shadows would seek bars. The patrons of these establishments were at times the most ostracized individuals in the Gay community (drag queens, the homeless, transgender individuals, males who were effeminate and male prostitutes), and they frequently visited these bars. Reasons for the riots could be that these hated individuals had nothing to lose, and the Stonewall Inn was home to these outcasts.

Police raids on gay bars were routine in the 1960's, and the patrons came to expect them on a regular basis, usually once a month. It must be noted that many bar owners and managers were rarely gay. Like many other Gay bars in New York, the Stonewall Inn was owned by the Mafia. The managers of the bar usually knew about the raids due to "tip-offs" from the police. However, in the early morning hours of June 28, 1969, the police turned on the lights, turned off the music, and made the 250 patrons' line up. The patrons knew they were to take out their identification cards to be checked. Anyone in full drag was immediately arrested. Some of those who were in what was deemed proper attire were allowed to leave. Recollections were that women had to wear three pieces of clothing that was judged as feminine. If the clothing was deemed inappropriate; they would also be immediately arrested.

On Saturday, June 28, 1969, at 1:20 a.m. there were four plainclothes police officers and two uniformed officers who entered the double doors of the Stonewall Inn and announced their presence. Rumors had spread that the raid would occur; however, the raid took place much later than usual. The management's tip of the raid had been inaccurate. When the raid occurred, the officers called for backup utilizing the Stonewall Inn's pay telephone. They then secured and fastened the doors, but the designed raid did not go as planned. What was unusual about that night was that those who were not arrested and released at the front door did not leave. Those individuals who stopped outside and refused to leave created a crowd that began to grow to about 100 to 150 people.

What happened next was the birth of a new revolution that marks why Pride is celebrated around the world. The police began to kick more patrons out of the Stonewall Inn, but some began to make effeminate poses and salutes with limp wrists as they mocked the police. When the first paddy wagon arrived, the crowd had grown to 500 or 600 individuals who possessed intense anger, resentment and opposition. Pennies and bottles of beer began to be hurled at the police wagon. Then, one of the officers picked up and shoved a "butch" Lesbian who tried to escape from the wagon; she was hit on the head by a baton. This incited the crowd. This is when onlookers joined in the uprising. They assisted in turning this into a full-fledged riot. The police tried to confine the crowd, and because of this it encouraged the onlookers to fight back. This novel, historic, engagement against the status quo would change the course of brutality, injustice and non-acceptance for this segment of the population that society had reviled.

The police tried to control the crowd; however, it was too late. The police had to retreat and barricade themselves in the Stonewall Inn from the mob outside the doors. Rumor spread through the crowd that patrons still inside the bar were being beaten. This haven for gays had now become a haven for the police. Parking meters became battering rams. The mob next lit garbage cans on fire and broke the windows of the bar. The police tried to put out the fire, but the hose had no water pressure. The police inside were ready to use their weapons when the New York City Police and Fire Department came to their rescue.

Upon their arrival, they tried to assist the police who had been imprisoned in the bar for their safety. The police attempted to disperse the mob with a formation of force, but the crowd only mocked them with their own formation which was a chorus line with high kicks. The police rushed the group and began to bash their skulls with their nightsticks, and chaos ensued. The mob stopped cars and began to overturn them. This provoked the police who began chasing the angry protestors, but the protestors began retaliating by chasing the police.

Not until 4:00 a.m. did the first night of the riots end. Onlookers from the stoops and individuals gathered in Christopher Park. An amazed skepticism took place whether what had occurred was real or not, but the excitement lingered on. Thirteen brave individuals had been arrested, and some others were taken to hospitals for injuries along with the four traumatized police officers. The Stonewall Inn had been destroyed, but its foundation and walls survived and would be rebuilt. This revolution would ultimately become the foundation of Albuquerque Pride and other Prides in the world who would honor and never forget this powerful act of civil disobedience.

It is necessary and crucial that the Gay community realize that there is more to this historical event. Many recounts the story of the Stonewall Riots as one riot that took place in the wee hours of Saturday morning, June 28, 1969. It is important to realize that the riots continued Saturday during the day and many days that followed. This was a time when there were no cell phones, internet, tweeting, texting, or social media, which is the primary way now to gather and support one another immediately especially for Pride. Other riots would take place after the first one Saturday morning because it took longer to get the word out to the community about what had happened at the Stonewall Inn. Many had heard from others about what was happening in the Village. They showed up to see what all the commotion was about. Some wanted no part of this monumental event. Others believed that what they heard was untrue and wanted the see it firsthand. These reasons and many more would assist most of them in becoming part of this historical Gay movement.

All day Saturday people came to look at the burned-out shell of the Stonewall Inn. Graffiti was written on the walls of the bar with slogans of power, victory and accusations. Thousands had assembled in front of the Stonewall which surprisingly had opened its doors for business. This occurred because of the many supporters who decided to immediately rebuild the bar and show the power and unity of the Gay community. The only direction of the rebellion was to move forward with the realization that there was no turning back.

The next night, rioting resumed. Fires were started in garbage cans. Buses and cars were moved back and forth for those who did not support the demonstration. Others were harassed who were not there to support the revolution. Hundreds of police officers were present, but the kick lines were again in full force. The second day of riots and "Gay Power" lasted until 4:00 a.m. Monday and Tuesday were intermittent because of rain, but there were still confrontations with the police. By Wednesday *The Village Voice* had reported the riots with descriptions that were faultfinding and unfavorable. Five hundred to 1,000 individuals threatened to burn down the newspaper building, and another clash took place with multiple injuries to the police and demonstrators. This incident lasted only an hour, and the community felt they had won. More protests took place the next evening and several nights after. The weeks following saw the residents of Greenwich Village organize and create activist groups to deter future persecution of the Gay community. Within six months there were two gay activist organizations formed in New York, and three newspapers were begun for the promotion of rights for gays and lesbians.

On June 28, 1970, the first Gay Pride Marches took place in New York, Los Angeles, San Francisco and Chicago in commemoration of the Stonewall Riots. Similar marches were organized in other cities, one being the march that took place June of 1976, in Albuquerque which would lead into the creation of Albuquerque Pride. Today, Pride events are held throughout the world to commemorate the Stonewall Riots.

Chapter 2

Pre-Pride in Albuquerque

For historical purposes it is important to discuss events that occurred previously to the inception and creation of Albuquerque Pride. As in other cities, there were few places for gays to meet in Albuquerque, yet it was even more difficult because of the small size of Albuquerque compared to other metropolises. Throughout the narration of the Gay movement, historians have debated the inception of the gay equal rights movement. In the 1920's there were many openly gay characters on the stage on Broadway, and in the 1930's there were massive "drag balls" in big cities that attracted thousands and few gay bars in the bigger metropolitan cities. However, during this period, many Albuquerqueans held vile views of homosexuality. There were no formal celebratory places or organizations that catered to a Gay clientele. In the 1940's the only places for gay men to meet in Albuquerque were in the hotel men's rooms of the Franciscan, Alvarado and the old Hilton. They met for sexual encounters; however, in some cases lifelong friendships were formed.

Establishments - "Gay Bars" in Albuquerque

Not until the 1950's, did businesses who catered to a gay clientele open their doors. During this period were "home" parties and the few gay bars were the only places where the Gay community could congregate. There was also a gay night club in Tijeras Canyon. While not exclusively a gay nightspot there was Bills' a large country bar which was also named *The Limelight* as a pseudonym located in the mountains east of town. There was also the Pelican Bar on North Fourth Street, and Duke's Cave Bar in downtown Albuquerque. Finally, in 1958, on the corner of Central and Montclaire was the Heights Bar (owned by a Gay male couple) which would include the surrounding area known as the "cruise" where Gays would drive in their cars hoping that one would encounter others for sex. Gay hustlers would also congregate in this area. The Heights Bar would be set on fire one evening by some supposed arsonist, though the incident has never been solved or even dealt with by any officials from Albuquerque. The club would eventually be rebuilt with community and monetary support.

On Saturday nights in the summer of 1967, one would be able to attend the local gay bar called the Newsroom. There was dancing and the juke box was loud. Now and then a male would dance with a female but preponderantly it was same sex dancing.

When it was a song that the patrons knew many of them would sing along with the juke box. Lesbians remembered the Newsroom, located on Seventh and Central which was sometimes referred to as the *Pit*, a dive bar. Patrons said it was an awful looking horrible dump, but many had lots of fun there. The *Lavender Baedeker,* the earliest gay bar guidebook, directed Gay men and Lesbians to the Newsroom as well.

Another bar called Okie Joe's, located on the same block and one block east from the Franciscan Hotel, was an early cruising spot for gay men. While some may have found their way to these places via the guidebook, most seemed to have discovered the gay bars by word-of-mouth. Other bars would "pop up" in the late 60's. There was the Upstairs, located along the Old Route 66, an after-hours club that featured drag queen performers; and Cricket's, a private club for women, owned and operated by a Native American woman in the suburban area of Central and east of Coors. Cricket's was identified as a working-class Latina bar. Another primarily catered to the Lesbian community was The Rusty Cork (also known as Corkys) on San Mateo, north of the freeway. In the summer of 1976, the first march in Albuquerque for Pride would have 25 participants assembled at the Warehouse, an "after hours" bar, just off Central. It would eventually become the bar known as Kapps.

In the 1980's there was the 8300 Club, R & S express on 4214 Central, which would become Climax Bar and then Voyagers Bar and Grill. In 1983 (originally known as the Heights Bar [1970]) became a private members' bar which opened as the Albuquerque Social Club (ASC) on Central and Aliso. Other bars located on Central were Adam's Den (4418), The Coffee Shop (4501), and Foxes Booze and Cruise on Central north of Eubank known for the best drag shows highlighting RISCLEE (The Royal Imperial Sovereign Court of the Land of Enchantment Empire) now known as the NM Imperial Court System which touted that going there, "you better make sure that your shoes don't stick to the floor, but if they do you got the best free chicken dinner on Sundays."

The Ranch (later becoming Sidewinders) opened in 1990 along with a Lesbian Bar named Champagne Taste on Paseo del Norte south of Wyoming. In 1993, the bar known as 999's (nines) would eventually become the AMC (Albuquerque Mining Company) which would go to many decorated changes, one being a motorcycle hung in the middle of the bar where one would order drinks. When the bar closed for each evening "last call for alcohol", this was a time when the bar as many of the bars would kick everyone out, and all would congregate outside in the parking lot. It was a time to really connect with friends, those who had become one's own family, and finally the police would arrive and make all those "family members" be forced to deal with reality, the rainbow would be dissolved, and all would head home or to be with someone else at their home.

In 1997 there would be a new night club at 4100 Central known as Pulse (previously known as De Ja Vu which was a Lesbian bar that had mixed nights [Gay and Lesbians] on Wednesdays. This was located across from Albuquerque Social Club. Also, in 1997, another bar opened known as Club on Central (CLUB COC "K") north of Juan Tabo on Central.

In the 2000's, Rene's would become Exhale Night Club (Lesbian) and the Empire Bar would open directly south of the Pulse Night Club. During the early 2000's patrons could go to the Pulse, ASC (now known as the SOCH) and Empire in one night. Central Avenue was packed with the GLBT community as they could safely walk from one bar to another. It was a time when one felt like a "big" city. In 2016, Lotus Nightclub (alternative bar) would become known as Evolution located downtown. Effex would also open downtown along with Martini Bar in Nob Hill who was the owner of the Pulse Night Club.

However, things would drastically change during the Pandemic of 2020 which would cripple the existence of our Gay Bars and the legacy that had kept all of us together providing a place of sanctuary, safety, saneness, and wholeness. And, despite this plague of despair, like the AIDs epidemic, we continued to build and rebuild. After the closure of the Ranch/Sidewinders, where Martini Grill was located this would eventually become the current location of Sidewinders, and as of 2025 there are only four bars that cater specifically to the LGBTQ+ community which are Sidewinders, Effex, the QBar (gay friendly), and ASC. Currently, and sadly but only for the loss of the exclusivity of bars for the GLBTQ+ community, nightclubs have been able to accept all of us, all or our colorfulness, all our rainbow brilliance. Most "straight" bars in Albuquerque now accept those form the LBBTQ+ community and do not "bat an eye" when we choose to hold hands, dance together, of express our undevoted love on the dance floor.

For many years gay bars have always been sanctuaries for our community. They became the only place or "home" for the GLBT community to safely congregate. Upsettingly, gay bars have also been places for other individuals from society to persecute, harass, and execute hate crimes. Recently, there have been many closures of "gay bars" and a decline in LGBTQ+ clientele. Speculation for the possible demise of the "gay bar" has been attributed to social media, numerous individuals who now find it easier to come out of the shadows, and the general publics' positive views of homosexuality. There are also many other places for the LGBTQ+ community to meet. Many feel that the bar environment which had been for many years a positive separate gathering place for the GLBT community is no longer needed. Despite the current trends of these establishments honor must be given to the significance of their place in the gay historical movement. This includes all the "gay bars" past and present in Albuquerque instrumental in the formation of Pride in Albuquerque. Bar owners, managers and bar staff must all be acknowledged to play a big part in contributing to the groundwork of Albuquerque Pride.

Gay Organizations

The Mattachine Society was founded in 1950 by Harry Hay who would be instrumental in the second Pride March/Rally held in Albuquerque. The Mattachine Society was one of the earliest Gay rights organizations in America. At that time Gay rights organizations were known as homophile organizations. During the 1960's, numerous unaffiliated Mattachine Societies were started in the United States. San Francisco and New York Mattachine Societies became some of the strongest Gay rights groups in the United States, especially, following the Stonewall Riots; however, the Mattachine Society apparently never formed a chapter in Albuquerque.

The Stonewall Riots had sent a powerful message that eventually reached the borders of New Mexico and the University of New Mexico's (UNM) campus. A group proclaimed as the Gay Liberation sought a charter from UNM in the fall of 1970 which would become the first Gay organization in Albuquerque. The group tried to get a charter from the Associated Students of UNM using the name Gay Liberation which changed to the Gay Liberation Front (GLF) which was named for the ongoing positive developments in New York. This name change was to express a shift that the organization would no longer exist in the quiet resolve that the Gay community had experienced prior to Stonewall, but it would be a loud part of a new proud and out force destined to support the new political radicalism of the left. The GLF also published a newsletter; unfortunately, no copies have been located, and the organizations charter is no longer recorded at UNM.

The alternative Albuquerque newspaper during this time, known as the *Seer's Catalogue*, (located on microfilm at the Miami University Libraries) had a few stories that reported that the Albuquerque aided the national gay liberation movement by starting the Gay Liberation Front (GL-NM) in Albuquerque which promoted social gatherings, speakers and support groups run by a handful of gay and lesbian students. The *Seer's Catalogue* also noted that the organization evolved into the Gay People's Union. After receiving a charter from the University of New Mexico (UNM) on February 16, 1971, the organization put an article in the student newspaper welcoming gay, lesbian, bisexual, and heterosexual students to join. President Dan Butler posted flyers on campus and passed out handbills at local gay bars to gain interest. However, Butler lamented that "some of the other gays do nothing by go to the bars, and don't attend meetings. They're just not willing to stick out their necks." This could be due to the older New Mexican GLB's who in the past dealt with secrecy and a fear of involvement in an organization that identified someone as gay and would unmask their sexual orientation to family members and employers.

It is during the 1971-72 academic school year at UNM that the GL-NM President Mark Youtzy would expand the groups aims to self-acceptance, social acceptance by heterosexuals and fight legal problems. The GL-NM would follow suit and change its name to the Gay People's Union which would wither away but would be followed by Juniper in 1974 and then the Gay Co-op in 1976. Future organizations for Gay men and women would have many transformations.

It is important to recognize Juniper's existence in 1974 as this would be the organization that would be one of the founding organizations to put on the first Gay Pride March in Albuquerque. The logo for the group was a drawing of a small evergreen gripping the New Mexican soil. It is believed that the name change was to acquire more members who did not want to be outed with the word Gay as well as allies who wanted to join. One of the focuses of Juniper was to counteract counseling organizations and medical establishments who did not appropriately serve the needs of the Gay community. They put in a proposal for office space for counseling and a place for support groups to meet. At this time, there was a divide between the women and the men of the group on how to proceed. Further, difficulties for Juniper took place when the group approached the student government of the University of New Mexico for a request of $670 and space for an office which was approved. One of the UNM senators rejected the request based on personal moral reasons. Juniper resubmitted its charter to the Graduate Student Association where the budget was approved. The importance of this victory became the foundation for future Gay organizations including Albuquerque Pride.

Gay Religious Organizations

The flood of activism spread beyond the university, with the foundation of the Gay Co-op and the Metropolitan Community Church –a denomination of Christian churches noted for its outreach to gay men and lesbians. The years of 1974 and 1975 were extremely important for the Gay community in Albuquerque, New Mexico. With Juniper formally approved as a gay organization and sanctioned by UNM, they were able to provide some assistance in the formation in 1975 of the Metropolitan Community Church of Albuquerque.

The Universal Fellowship of Metropolitan Community Churches (MCC) was founded by Reverend Troy Perry in 1969. Perry who was a married Baptist/ Pentecostal pastor in California realized he was gay. He began to confront the contradictions that existed with Christian theology. This would lead him to divorce his wife, separate from the church, encounter suicide and eventually have a spiritual revelation that God loved him and all homosexuals. Because of his metamorphosis and revelation of unconditional love for homosexuals, he needed to proclaim the word of salvation, love and acceptance for all. This would become the cornerstone of the MCC chapters which began to spring up throughout the United States. Seven years later after the original formation from Reverend Troy Perry the Gay community would experience this faith-based organization in Albuquerque. His faith positively contributed worldwide to the GLBT movement and Pride in Albuquerque. Because of his positive contributions Reverend Troy Perry would become a speaker and honored dignitary for Albuquerque Pride. Metropolitan Community Church of Albuquerque is currently the oldest GLBTQ+ organization in the State of New Mexico, as Juniper no longer exists. Reverend Kris Dodds would become the first pastor of the Albuquerque MCC. The importance of a female pastor in New Mexico is noteworthy because it denounced traditional Christian denominations that refused the ordination of women. The church not only became a place of worship but became a well needed community center for the Albuquerque Gay community. The Albuquerque MCC would establish the first chapter of Albuquerque Alcoholics Anonymous for Gay men and women.

Under the direction of Dodds, a small study group began meeting in the living rooms of Albuquerque homes and eventually at the few gay bars, the Wellington, Foxes Booze and Cruise, and the two bath houses located in Albuquerque on Central by Aliso and on Central between Pennsylvania and Wyoming. Two years later in 1977, they had enough members to officially become a chartered church of MCC with its first official location at the corner of 120 Morningside Drive and Copper Avenue directly north of Central Avenue. Meeting at various places continued until 1980 when the small congregation moved into their first church building. Despite this milestone of having an actual building to congregate, the church did have many difficulties throughout the decades. The church experienced an intense separation in which the congregation was divided into two factions. Some members had reported the separation of the church was because of the infighting between the Gay men and Lesbians and others had stated the separation was due to different spiritual beliefs. For whatever reasons for the divide, it occurred. The actuality of two MCC churches existed in Albuquerque. They would be known as MCCA (Metropolitan Community Church of Albuquerque) and EMCC (Emanuel Metropolitan Community Church of Albuquerque). Not until 2000 would both churches finally become one united church again.

Arguably, MCC-ABQ's most important contribution to the gay and lesbian community was its cooperation in organizing Albuquerque's first Gay Pride March in 1976. Juniper, the gay and lesbian organization that formed in the wake of the Gay People's Union's demise, would work with MCC-ABQ to coordinate the march. Twenty-five pioneers marched in the parade that launched New Mexico's entrance into national pride celebrations.

Chapter 3

The Birth of Pride in Albuquerque

The Gay community of Albuquerque realized the importance of being visible to the greater Albuquerque community and understood that a parade would be a crucial opportunity to reach out to others who were not yet ready to make such a visible public statement. In 1975, talks began about entertaining the need for a Gay Pride march. The Gay and Lesbian Student Union proposed that a Christopher Street Celebration be held in June of that year. According to an announcement in Juniper's newspaper, *The Lavender Wing,* the event would consist of an art show, poetry reading, a dance, an Open House, a picnic, and a sexuality workshop. Despite these ambitious plans, the event never took place. One reason why the event did not occur was the group had several transformations. The formation of the original group was known as the Gay Liberation. Then it was changed to the Gay Liberation Front, and the final transition to the group known as Juniper. Each transitional change encountered a shuffle of leadership, loss of members, and obtaining new members with different visions and priorities. Finally, difficulties arose from not receiving official status as an organization from the UNM Student Associations. This caused Juniper to focus on the issue at hand which prevented an event from taking place in 1975.

It was not until the summer of 1976, that the newly formed Albuquerque MCC and Juniper worked together to organize the first Gay Pride march in Albuquerque and the State of New Mexico. This would be titled and themed as "Christopher Street Celebration." In 1975, other cities in the United States were having numerous marches which attracted thousands of Gay men and women who marched to honor the Stonewall Riots. The nearest Pride to Albuquerque during the 1970's was Denver, Colorado, which had its first Pride in 1974 experiencing thousands of participants.

The lack of experience of Juniper and MCC in producing large events in the past caused them to run into problems. They lacked the "know how." Also, there was a lack of organizational leadership. Who or what organization would be in charge, and who would be responsible, may have caused complications. Both groups did not know about the laws and permits needed to successfully produce a Pride march or any march in Albuquerque legally, especially one that would be so visible and "in-your-face" about Gay rights.

It is also important to remember that at this time both groups trying to create a Pride event in Albuquerque had no legal counsel and did not know how to petition the City Council. They also had no representation from the various departments of the City of Albuquerque who approved marches/rallies/parades, including Mayor Harry Kinney who was unaware of the actions being conducted by MCC of Albuquerque and Juniper. Mayor Kinney (Republican 74-77) would eventually become an important advocate and supporter of Pride events in Albuquerque.

Further stumbling blocks in making this first Pride event happen was that Juniper had experienced institutional struggles the year before, and MCC of Albuquerque, a newly established church, was also trying to define and develop their foundational purpose. Because of this, the outcome was a parade/march resulting with only twenty-five participants. Although this number was significantly low compared to what was happening around the country, it must not be seen as a negative, but as a positive. It was a start.

There have been many discrepancies on where the actual march took place. Reported facts were that it was on the north side of the sidewalk on Central Avenue; however, some have stated that it was somewhere between Washington and Aliso. Others have remembered that it was by San Mateo Boulevard. Researching this event has evidence that the many scenarios can be validated because participants had stated that marchers would be coming from various directions from Central and surrounding streets.

It was noted by some MCCA members that in the summer of 1976 (actual day unknown), congregants assembled at the Warehouse, an "after hours" bar, just off Central. MCCA would sometimes have church service at this establishment. The Warehouse would later become the bar known as Kapps. Eventually, all would meet and these twenty-five brave individuals marched for several blocks on the sidewalk of Central Avenue garnering no attention from the larger community and media and headed west to Yale Park (where the current UNM Bookstore resides).

Harry Hay founded an organization called the Lambdas de Santa Fe in 1977 but was a featured speaker at the first pride parade in 1976 in Albuquerque. Hay, one of twenty-five participants at the parade, conducted a speech and presented his radical new theories on "gay consciousness" to New Mexican Gay men and Lesbians. While living in New Mexico, Hay spent much of his time writing theories on "gay consciousness" in which he argued that Gays and Lesbians as "a separate people" had "unique contributions to make to the straight world."

Mimicking Lesbian separatism, Hay believed Gay men needed to discover homosexuality (especially creative growth and spirit) without the imposition of heterosexual norms. Hay's speech addressed the rise of the new right and the need for coalition politics to combat them: "A coalition of America's Scapegoat Minorities, working on consensus, can become a real force not only for holding the line against regression but for the grassroots impetus towards constructive social change." Hay's development of an analysis that linked sexism, racism, and homophobia resonated with the lingering radical contingent of Gay liberation politics in New Mexico.

Hay went on to explore how, "all Gays, women and men alike, had to learn to look at their world through the Hetero window using hetero-evolved language and hetero-male-evolved patterns of thought." As a result, Gay men and Lesbians viewed their world through the gay window – a shared perspective that linked all Gay men and women together. Not everyone bought into Hay's radical theories. "The gay window idea sounds just a little mystical," commented Bill (last name unknown) after the rally, "but I hear in it an idea of homosexuality as being something more than a description of who you're having sex with– that homosexuality may be an attitude." In the feminist lesbian community, the phrase 'woman-identified-woman' implied an ideology rather than a simple sexual preference.

Hay articulated a counterpart that embraced both genders. As the Gay Liberation movement sought to crystallize specific problems related to sexual identity and ways in which to combat them, radical ideas continued to ferment in gay and lesbian liberation politics. Hay attempted to bridge divisions between lesbian feminists and male gay liberationists by giving them a unified conception of oppression.

After the rally concluded, the brave participants went in different directions some went home, some to nearby bars; others back to the Warehouse where MCCA congregants would have a prayer service, and others to Morningside Park to rest and talk about what had occurred. A few of the individuals who did not know that the event was scheduled had just happened to be walking on Central Avenue and decided to join in. Michael (Midnyte) Telles remembers walking with friends on Central Avenue and stumbling across the march. He knew some of the individuals marching and decided to join them in their courageous chants. When it was over, and the protestors separated in different directions, Midnyte and a few decided to pick something up to eat and go to Morningside Park. Midnyte remembers that what they had just experienced did not seem to have any resonance at the time and figured it would not have any future significance. This is similarly how many of the protestors who participated in the Stonewall Riots had felt. These few brave individuals did not realize the significance and power of their voices. Their chorus of voices would start off meek and would eventually become one mighty voice, part of history, and be the start of Albuquerque, New Mexico's own historical Stonewall Riots.

Currently, there are only two art sculpture monuments dedicated to Gay Pride in the United States. There is a sculpture located outside at 51-53 Christopher Street in New York City adjacent of the Stonewall Inn in New York. The other is in Albuquerque, New Mexico at Morningside Park to commemorate the first march held in 1976. The significance of this monument, dedicated by Mayor Martin Chavez and the City Council, solidified the importance of that historical march and the Gay Pride movement in Albuquerque. The memorial's intent is to honor and commemorate all those heroic marchers who fought and gave their life so that Pride could exist in the city. One must not forget the importance of this event and must realize how significant this act of non-violent demonstration was. It was attempted despite the views of society towards homosexuality in the 1970's. Ultimately, one must remember that this feat was attempted, completed and would reverberate success for the future GLBT community in Albuquerque and the state of New Mexico.

Chapter 4

Pride in Albuquerque

Those twenty-five brave individuals who marched on Central Avenue in the summer of 1976 committed an act of non-violent demonstration protected by the First Amendment of the Bill of Rights. It states that Congress can make no law hindering the right of the people to peaceably assemble. The right to peaceably assemble for Gay Pride in Albuquerque has never been "out rightly spoken against" or viciously questioned by any elected city officials throughout the history of Pride in Albuquerque or at least not recorded in print, television or on the internet. Also, remarkably, throughout the years of celebrating Pride in Albuquerque, the march/parade has encountered limited opposition from the citizens of Albuquerque, many of the departments in the City of Albuquerque who approve events, and the many elected past mayors and city council members.

Dr. PJ Sedillo, a native of Albuquerque, and a past president, incorporator of Albuquerque Pride has provided a summation for this repeated occurrence for the limited opposition of this event, as well as a possible reason for this acceptable mindset that most Albuquerqueans hold. Sedillo has stated that "Albuquerque has always been a "mañana town" [town of tomorrow] or a "live and let live city." Numerous reporters who have interviewed Dr. Sedillo have noted this jokingly response to clarify his statements. When asked why there was a limited number of negative demonstrators who would be protesting the Pride event, Sedillo would respond "not that many protestors would be in attendance. They would be too busy making their signs the week after the event." Dr. Sedillo believes that this populous mentality has been one of the reasons why success has been secured for this annual event.

These simplified assumptions pertaining to others negatively demonstrating against Pride is somewhat true; however, Albuquerque which has always been known as a "mañana town," would also have its citizens come to an understanding that Pride in Albuquerque would always occur in June so "live and let live." Despite Albuquerque's citizens somewhat acceptances of a Pride march happening each year, the event has experienced hate from a few select churches and individuals. Adverse demonstrators have come out each year with limited support to try to stop the event by providing statements of damnation carved upon their vicious signs and verbally spewing hate reverberating from their megaphones. These repulsive acts have never stopped a Pride in Albuquerque from happening for 50 years. In turn, these demonstrations propelled against Albuquerque Pride have assisted the event to flourish by using outright disapproval to be revamped into becoming a positive force. This positivity is a creative aspect to the success for the Gay Rights Movement which has helped Pride in Albuquerque to produce each year an event that started off small but has become victoriously mighty.

It must be stated again from the first known article written about Pride in Albuquerque in the 1977 *SEERS Rio Grande Weekly* which reported, "For those who did attend, the march symbolized the growing solidarity among gays in Albuquerque, Santa Fe, and across the nation as a whole" thus indelibly infusing the eternal beliefs continued throughout the forty years. Notably, there has been a Pride event always scheduled on Central Avenue since 1976. Albuquerque Pride has become the oldest, continuous parade on Central Avenue even older than the New Mexico State Fair Parade which for some years did not have its event on Central Avenue.

Albuquerque Pride became its own entity in 1996, twenty years after the first march, after many GLBT organizations had dissolved. Albuquerque Pride has been distinguished as the most instrumental, influential GLBT organization in New Mexico whose parade rivals other Pride events held in the Southwest because of population differences. The Pride Parade has become one of the most beloved parades in Albuquerque catering to the GLBT community as well as mainstream Albuquerqueans. It has out shown other parades in Albuquerque, including the (EXPO) New Mexico State Fair Parade which Albuquerque Pride has also participated in with entries. From humble beginnings of a Pride March with twenty-five people walking defiantly on the sidewalks of Central Avenue in 1976, to forty years later, on the second Saturday in June, Albuquerque Pride delivered a three-mile parade with over 200 entries. Lanes on Central have been closed off and over fifty thousand spectators have been in attendance.

Albuquerque Pride's main purpose from its inception has been to be a positive, visible force and be the voice for all those individuals who have had to hide in the shadows of darkness not ready to burst out and be part of the rainbow. Even though Albuquerque Pride has developed and flourished, this organization, like so many others, has had many "ups and downs." In some cases, there have been controversial proposals to Pride, questions of ownership, visibility issues, leadership difficulties, and mistrust in finances. Pride in Albuquerque since 1976 would encounter many other difficulties throughout the decades.

Throughout the history of the Gay Rights Movement in Albuquerque, light must be shed on the many Gay organizations that began, ended and/or were reformed, the multiple disagreements and different agendas between the Gay and Lesbian community, the pitfalls in the city, politics and political views, the AIDS crisis, the devastating deaths of some of the most influential Gay leaders, the hate crimes committed, and the unconventional laws and ordinances against the Gay community.

These circumstances were at the forefront of what could have become the possible destruction and ruination of Pride in Albuquerque. Struggles plagued Albuquerque Pride throughout the years and some of these would outright drive a wedge and separate the very heart and spirit of the Gay community. The possibility of not having a Pride in Albuquerque each year could have easily happened, but luckily it did not. The significance of recording, revealing and presenting the history of Pride in Albuquerque has been to bestow information concerning how intricate, volatile and fragile it has been for this organization to even exist and for the Pride Parade and event to have taken place each year.

SEERS Rio Grande Weekly 25¢

Out of the Closets — into the Streets

Overview page 2

1977

This newspaper article highlights "Albuquerque's second gay right's march." Albuquerque Pride has found no other articles pertaining to the 1st gay rights march.

<Pride Fact

Gay Rights Overview

The Closets Aren't Empty—the Streets Aren't Easy

First known article written about Pride in Albuquerque in the 1977 SEERS Rio Grande Weekly

Chapter 5

Pride in Albuquerque in the 70's (1977-1979)

In the face of all these complexities for Pride in Albuquerque, the function and purpose of this event have endured and has become a phoenix or 'roadrunner' (New Mexico's State Bird) rising out of the ashes to ensure that a Pride Parade and event in Albuquerque would take place each year, successfully for 50 years. This accomplishment shepherded in a city located in the desert Southwest should be shouted with praise and acclamations from the peaks of the Sandia Mountains.

Pride in Albuquerque, 1977

In 1977, Albuquerque's second Gay Pride March would have one hundred marchers, and Gay Pride Week would be celebrated from June 19th to the 26th; however, no documents have been located to support what events took place during that time-period beside a march and rally. It is evident that the few homophile organizations that existed in Albuquerque especially with the leadership of Reverend Kris Dodds, the pastor from MCC of Albuquerque and congregant Dan Butler. They were able to successfully produce a Pride event that symbolized the growing sense of Gay, Lesbian, Bisexual (GLB) Pride in Albuquerque.

During the post-parade rally, Rev. Dodds (MCC-ABQ), Dan Butler (Gay Co-Op), Katherine Davenport (Santa Fe Lambdas) and Harry Hay (Circle of Loving Companions) addressed the crowd. The parade brought together activists from all over the state and provided and an arena for diverse gay men and lesbians to come together proudly. For example, Bobby Maestra, born June 6, 1957, in Santa Fe, New Mexico grew up in a large Hispano family. Maestra attended Albuquerque's second pride parade. He would state "that it was time for him to step up even if it meant losing his family, job, and life." It is those many brave individuals who have been forgotten in time because our history has not been recorded and sometimes literally destroyed. Rev. Dodds of MCC-ABQ led the parade stating its purpose was to:

> Make gay people visible in the community. You can't obtain your rights without visibility. We would like to have job security. We would like to go into open housing. We would like our gay parents to be able to retain their children.

Reverend Kris Dodds (noted as Reverend Chris Dodson in the *SEERS Rio Grande Weekly*) stated, "There is a lot of work ahead of us, but when we get a 400% increase in one year, I know that we are on the right track." Reverend Dodds, realizing the importance of the march also stated, "I'm thinking about those of us who aren't here marching, who're unable as yet to come out, and I'm thinking about next year."

Permits were not obtained for this march which began at MCC of Albuquerque's location (Silver and Morningside) and followed a three-mile route westward on the sidewalk of Central Avenue crossed the street and then proceeded back eastbound on the southside of the sidewalk on Central Avenue to Morningside Park. As reported in Seer's Catalogue the march drew little attention as participants chanted "two-four-six-eight, gay is just as good as straight, A-B-C-D, gay's the way I want to be, and out of the closets and into the streets!"

Unlike the first Pride event held in Albuquerque in 1976 that garnered twenty-five participants, this unaccustomed and unusual spectacle would be the first real encounter that Albuquerqueans would have to confront and deal with an openly homophile organization and Gays who could be their neighbors, co-workers, teachers, friends and family members. The greater community of Albuquerque, which involuntarily experienced this march, stared with bewildered and amusement. Some onlookers would thrust an occasional harassment with professed hecklings, boos, and name calling which at one point would become physical thrusts of harassment resulting in eggs being hurled at the group. Rev. Dodds stated that, "They can't shame us and they can't stop us." Those who did attend the march would symbolize the growing solidarity among Gays in Albuquerque, Santa Fe, and across the nation.

To receive more visibility from the mainstream media the Gay community would invite the North Valley Gospel Church to participate in the Gay Pride March. This ultra-conservative church would show up with protesters in hand. Pamphlets were distributed proclaiming, "I Was Gay, But Jesus Set Me Free."

After the march a rally took place at Morningside Park. Albuquerque's Gay community would host the founder of the Mattachine Society at the second Pride march and the first official Pride Rally held in Albuquerque. Harry Hay (noted in the *SEERS Rio Grande Weekly* as Henry Hay) would speak at the rally. He would receive a standing ovation and talk about how the exclusivity of Gay neighborhoods would be the detriment to the Gay movement.

His statements were reported in SEERS alternative newspaper as follows: "The world that we see beyond, through our gay window, calls us to engagement and responsibility. We are forced to struggle ceaselessly and with utmost alertness through an unmapped world full of traps and hazards. Among these is an invitation to self-betrayal particularly cruel, the 'gay ghetto' with its agony under the tinsel, dealing out death to the spirt but surfaced with glamour." His harsh remarks pertaining to the pitfalls of gay neighborhoods tried to be an important message; however, he did not realize that Albuquerqueans had never had a specific 'gayborhood' (gay neighborhood) or specific section of the city that was inhabited solely by gays. The Nob Hill District could essentially be noted as the "gayborhood" in Albuquerque; however, this has never been proclaimed or substantiated. The participants at the rally had a limited understanding of the impact of Gay neighborhoods and were somewhat confused at the point he was trying to make during his speech. The most important message received was that the Gay community had no control over any section of the city.

Juniper and MCC of Albuquerque would be able to beam in the spirit and success of the march despite some of the friends and lovers who had declined to march out of fear of identification. After the event was concluded, some would go back home, and others would return to the MCC parking lot to discover that their cars had been egged. One lesbian marcher responded, "That's okay, 'straights aren't used to us—we've been invisible or socially ghettoized for centuries. But our time has come. The homophobes and hatemongers will just have to look out because we're coming out and we're not going back."

By 1977, several members of Juniper decided to reach the greater Gay population than solely servicing the students, faculty and staff at UNM's campus. Another group was created and become the Gay Co-op which would open its doors as an alternative community center located on the corner of Girard and Central Avenue. The chief purpose of the Gay Co-op was to be a beacon to serve the entire Gay community of Albuquerque which was the similar definition of Juniper; however, the Gay Co-op tried to provide services to Gay people throughout the city. The Gay Co-op also tried to actively communicate to the community by publishing a newsletter that was distributed throughout the various gay bars in the city. It, thus, became the first organization to reach out and educate individuals about the important and current issues facing the Albuquerque Gay community.

One of the newsletters in 1977 reported the overwhelming frustration for the organization to incorporate and become a non-profit organization. The idea for the Gay Co-op to incorporate and become a non-profit would be the ultimate destruction of this organization as would many Gay organizations for decades to follow because of wanting to incorporate. This would include the backlash from the Gay community when Albuquerque Pride became incorporated to file for their non-profit status.

In, 1977, the community tackled two concerns for the Gay community which was highly promoted during the Pride event held in Albuquerque. Foremost, Albuquerque Gay activists created the first Gay Voter Guide. This was significant because the Gay community became part of the "politics" of Albuquerque to proclaim which candidates supported their endeavors with verbatim quotes. The Voter Guide presented the following brief paragraph:

> This guide has been compiled to inform Gay people of the status of Gay rights in this municipal election. All city council candidates were asked whether they would vote in favor of the pending expansion of the city's Human Rights ordinance to prohibit discrimination on the basis of sexual or affection preference and marital status. Each of the candidates understood, that his/her responses were intended for publications. All candidates for mayor were questioned at a mayoral forum if they would support the amendments.

Several candidates were positive about the voter guide and would participate with the 1977 Pride event. The mayoral incumbent, Harry Kinney, stated in this pamphlet "[he] does not believe that discrimination exists." The Mayoral Candidate, David Rusk, responded in the Gay Voter Guide "I will work for passage of both amendments." David Rusk would be declared Albuquerque's next mayor. There is no data that supports that this Voter Guide assisted in David Rusk becoming Albuquerque's Mayor. However, there were also many negative responses from those who participated in the Gay Voter Guide.

Paul Demos, a Mayoral candidate, emphatically opposed both amendments and stated, "if this will help homosexuals, no, never!" Robert Welsh, a city council candidate from District 7, stated that he was "absolutely opposed to gay rights, [Gays] will infect schools."

The second issue facing the community was known as The Anita Bryant Affect. Anita Jane Bryant was an American singer, former Miss Oklahoma beauty pageant winner, and former spokeswoman/brand ambassador for the Florida Citrus Commission which markets orange juice. In 1977, she was notably recognized in the GLBT community as an outspoken opponent of Gay rights. Her "Save Our Children" campaign to repeal a local ordinance in Dade County, Florida would have prohibited discrimination on the basis of sexual orientation. It spread across the nation with evangelist Jerry Falwell assisting her. During the campaign Anita Bryant stated, "As a mother, I know that homosexuals cannot biologically reproduce children; therefore, they must recruit our children." She also declared, "If gays are granted rights, next we'll have to give rights to prostitutes and to people who sleep with St. Bernard's and to nail biters." On June 7, 1977, Bryant's campaign led to a repeal of the Dade County anti-discrimination ordinance by a margin of 69 to 31 percent.

The success of Bryant's campaign galvanized her opponents, and the Gay community retaliated against her by organizing a boycott of orange juice. Gay bars all over the United States took screwdrivers, a drink made with vodka and orange juice, off their drink menus and replaced them with the "Anita Bryant," which was made with vodka and apple juice. Sales and proceeds went to Gay civil rights activists to help fund their fight against Bryant and her campaign. In Albuquerque, a handout was passed out during the Pride event. It was titled "Squeeze Anita, take the Pledge." The handout stated:

> The Florida Citrus Commission has consistently refused to end job discrimination against Gay People. The President of the Florida Farm Bureau Federation has issued a statement supporting the bigoted views of Anita Bryant, the nationally known peddler of Florida Citrus products. Do you really care who picks your oranges?
>
> If you believe in Human Rights, boycott the following brand name Florida Citrus products:
>
> MINUTE MAID - SNOWCROP - DONALD DUCK - BLUE BIRD - TROPICANA - ASTER - TROPICALO
>
> Every lesbian and Gay man should ask their grocer if they sell Florida Citrus products or produce. Ask at restaurants that you frequent if they use Florida Citrus products or produce.
>
> If you know establishments that are trafficking in Florida Citrus, please contact
>
> SCURVY FIRST! COMMITTEE 842-XXXX
>
> The following are some of the local supermarkets that presently carry Florida Citrus fruits:
>
> BAG & SAVE CAMPUS MARKET EL CAMBIO NOB HILL
>
> Let She Who is Without Sin Cast the First Orange.

Albuquerque's GLBT community was only one of the many Gay communities with counter campaigns across the nation which tried to stop this hateful campaign from spreading throughout the United States. The Gay activists boycott would also become an issue at every "dinner table" conversation especially when prominent celebrities like Barbara Streisand, Mary Tyler Moore, Bette Midler, Charles Schulz to name a few, supported the boycott. Ultimately, her involvement in this anti-gay campaign significantly affected her popularity and career in show business. She had multiple bankruptcies and was fired from the Florida Citrus Commission.

The bars in the Gay community had become essential meeting places and supporters of Pride in Albuquerque. In 1977, after selling the Foxes Booze and Cruize, Dave Mauer opened the Albuquerque Social Club (ASC) on Morningside and Central where Mildred's (bar) used to be. He had been paying on a leased alcohol license and decided not to waste his money; therefore, he bought a private club license. At that point Dave Mauer became the lifetime member, and everyone else was sold a yearly membership at $10.00 which allowed them to access the club all year. This became "the" disco in town. Shows and dancing and afterhours made this the "it" place in town. During its heyday, the ASC hosted a bath house type area, after hour's discos, coffee house, restaurant, and leather room. The ASC also had a porn theater with a screen and theater chairs and a room that sold sexual "toys" and videos.

Sometime in 1977, Adams Den appeared on the scene. It was housed in the same building on Adams and Central where The Office was. It was noted as "trash" but lively and had a very accessible bar which was completely opposite from the restricted and regulated bar known as The Office. Adam's Den housed a high-tech light show that only worked half of the time. The ASC and Adams Den would host Pride events in June and be the place to go after the march.

Pride in Albuquerque, 1978

In 1978, members of the Co-op debated incorporation issues. This is important because this issue would face the demise of future GLBT organizations in Albuquerque, one being Albuquerque Pride. The Co-op pleaded to the community that the organization needed to incorporate so that it could then seek non-profit status; however, the community did not want the organization to become a business. Because of this, the organization proposed to change its name to GALA (Gays and Lesbians of Albuquerque Inc.). This change of name also presented a clear distinction between the men and women of Albuquerque. During the meeting to change the name, there was hostility especially with individuals expressing that the name was likened to a faggot organization. After the intense meeting, the final selected name would be GLCAA the Gay and Lesbian Community Association of Albuquerque.

The next step would be to talk about the organization becoming incorporated. This would be a controversy that divided the gender lines between Gay men and Lesbians. Russel Gray, a lawyer, led the movement to incorporate. Professionals Jon Hull and Richard Koteras also led the charge for incorporation to end the secrecy of membership. Jon Hull felt that pseudonyms would no longer benefit the future of the organization. Eventually the opposition to incorporation would lead to the demise of the organization.

Despite the turmoil happening in the community, Pride was celebrated in 1978. Gay Pride Week would be scheduled for June 18-24, and the Gay Pride Week Committee would meet in April to prepare for the annual event. Since the event had grown, a committee needed to handle all the events. Also, a social group started in 1978 known as Hijos del Sol, which was only open to Gay men. It assisted with the planning of Pride as well. The group would later change its name to the “New Mexico Outdoors” group. Individuals from the committee met during each week at The Rusty Cork (AKA Corkys) a pool bar, which primarily catered to Lesbians. It was off San Mateo behind Denny's.

1978 the first motorized unit was added to the annual march. The Parents and Friends of Lesbians and Gays decorated a van owned by John Wright and John Hunt with a sign that read “Proud Parents of Gays and Lesbians,” and John Hunt's mother, Betty Hund, rode up front to demonstrate her support. The '78 march began at the Heights Bar, now the Albuquerque Social Club headed down Central and ended at Roosevelt Park with a rally. Harry Hay was again the featured speaker at the rally. The owner of the Heights at the time, Dave Maurer, provided free coffee and donuts to the marchers. One of the other speakers at the rally was Reverend Troy Perry. Crickets, a women's club opened on 4th street, became one of Pride's first official sponsors of the event with its provided financial support. Crickets would eventually relocate to 55th and Central and became the meeting place for the West Side.

Despite the turmoil of the various Gay organizations, the community was able to have the Pride event in 1978. Notably in 1978, Gilbert Baker a San Franciscan would create the rainbow flag. The original Gay-pride flag was hand-dyed by Baker. It first flew in the San Francisco Gay Freedom Day Parade on June 25, 1978. Gilbert Baker would be honored as a Grand Marshal for Albuquerque Pride in 2010.

Pride in Albuquerque, 1979

In 1979, the Pride event held in Albuquerque was organized by The New Mexico Coalition of Lesbian Rights Organizations. The event was entitled Lesbian & Gay Pride Week and was held from June 24-30. The events consisted of a Sunday Memorial Service at the UNM Alumni Chapel. The event was held in memory of the 1969 Stonewall Riots, San Francisco Supervisor Harvey Milk, and all the unknown Lesbian and Gay martyrs. This event was sponsored jointly by the Metropolitan Community Church and Integrity & Dignity (a non-sanctioned group from the Catholic Church). Monday there was a Sign Making Party at the Albuquerque Social Club. It was suggested that participants bring their own supplies which included paper, paint, banner material, sticks, and "refrigerator" boxes with which to construct portable closets.

On Tuesday, there was a Potluck Dinner at the Rusti Cork where those who attended took their favorite dish with the intention to meet some new people. There was also live entertainment at the event. Wednesday there was an event of Drama, Music & Poetry held at the Kimo Theater. The program consisted of one-act plays, comedy routines, poetry readings, and musicians. Thursday, June 29, the event was Films at The Kimo where they showed *In the Best Interest of the Children* and the *Word Is Out* at the Kimo Theater. Friday's event was a Sok Hop Dance held at the SUB Ballroom at UNM. There was also a dance and best dressed contest. It was noted on the flyer that a famous guest disc jockey would be at the event (no records have been located on who that famous guest disc jockey was).

Saturday, June 30, was the march entitled Parade & Demonstration which was from 8:30 am to 10:30 am, with free coffee and doughnuts at the Albuquerque Social Club (ASC). The march left the ASC and proceeded west on Central past UNM to Sycamore and then headed south on Sycamore to Roosevelt Park where the celebration would begin. Artists were asked to bring their wares for display and sale. The march itself was much the same as the one held in 1978, except that Lucia Valeska, who had just been named the Executive Director of the National Gay Task Force was the featured speaker.

Sponsors of the event were Adams Den, Albuquerque/Santa Fe Chapter of the National Lesbian Feminist Organization, Albuquerque Social Club, The Coffee Show (noted as a new establishment on 4501 Central), the Gay Co-op, Integrity, Juniper, Metropolitan Community Church, and the Rusti Cork. It was noted from the organizers that all funds received over cost would go to financing future events.

Chapter 6

Pride in Albuquerque in the 80's

In 1980, several members of the Gay Co-op were frustrated with what they perceived as the inaction of the group. The group consisted of several Gay men who reviewed the consensual style of decision making. They also felt that the Co-op's agenda was too concerned with feminist issues and the proposal for incorporation which led to the demise of the organization and the creation of Common Bond in 1980. The Gay Co-op's (AKA Alternative Community Center) last attempt to survive was a mass mailing to its (authorized and avowed) members, Gay bars, other Gay organizations, and businesses.

Pride in Albuquerque, 1980

In the 1980's different segments of the Gay community were frustrated by the inaction and indecisiveness of the Gay Co-op and formed another organization known as Common Bond as mentioned above. This was a significant change in the Gay leadership in Albuquerque. Richard Koteras, one of the founders of Common Bond (which was created after the demise of the Gay Co-op), praised the diversity of the Gay Co-op; however, the organization was lacking in providing a forceful movement, one that acted (eventually, this would lead to the downfall of the Gay Co-op in 1981). Russell Gray, Richard Koteras, and others would endure the controversy of incorporating and the internal strife between the Gays and Lesbians. The community felt the next organization needed to be more out, inclusive, uncensored and accepted. This resulted in the creation of Common Bond Inc. (note that it was incorporated). The stated goal of Common Bond was as follows:

> To enrich the community and the quality of life for all persons regardless of sexual or affectional orientation by providing educational programs, public services, peer support, consciousness-raising, and social activities.

Common Bond would covey that this would be an organization for both men and women, and it incorporated in 1981 as a non-profit - a controversial topic. Common Bond would eventually become the foremost Gay organization in the 1980's and well into 1996. Common Bond would be the leading GLBT community organization to create and support the numerous GLBT organizations that are still in existence today, some being the New Mexico Outdoors Group, the New Mexico Gay Rodeo Association, and most importantly Albuquerque Pride. One of the first organizations formed under the auspices of Common Bond was an all-male chorus. The group was originally founded as the "Brash Ensemble" which later became the New Mexico Gay Men's Chorus. It must be noted that Common Bond Incorporation acquired its name from a classical music concert that took place in the early summer of Gay Pride Week celebrating its 5th anniversary.

Common Bond also had a newsletter/magazine entitled *Common Bond Ink*, which became the most important means of allowing the community to disperse information. The primary focus for Common Bond was political action and securing civil rights. This would all change with the dawn of AIDS in the early 1980's, and so would the focus of Common Bond and other Gay organizations.

Gay Pride in Albuquerque would be hastily organized in 1980 and would have a march and rally because the Gay Co-op and Common Bond could not come to any mutual agreements on the event still being produced by the Gay Co-op. This would be a great divide in the community. The community was eventually notified that the event would start at the Albuquerque Social Club down Central Avenue and would end at Roosevelt Park. There has been little recorded on this year; however, it was noted that an event did take place. After this event took place, Common Bond would realize the importance of Pride and would begin meeting after its conclusion and unsuccessful event in 1980. The Gay Co-op would also begin meeting to put on Pride in 1981; however, Common Bond would ultimately succeed. Therefore, Common Bond would attempt to produce the most successful Prides in Albuquerque in the 1980's despite the great divide in the community with various organizations and the issue of Gays vs. Lesbians.

Pride in Albuquerque, 1981

Since 2019 (except 2020 during the Pandemic) the only artifacts that have been showcased at the Albuquerque Pride Pridefest have been the past official t-shirts. The oldest t-shirt located is from 1981. Through extensive research there were no T-Shirts made prior to that year. Therefore, this book is intended to showcase those t-shirts and have them proclaim, *If These T-Shirts Could Talk…50 of GLBTQ+ Pride in Albuquerque 1976-2026.*

The 1981 t-shirt design was very simplistic and only in white with a tan collar and sleeve. The words written in a circular motion stated Lesbian and Gay Pride Albuquerque with NM in the center. This was unique in the fact that the word Lesbian was put before the word Gay. Research from individuals who donated this shirt had said that a female couple had purchased the t-shirts to sell for Pride and stipulated that the word Lesbian would come first. It is not known if this became a controversy for the GLB community in Albuquerque.

1981

The first annual meeting and dance for Common Bond, Incorporated (Inc. stressed in the newsletter) was held Sunday, September 27, 1981, at the First Unitarian Church. The importance of this meeting was that the first board of directors for the corporation would be elected. Refreshments were served after the meeting and a dance commenced at 9:30. Voting member ship cost $10.00 a year which supported the business as well as Gay Pride Week activities. The success of the year and annual meeting proclaimed victory for the formation of this corporation which assisted in producing a great Pride event for 1981.

Pride in 1981 was entitled Lesbian & Gay Pride Week scheduled during June 17th-28th: it was still produced by the Co-op. The poster was drawn by Raymond Sandoval (Albuquerque Pride Arts Honored dignitary in 2006.) Wednesday, the 17th, Common Bond sponsored an evening of piano, fluted and vocal music including the works of Gay and women (lesbian not used) composers. The event was held at the Unitarian Church on Carlisle and Comanche. On Tuesday was the Lesbian/Gay Community Night. This was an open house sponsored by Common Bond which was an information gathering of community groups such as the Gay & Lesbian Co-op (Common Bond's rival), Metropolitan Community Church, the local chapter of the National Lesbian Feminist Organization and Parents of Gays (which eventually became PFLAG Albuquerque). The event was held at the SUB (Student Union Building) at the University of New Mexico.

Wednesday's happening was Roller Disco. This was one of the biggest successes of 1980's Pride Week. The Roller Disco was held from 9:30-11:00 p.m. at the Roller Drome on 204 San Mateo. Parents of Gays and Lesbians also had an Open House at 1028 Georgia Street from 7:00 to 9:00 p.m. Thursday, the 25th, there was a Coffee House which was an evening of old-fashioned musical entertainment, poetry-reading, and refreshments held at MCC located at 116 Morningside. Saturday, June 27, was the 6th anniversary of Pride in Albuquerque. The event entitled March! Rally! Picnic! gathered at Yale Park (Central at UNM) at 9:30 a.m. The tradition of marching from the University of New Mexico west on Central downtown to the Civic Plaza began in 1981. For the next four years this route was used except in 1982 when a detour had to be made down Grand Avenue to avoid road construction.

The march began at 10:00 a.m. proceeding down Central to Civic Plaza with a rally with speakers and entertainment from 11:00 to 1:00. This was the first march to have a massive counter demonstration. That year members of the North Valley Gospel Church tagged along shouting anti-gay slogans and urging Lesbian and Gay marchers to "repent." Although previous marchers had received some television and press coverage, the presence of the counter demonstration brought even more extensive reporting of Gay Pride Week activities and provided a sharp contrast to the happy and festive spirit of the Lesbian and Gay Pride march. Mike Shearer, one of the organizers of the Albuquerque Lesbian and Gay Speakers Bureau, gave a particularly militant speech at the rally at the Civic Plaza. Afterwards, there was a picnic held in the Manzano Mountains proclaiming to bring all your friends, straight or Gay!

Pride in Albuquerque, 1982

Within Common Bond's first year, a wide range of other social groups covered the spectrum from long distance runners to Gay men interested in leather and motorcycles. In the political arena, the formation of the New Mexico Gay Rights Lobby (NMGRL) was formed. NMGRL had numerous successes at the local and state level. This organization eventually became the New Mexico Lesbian and Gay Political Alliance in 1983. Common Bond's approach was to be visible in order to outreach the greater community. This was a departure and different vision held by the Gay Co-op. However, Art Showings would occur at the community center that would divide the community. Leaders from the lesbian community would debate whether the art shown was pornographic, sexist, and inappropriate for the community center. Many had said that some had experienced being "rape" by the artwork profiled each week. Art showings would plague future Pride events on what would be deemed appropriate.

Steve Slusher would be noted as the first president of Common Bond, which would be inconsistent with many who believed that Richard Koteras, who was one of the founders was the first president. It is at this time that many individuals who were part of many Gay organizations infused lines that had become diffused. Despite this inconsistency Steve Slusher, noted as Common Bond's first president called for a greater visibility of the community despite objections from others. He zealously stated that "only through (full) exposure can acceptance be obtained, and that no longer others would ignore the Gay and Lesbian community without full acceptance with any room for rejection." With this new foresight, Common Bond under the direction of Steve Slusher began planning the most all-embracing Gay Pride Celebration that Albuquerque had ever experienced. Gay Pride Week 1982, in Albuquerque, would become the most extensively planned Pride held in all of New Mexico from its inception. Russel Gray, Common Bond's vice-president would be interviewed on three radio stations KRKE, KOB and KZIA about the plans for the week.

Common Bond would sell Pride Week '82 T-Shirts. The design of the shirt consisted of the Zia Sun symbol with the words "Pride Week '82 and was printed in red ink on a yellow T-Shirt. Gay and Lesbian buttons were also sold for wearers to display the "exact nature of their pride." In *Common Bond Ink* it was noted that sixty-one people had ordered the shirts, and it was suggested to get them early before they ran out. The shirts sold for $5.00 and those interested contacted Russell Gray. The shirts would also be sold at all events during Lesbian and Gay Pride Week '82.

Notably, decades later, Russel Gray would be given the title as New Mexico's Harvey Milk; however, until this book was written he had not been given the respect of his noteworthy contributions to New Mexico. Russel Gray would recount that he and his mom decided in 1976 to march with a butch lesbian know as P.M. Guffy who had run for homecoming queen at UNM in 1976. The recount of the 1976 march, the first march, would be proclaimed by Russel Gray and be used countlessly throughout this historical account. He would be the individual whose statement would be accounted in SEERS newspaper (the only article written about the event in 1976 and 1977). He would recount that in, "1976, the first Gay Pride Parade in Albuquerque, composed of only 25 people, marched up Central Avenue." In other documents obtained he would state that "The second Pride Parade in 1977—which drew a larger crowd of 100 marchers and enlisted Mattachine Society founder Harry Hay as its Grand Marshal—garnered more public attention and provoked mixed responses…while some observers showed support, others hurled eggs at the marchers."

1982

Russel Gray would further state that, "When my mother left Albuquerque to attend law school in the late '70s, she left behind a city still in conflict over how to include its emerging Gay community. When she returned to Albuquerque nearly a half decade later to work for the Bernalillo County District Attorney's Office, my mom met the man who had taken the lead in organizing and advocating on behalf of Albuquerque's Gay community."

Lawyer Russell Gray would work with District Attorney Steve Schiff (who would become a congressman). It would be Gray's mother who would state that her son "Russell was much more than just gay. And by that point, he had established himself as the city and state's leading Gay rights activist."

Unfortunately, Pride in Albuquerque would lose an important individual whose life was taken too early. His mother would speak at his memorial service, which was attended by a large crowd of people from the GLBT movement, the Gray family, the D.A.'s Office and many others from the larger community. Russell's parents at the funeral, Russell Sr. and Edith were open about discussing their son's sexuality and the way he had died during a time when gayness and AIDS were both stigmatized in society. His contributions and expertise would produce Gay Pride celebrations with participants numbering in the tens of thousands, and he had many more contributions to the future creations of Gay organizations that would emerge, such as Equality New Mexico and Albuquerque Pride that would follow the lead of Common Bond. These organizations would become capable of addressing the diverse needs and causes of the broader queer community in Albuquerque and New Mexico, and because of his contributions to the Gay community, the Common Bond Foundation would annually award the Russell Gray Lifetime Community Service Award to New Mexicans who have contributed significantly to the LGBT community and movement.

Russel Gray's importance to Albuquerque Pride was instrumental; however, the event that took place in 1982 would need to proceed and honor his contributions. The New Mexico Coalition of Lesbian and Gay Rights Organizations (led by Jon Hull from Common Bond) met in April to plan "Lesbian and Gay Pride Week '82." The Coalition was composed of representatives of Common Bond, the Gay and Lesbian Student Union, Hijos del Sol, the Lesbian Political Caucus, the Metropolitan Community Church of Albuquerque (MCCA), and the Speakers Bureau. Lesbian and Gay Pride Week '82 which was observed from June 12th through June 20th was set in motion to not conflict with the observance of similar Gay Pride activities in larger cities. Albuquerque's 1982 Gay Pride Celebration would include three noteworthy individuals who nationally had positively moved Gay rights in America.

On Saturday June 12th, Lesbian and Gay Pride Week began with a day-long workshop "Building Alliances Between Lesbians and Heterosexual Women" with Becky Bosch and Judy Ley from the Albuquerque Counseling Co-op. The workshops were held at 722 Silver from 9:00 a.m. to 5:00 p.m. Next, there was a kick-off address by Leonard Matlovich a former United States Air Force sergeant. His speech was covered by KOB-TV and KOAT-TV. Matlovich attained national notoriety when he deliberately took on the Air Force's longstanding ban on homosexuals by openly declaring that he was Gay. He first lectured to the members and friends of Common Bond with a $15.00

reception/fundraiser that followed. The reception/fundraiser was held at Jacques and Kirk's home (unknown). Those individuals who wanted to attend needed to call for directions. Matlovich, the guest of honor would also speak at services held at MCCA on Sunday, June 13th at 10:50 a.m.

On June 14th, the *Albuquerque Journal* ran a feature story on Matlovich which was written by Common Bond member Steve Penrose. In the evening, there was a Women's Sports Festival with softball, volleyball, and kite flying. This was sponsored by the Lesbian Caucus of the NM Chapter of the National Women's Political Caucus and Full Circle Books. Next, the Roller Disco sponsored by Hijos del Sol at the Skate Ranch on 5105 McLeod was from 4:30 p.m. to 6:30 p.m. Finally, the day ended with the 2nd Annual Common Bond Concert at the First Unitarian Church.

Also, June 14th would be an hour-long filmstrip with a discussion conducted by the Albuquerque Counseling Co-op. The movie was "Straight Talk for Lesbians" and was only for Lesbians. This same event would be open to everyone on Thursday, June 17th. On Tuesday, June 15th was the only event, a Potluck at the Rusty Cork.

Wednesday, June 16th, Lucia Valeska, the executive director of the National Lesbian Gay Task Force (NGTF), lectured on "The Current State of the Revolution" at Full Circle Books at 2205 Silver. The presentation was sponsored by the Lesbian Caucus. Valeska was selected from thirty-four applicants as co-executive director of the NGTF in July of 1979. Following the Task Force's reorganization in 1981, Valeska became the organization's sole executive director. This would be her second time speaking at a Pride event in Albuquerque.

Thursday, June 17th, there was a Potluck at Crickets' Country Club. Friday, June 18th, Rev. Troy Perry, the founder of the Universal Fellowship of Metropolitan Community Churches, spoke at the Metropolitan Community Church at 6:30 p.m. In October 1968 the MCC was founded with a service held in Perry's Los Angeles living room and attended by twelve people. Within six months after this inauspicious beginning, the church had two hundred members. By the end of the first year, it swelled to six hundred. In 1982, MCC had 172 churches with 27,000 members in the United States and eight foreign countries.

"Caught in the Act" a Variety Show was also on Friday. The show was held at Numbers After Hours Disco located on 3600-D Menaul NE. There were two shows one at 7:30 and another at 9:30. This variety show put on by Common Bond for Gay Pride Week played to an audience of about 170. The director of the show, Jon Hull, stated that he was "proud of the work and performances of the cast." Audience comments ranged from "outstanding" to "sexiest." Some of the performers were Darby Fegan virtuoso pianist, actors in a short play entitled "The Body Shop," Galt Johnson, and George

Arellanes with Brian Lanter singing a song entitled “Furtive Glances at the Gym.” The Brash Ensemble (which would become the NM Gay Men’s Chorus) also performed, and Glen Samson gave a slide presentation entitled “Our Town” with electronic music played by Scott Amspoker. *“Caught in the Act”* would last for 13 years. The significance of this show was that money made from the event benefitted Common Bond which assisted in opening its doors as a community center and keeping its doors open which gave a place for future Gay Prides in Albuquerque to be planned and executed.

Saturday, June 19, 1982, was the MARCH! RALLEY! PICNIC! CELEBRATION! Participants gathered at Yale Park (on Central at UNM) at 9:30 a.m. The march began at 10:00 a.m. using the sidewalk and not the street. It ended at Civic Plaza with a rally from 11:00 a.m. -12:30 p.m. All four local television stations covered the event. The parade of marchers exceeded 200; however, there were 130 counterdemonstrators from the North Valley Baptist Church. They shouted, “Hell is Hot.” The marchers replied with rather more reliable information “so is Albuquerque.”

Common Bond’s President, Steve Slusher, would talk first and give credit for the success of the march and rally to the “unified effort of several lesbian, gay, and sympathetic groups, the crowd, led by a group of lesbians, bannered, placarded, ballooned, flower wielding, flag bearing, holding hands, embracing, kissing and laughing: proudly Albuquerque lesbians and gays marched in celebratory, like a sinuous animated blossom flecked with bright yellow scales of official Lesbian and Gay Pride Week ’82 T-shirts, flanked by a somber withered calyx in black and white dresses.”

Lucia Valeska, Troy Perry and Leonard Matlovich spoke to a crowd that had swelled to nearly 500. Matlovich talked about being discharged from the military where he said, “they gave me a medal for killing two men and then discharged me for loving one.” Reverend Troy Perry spoke about how the Gay community had grown since his last visit in 1978 when there were only two major Gay organizations in Albuquerque that being MCC and the Gay Co-op. Lucia Veleska spoke about the success of the political Gay Rights Movement. She stated, “We can’t afford to remain isolated from one another.” It is important to note that this being Common Bonds first sponsored Gay Pride rally had a prominent woman speak at the rally, even though Common Bond was an organization that many Gay women (Lesbians) felt excluded from. The rally closed with the traditional Gay anthem of hope, “Somewhere over the Rainbow.”

Saturday evening Reverend Troy Perry would lecture at MCC at 6:30 p.m. An Open House sponsored by Parents and Friends of Lesbians and Gays was also held at the same time. The week culminated with its final event, which was held on Sunday, June 20. There was a Charter Service for Metropolitan Community Church of Albuquerque at 10:50 a.m. Reverend Perry again spoke at 6:30 p.m.

The New Mexico Coalition of Lesbian and Gay Rights Organizations, led by Common Bond, had successfully produced an event that equaled other Pride events held in cities that were larger and more populated. In fact, many cities that held Pride events only had one day whereas Albuquerque had a week-long celebration. Gay Pride Week of 1982 had become the communities' premiere Gay event which would become the foundation for future years of Pride in Albuquerque.

In July of 1982, the month of Pride Week, *Common Bond Ink* (newsletter) reported about Gay Sex & Cancer. This cancer seemed to be targeting Gay men in San Francisco and New York. There were no reported cases of Kaposi sarcoma in New Mexico in 1982. However, the first AIDS fatality in New Mexico would be in 1981. It would later be uncovered that this individual did not get the cancer in New Mexico but had come home to die. The GLB Albuquerque community was not organized or aware of the disease. Furthermore, in 1982, AIDS was a distant and unclear risk to New Mexicans. By 1985, the awareness of AIDS would become the focus of the Gay community which eventually affected and shaped events for Albuquerque Pride.

Pride in Albuquerque, 1983

Jon Hull, Common Bond's Director of Special Projects would be the principal coordinator of Gay and Lesbian Pride Week 83. Lesbian and Gay Pride week demonstrated a strong emerging Gay culture in New Mexico. The diversity of that culture was illustrated in the variety of ways in which Gay men and women celebrated the week of Gay Pride June 17-26. All Pride events held in Albuquerque did not have an official theme (except for 1976 entitled Christopher Street Celebration). There was one for 1983, and it was Albuquerque Galesbian Pride Week '83. The logo would be a circle with the wording Galesbian Pride Week '83 at the top and the word Albuquerque at the bottom. Within the circle was the lambda symbol. The term "Galesbian" was coined that year to express the solidarity of the Lesbian and Gay community as well as to recognize the unique aspects of its many groups. Because of this, Common Bond decided to change its administrative procedures to require that the presidency of the organization alternate between a man and a woman from year to year.

This new paraphrased theme Galesbian would be shunned by many members of the community. There was a cartoon entitled *Burying the Hatchet* located in the calendar of events for *Common Bond Ink*. It showed a man and woman talking to each other sitting on the sidewalk after the march. The male responded "Well, we finally agree on one thing…" and the female responded "Yes, we both HATE the word "Galesbian!" Others would write letters to the editor of *Common Bond Ink*. One such editorial stated "I have become more and more bothered recently by the foolishness called 'separatism.' My sense of disgust is furthered by the local gay organization's use of the hideous theme

'Galesbian'." Even though some of the community loathed the theme, the Pride Planning committee tried to showcase the diversity of the Galesbian community as reflected in the wide variety of events planned. There were no merchandise or logos created using the theme "Galesbian" and the t-shirt that were sold that year were simplistic. The shirt was only in yellow with content in black that had a circle with a Lambda in the middle surrounded by the wording Gay and Lesbian Pride Week '83-Albuquerque.

1983

Common Bond Ink (Roy Reini Editor Publisher – later known as Out! Magazine) would note the event as Albuquerque's ninth annual pride march; however, it must be noted that this was the eighth annual march. This would be problematic for when Pride started in Albuquerque. Notably, there was a march attempted in 1975; however, it never came to fruition.

The week's events included a posh party, march and rally in honor of David Kopay, an old-fashioned picnic, a classical and popular music concert, a political forum on Lesbian and Gay rights, a wild variety show, roller skating, a soft ball game pitting the men against the women, and a few special buffets, potlucks, lunches and open houses. This is also the first year that a large selection of Pride memorabilia was sold. T-shirts, buttons, and posters were sold at all the events throughout the week.

This was the second year for "Caught in the Act," the variety show sponsored by Common Bond. Over 400 people attended this annual Gay Pride event, making it one of the largest audiences to view a Gay cultural event in the state. Producer Jon Hull stated, "The show gives gay women and men an opportunity to demonstrate their talents, and the community as a whole to have a good time."

The 1983 Gay Pride concert, known as "Classics and More," revealed that Albuquerque had many accomplished Gay composers and musicians of its own. This concert featured the works of local composers like Alan Stringer. The Brash Ensemble also sang a love song composed by Brian Lanter, an Ensemble member. In addition to these compositions classical music was performed ranging from Mozart to Debussy. This event was performed by all local and talented musicians.

Over 200 Gay men and women participated in the march despite the hostile attitude again from the counterdemonstrators from the North Valley Gospel Church who did not stop the march from reaching its destination at Civic Plaza where David Kopay was the featured speaker. In 1975, David Kopay was the "first" player in the National Football League to publicly reveal that he was homosexual when he told a newspaper reporter that he was gay. This interview made him an over-night celebrity and an instant spokesman for Gay rights. At the rally, David Kopay would encourage the participants to speak out for their rights and, "watch out for those in the Gay community who refuse to come out because they are the ones who may turn against you."

There were many Gay and Lesbian political events during the week. There was a civil rights forum entitled "Unequal Protection Under the Law: Lesbian and Gay Rights." This was held at the downtown YMCA. Prior to the civil rights forum the Gay and Lesbian Student Union hosted an organizational information exchange. Over sixteen Gay organizations were in attendance. The event also had STD Screening Services of New Mexico conduct testing. NMGRL (New Mexico's Lesbian and Gay Rights Lobby) circulated petitions urging New Mexican elected officials to support legislation prohibiting discrimination on the basis of sexual or affectional orientation. The week garnered 500 petition signatures.

The Acquired Immune Deficiency Syndrome (AIDS) became a major topic of discussion throughout Gay Pride Week that year. The NM Physicians for Human Rights, the STD Screening Services of New Mexico and others sponsored an AIDS benefit show at Foxes Lounge. The show raised over $900.00 for the AIDS Coalition which was lobbying the U.S. Congress for more funding for AIDS research. All involved had expressed a deep concern for the medical, emotional, and financial needs of persons with AIDS; however, in 1983 AIDS was still not seen as an important concern for many.

Numerous social events were held throughout the week. Kopay was honored at a party at the Tamarind Restaurant sponsored by Common Bond. Potlucks and buffets were held at the Rusti Cork, Cricket's Country Club, The Albuquerque Social Club, and the 8300 Club. Parents and Friends of Gays held an open house, and MCC Albuquerque sponsored a picnic following the Gay Pride March and Rally. Hijos del Sol hosted its fourth annual roller disco. MCCA observed Gay Pride Week with a special service in which David Kopay was the featured speaker. He told the congregation, "We are all sexual beings, and the important thing is that we all be true to ourselves."

For the first time Gay Pride Week was also observed outside Albuquerque. The Santa Fe Support hosted a luncheon for Dave Kopay, and a special meeting was held in Chimayo, where Elizabeth Canfield led a discussion on how to set heterosexuals "straight" about homosexuality. In 1983, Liz Canfield, a counselor and sex educator, also organized Project Straight Talk. Canfield had been approached by a high school teacher who recounted her story of a student who had been harassed by his classmates for being openly Gay. The abuse led the student to commit suicide. As a non-gay professional, Canfield was not subject to accusations of recruitment or exploitation. Canfield had worked on similar projects in Southern California; thus, she was able to borrow from previous experience to launch the effort in Albuquerque. This would serve as the predecessor to Common Bond's Under 21 group.

Gay Pride Week in Albuquerque had extensive coverage. Both the *Albuquerque Journal* and *Albuquerque Tribune* included all Pride week events in their community calendars. Television stations KOB and KGGM would cover the march and rally. Jon Hull, Common Bond's Director of Special Projects and the coordinator of the Gay and Lesbian Pride Week, felt that it was tremendously successful due to the participation and support of hundreds of individuals.

Pride in Albuquerque, 1984

Common Bond members Ruben Garcia and Jeffrey Kraybill representing Pride Week in Albuquerque, joined delegates from seventeen other United States cities holding Pride events at the Lesbian and Gay Pride Week Coordinating Committee (which would become InterPride) conference held in San Diego. Doug Moore, San Diego's host committee spokesperson provided a learning experience and an opportunity to meet Lesbian and Gay men like themselves, who continued to promote Pride. During the conference, Prides were able to share any difficulties, successes, and find a common desire to help new cities begin their own style of celebration as well as forming a supportive nationwide network.

Ruben Garcia would state the differences between small and large Prides. He stated, "The large cities concentrated their efforts on a single large celebration, while the smaller cities tended to have a more political focus to their festival with multiple events." Jeffrey Kraybill would tout that, "Albuquerque has suffered so few of the problems encountered by larger cities such as New York and San Diego… Much of the success of Albuquerque's past celebrations has been due to the successful communication between the Pride Week organizers, the city and news media…. larger cities had a difficult time attracting the attention of any news media." He would further state, "Although many cities have much larger and more spectacular Pride Weeks than Albuquerque's, I (Jeffrey) discovered that ours is one of the most well-rounded and balanced." This sentiment would be one of the cornerstones for future Prides in Albuquerque. At the conference the National Pride Week Theme for 1984 would be "Unity And More In '84," which would also become the suggested theme to be utilized in Albuquerque, but eventually not used.

Garcia and Kraybill's excitement would be evident in the planning for Albuquerque's Pride Week '84 celebration. The planning began with a meeting on Sunday, November 6, at 7:30 p.m. at Albuquerque's Federal Savings and Loan on 4901 Central N.E. Planning would occur 6 months before the actual event would take place. Russel Gray was named as acting chair of the Coordinating Committee, Jay Bagi as acting publicity chair, and Mike Owens as acting secretary. Eventually, Ruben Garcia would be elected the permanent chairperson for Gay and Lesbian Pride Week '84. The newly elected officers would be Jeffrey Kraybill, vice chair, Make Owens-secretary, Jon Hull-treasurer, Ross Porter-promotions and member Jay Bagi. This was noted as the Eighth Annual Lesbian & Gay Pride Week held from June 16-24; however, this was actually the ninth annual event. The 1984's theme was "We Celebrate Freedom." A contest was held to give Albuquerque Pride Week a face. Eight local artists submitted entries that featured both the national theme of "Unity and More in '84," as well as the local theme "We Celebrate Freedom" also translated in Spanish "Celebramos la Libertad." This is the first time mentioned that Pride in Albuquerque would be associated with the International Associations of Pride. Other flyers passed out also deemed this year's event as "Freedom Week Celebration."

The logo chosen would be featured on the first ever program for Albuquerque Pride Week history. The winning design was from Jeffrey Kraybill. The logo chosen had a

"Greek" motif. The logo was two concentric circles that had two figures joined at the top and bottom of the circle. On the top and bottom were a male and female conjoined. The men and women would be arched around the circle touching with a gazing stare into each other's eyes. In the center of the circle was the words written "We Celebrate Freedom." The Pride Week winners were announced at the bar 999's (pronounced nines). The week-long festivities would be fully listed in a colorful twelve-page program. Programs were distributed throughout the community. Also, another first was a television public service announcement for Pride Week events produced by Common Bond in cooperation with KOAT TV who announced the events. This 30 second spot incorporated past Pride photos and was broadcasted by all local commercial television stations during June.

T-shirts, and buttons that were made available for sale at the Gay and Lesbian Art Show held on May 20th before Pride Week. The t-shirts would use the motto "We Celebrate Freedom" and be sold that year which would be available in Black and White with some being sleeveless. The t-shirts would not include the word Gay or Lesbian to sell more t-shirts to others who were not yet "out" or allies. This new marketing tool would help promote future t-shirt sales that would be one of the primary merchandising items to help produce the event each year.

A week before the Pride March on Saturday, June 16, PFLAG (Parents Friends Lesbians and Gays) had an Open House and there was a Women's Dance in the Spanish Village at the State Fair Grounds. For $2.00, there was a DJ, dancing, and a statement "Women only, please." This event was produced by Women in Movement in New Mexico (WIMIN). This organization was founded after a group of women were thrown out of Corky's for complaining about watered down drinks. The significance of this Women's Dance held at the Spanish Village would open the doors for contracting with the New Mexico State Fair for future Pride events in Albuquerque to take place. Also, on Saturday there would be a Stonewall Day Pool Party at Sunport Pool at 2023 Columbia SE from 5:30 to 9:30 p.m. which was only for men. On Sunday, Common Bond had a volleyball tournament and a camping competition; Hijos Del Sol again sponsored its Roller Disco event at 2 p.m. and at 8 p.m. Foxes had the Jennifer Jones Show and Common Bond's Chamber Music Concert took place.

Monday at 11:30 there was a Women's Luncheon featuring Flo Kennedy who worked for civil rights spanning a rainbow of interest groups. She had appeared on *60 Minutes*, the *Phil Donahue Show* and *Good Morning America*. She would also speak that evening at the University of New Mexico's Kiva Auditorium. Tuesday at 8 p.m. at Corky's there was a Boy George Look-Alike Contest. The flyer stated, "Fashionable Androgynies Compete for Prizes! Bring your 'look' for the 80s." On Wednesday evening, June 20, the GLSU from UNM had an Open House at the YMCA Downtown. After the event there was a Political Forum for newcomers to New Mexico. Next was a question-and-answer session following a panel discussion for any issues facing the GLB community.

1984

Thursday, Crickets Country Club had a buffet where "Everyone is welcome to Cricket's Friendly Feast to Celebrate Freedom!" Friday, there was an event scheduled in Santa Fe entitled as the "The Chase Event." The Chase was a bar located in Santa Fe at 6800 Albuquerque Highway ½ mile toward Santa Fe after taking Cerillos Exit off northbound 1-25. The bar was on the east side of the highway. There was a $3.00 cover which included a buffet, show, and an all-nighter dance floor with door prizes and more.

The Lesbian and Gay Pride march was stated to be more than a stroll down Central Avenue. It would be a parade. Arb Arbanas, one of the organizers, had proclaimed that there would be a parade. This is also the first time that the march had been called a parade. Arabanas welcomed every kind of entry. He invited convertibles, decorated cars, marching musical groups, balloons, banners, floats, motorcycles, antique cars and especially hundreds of people. Trophies were awarded to the best entry in each of the following categories: Commercial, Non-commercial group, and Individual.

The Albuquerque Pride Parade was tentatively scheduled for Saturday, June 16th, and all were encouraged to use the theme "Celebramos la Libertad." In the souvenir program it is important to note that it was touted as the EIGHTH ANNUAL LESBIAN & GAY PRIDE WEEK PARADE! Again, this is significant because the event had moved away from being a march and was now a parade which is more celebratory than political. The Parade of Colors Assembly would meet at Johnson Field at 8 a.m. This is significant because the starting line-up would take place at a major university where permits were needed to be obtained. At 8 a.m. individuals could paint their posters, set up banners and complete the assemblage of their float. At 9 a.m., instructions were given for a safe and orderly procession, and the Parade went down Central Avenue from UNM to Civic Plaza.

A record number of participants, over 300, came out to celebrate their Pride. It was the first time in Pride history that the parade featured decorated cars, floats, and a one-hundred-foot unity banner which snaked down Central Avenue. Don Durham won the Pride Parade's Individual Award for his cowboy clown costume. The North Valley Gospel Fascist Church float took the award for best entry by a non-profit group, and the theme banner, designed and produced by Bobbi Hubert received a special award from the parade's judges: Reverend Dona Lockridge, Gabe Kruks, and Thad Garvin. One of the most unique entries in the parade was a float with paper mâché heads of each of the current justices of the US Supreme Court. The float was designed by Wayne Bennet, Jeff Moses, and Don Schmidt, members of the New Mexico and Gay Political Alliance. Miss Gay New Mexico, Candy Lee, was featured on a float sponsored by the city's newest bar, Cleo's Pyramid Lounge.

The Gay and Lesbian Student Union (UNM), Common Bond and various individuals entered well decorated vehicles. At Civic Plaza the Rally would commence when the Parade reached its destination. Originally, the rally was to be held at Downtown's newest pedestrian mall known as "The Crossroads" located on Fourth Street. This did not happen, and the rally took place on Civic Plaza.

After the rally, from noon to 6 p.m. the Albuquerque Social Club had a Tea Dance and Buffet and hyped that it was "an excellent post-parade Whistle-Whetter!" At 12:30 p.m. MCCA had a Pride Week Picnic located at Holiday Park near Comanche and Tramway. From 5-7 p.m. happy hour was celebrated at Foxes. Finally, at 8 p.m. "La

Cage Aux Folles" Youth Dance at Penn Hall located at 111 Pennsylvania SE offered a trendsetting youth celebration with New Music, DJ, and dancing with No Alcohol. This would be the first ever Pride event for the youth of the community.

The culminating events would be held Sunday at MCCA which would celebrate the Second Anniversary of its Charter. There was an ecumenical Service held in honor of the landmark occasion at 120 Morningside NE. At 8 pm. Common Bond's "Caught in the Act" Variety Show at the Kimo Theater would produce a traditional Pride Week crowd pleaser featuring the talents of many.

The year 1984 would be a year of many 'firsts' for Pride which would become one of the most attended events for the community; however, because Pride had moved into mainstream Albuquerque, the mentality of "mañana" would encounter the mentality of fear and of the acceptance of the unknown. Pride in Albuquerque had been very successful for 9 years; however, in 1985 AIDS would hit the community hard and the "in-your-face" divisiveness revealed during the events scheduled in 1984 between the Gays (men) and Lesbians (women) would come to light for future Pride's in Albuquerque.

Pride in Albuquerque, 1985

Pride Week '85 planning began when the Committee Chair Ruben Garcia, who attended the Third Annual Gay and Lesbian Pride Week Coordinator's Conference in October of 1984 where the theme *Alive With Pride In '85* was selected, would share how to make pride better with what he learned at the conference. The first meeting was held November 10th at 1104 Standford N.E.

New Mexico's premier gay and lesbian newspaper was now *Common Bond Ink*. The newspaper proclaimed ALBUQUERQUE CELBRATES TEN YEARS OF GAY PRIDE, even though the prior year, in 1984, the event was proclaimed as eight years of Pride. Announcing the years of Pride has always been contentious for Pride and other events. The first Pride held in Albuquerque was in 1976, was which cannot be noted as annual. In 1977, the march became the 2nd Annual Pride event. Technically in 1985, the event was celebrating the beginning of 10 years. The year 1986 would be the completion of ten years. Therefore, in 2016, to celebrate 40 years one needs to subtract 1976 from 2016 to get the completion of 40 years of Pride in Albuquerque.

The 1985's Pride Coordinator was Ruben Garcia. According to the minutes from a meeting held March 7th, it was proposed that Joe and Mary of Dignity would have a candle-light Interfaith Service at the Spanish Village at dusk. The budget approved for Pride was $2180 which was for a total of two-hundred and one t-shirts, as well as printing for the program, posters, and banners. Ruben Garcia would write a letter to the North

Valley Gospel Church and cordially inform them of the change of the parade route. This is significant because protestors would be notified to be part of the event. Rob De Vries, the Parade Consultant, presented a budget for $150.00 for materials that would be used for enhancing the aesthetics and impact of the parade. The entire budget for that year would be $2,180.

1985's theme was *Alive With Pride in '85,* which was also the national theme. The event was also known as the *Gay Pride Fiesta* and *Around the Fairgrounds.* The community would ultimately be upset, and many outraged by the posters, programs, brochures, flyers, and calendar of events' page produced by the Pride Committee. The graphics created looked as if blood had been splattered over the content and text of the document. The design would be extremely controversial because AIDs had become the foremost problem facing the GLB community in Albuquerque. For some individuals, these promotional materials would expose a scared intensity and an "in your face" reality of what the community was experiencing.

Despite the outcry of the poster, t-shirt sales would sell including all two-hundred one that were purchased as the design was offered only in red with the entirety of the shirt that had small pink triangles that covered the shirt with the motto, "Alive With Pride in '85". This would be a time in our GLBT history that being alive was not only a struggle but a fear and concern for all New Mexicans. AIDS had hit our community hard and the thoughts of putting another Pride on in Albuquerque in 1986 and the future would be a major concern.

Despite the "horrors' that hit our community the event started on Friday, June 14th with a dessert, potluck, and parade planning party at the Common Bond Community Center located at 1101 Cardenas, NE. This event's intent was to have fun and make banners and flags. Saturday, June 16th, the parade line up started at 9 a.m. at Gate 11 at the New Mexico State Fairgrounds. The parade with 300 participants proceeded south on Louisiana, went right on Central Avenue to San Pedro, and then entered Gate 3 at the Spanish Village at the New Mexico State Fairgrounds. This would be the shortest Pride Parade held in Albuquerque.

Record numbers of people participated in June's Gay and Lesbian Pride Fiesta. KOAT-TV reported that approximately 400 people marched in this year's Gay Pride Parade noting that non-gays from PFLAG and the Peace Center participated. The parade experienced more confrontation than years past from the North Valley Gospel Church who tried to silence last year's march. The Peace Center was instrumental in assisting by holding hands in-front of the hatred by providing a wall of love and acceptance. The Gay and Lesbian Pride Fiesta Coordinating Committee would award the Peace Center the prize for "Best Group" in the parade. Jim Hobson would also be recognized as a winner for presenting two years in a row his parody of the counterdemonstrators. Hobson would be dressed in a polyester leisure suit and greased back hair declaring the absurdities of the protestors. MCCA members who wore paper bags on their heads (with labels of different professions i.e. teacher, lawyer) won best all-around award.

1985

The new parade route around the State Fair Grounds brought greater public exposure for the annual demonstration. Previous years down Central to Civic Plaza brought forth limited spectators. By moving it past the NM State Fair Flea market goers and by going by the heavy Saturday traffic along the route, the marchers were provided a large audience. Instead of a rally at the conclusion of the parade, a Gay Fair was held.

This would be the foundation of PrideFest which would become a staple held after the parade.

More booths than expected showed up at the Gay Fair. Music was provided by Common Bond's Gay Men's Chorus (1st noted this year) and the Brach Ensemble which added to the festive atmosphere of the fair. Common Bond's dunking booth was more popular with those who wanted to cool off by being dunked than with those who wished to show off their pitching skills. Someone dressed as Jesus wearing a sign that "hell is hot" would be continuously dunked. Cold drinks, Mexican food, sandwiches, hot dogs, and t-shirts sold quickly. The information booths that were set up had numerous Gays and Lesbians who would be recruited as new members. The activities of the groups would be recognized, supported and spread to others in the community who did not attend.

Midway through the fair, the participants took time out for an Inter-faith religious service. AIDS had become a division and element of Albuquerque. Alan Kaiser spoke for the Jewish faith. Others included Reverend Layton Zimmer of St. Aidan's from the Episcopal Church and Donna Lockridge of MCC Albuquerque. Joe Medina started with a religious chant, and Joe Sinico said a few words on behalf of the Catholic Community. A candle-light vigil was part of the event. Upon conclusion, the festive spirit of the parade and fair continued with entertainment and events throughout the evening. For the first time, men and women danced together at the Spanish Village for the benefit of Pride in Albuquerque. A professional DJ played the music provided by the committee member Don Carlos who organized this dance under the stars.

Common Bond's Forth Annual "Caught in the Act" event was celebrated from its inception at a bar known as Numbers in 1982. The Sunday event drew a near capacity crowd at the Kimo Theater. Jon Hull, the producer of the show, brought together twenty-one performing groups for the longest and smoothest running show in the four-year history of "Caught in the Act." The week's entertainment was not over when certain performers from "Caught in the Act" performed at Crickets bringing forth the illusions of Joan Rivers, Diana Ross, and Prince by Lorenzo Colorado which held in the evening of Pride on Saturday.

Pride would continue Monday, June 17th, with a meet and greet and a lecture with Mayor Harry Kinney, Governor Tony Anaya and Representative Bill Richardson. On Tuesday, at 7 p.m. there was a bring your Favorite Dish Potluck at the Rusti Cork; finally, Wednesday an Open House at Common Bond was held with Jerry Cosh who trains volunteers in Los Angeles answering questions on AIDS and its treatment at the community center. At 7:00 p.m. there was a Gay Pride Pool Tournament at the R & S Express (Gay bar) on 4214 Central.

What also must be discussed during the era of 1985 was the horrific, head rearing destruction of AIDS. On September 17, 1985, President Ronald Regan finally mentioned AIDS in public for the first time, and Ryan White an Indiana boy with hemophilia and AIDS would be barred from attending public school.

New Mexico AIDS Services (NMAS) would be founded in March of 1985. Don Schmidt, who was a Gay HIV positive man, and Dr. Jim Waltner, who was from the NM Public Health Service, would meet to present specific goals to be articulated to the community. These specifics would become political for the organization. Russel Gray, Common Bond's President, would become a vehement advocate of NMAS who believed that AIDS would eventually affect all New Mexicans, and so it did. Russel Gray warned that the denial of the problem of AIDS would only get worse and that the Gay community had only begun to believe in the concept that AIDS posed a public health crisis that would be the destruction of Gay Civil Rights. Russel Gray and the Gay community would link the recrimination against Gay people and those who would not seek testing or treatment.

Through an intense discussion, reiteration, proclamations of hatred and acceptance during the State Legislative Session with bills introduced for and against AIDS, Tony Anaya, a liberal Democrat in April of 1985 acted on the request of the advice of NML/GPA (New Mexico Lesbian/Gay Political Alliance) to issue an executive order banning discrimination on the basis of sexual orientation in State government. This would ultimately end the certainty of some NM State Legislators whose horrible anti-gay sentiments blamed Gay people for bringing AIDS to New Mexico.

Pride in Albuquerque, 1986 - 10 years

In April of 1986 the "Committee 100" announced plans for a new larger community center at the corner of Central and Aliso, NE. The center would open on the 15th of April. Due to hidden property costs the community center finally moved to its location at 107-A Tulane SE. Another first was the formation of the New Mexico Gay Rodeo Association.

Prior to Pride Week, Michael Kerns, a Los Angeles actor, director, playwright and producer, would appear on Sunday, June 9th, at the Voyagers Bar in a fundraising event for Pride in Albuquerque. Special guests would be the incomparable CJ Diamond "Drag Illusionist," Ron, Greg & Greg, Richard Garcia and back by popular demand OLGA SOMEVABICH! Pride in 1986 was scheduled from June 14-22. The theme was "Come Out with Pride" for the "New Mexico Gay Fiesta." In keeping out with the "coming out" concept, groups and organizations planned events that would encourage more people within the lesbian and gay community to "come out" and see what was happening in New Mexico from June 14-22. The Pride Committee consisted of Ross Porter, Daniel Kemp,

Vangie Chavez, and Tina Caton. At a planning meeting a list was presented for what to experience at this year's Pride. It included the following:

- Social occasions (a skating party, a pool party, dance for women, special events at Albuquerque's gay and lesbian bars)
- Talent ("Caught in the Act" is June 22nd at the Kimo and auditions will be next week)
- Parents support
- The fight against AIDS
- "Soul Support" – the quest for spirituality
- Politics and Self-Knowledge

1986

Pride T-Shirts were made available for $7.00. They were all-cotton T-shirts in white (sleeves) or turquoise (sleeveless). The shirts featured the distinct landscape (Sandia Mountains with the sunrise) and the theme "Coming Out With Pride, New Mexico Gay Fiesta, 1986." Friday, June 13th, there was an evening party and Pride fundraiser at the Climax Bar at 4214 Central SE. Voyagers Bar & Grill would also have on the 14th and 15th a Patio Party, on the 19th a T-shirt Nite Gay Pride Week where people who wore the official Albuquerque Pride t-shirt got drink specials, and on the 29th the Band Show III Variety talent contest would take place.

Crickets Country Club (bar) would also have on the 14th the Carmen del Rio Show and on June 22nd a picnic for members and non-members. Notably, the bars would realize the importance of latching onto Pride to become more lucrative making money on the "tailcoat" of Pride in Albuquerque. This would become a problem in the future that would have to be handled.

The parade assembled at Johnson Field at UNM at 4:00 p.m. beginning with a rally, June 14th. The parade started at 5:00 p.m. and made its way west on Central Avenue past the University of New Mexico and turned right on University to Grand (now known as Martin Luther King). The parade concluded, and the Fiesta would start at 6:00 p.m. at St. Thomas Episcopal Church. This change had a few community members from various organizations upset because the event was going to be more sacred than secular; however, the overall change was made by the many Albuquerqueans who were dealing with AIDS: either from someone whom they knew, they had lost, or who was currently in their life and not knowing what to do. This need and request from most of the community, ultimately revealed the intense need for support and opportunity for the Gay community to come together for healing. This would occur by having the Gay communities' spirituality experts provide the opportunity for healing, reconciliation, recovery, and rebuilding.

About 400 people marched to the church where the Fiesta began at 6:00. Members of several churches in the Albuquerque and Santa Fe area were invited to participate and be spectators during the parade. Parade organizers would state that those who were part of the parade were looked upon as the Christians being sent to the lions. Those against the event would outnumber those who were in the parade, this year. It must be recounted that marches in the past had encountered those on the sidelines who spew hatred. Countless marchers have stated that whether this is one's first experience or their last, they need to get enough strength to react with love and restraint when they encounter so much hatred. However, sometimes it becomes an overwhelming problem, that boiling point, when one must finally fight back. Ultimately, this is what the opposition wants. This is an issue that has plagued Pride in Albuquerque the entire 50 years of Pride's existence.

A shuttle was provided to ferry participants back to their cars parked at the beginning of the parade. An Interfaith service began directly after the Fiesta/Parade. Then, on Sunday, June 22, the Metropolitan Community Church invited the community to a breakfast directly after their morning services.

The year of 1986 marked an emergence of the exploration of spirituality for Gay and Lesbian people. For a variety of reasons and the onset of AIDs hitting Pride in Albuquerque hard in 1986, the community was urged to tie together and thread religion and spirituality for Gays and Lesbians. Members of the New Mexico Community had ample opportunity to explore spirituality for themselves during the 1986 New Mexico Gay Fiesta.

Another aspect added to Pride Week was the start in the area of support for AIDS patients and their families and friends. An initiative began by the New Mexico Council of Churches that resulted in a day-long conference in Albuquerque for members of the clergy and interested persons. All members of the New Mexican Lesbian and Gay community were welcomed to the ecumenical religious service which concluded the conference. Also, there was a two-hour program at the UNM Law School for those who were curious about the story of AIDS in New Mexico, and who wondering about NM AIDS Service and how they could help.

Pride in Albuquerque, 1987

Common Bond Ink publicizes an article entitled "Albuquerque Gays and Lesbians Celebrate Twelve Years of Pride;" however, it was only eleven years. The theme was "Share Our Pride" scheduled from June 12-21. Sherry Clancy became the 1987's Pride Week coordinator and was pleased with the diversity of events and the participation of all segments of the community in 1987's Pride activities. It was proclaimed as an event that would be completely different.

There were events prior to the announced Pride Week. Common Bond had at the center an art show June 4, 1986. Some of the highlighted artwork was from Harmony Hammond. (She would become Pride's Grand Marshal in the year 2005.) Friday night was an evening to make banners and signs for the Pride Parade. Common Bond provided refreshments at the Community Center at 107 Tulane SE. The Lesbian/Gay Film Festival also opened at Don Pancho's.

Saturday, June 13th, would be the Lesbian/Gay Pride Parade. At 10 am at the Community Center line-up took place. The Pride Parade traveled up Central to San Pedro NE and entered the New Mexico State Fair Grounds. Many non-gay groups also joined in the parade this year. They included: Peace Center representatives, New Mexico

Progressive Political Action Committee, members from the Quakers, Unitarians, Congregationalists, and PFLAG. Cricket's Country Club, Albuquerque's west side Gay and Lesbian bar, challenged all other organizations, bars and businesses to enter a float to try to "out-do-them." For the second year there was the Brown Bag Brigade that demonstrated and marched that not all Gays and Lesbians can come out of the closet. Others had the opportunity to participate in the parade and were urged to wear a brown bag over their heads with a name of their occupation on a placard or on a sign.

There would be a Fiesta from noon to late afternoon in the Spanish Village with booths, entertainment, and a space to picnic. This move to the Spanish Village (New Mexico State Fair) would be the contention of future debates whether this should be the place that the parade should end. Kate Clinton, a lesbian/feminist comedian, was the guest speaker at the Fiesta and with Harmony Hammond –Artist would be deemed as Co-Grand Marshals for Pride, but this would not be announced until the day of the event.

In the evening there was a potluck from 6-10 p.m. at Metropolitan Community Church at 120 Morningside, NE. There would also be a Gay game night at the Community Center. A WIMIN's Dance was from 9 to Midnight for women only also at the Spanish Village. This event would become controversial because some Gay men in the community felt that the Fiesta did not provide or offer anything for the men. Some Gay men felt that since the Pride coordinator was a woman, she favored the event "happenings" to be mainly for females, even down to selecting the main entertainer who was Kate Clinton. That evening, some Gay men tried to enter the WIMIN's Dance, but they were denied access. Shouting between the men and some women attending the dance would occur. The Gay men were escorted off the premises by security from the New Mexico State Fair.

On Sunday, Common Bond sponsored a Lesbian Brunch (potluck) at 11 a.m. MCC had a Pride week brunch at 1 p.m., and at the Friends Meeting House at 1600 5th NW there was a Lesbian/Gay Pride Poetry Reading from 2-5 p.m. At 6 p.m. at Common Bond there was a Pride Week Movie event which showed the "Life and Times of Harvey Milk," "Before Stonewall," and "Pink Triangles." This event was free and opened to the public. Finally, Common Bond Classics (and More) Patio Concert was at 7 p.m. at 1104 Stanford, NE.

There were no events planned for Monday; however, on Tuesday there was a Disabled Lesbian & Gay Panel Discussion at the UNM Law School. The first part of the discussion from 7-8 p.m. was only for women, and men were welcomed at 8 p.m. Again, events like this had shown a division between the genders in Albuquerque. Wednesday, AIDS and Acupuncture; Prevention & Treatment discussion took place at Common Bond's Community Center at 7:30. Thursday, a discussion with attorney Ruth Cohen presented Lesbian/Gay Lives and the Law. On Friday, June 19th, Parents & Friends of Gays and Lesbians had an Open House at 1028 Georgia Street. There was a buffet dinner at 6:30 p.m. which was free. Saturday, there was a CHEM-FREE (No Alcohol, No Smoking) Pride Week Dance at 9 p.m. at Friends Meeting House. This was for both men and women. Finally, on Sunday, June 21st, there was a Pride Week Interfaith Service at 4 p.m. at MCC. At 7 p.m. the annual variety show known as "Caught in the Act" was held.

1987

It must be noted that 1987 marks the formation of the Lambda Car Club. This car club has been instrumental in assisting and providing vehicles for honored dignitaries, and grand marshals. The club is also known for showcasing the beauty and pride of their vehicles in the parade.

Pride in Albuquerque, 1988

For 1988, the national and Pride in Albuquerque theme would be "Rightfully Proud!" *Common Bond Ink* would provide extensive coverage in the newsletter pertaining to Gay & Lesbian Pride Week 1998 with one headline reading "RIGHTFULLY PROUD Parade marks the city's Thirteenth Annual Gay Pride March." The article provided a history of Pride in Albuquerque and stated that in May of 1975 Juniper planned an event; however, despite their ambitious plans, the event never took place. The article further mentioned that the first event was held in June of 1976. Therefore, the event should have been celebrating twelve years instead of thirteen. This also marks the first time that the Gay Pride Parade would begin Pride week with other events that would follow during the week after the parade.

The event was led under the direction of Russel Gray-Common Bond's Executive Director, Neil Isbin-Board Member, and Treasurer- Kent De Jong. He would submit his Treasurer's Report noting that Gay & Lesbian Pride Week '88 would be budgeted for $1475.00. Tony Bucci would be the Committee Chair Gay & Lesbian Pride Week '88. Kathy Staruska would be the organizer of Desert Dynamite.

Desert Dynamite was the new name given to the Gay Pride Fiesta. This team would try to "mend" the different factions between Albuquerque gays and lesbians, after what had happened in 1987. There would be an unveiling, sampling, and preview of Desert Dynamite at the bar Champagne Taste on Sunday May 1st at 6:00 p.m. (located at 8201 San Pedro, NE). At this event, people were able to take time to meet with the planning committee and be the first to know what was prepared for Pride Week '88 showcasing Desert Dynamite that claimed would have more events and excitement for the entire Gay and Lesbian community. Desert Dynamite would be held at night instead of during the heat of the day. A dance would be held in conjunction, and all Gay and lesbian organizations would have booths. This preview of Desert Dynamite would also serve as a fundraiser for Gay & Lesbian Pride Week '88.

This would be the second year where a program would be produced by Common Bond by the 1988 Gay and Lesbian Pride Week Committee and the Common Bond Publications Committee. Pride week in 1988 would be scheduled from June 17-26. On Friday, June 17th, the event scheduled was Friday Night Out at the Community Center from 8 p.m. to 1 a.m. Banners and other March paraphernalia were prepared in a pep rally atmosphere. Cars and floats were also decorated.

Saturday, June 18th, was the twelfth annual Gay and Lesbian Pride Parade. Individuals assembled at 9 a.m. at Morningside Park, with the parade starting at 10:00 a.m. The route was along east Central through the heart of Nob Hill where many businesses supportive of the lesbian community were located. It then headed west on Central to Yale Park on the University of New Mexico campus (Yale Park was located there prior to the building of UNM's Bookstore).

The event proclaimed that Reverend Freda Smith, Grand Marshal, along with other speakers would close the Gay Pride March with a bang! Reverend Freda Smith had been actively involved in the Gay and Lesbian Rights Movement. She served on the California State University, Sacramento Gay Studies Board, was chair of the California Committee for Sexual Law Reform, served as Co-Chair of the Whitman Radclyffe Association and moderated the State-wide California Conference for Law Reform in 1973. She would eventually join the Universal Fellowship of Metropolitan Community Churches in 1971. As a Grand Marshal, she believed that her visit to Albuquerque would assist her in conducting a Spiritual Renewal for the members of MCCA and the community at large.

Sharon Kowalski was named as an honorary parade Grand Marshal, and many Gay Pride Parades across the country would honor her. In November of 1983 Sharon's car was struck by a drunk driver, and she experienced a serious brain stem injury which resulted in a coma. Her 'lover' of four years, Karen Thompson, wanted to help nurse Sharon back to health and be close to her to assist her with anything that she needed. Sharon Kowalski's parents found out about the relationship and tried to prevent Karen from seeing and caring for their daughter. Karen Thompson would sue for guardianship of her partner Sharon in 1984; however, Sharon's father Donald Kowalski would be named as her guardian. Karen would be barred from ever seeing Sharon. Since 1985 Karen Thompson would fight the courts for her right to care and visit her 'lover.' In 1988, Pride in Albuquerque, would honor Sharon Kowalski with an empty wheelchair to celebrate the spirit of being "Rightfully Proud." Common Bond would also provide more information and suggestions on how to assist Karen Thompson to fight for the rights to love, honor and support her partner.

This would also be the first year that Common Bond would honor a community member for his dedication to the Community Center. The "Grand Marshal's Award" would be given to George Mead who had dedicated and volunteered since the inception of Common Bond. He would give a moving speech at the rally at Yale Park. He called everyone to action and the need to be out to all, including family, friends, and co-workers.

The Gay and Lesbian Pride Week '88 "Rightfully Proud" Rally would begin at 11 a.m. at Yale Park on the University of New Mexico Campus. Reverend Smith would speak, and a moment of silence would take place for Leonard Matlovich who died of complications resulting from AIDS. Matlovich had been a Grand Marshal and had spoken at the rally after the parade in 1982. Awards were given to the best parade entries. Three judges would select the winners of the Grand Marshal's Award, The Rightfully Proud

Award, and the Community Award. There would also be the first-ever Lesbian and Gay run from Albuquerque to the steps of the New Mexico State Capitol in Santa Fe. The run, which was over 56 miles long, would be completed by relay teams to draw attention to the week's activities and the Gay and Lesbian community's struggle for civil right protections.

1988

"Rightfully Proud," the national theme for Pride Week '88 had been selected by the Albuquerque planning committee to serve as the overall theme of the week-long celebration. In addition to the primary theme again, Desert Dynamite would also serve as the name for what had traditionally been known as the Pride Week Fiesta (now known as PrideFest).

Kathy Staruska, the organizer, proceeded with a new change that would be a street fair. Flyers noted that the event would be, "An evening of dancing, eating and raucous good time [that] will be had by all at the first-ever Desert Dynamite." This year the night-time event would feature music provided by disc jockey Chris Martin, popular disk jockey from WIMIN dances numerous food booths, entertainment areas and an opportunity for a good time. The event would take place from 6 p.m. to midnight at the Spanish Village at the NM State Fairgrounds, and there would be a $5.00 charge. The significance of this event was that it would bring the Gays and Lesbians together for an event which had previously only been a dance for Lesbians. This would also be the first time that individuals would have to pay to go to the event (PrideFest) held after the parade and rally.

On Sunday June 19th, MCCA had a Gay Pride Week religious service. The church had moved to its new location at 2404 San Mateo Place, NE. Following at noon there was a Pride Week lunch which had a $3.00 admission. At the Vienna Coffee House located at 324 Hermosa, SE there was a classical concert at 6 p.m. with an admission price of $5.00. This annual Gay Pride Week event was held at one of Albuquerque's known architectural masterpieces, the "Kelvinator House" (AKA the Frigidaire House) owned by Common Bond member Dan Schaller.

Mid-week the New Mexico Lesbian and Gay Political Alliance (NML/GPA) would have its annual Pride Week political event. Thursday, June 23rd Romanovski & Phillips would give a concert in Santa Fe. This group began their career in San Francisco in 1982 and would be noted as "the" Gay musical group in North America. The event took place at the St. Francis Auditorium at 8 p.m. The Gay singing duo performed their new repertoire of sassy folk-inspired music and comedy. Friday Night Out at the Common Bond Community Center (CBCC) would take place from 8 p.m. to 1 a.m. This would be Pride Week T-shirt night with movies, games and a safe place for all to attend for those who did not want to go to the bars.

Saturday, the Gay and Lesbian "Rightfully Proud" film festival took place at the CBCC. The event began at 5 p.m. and lasted until midnight with $1.00 admission and refreshments. The movies shown were the documentary *Before Stonewall, Desert Hearts,* and *Prick Up Your Ears*. PFLAG also had an Open House at 6 p.m. where Betty Hunt would open her house for the event. Corky's at 9 p.m. would present, "The Dating Game" where the winning couple would win a dinner for two and movie passes. Finally, on Saturday there would be Candlelight Remembrance & Celebration of Santa Fe's Lesbian and Gay Community at the Plaza at 9 p.m. It must be also noted that in 1988 for the first time Santa Fe would formally observe Gay and Lesbian Pride Week with its own events.

Sunday, June 26th, would be the end of Gay and Lesbian Pride Week with the annual celebrated show "Caught in the Act." The event would again take place at the Kimo Theater with a $5.00 advanced ticket price and $6.00 at the door. The event was advertised as New Mexico's premier Gay and Lesbian event with laughing, cheering, and talented performers. This would be the largest event held during Pride Week.

Pride in Albuquerque like other Prides in the United States had successfully survived the AIDS epidemic. On a positive note, the loss of so many loved ones would eventually provide unification between the Gay and Lesbian community.

Pride in Albuquerque, 1989

Russel Gray, founder of Common Bond, New Mexico's Gay and Lesbian community center would pass away on July 4, 1989. He had assisted with the Gay Pride Movement in Albuquerque and was instrumental in the formation of the annual Gay and Lesbian Pride March. Russel Gray had served as an Assistant District Attorney for three years and was the first openly Gay person to represent New Mexico at the Democratic National Convention in 1984.

Common Bond INK would ask the community to submit ideas for the 1989 Gay Pride Week theme; however, Kathy Staruska would oversee the event and choose "Out & About." The graphics would have a triangle with the wording "Out & About" on top. Within the triangle was a coyote baying at the moon with the mountains in the foreground. The logo was designed by Jennifer Northrup, and it was available on posters and T shirts to be purchased at Full Circle Books. No T-shirts have been located with this logo for the Albuquerque Pride Archives.

The organizing committee for *Out & About* Gay Pride Week '89 was Tony Bucci, Greg Ferran, Diane Gibson, Marsha Lohman, Maria Lopez, Nyira Lopez, Steven Lopez, Jennifer Northrup, Babe Pobst, Chuck Smith and Kathy Staruska. This would be the first year that the team putting on Pride would be noted as the Common Bond Gay Pride Week Planning Committee. This is significant because Common Bond would claim possession to this event. The budget would be $2,209 with most of the money to be spent on the featured performer Margo Gomez at Desert Dynamite.

Metropolitan Community Church of Albuquerque would begin the celebration of Gay/Lesbian Pride Week with a weekend of Spiritual Renewal with Reverend Elder Freda Smith who was the Grand Marshal in 1988. Her dynamic and popular preaching style would start off Pride in Albuquerque at MCC at 7 p.m. On Sunday, MCC would celebrate their Seventh Anniversary of its chartering with the Universal Fellowship of Metropolitan Community Churches.

1989

Kathy Staruska, the Pride Chair, would state, "We will use the traditional parade route, starting at Morningside Park." The Gay Pride Week parade began at 10 a.m., on Saturday June 17th, and left Morningside Park and continued Aliso to Central Avenue and then to Yale. Individuals were asked to assemble for the parade at 9 a.m. and needed to contact Kathy Staruska so that no confusion would take place during lineup. This is the first year that the parade marshal would carry one of the New Mexico State flags. There would be 21 flags, one for each county in New Mexico. Future Albuquerque Pride parades would locate a notable Gay or Lesbian individual from each county to hold one of the New Mexico State flags. There would be a short rally and picnic following the parade at Yale Park. In 1989, the Gay & Lesbian Pride Week Parade would grow to 500 participants.

The Second Annual Desert Dynamite (eventually known as PrideFest) would be held in the evening at the Spanish Village. The show was highlighted by San Francisco's "1988 Entertainer of the Year," Margo Gomez. As a veteran of stage and television, Margo Gomez had found a wide appeal among audiences since her act began at the Valencia Rose, a popular club in the Gay community in the Bay area. She had toured on the nightclub circuit and had appeared at Gay festivals, conventions, colleges and even prisons. Gates at the Spanish Village on the west side of the State Fairgrounds opened at 6:30 p.m. The show started at 7 p.m. with dancing that followed.

Sunday, MCC Albuquerque would have its Anniversary Service with a Gay Pride Brunch. That evening would be the 8th Annual "Caught in the Act" at the Kimo Theater. Monday, June 19th, was a Mush Ball Game at Bataan Park at 6:15. It was suggested to bring a sense of humor and a friend. At 7 p.m. Common Bond Community Center (CBCC) had an Art Show. At the UNM Law School a short vignette, *"Why Should I Worry About AIDS?"* was presented by New Mexico Association of People Living with AIDS.

Tuesday there was an event entitled, "Gay Olde Time in Old Town" held at the Old Town bandstand at 6 p.m. This was a night of fun and frivolity where individuals could buy a button at the band stand before shopping to show the unity and money power of the GLB community. From 7-9 p.m. there was a showing of the Quilt panels from the Names Project. This would be the first display at MCC Albuquerque. Wednesday, the UNM Law School had a seminar pertaining to legal considerations for Gays and Lesbians, and on Thursday, June 22nd, there was Gay/Lesbian Bowling at Fiesta lanes. Friday Night Out at the CBCC took place where individuals were asked to bring their favorite pie or dessert. Saturday, at the CBCC at 12 noon there was the Gay & Lesbian Movie Festival showing: *Torch Song Trilogy, Before Stonewall* (documentary), *Desert Hearts,* and *We Are Family* (documentary). Finally, on Sunday, June 19th, there was a Champagne Brunch at CBCC, a Nondenominational Healing Service at MCCA and a Classics Concert at Joe Walker's home at 4 p.m. which highlighted the New Mexico Gay Men's Chorus performing works of gay composers.

The 1980's community experienced the devastation of AIDS. This was a time when the segregated community of Gays vs. Lesbians existed, but somehow unity came forth because of this horrible epidemic. Pride in Albuquerque continued under the direction of CBCC, who would try to thrive and make improvements each year, despite the AIDS pandemic.

Chapter 7

Pride in Albuquerque in the 90's

The 1990's would become a transition year for Pride in Albuquerque. This year, the event would leave Common Bond Community Center, and it would also move forward with the formation of Albuquerque Pride as its own entity, business, corporation, and finally a non-profit. Albuquerque Pride would encounter similar struggles as other past organizations. One hurdle being the opposition to it becoming incorporated. As in the past, many Gay and Lesbian organizations in Albuquerque tried to incorporate, but none would be successful.

Pride in Albuquerque, 1990

The planning committee for Gay & Lesbian Pride Week had their first meeting March 4th at 3 p.m. Neil Isbin oversaw obtaining the parade permits. Toni Bucci and Maria Lopez were responsible for Fairground permits. Both would be appointed as co-chairs. Paul (PJ) Sedillo would become the Pride assistant to the co-chairs. The next meeting was on April 1st, when the Grand Marshal selection would be finalized.

Don Schmidt was chosen. He was an openly Gay minister from the United Church of Christ in Hawaii. His congregation had come to know and love him as their kahu (minister). Finally, at the meeting, judges was selected for the parade. They would be past CBCC presidents who would give awards for the most creative, most outrageous, and most festive.

To pay for Pride there was a Spaghetti Dinner scheduled for April 7th and a Mexican Dinner on May 5th. In addition, T-Shirts, raffles, flag sales, commenced, plus a fundraiser at the bar Crickets would also assist in paying for Pride. There would also be a small fundraising event at the newly opened bar known as The Ranch by J.C. Moore and Don Denario. It was the first all-western club riding in on the tails of the big Country Music resurgence. It must be noted that Gay Pride Week in Albuquerque was budgeted for $3,921.25; however, the total expenses for the entire event would be $2,209.06.

Gay & Lesbian Pride Week 1990 was entitled "Look to the Future." The logo designed would have a pink triangle with multiple black and gray triangles ending in the year 1999. The event was scheduled to begin at the CBCC's Friday Night Out from 8 p.m. to 1 a.m., where posters and cars would be decorated for the next day's Saturday parade. Marchers and floats lined up at 10 a.m. at Morningside Park. The parade went west on Central Avenue to Yale Park where the Gay & Lesbian Pride Rally took place at noon with speakers, music, and a picnic in the park. However, the parade date would be moved to accommodate the Sirens (Lesbian Motorcycle group also known as [Dykes on Bikes] which usually leads Gay Pride Parades across the nation) because of a Trip to San Francisco's Pride and the Women's Solstice. These changes would also make it difficult for the Motorcycle Men of Albuquerque to participate.

1990

To avoid conflict, the date for PrideFest '90 Parade would be scheduled for Saturday, June 9th. This announcement is important because the many GLB organizations that existed in Albuquerque needed to come together, thus so the date would be changed officially to June 16, 1990.

That evening would be the Third Annual Desert Dynamite from 7 p.m. to 11:30 p.m. at the Spanish Village. The event featured a Bay Area Comedian, Danny Williams, a well-known comedian and AIDS activist. In 1989, he started working for RSVP Cruises, known for their gay clientele. He entertained on board hosting costume parties, pool parties, and gay spoofs of shows like, "The Dating Game" and "Newlywed Game." This would be an "olive branch" offered to gay men so that they would be welcomed at the event. Also, at 7:30 p.m. that evening was a MCC Spiritual Renewal Worship Service with Reverend Elder Don Eastman.

Pride events would continue for the weeks following. On Tuesday, NM AIDS Services (NMAS) had a wine and cheese open house, and a community forum took place at the NM Law School. Wednesday the NM Lesbian & Gay Political Alliance (NML/GPA) had a seminar on *How to Argue for Gay Rights.* Thursday, June 21st, at Full Circle Books there was a Gay & Lesbian Pride Week Solstice Party with refreshments. Also, on Thursday there was a concert with the Blazing Redheads, a hard bop, mainstream group who played pop-flavored originals. This group made of women instrumentalists consisted of reeds, drums, and Latin percussion infused with a bass and piano. The concert would be at the Indian Pueblo Cultural Center and tickets and cassettes could be bought at Full Circle Books. Friday, June 22nd, at Crickets Lounge there was Leather and Lace Fashion Show and a slumber party for Friday Night Out at the CBCC.

Saturday, June 23rd, at the CBCC was the Gay & Lesbian Pride Week Film Festival featuring *Torch Song Trilogy, We are Family, The Virgin Machine,* and *Dona Herlinda and Her Son*. That evening was a Black and White Ball from 8 p.m. to 1 a.m. at the bar known as Champagne Taste. This would be a fundraiser for NMAS.

Friday, the week after PrideFest, June 29th, an event sponsored by NM Lesbian and Gay Political Alliance was a Pool Party for Pride Week located at Sunport Pools. On Saturday June 30th, Gay Pride month would have the Ninth Annual, "Caught in the Act" variety Show. Sunday, MCC would have its annual Pride service which followed with a MCC Gay & Lesbian Pride Brunch. Also on Sunday, there was an Under 21 Tea Dance at 2 p.m. This would be the first event held for our GLB youth for Gay Pride Week in Albuquerque. At 4 p.m. would be the annual Gay & Lesbian Pride Week Classics Concert.

Pride in Albuquerque, 1991

As noted previously in the archival records, past Pride committees celebrated an 8th annual event and the next year's Pride Committee would declare it to be Albuquerque's 10th Anniversary event. Past Pride history does not have a year nine designated. The year 1989 claims to be the 14th annual event. In 1990 and 1991, records found do not indicate an anniversary year on any of the documents produced during these years. Therefore, in 1990 and 1991 because no year was noted, the Pride events that proceeded after 1991 documented the proper anniversary year.

In 1992, the archival records claim the event as the 16th Annual Gay Pride Parade and PrideFest thus putting the celebration right back on track. This would be the first year that the official wording of "PrideFest" would be used and many different spellings would occur in the future such as *Pridefest, Pride Fest*, and *pridefest*. The week would be entitled Together in Pride: PrideFest '91, Gay & Lesbian Pride Week 1991.

1991

There would be no t-shirts produced this year, and no logo has not been identified for 1991. The budget for the event would be $1281.19, and the total expenses would be $1238.47, which included a donation from the Albuquerque Social Club in the amount of $400. This money deemed as a sponsorship would be the first recorded in Pride's history; although, Crickets had given sponsorship money years before.

Sine 1978, securing the Gay Pride Week Parade Permit was an arduous task, and it would become more difficult as the years progressed. In 1991, the permitting process would be as follows:

1. Secure application from Traffic Headquarters at 401 Menaul NW
2. City officials required proof of a parade route map, insurance form, insurance receipt, barricade permit fee, barricade rental agreement, and parade notice (Public Notices) form to area merchants- all must be provided to proceed.
3. Secure signatures in order on application from:
   - Operations Manager of Suntran (on Yale)
   - Barricade-Traffic Engineer, 1 Civic Plaza, 5th floor
   - Police Area Commander, SE division, Louisiana & Kathryn
   - Traffic Commander, 401 Menaul NW
   - Chief of Police, downtown office

At any time, any of the individuals responsible for "signing off" could make it difficult and refuse to sign, or the application would be left at each location to wait for a signature to be processed. Pride realized that copies of the application would need to be made at each step of the process. Sometimes the different agencies would not offer to make a copy of the document, which meant that the representative from Pride would have to make a copy and go back to leave the original document. Consequently, the original application form would be lost many times and multiple copies would become collected and submitted with all the needed signatures. This process would take up to 2 months to complete resulting in a pile of applications with the numerous required signatures.

Public notices would need to be hand delivered to every business and home that would be along the parade route. This public notice was a requirement posed from the City of Albuquerque. For many years, many brave individuals would walk up and down Central Avenue to hand deliver the public notices. Many businesses, especially in the Nob Hill District were very supportive; however, at times many businesses were extremely caustic to those who delivered the public notices in person (sometimes life-threatening). The many Pride volunteers who knew which business would be the most difficult to deliver the public notice would make sure that a group would go together, hand in hand to face the owner or manager of the business. Information printed on the public notice stayed consistent for many years with only the contact information changed. The following information was on the public notice:

SUBJECT: GAY PRIDE WEEK PARADE
DATE: SATURDAY, JUNE 22
ROUTE: from Morningside Park, down Central to Yale Park

Per instruction from the City of Albuquerque, this is an official notice of the Gay Pride Week Parade. As the parade passes by your business, there will be a slight delay (about 15-20 minutes) in access to your business by traffic moving West on Central. We appreciate your cooperation.

The fight for freedom and liberations from oppression begins with self-liberation. Gay Pride Week is a time when gay men and lesbians reject both society's homophobia and their own internalized homophobia to celebrate their personal freedom and pride in being gay. Please feel free to demonstrate your support for freedom, liberty and equality by welcoming and encouraging the individuals participating.

Local Contact: Neil Isbin, 275-XXXX

Neil Isbin's phone number was located at the bottom of each public notice. Notably, it must be acknowledged that this endangered Neil Isbin as it was his own personal home phone number. Neil Isbin would always make light of the numerous hate speeches left on his answering machine or actual live phone messages that he would encounter. For many years public notices were distributed to all of those along the parade route. These instructions per the City of Albuquerque were never questioned. Until 2009, the public notices would be distributed to businesses and homes along the route of the Pride Parade. This notice distribution had become a traditional rite of passage for those who volunteered for the event.

It is 1991 that Neil Isbin would mentor PJ Sedillo about the "ins-and-outs" of the parade permitting process. Technically, because of Neil's health issues, Neil would have PJ Sedillo fulfill and learn the requirements for obtaining the permit for the parade. Neil Isbin's mentorship and "larger than life" being, would be instrumental in developing PJ Sedillo's leadership capabilities.

Under the mentorship and direction of Neil Isbin, PJ Sedillo, a newly hired teacher for the Albuquerque Public School System, would attend an APS Board meeting in 1991 to ask for "wording" to be included in the negotiated contracts for all APS teachers that would include non-discrimination for sexual orientation. Neil Isbin, as the great orator he was, would successfully present the case to the Board, and PJ Sedillo would reveal his fear of being fired because he was Gay. Neil Isbin would demand that the APS School Board vote to ensure that they would honor all of their employees. The school board voted unanimously to ensure that a non-discrimination clause would be included. This mentorship would be the start of PJ Sedillo's twenty-one years of volunteering for Common Bond, Pride in Albuquerque, and ultimately assist in the formation of Albuquerque Pride.

Saturday, June 15th, would be the kick-off of Pride with a Black & White Dance with music by Madie Mirabal & High Fashion at 7 p.m. at the Albuquerque Old Airport. Madie Mirabal assisted with her DJing expertise for future Pride events. Entertainment at this Black & White Dance was provided by the first organized Gay and Lesbian Dance Troupe in Albuquerque known as Albuquerque Beat. The choreographer and owner of this dance troupe was PJ Sedillo.

The week following on Saturday, June 22nd, would be the 15th Annual: PRIDEFEST' 91 Parade, Rally & Picnic. Notification to those who would like to participate would be sent out to the community. Common Bond's President, Neil Isbin, and Chair of PrideFest '91, Tony Bucci, would state the following in their notifications:

> Participating in the annual Parade is a rite of passage for gay men and lesbians in the process of coming out. For those who are "out," participating in the parade is an annual reaffirmation of one's pride and self-confidence and an opportunity to warmly embrace and encourage those struggling with the fears of coming out. For those who are not gay, participating in the parade is a visible sign of support.

Line-up began at 10 a.m. at Morningside Park (Aliso and Lead), and the parade started at 11 a.m. The parade proceeded down Central to Yale Park where there would be a Rally and Picnic. Desert Dynamite, which had previously been held in the evening after the March and Rally concluded, would take place, but it would be part of another committee that did not report back to the Gay & Lesbian Pride Week Committee; thus, limited articles publicized the event. The next event would be scheduled for Sunday, June 23rd, with MCC's annual Gay Pride Brunch. Monday, June 24th, there was a discussion held at MCC on, "Homosexuality –What the Bible Does and Does Not Say" from 7 p.m. to 9 p.m. On Tuesday Common Bond held a workshop entitled, "Our Identities & Relationships" at the UNM School of Law, and on Wednesday NML/GPA conducted a Forum on, "How to Mobilize to Win our Rights" at the same location.

Saturday, June 29th, the 10th Annual Variety Show- "Caught in the Act" was held. The show would be the primary fundraiser for the CBCC. The event, ultimately, assisted in paying for the rental space, other events, and Pride in Albuquerque. On Sunday, June 20th, the Gay Pride Carnival was held at 7:00 p.m. at The Great Catsby in Santa Fe. It was promoted jointly with Pride in Albuquerque. The event had a full day of events with booths, fun, and entertainment. This event was also part of Santa Fe Pride's closing events.

Pride in Albuquerque, 1992

Saturday, June 13th, the PrideFest Parade, Rally & Fiesta would embody the theme PRIDE = POWER which would be led by the Chairs of PrideFest, Karen Severino & Steve Lopez. The t-shirt would be in black with the logo printed in white. PRIDE = POWER, the theme for 1992, invited organizations and the community to partake in the reality that if "we lose each other, there is no Power." The community in New Mexico had suffered intense discrimination, death in the face of homophobia, and remorse in the many who had vanished from the community's lives due to the AIDS pandemic. The theme dictated the community to become empowered.

The Gay and Lesbian Pride Committee had sent out a letter on April 2, 1992, to the community for participation. The letter declared, "As you know, for many years, the Gay and Lesbian community in New Mexico has been fractured through many different organizations and opinions. We believe the community, although there are differences, has a bond and a common cause when it comes to Gay Pride and Gay Power." These sentiments have been continuously cited as the foundation of Pride which originated from those brave individuals who fought back at Stonewall and those twenty-five individuals who came together as one in 1976 in Albuquerque, New Mexico. These sentiments follow the continued Pride celebrations in Albuquerque and all Pride events that take place around the world. Despite all differences, this singular event has unified the GLBT community as one whether during a month, a week or a day.

Saturday, June 13th, the parade lineup began at 10:15 a.m. at Morningside Park and the parade started at 11:00 a.m. The Gay Pride Parade proceeded west on Central to UNM Johnson Field. Once at Johnson Field PrideFest '92 would begin with a six-hour Fiesta with live entertainment, a dee jay, food, and beverages. Each organization was invited to attend and participate. Booths were set up around the perimeter of the field where organizations/businesses sold items, advertised, or raised awareness about their group/business. It was highly suggested for those who had a booth to have and sell merchandise to raise money for their respective organization. Each booth was required to donate to PrideFest '92, which was a new idea. However, the importance of "pushing" for booths would produce a change that would be the cause for future Pride's in Albuquerque to have booth procedures, regulations, and fees. Organizations, business, and information booths to name a few, would become an integral part of PrideFest; thus, ensuring that Pride in Albuquerque would continue to exist.

1992

Posters for the '92 event stated that this was the "First Annual Fiesta." At the event the guest speaker would be one who had graced the stage multiple times for Albuquerque Pride. Troy Perry the founder of Metropolitan Community Church spoke at the rally which started immediately once the parade from Morningside entered the grounds of Johnson Field.

The budget from Common Bond for Gay & Lesbian Pride Week was $2,116 and total expenses would be $1,475. The original budget had an itemized expense for the Spanish Village of $300. This was not used because the event would cost nothing for the use of Johnson Field. This expense was noted in the total expenses even though the amount was never utilized. The PrideFest '92 Committee wished for the Gay and Lesbian Pride Parade and Fiesta to be a big success by not charging a fee for participation in either the Gay Parade or Fiesta. In the past the event known as Desert Dynamite, precursor to PrideFest was held after the parade in the evening at the Spanish Village with an entrance fee charged. The committee had made a commitment to have those who participated donate whatever they could, whether through time, money or both. This participation was key to the success of the event. After the conclusion of Pride in Albuquerque in 1992, Karen Severino and Steve Lopez, the chairs of PrideFest's '92, would tout the "Power belongs to us!"

Pride in Albuquerque, 1993

After the 1992 PrideFest Parade, Rally & Fiesta concluded, many community members, businesses, organizations and participants were disappointed and let down about the Pride event. Many had felt that there was lack of organization, and that the location at Johnson Field was unbearably hot in the month of June (lack of trees). There also was no grand marshal, and the parade lacked its usual "pomp and frivolity." Many left early after the rally because there were few booths and limited entertainment. Most had also come to expect an event in the evening, and this time the only choice was to go to the bars.

This outcry from the community made Common Bond strive to produce a better-quality event for the community in 1993. Planning meetings for Pride in Albuquerque were now to be held once a month from September to December. From, January to April planning meetings was held two times in the month. By May to June 11th, meetings were held weekly. This preparation would assist in producing a well-orchestrated event.

The public notices distributed to businesses along the parade route for Gay & Lesbian Pride Week Parade would proclaim, "The fight for freedom and liberation from oppression begins with self-acceptance and self-liberation." This would be the first Pride Parade in Albuquerque to march from Morningside Park, head east on Central, north on

San Pedro into Gate 4 of the New Mexico State Fairgrounds. Future Prides in Albuquerque would take a similar route.

In 1993, President of Common Bond was PJ Sedillo who was also Parade Chair. Neil Isbin, past president of CBCC, would become PJ Sedillo's mentor and assist him with the ins-and-outs of obtaining the ever-dreaded parade application from the City of Albuquerque. A big difference for '93 was the number of barricades required along the route, and the City of Albuquerque Parade permit would cost $387.30. Also, this would be the first year that State Police officers would be required, as the event entered the NM State Fair Grounds.

Albuquerque Police officers and State Police were needed, hired, and paid for their services for the protection of the spectators and participants. Many did not realize that this was a huge expense needed for the parade to take place. Many assumed that the police worked the event because they work for the City of Albuquerque. The expense was more costly because Pride paid the police officers for overtime. Many police officers who assisted with their services had chosen to protect and serve the community at this yearly event. Many had gay brothers and sisters, uncles, aunts, or were in the closet themselves. Yet even though they were paid, they volunteered their time to be there as this was an extra duty and not forced upon them. Therefore, those who signed up for the event have always been willing to serve the Gay community and protect everyone from harm's way.

This year, Gay Pride Month would begin June 11th with an Art Show Opening at the CBCC with an Open House the next day. "Bar Week" was scheduled from June 15th through the 20th. Corkeys had a town meeting on the 15th, and on the 16th Foxes Lounge had a drag show and raffle to benefit Gay Pride. The Social Club had the Wild Bunch Square Dance group provide lessons. The Albuquerque Mining Company held a benefit with a $1.00 cover charge for Gay Pride June 17th. On the 18th there was a traveling drag show that went from the Westside to the Eastside. The show began at Crickets at 7:00 p.m. to 9:00 p.m. When the show was over, a caravan drove to the Ranch to perform at 10:00. The headliner for the event was none other than C.J. Diamond one of Albuquerque's premier female impersonators, or as she called it, "female illusionist." That evening Common Bond would also have a booth to answer any questions about the parade and to accept applications for booths and parade entries.

June 18th – 19th would be the Women's Summer Solstice in the Jemez Mountains. Friday, June 25th, was Youth Night at the CBCC, and Saturday would be the ever popular "Caught in the Act" variety show. This would be the first parade to be held on a Sunday. The event started at 11:30.

The Pride Theme was Fiesta de Colores (Party of Colors). This is the second Pride in Albuquerque that only a theme was used without a logo created. There was also no merchandise that was made to sell. It would be mentioned at one of the board meetings, but it was too late to get any merchandise. CBCC Board of Director minutes would mention this so that future Prides would not miss out on this lucrative item to assist and produce Pride in Albuquerque with this needed monetary support.

1994

This would, however, be the first year that there would be an actual Pride Parade Line Up. In the past people interested in having a car, float or marching would just show up and the line-up took place. Seventeen registered and turned in applications; however, several groups/businesses had signed up during the morning of the event. The final list had the following 23 parade entries:

1. Sirens (Dykes on Bikes)
2. Horses
3. Motorcyclemen of New Mexico
4. Emmanuel MCC
5. Grand Marshal – Dusty Pruitt
6. Common Bond Float (Albuquerque)
7. Women on Stilts
8. Under 21 (CBCC)
9. PFLAG Albuquerque
10. Lesbians for Change
11. Sandia Leather
12. New Mexico Outdoors Group
13. Wilde Bunch (Square Dancers)
14. Feminist Lesbian Art & Police
15. Full Circle Books
16. Metropolitan Community Church
17. Food Fun & Thought (NM People Living with AIDS)
18. Dignity
19. Common Bond (Portales)
20. Albuquerque Mining Company (AMC)
21. Foxes Lounge
22. The Royal Imperial Sovereign Court of the Land of Enchantment Empire
23. The Ranch – NM Gay Rodeo Association's Royalty

This would be the first year for so many groups to participate in the parade and so many spectators to watch the parade. The increase in numbers was primarily due to the increased amount of publicizing of Fiesta de Colores. The parade was a huge success primarily because the parade went through the Nob Hill District. Albuquerque has never had a "gayborhood." The closest would be the Nob Hill District. This would be a parade first. The parade would march up Central Avenue through the most acceptable and supportive area in Albuquerque. Thousands came out to cheer and line the streets with support, and many local businesses put out the Gay Pride Rainbow Flags.

The Grand Marshal for 1993 was Dusty Pruitt. Dusty entered the Army as a second lieutenant in 1970 where she came to understand that she was gay. She was later introduced to the Metropolitan Community Church in Atlanta, Georgia, and when she was transferred from active duty to the Reserves in 1976, she began studying theology. She was the first openly gay or lesbian person to graduate with a Master of Divinity degree from the School of Theology in Denver, Colorado. She then began pastoring at the MCC in Long Beach, California. Dusty Pruitt gave an interview to the *Los Angeles Times* about her work with MCC and as an Army Reservist. The article was picked up by Pruitt's commander who initiated an investigation her for being Gay and immoral. The investigation would ultimately take away her promotion to Major and result in an honorable discharge. This started her on a twelve-year legal battle that would eventually be resolved in1995 with Duty Pruitt's reinstatement issued by the U.S. Supreme Court. She would be named the first *Advocate* Woman of the Year in 1991.

The parade would enter the New Mexico State Fair Grounds and individuals would head to the Spanish Village. The event was free; however, volunteers with buckets were at the gates to take any amount of monetary donations. Once in the Spanish Village, booths were set up. The music was thrilling, and multicolored balloons and decorations filled the space. The environment was full of excitement. Throughout the day there was entertainment. The rally and PrideFest ended about 6:00 p.m. Many who participated gave thanks to Common Bond for a successful Pride event in Albuquerque.

On a negative note, Gay Pride Week would cost $3,377.79 and only $1196.58 was raised from donations to support the event. Subsequently, fundraisers were held from July to September to offset the cost. Even with the fundraisers that took place this would be the first time that there would be a loss of $379.21. Money from the variety show, “Caught in the Act” would make up the difference so that the event would take place in 1994. Despite this loss, the success of the event would have the Pride Committee analyze the positives and negatives of the event so that next year's event would be better than Fiesta de Colores.

An interesting Pride fact for 1993 was that Rush Industries Inc. wanted exclusivity with their product for sponsorship of the parade by offering $500.00 to secure the event. Needless to say, Common Bond and the Board of Directors turned them down because they did not want “Padded Briefs” to have sole sponsorship of the event.

Pride in Albuquerque, 1994

On June 27, 1969, the crowd gathered at the Stonewall Inn and had no idea what was about to happen, in fact, one bar patron later was quoted as saying, "They said we were making history, but I just wanted a cocktail." But what started out as just another New York Police Department raid on just another Greenwich Village gay bar soon erupted into a full-scale riot, and the Gay and Lesbian Civil Rights Movement was born. In 1994, Albuquerque Pride and Pridefest (official spelling for future Prides in Albuquerque) along with other cities would celebrate twenty-five years of this historic moment.

The theme for the event was, "Stonewall 25-A Global Celebration" which was also the International Pride Theme. Albuquerque Pride would make sure that a logo was created to produce merchandise to help pay for the events. The logo designed for that year incorporated letters that spelled Stonewall in the shape of the earth. On the top of the sphere was the wording, "A Global Celebration" and at the bottom, "25 years." The importance of this logo was that merchandise which included T-shirts would be sold to sell and raise money to put on the event. Pride T-Shirts were sold at Full Circle Book and Sister & Brothers Bookstore (located directly east of the CBCC) and at the In Crowd, a gay friendly novelty store located in the Nob Hill area. The budget proposed for 1994 would be $1,500.

This year, the chair for the entire event would be PJ Sedillo who was also a Common Bond Board Member. He was asked to become Vice-President instead of President due to his many duties. This would be the start for PJ of decades of service producing and leading Albuquerque Pride into the future. PJ would reiterate through his tenure and was quoted in 1993 as saying, "A lot of people show up to be in the parade, but the work is all done by four [few] individuals. This is a similar lament among those who plan Gay/Lesbian events in their town… the whole parade takes about an hour, but it's nine months of work."

Pride week in Albuquerque would begin on June 4th. Common Bond and NM Gay and Lesbian Political Alliance would staff a booth for the Human Rights Day Celebration/A Taste of Summerfest Downtown. This would be the first time that the Gay community would have such a visible booth at a "mainstream" event held by the City of Albuquerque. June 10th would be the annual Art Show and Open House at the CBCC.

1994

The parade would be moved to Saturday, as many of the churches in Albuquerque who were supported wanted to participate and could not if the event was again held on Sunday as in 1993. The Pride Committee had met extensively throughout the year to put on an event that was better than 1993; however, roadblocks would be encountered, and these roadblocks would be daunting.

In the summer of 1994, the City of Albuquerque decided to precede with extensive road construction and maintenance on the main artery of Albuquerque, Central Avenue. This would pose problems for the Pride Committee to continue the overwhelming positive response to continue the route for the parade that was held in 1993. Most of the support came from the Nob Hill District. This support would ensure that future Pride parades in Albuquerque would be on Central Avenue.

Interestingly, the Pride Committee had many options presented from the City of Albuquerque. Many of these options were to move the event off Central Avenue. The Pride Committee was adamant about not moving the parade off Central Avenue especially with this being the 25th Anniversary of Stonewall and having the necessity to honor those past brave individuals who marched in 1976 on Central.

In the end, the parade route line-up would start on Aliso and Central Avenue. The parade would move west on Central past Carlisle and turn left on Richmond. It would then make a left on Silver Avenue and proceed to Morningside Park located on Aliso where the Pride week Fiesta and the rally would begin. The parade had technically made a square for this year's route, but the march/parade still occurred on Central.

Grand Marshals for the parade were State Senators Tom Rutherford and Liz Stefanics, two key sponsors of a 1993 bill to add sexual orientation to the State's Human Rights Act. The number of parade entries had doubled in size with thirty-nine registering and with eight more showing up on the morning of the event to register. It was estimated that 900 participants were in the parade with 1,300 spectators.

The '94 Pride Committee would extensively advertise the Fiesta as an event that would honor Pride's roots, where the event began in 1976 at Morningside Park. This idea of grandstanding would be tied into twenty-five years of Stonewall and to Albuquerque's own "Stonewall." In essence, this celebration and those who participated would recount that the construction on Central was "meant" to happen which assisted the community to come "full circle" its own little corner of Gay rights in the world.

The Fiesta would be decorated in multicolored balloons. Many organizations and businesses had booths that surrounded the entire park. The Nob Hill Association would overwhelmingly support the event with advertisement and booth participation. The association had also asked to be part of the planning stages for Pride in 1995. Over 2,500 individuals were in attendance, which overpowered this little corner park on Lead Avenue, Aliso and Morningside. At the rally PJ Sedillo spoke the following message:

Hello, my name is PJ Sedillo.

I am your 1994 Gay and Lesbian Pride Parade Chairman. Many people have been asking why the parade is ending at Morningside Park. Despite the wonderful orange barrels on Central and San Mateo prohibiting our way to the State Fair there is another reason. We are celebrating 25 years of hardship, pain and joy which was led by a handful of Drag Queens, Lesbians and Gay men, what I am referring to is Stonewall the birthplace of our Civil Rights. Well believe it or not we have had our own little part in that history in the making at Morningside Park which had a lot to do with it.

Eighteen years ago Albuquerque had 25 remarkable individuals who had the guts and determination to march several blocks along Central Avenue drawing little public attention and no notice in the local media, but it was an important milestone. The following year which was 1977 Albuquerque's second parade drew one hundred marchers, symbolizing the growing sense of community in Albuquerque. The march followed a three-mile route from the Old Metropolitan Church westward to Central Avenue to Morningside Park.

Marchers were taunted with abuse from passersby and at even one-point eggs were hurled at the participants. After the march the group held a rally here at Morningside Park where they listened to Harry Hay the founder of the Mattachine Society. Another prominent speaker was Reverend Troy Perry who had contributed immensely to our community. In a sense the ground that you are standing on represents many years of history within our own little "Stonewall" here at Morningside Park. I will fight for future plans with the Pride Parade Committee to work on establishing this park as the birthplace of our civil rights with a permanent statue or plaque commemorating those brave individuals who marched proudly 18 years ago.

I leave you with this final message that Harry Hay said 17 years ago at this park. The world that we see beyond, through our gay window, calls us to engagement and responsibility.

Thank you.

The event left all the community full of excitement which would continue for the events for the week. Sunday, June 12th, there was a fundraiser dance at La Posada de Albuquerque Hotel for Senate Bill-91 which was to support civil rights for Gays and Lesbians in New Mexico. Tuesday was a lecture by Lesbian Katherine Forrest at Full Circle Books. June 17-19 would be the annual Women's Summer Solstice. The same dates would be the NM Gay Rodeo Associations weekend held north of Santa Fe.

On June 18th would be an event held by New Mexico Motorcycle action culminating on June 19th when the NM Motorcycle Man "Poker Run" took place. An event that had not taken place in a few years, but had become a staple for Pride, was held again on June 24th at the Rainbow Garden Roller Drone. This roller-skating event was held from 7:30-9:30 p.m. Everyone was asked to bring the entire family.

The final event scheduled for June 25 would be the ever popular and ever expected event for Pride, "Caught in the Act." The event had moved into "mainstream" Albuquerque and now had been attended by not only the Gay and Lesbian community but the heterosexual community at large who might or might not have supported Gay rights. Most of those individuals attended because of the fantastic entertainment on the stage. This would become a crucial event that would assist in "normalizing" the Gay community to the greater public in Albuquerque.

Pride in Albuquerque, 1995

Twenty-six years later, Albuquerque would celebrate the historic moment with Pridefest '95 celebrating lesbian and gay pride. In 1995, the committee wanted to promote a better understanding of lesbians and gay men while celebrating the steps the community had taken towards achieving greater civil freedom. The Pride Committee would declare that this had occurred and was evident, "by the process of coming out to the entire Albuquerque Community." Therefore, this proclamation would support the theme "Pride from Silence to Celebration." This would also be the International Pride Theme.

The logo for merchandise and t-shirts would incorporate pink and black tringle symbols from the Holocaust. The pink triangle is a symbol for the GLBTQ+ community and was intended as a badge of shame and later reappropriated as a positive symbol of self-identify. It originated in Nazi Germany as one of the badges to distinguish those imprisoned because they had been identified by the authorities as gay men. The black triangle was also an identification badge for those women who were deemed to be anti-social which included lesbians and others deemed nonconformists.

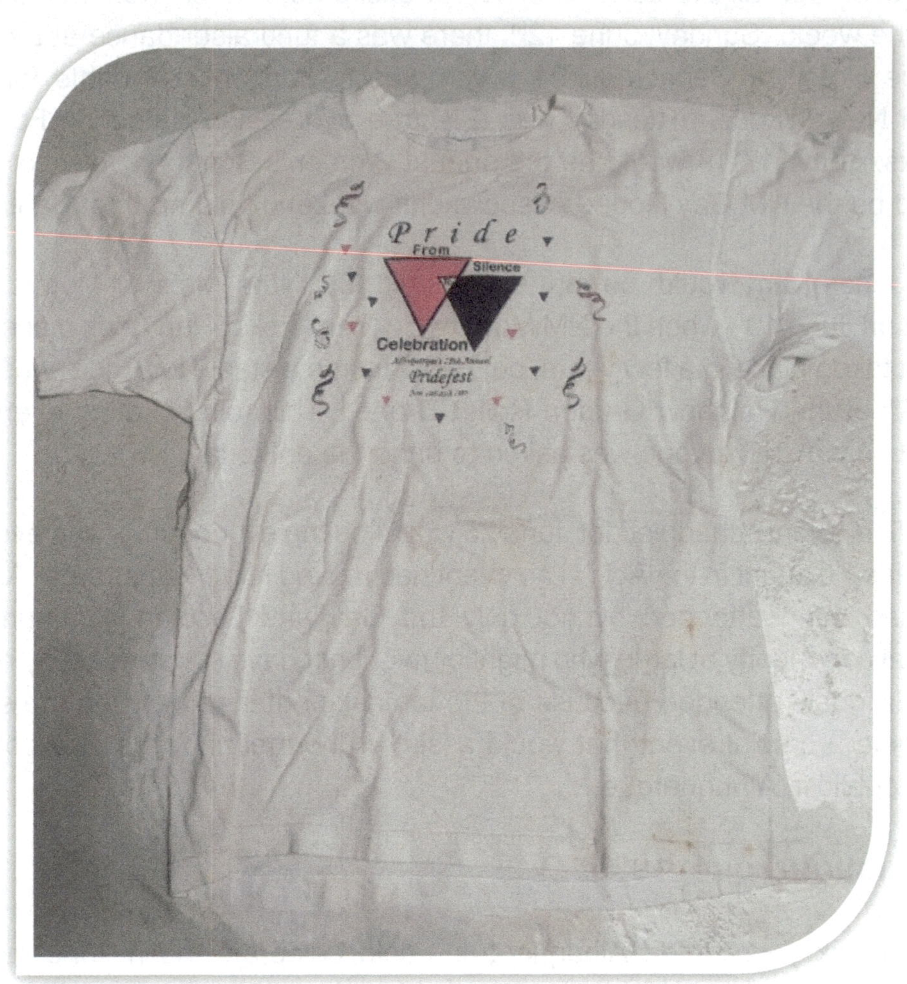

1995

Andy Najar (instrumental in solidifying the Under 21 youth group at the CBCC) and PJ Sedillo would become the Pridefest Chairs. PJ Sedillo would again assume the duties as President of Common Bond. The most drastic change that was made in 1995, was to solely concentrate on the parade and Pridefest event. The Pride Committee had realized the difficulty in producing and orchestrating an entire week or month of Pride events which ended up taking away from focusing on the "main" event. In the past, several businesses/organizations who had stated that they would produce events ended up not producing them, and Common Bond would be blamed for the events not taking place. Also, if the event was unsuccessful and declared a "bomb," Common Bond would be associated with the event and would be required to answer about the mishaps. Therefore, the committee would vote and decide that its primary function would be to produce the parade and the event that took place after. The year 1995 would necessitate Specific

Parade Guidelines which were presented to those who wanted to participate. Guidelines to those who wanted to participate would state the following:

> "The Pridefest '95 Parade will be the largest lesbian and gay event in the history of the state of New Mexico with expectations of 1,000 or more participants and we are doing it right this year. The parade will be escorted by the Albuquerque Police Department-yes we have licenses and the cooperation of the City of Albuquerque. The police are followed by floats, dancing groups, motorcycle troupe and dignitaries in flashy convertibles. The second part of the parade honors the roots of our celebration when gay people would march boldly up city streets shouting civil right chants. Groups with banners will also be invited to join the parade."

This would be the first time where there were parade guidelines that would require the participants to provide a signature as a, "hold harmless agreement." Signatures would be obtained once the entry form was submitted to participate in the parade. Those who showed up on the day of the event needed to sign off on the same, "hold harmless agreement." Participants would sign this statement "that the Pride committee has the right to refuse any entry that infringes upon the guidelines of the parade or the agreements with the city or state agencies." The importance of this position was the realization mentioned from other Pride events happening in the United States that individuals from the religious right, skinheads, Neo-Nazis or those who beliefs were adamantly against Gays and Lesbians could obtain an entry form and submit the application to participate. In the past, the event had openly and actively invited those who were against the Gay community; however, in 1995 Pride in Albuquerque needed to be aware that those groups/individuals could have the opportunity to participate openly. Consequently, the community should have been educated why this change in guidelines took place, but it did not occur.

The Parade Committee and the Board of Directors of Common Bond also were amazed by the large amount of people attending the event, numbering over 2,000. However, there was a revelation that those who were in the parade, or were a spectator, could possibly sue the Pride Committee/CBCC for any mishaps. This would move the Board of Directors of Common Bond to acquire liability insurance for the Pride event.

This would also be the first year that the Pride would require a fee. The committee let the community know that the Pridefest Committee would diligently work to include anyone who wished to be part of the parade and that the fees were needed to cover the tremendous expenses involved with a professionally organized event. Gay and Lesbian organizations/businesses were encouraged to support those who could not afford the fees, and some participants were requested to try to locate a sponsor willing to contribute to their entrance fee.

The *Albuquerque Tribune* would provide an article on June 8th two days before the event. The article was entitled *Doin' it for Judy and God.* The article had been written about the misconception that Stonewall took place because of the death of Judy Garland and the patrons of the bar who were upset that they could not grieve her death that day when the police harassment would start in the bar. The article also stated that "the Stonewall Riots [which occurred June 1969], which directly led to the Gay Rights Movement, means it's time [in June] for 1,000 or so members of Albuquerque's gay-lesbian-bisexual-transgender community to pony up Saturday morning and march down Central Avenue." This would be the first mainstream article that provided press prior to the event and acknowledged the GLBT (Gay, Lesbian, and Bisexual, Transgender) community including the identification of Bisexuals and those who were Transgender.

Andy Najar would state in the article that there was a marked increase involvement from churches. The Reverend Elder Harvey of the Universal Fellowship of Metropolitan Community Churches would be designated as a special guest speaker. Reverend Elder Jeri Ann Harvey served two years with the US Navy and was honorably discharged. She had written several articles, published poetry and recorded as a singer with the Nelson Riddle Orchestra in 1953. She became a licensed minister in Dallas, Texas in 1975 and was ordained in Denver, Colorado. Harvey was the first woman elected pastor of the founding church, MCC Los Angeles.

The Pridefest '95 Parade was scheduled for June 10th and was going to follow the same route held in 1994 with the event ending at Morningside Park. This was because the City of Albuquerque refused to sign off on the parade application because construction was being planned on Central Avenue by the New Mexico State Fair Grounds. The Pride Committee wanted the event to end again at the Spanish Village, which was also being requested and petitioned by the GLBT community. Because of this, the Pride Committee was called to action to try to postpone the planned construction.

The Pride Committee and the Nob Hill Business Association decided to meet with the City of Albuquerque to propose a possible postponement for the construction on Central and San Pedro. Mayor Martin Chavez who had been an important supporter of Pride in Albuquerque attended the meeting as well as the planning department from the City. It would be decided that construction would begin starting on Central Avenue and San Pedro on June 10th the same day as the parade; however, construction would start at 1:00 p.m. which was after the parade had concluded and entered the State Fair Grounds. Mayor Martin Chavez also had the City of Albuquerque pay for the barricades for the event because the City would be using them anyway for the planned construction.

At the meeting PJ Sedillo the Chair of the Pride Committee, would ask Mayor Martin Chavez for a proclamation. Mayor Chavez wholeheartedly supported the proclamation and would be presented at the Pridefest in the Spanish Village to read the decree.

The parade began promptly at 10:45 a.m. Those who sent in applications received notification about their position in the parade line-up. Line-up for the parade would start at the Common Bond Community Center at 4013 Silver Avenue. The parade would turn left on Montclaire, right on Central Avenue, and then left to San Pedro. The parade would head north on San Pedro and enter Gate 4. The police officers were led by Sergeant Sheryl Tiller and eight other officers. This would be the route utilized for a few more years until the line-up outgrew the space required for the large number of entries.

Notably, this year the Pride Committee decided to not have one individual as the grand marshal. The 1995 "Pride from Silence to Celebration's" grand marshal would be all those who had ended their lives, lost their lives to AIDS, were victimized and bullied, or who did not have a voice and were forced to be silent. A hearse would be draped in the Rainbow Flag. People were asked to march silently behind the hearse with signs signifying past loved ones with their names and pictures on the placard.

Once in the Spanish Village, participants were greeted with music celebrating the event. This would also be the first year where liquor sales would be offered. Therefore, there would be a Children's Area with games and inflatables and an Alcohol-Free Zone to support those in the community who suffered from addiction. In addition, 45 booths were purchased from businesses and organizations both for profit and non-profits. There was also a space designated for pets sponsored by Accent Pets. Entertainment was scheduled throughout the day, and it was estimated that there were over 2,000 people in the Spanish Village. The event was free and ended at 5:00 p.m.

At this time people were asked to proceed out of the Spanish Village where the event was transformed with new decorations for the evening event. Booths could stay if they chose. At 6:00 p.m. individuals who wanted to attend would need to pay a $5.00 entrance fee to be part of the Pride Day Concert and Dance featuring Too F.I.N.E. Minds. This band from Albuquerque was led by Storm Florez who would later move to the Bay Area. The group which had recorded two albums was known for its various folk-rock styles with dreamy tales of love, death, romance, and basic scorpionic woes. They performed across the Southwest and South at various bars, coffee houses, and LGBT pride events. The evening event would have about 500 people in attendance. Many individuals were excited about the evening activities; however, many would go home and get ready to go out to the bars. The Pride Committee would evaluate to decide if there should be an evening event planned in the future. This decision would plague future Prides held in Albuquerque. Despite the many that did not stay for the evening, the event was a huge success, and talks for next year's Pride began immediately after the conclusion in '95. One of the items discussed brought forth a possible next step for Pride to become a viable business, an organization on its own. This possible idea could have been the demise of Pride in Albuquerque.

Albuquerque Pride, 1996 – 20 years

In 1996, the Common Bond Community Center, had assisted individuals to put on a yearly Parade and Pridefest. However, CBCC was having financial and internal problems with the organization. That year Albuquerque Pride subsequently left Common Bond to become its own entity (many other organizations would follow, i.e., the Gay Men's Chorus, the New Mexico Gay Rodeo Association, the Rainbow Roadrunner Car Club, etc.). The event was sponsored by RISCLEE (The Royal Imperial Sovereign Court of the Land of Enchantment Empire) who had their own non-profit status. Because they were incorporated, they became the financial sponsor. Ian Gioseffi, a board member from RISCLEE, was instrumental in assisting the Pride event in 1996 and worked closely with PJ Sedillo, the Pridefest Chair. The Pride Committee consisted of Will Wroda, Maryanne Strickland, Doug Parkard, Greg Baca, Miguel Tavarez, Tony Ross, Ron Wommelsdorf and Allison MacIsaac. This would be the 20th Anniversary of Albuquerque's Gay and Lesbian Parade which was scheduled for Saturday, June 8, 1996. The theme was "Pride Without Borders."

The official Pride t-shirt was very striking. It had a barricaded wall with razor wire that was being broken through by an iron pick. The rubble had the words silence and hate. This would be a controversial t-shirt, designed by PJ Sedillo, but has always been a favorite. It won "People's Choice" for best Pride T-shirt in 2024 at the Albuquerque Pride Pridefest. An interesting fact about the t-shirt is when the color purple was printed it did not come out. Pride members individually painted 450 shirts to add the missing color.

The rainbow filled parade began at the corner of Montclaire, SE and preceded east on Central and north into the Spanish Village at the New Mexico State Fairgrounds. The parade included thirty-nine entries which was an increase of eighteen entries from the year before. The grand marshals for the parade were Elizabeth Canfield and Albuquerque PFLAG.

Pridefest was highlighted by an executive order from Mayor Martin A. Chavez declaring June 8, 1996, as Pride Day. The executive order was read by Bob White the City Attorney. Reverend Pat Langlois of Emmanuel Metropolitan Community Church delivered the invocation followed by an acapella rendition of the National Anthem sung by Pat Baillie. Mr. Ian Gioseffi served as the master of ceremonies. There was a children's play area, memorial balloon tie down, dignitary dunk tank, and volleyball court. The inaugural Mr., Miss, and Ms. Gay Pride New Mexico pageant would also take place. The winners of the pageant would be Mr. Gabriel Duncan, Ms. Diana Johnson, and Miss Victoria Vale. These would be noted titles under RISCLEE. Not until the next year would the titles be handed over to Albuquerque Pride. Diana Johnson and Victoria Vale would be Albuquerque Pride's first title holders who reigned for an entire year. Political speakers and exciting entertainment during the day would reveal the diversity of the Gay community. Information and retail booths more than tripled from past year. Publicity in the form of banners, t-shirts and gate give-a-ways were provided by Bud Lite courtesy of Premiere Distributors. Bud Lite would become the first official "beer" sponsor promoted by Albuquerque Pride.

1996

The budget for the entire event would be $3,189.80 which would be paid by merchandise sales, sponsors and donations. The event would make $1853.57 which was donated to the New Mexico Breast Cancer Coalition. The amount exceeded all expectations; however, there would be no monetary fund's given back to Pride to produce the event in 1997. The Pridefest Committee had a successful event, but on the horizon would be the most difficult struggles that Pride in Albuquerque would ever experience. The difficulties could have stopped future events. Others would try to start a new Pride organization in Albuquerque.

Four months after the successful '96 Pride event in Albuquerque, PJ Sedillo and Tony Ross, in October, attended the 15th Annual InterPride Conference held in Kansas City. There had not been a representative from Albuquerque since 1984. They would learn about how other Prides in the United States and the world put on their events. The Conference in Kansas City was instrumental in shaping how Albuquerque Pride would exist in the future. At the conference Albuquerque Pride became members of the international organization.

PJ Sedillo had incorporated the organization under the name the Albuquerque Gay & Lesbian Parade and Pridefest a.k.a. AGLPaP (pronounced ayygulpap), with the future in mind for the organization. Many community members were outraged that Pride had become a business, incorporated. The Gay and Lesbian newspaper in 1996 was the *New Mexico Rainbow*. It would publish an article in November pertaining to AGLPaP that PJ Sedillo was the owner of Albuquerque Pride and because of this article the community had jumped to the conclusion that PJ Sedillo was sole owner of the Pride Parade which was not true. Pride had been incorporated so that non-profit status could be obtained in the future. The board of directors of AGLPaP with the assistance of RISCLEE had a community meeting to discuss the future of Pride in Albuquerque and present the 1997 Pride Theme. Many attended the meeting and some were outraged, especially from the leaders of Lesbians for Change, but only a few stayed on to help produce next year's event in 1997.

In December the *New Mexico Rainbow* would permit Albuquerque Pride to write a rebuttal to clear up any misunderstandings. The article stated that the Albuquerque, Gay & Lesbian Parade and Pridefest had been incorporated but not for the reasons reported in the November 29, 1996, issue of the newspaper. Upon attending the InterPride Conference in October, PJ Sedillo and Tony Ross had heard stories from other Pride organizations in the United States who were not allowed to use the word Pride for the event. Many religious right organizations were buying the title of Pride and planned to sue events that used the word Pride. That was one of the primary reasons for incorporation. The second was for the entity to become a non-profit which cannot be obtained unless it is a business. The response from Albuquerque Pride also stated that the article appearing in the newspaper prior to the meeting only added to misinformation and projected an unfair and biased image of the intent of the officers and incorporators, none of whom were even interviewed.

More dissent would come out over next year's theme. The 1997 InterPride theme that would be proposed to be used was, "Equality through Visibility." Additionally, some of individuals who attended the meeting were upset that the event would be at the Spanish Village which was an enclosed compound out of sight of passersby (this sentiment still exists today). The event held at the New Mexico State Fair would be debated for many years to follow. The article ended with the hopes that the newspaper would stop negatively reporting the event which could prevent any individual or group from entering into and helping create the future of this major community event. The *New Mexico Rainbow* would respond that PJ Sedillo, Marianne Strickland, and Ian Gioseffi were not owners of AGLPaP. They were in fact, incorporators and officers.

Albuquerque Pride, 1997

Despite the rocky start, Pride would have an extremely successful year in '96. Those who had opposed the incorporation of Pride would come to understand and realize why it happened. Albuquerque Pride had survived unlike the many past victims of Gay organizations that had tried to incorporate, but the community would not let them move forward. The year 1997 would be the first time the event became its own entity. It was a business and corporation that stood proudly on its own newly created foundation. In January of 1997, seventeen members of the community met at the first Pride Committee planning meeting. The word was put out in the community newspapers that key volunteered positions would be filled by election at the meeting. The following were elected: PJ Sedillo-President, Marianne Strickland-Vice President, Ian Gioseffi-Secretary/ Treasurer, John Daly-Education, Denise Grey-Entertainment, Pat Ballie-Media, Tony Ross-Permits, and Bodi Guevara-Publications/Program. Pride would be scheduled for June 7th. Steps would also be taken to move forward to have the Parade and Pridefest become a 501(c) 3 nonprofit organization. Steven K. Homer (Attorney at Law) would eventually obtain nonprofit status for AGLPaP. A budget would be voted on for $5,450.

At the meeting there would also be a discussion about where the event should take place. Many had wanted a more visible location than the Spanish Village. Some wanted Civic Plaza or Morningside Park. Others wanted to have the streets closed from the Pulse Nightclub to Morningside Park. Plans would be looked at and brought to the meeting at the end of January with possible suggested locations. These were some of the possible suggested parade routes and Pridefest locations:

1. Parade forms on Silver Ave. between Yale & Harvard in front of Full Circle Books. The parade would move onto Harvard to Central Avenue and then to Morningside Park.
2. The Parade starts at Common Bond or at Full Circle Books and heads west on Central Avenue to Civic Plaza.
3. Parade continues the route that was completed in 1996 which ends at the New Mexico State Fair Grounds Spanish Village.
4. Parade starts at Common Bond on Silver Avenue and heads east on Central to Full Circle Books where a street fair would take place.
5. Parade starts at Full Circle Books and goes to Tiguex Park near Old Town.
6. The Pulse Nightclub had declined to assist with a street fair which was previously presented as a final location

Costs were submitted. The amount of money that would need to produce a successful event was extremely high for the locations that did not end at the Spanish Village. All the amenities would have to be built or brought in at the locations in order to successfully produce what had happened in 1996 without limiting or taking away items. The actuality of bringing in port-o-potties, electricity (if available), and noise permits, concert staging to name a few items produced a list of overwhelming budgets that could not be obtained. Liquor would also not be available at any of the locations except for the Spanish Village.

This would be the first year that there was actual data collected about the importance of utilizing the State Fair Grounds. The Nob Hill Business Association would also attend an AGLPaP Board meeting. They would plead with the Board of Directors to continue the event on Central Avenue to the New Mexico State Fair Grounds. The Board of Albuquerque Pride would make the decision to use the same route conducted in 1996 where Pridefest would be celebrated in the Spanish Village. The community would be involved in the decision-making process; however, many would be upset and refuse to participate in the event because the event would be at the New Mexico State Fair Grounds. Unfortunately, these individuals would hold a grudge for many years to come and boycott the event.

Despite these challenges, the Albuquerque Pride Board was stronger than ever and ready to produce a successful event. The theme was “Equality through Visibility.” The logo was a triangle that had multiple profiles. Alternating faces were the colors of the rainbow while the others were without any color. The illusion of the logo showed a uniqueness of those who were not visible in our community.

1997

After many years of not producing a program, Albuquerque Pride was successful in getting out to the community an official program presenting all the events. This program could be obtained a week prior to the event at all the bars, the Frontier Restaurant, and many businesses located in the Nob Hill area. Signing up for the parade needed be done by May 15 to be included in the early press releases and no later than May 30th to be listed in the program. Program ads were sold which proved to be profitable.

This was the first time that the community would be inundated by the massive number of promotions and advertising produced by Albuquerque Pride. Posters and flyers were in almost all the businesses in the Nob Hill area, UNM, gay bars, MCC and even at other businesses who were gay friendly throughout the greater Albuquerque area. All the major newspapers, radio stations and television stations were notified so that articles could be produced the week before Pride. The *New Mexico Rainbow,* who had published negative articles in the past about AGLPaP, were now "on board" and reporting numerous positive articles about the events that would take place at the '97 Albuquerque Parade and Pridefest.

The Pride Committee would sponsor the Miss, Ms. and Mr. Gay Pride Pageant. The contest would be held for one night on May 31st at the Ranch. The winners would be riding as dignitaries in the Parade. Martinique Bouvier would be crowned as the first Miss Pride under Albuquerque Pride, Inc.; however, she would not be the first. Miss Pride Victoria Vale had been crowned in 1996 under RISCLEE and the title handed to Albuquerque Pride. This would also become a debate for future pageants as to who was the first Miss NM Pride. The Albuquerque Pride Board in 2016 would honor Victoria Vale with an honorary twenty-year crown and sanction her as the first Miss NM Pride. There would also be a Youth Essay Contest for those who attended Under 21. The winner would have his or her winning essay put in the official Pride Program and would be given $50.

Albuquerque's 21st Annual Gay & Lesbian Parade and Pridefest would be scheduled for June 7. The event's starting location would be on Richmond between Central and Silver. This new location was needed because of the vast number of entries in the parade. Check in would be on the corner of Richmond/Central by Pick up Your Toys, a gay friendly business, who offered free coffee and donuts to those who had registered. Registration/check-in took place between 10:30 a.m. and 11:45 a.m. Anyone that registered on the day of the event had to pay a $10 late fee. At 11:30 a.m. the first ever Albuquerque Pride Press Conference took place. Two local news agencies were there as well as all the major newspapers.

The Pridefest '97 Parade would begin at 12:00 p.m. with a ribbon cutting ceremony. The Pride Titleholders (Ms., Miss, and Mr. Pride) would hold the ribbon, and the grand marshals would cut the ribbon with the crowd and participants all cheering while the Dykes on Bikes revved up their engines.

The community had received, and acted upon, "the word/messages" about attending and participating in the event. This would result in forty-three pre-registered entries in the parade and ten entries that registered on the day, making it a total of fifty-three entries proceeding up Central Avenue. Most of the entries were floats, which was "pushed" by the Pride Committee for those who participated. The Albuquerque Pride Board would attend, as many GLBT organization meetings suggested that they produce a float for the event. The increased number of floats would change the event from not just a march but to an actual parade for all to see. Musical Theater Southwest, a local theater production company, would have a float promoting their show *La Cage, Aux*

Folles. In the end, it would be estimated that between 1,500 and 2,000 spectators watched the parade.

To this day the greater Albuquerque community, whether GLBT or "straight," attend the Annual Pride Parade to view and experience the wonderful and exciting floats that tend to surpass all the other parades that occur in Albuquerque throughout the year. This can be attested to by the floats that were showcased in '97.

The Grand Marshals were Lois Dickerman and the Under 21 Group. Lois Dickerman had worked in several arenas to promote an understanding of gay/lesbian/bisexual people and their issues and the passage of equal rights legislation in New Mexico. Lois had been an "out" counselor in the Albuquerque Public School System; a member of the Gay, Lesbian, Straight Teacher's Network; facilitator of a weekly Under 21 group of gay and lesbian teens; a former and founding member of the Statewide Coalition for Gay, Lesbian Civil Rights; and a former member of NM Lesbian/Gay Political Alliance.

The Under 21 Group, also awarded as Grand Marshal, had begun about September of 1989 with Joseph Zummach being one of the facilitators. There were three to five youths who would meet at the old Common Bond Community Center on Tulane. Andy Najar would join as a facilitator, and the group alternated with a social one week and then a week with an educational format. This would be a place youth could talk about the oppression they found in their lives and could get much needed validation and support from each other in their sharing.

In 1992 the Co-Grand Marshal, Lois Dickerman, would be involved with the group and began to work with Neil Isbin to bring schoolwide in-services for counselors and administrators in the Albuquerque Public School System. PJ Sedillo, who had worked with Neil Isbin in the past to obtain non-discrimination for all APS teachers, would be asked to assist.

Twelve to fifteen youths were willing to go on camera. Lois videotaped their conversations so that there would be "faces" to the problem that APS counselors would encounter. This would be a powerful video tape for counselors and would also be released to the APS school board who would see and hear Erin, Robert, and John talk about their experiences in the public schools and the need for youth to have an 'antennae out" for anything positive to latch onto for hope. APS would move forward to adding in-services to occur at every school in the district for educators, parents and students to view the video tape.

This would result in the Under 21 group growing in numbers of attendees and undeniably saving lives of gay youth. Parents and Gay youth were now aware through the viewing of the Under 21 videos that there was a place in Albuquerque that was a safe and inviting place for GLBT youth to participate weekly where those who attended would meet and not hide who they were. This haven would be praised by many parents. It is interesting that most of the youth would ask their parents to drop them off and did not want them to go inside. Interesting enough, what was great about this scenario was that this was typical "normal" behavior for teenagers who do not want their parents to meet their friends or might be embarrassed by what they might say.

During 1993-1994, the under 21'ers wrote letters to key state legislators about SB91, the non-discrimination act. Two members even testified to a joint chamber session with the full gallery. Two film crews from Public Broadcasting System (PBS) projects came to Albuquerque to interview the group. They appeared on *Testing the Limits* and *Road Trip Productions*. By 1995, most of the original members had graduated, and the group became smaller; however, in 1997 the group would thrive with 40-50 people with around 25 showing up on any given Friday when they met. The Albuquerque Pride Committee had chosen these grand marshals to celebrate the youth and their families; therefore, promoting the theme "Equality through Visibility." This was especially important as the youth had not been given the chance to become visible in past Prides. Many parents from the Under 21 group, both past and present, would ride down Central showing a positive image of families in the community who gave Pride a look at a positive future.

The Pride Parade would enter Gate 4 at the NM State Fair Grounds where those who attended would experience beautiful multicolored decorations, booths set up and ready for all to view, and the main stage with music blaring Kool and the Gangs song *Celebration*. The next song would be Sister Sledge's *We Are Family*. John Hull, producer of the famed, "Caught in the Act" variety show would provide, free of charge, the sound system for Pridefest. He would continue to do this for many years because of his support and love for the event.

There would be no fees to enter Pridefest, and volunteers would be stationed at the entrance with buckets to ask for donations to assist with paying for the event. Upon entering the Spanish Village there were forty-five booth registrations and twelve that registered on the day of the event. Albuquerque Pride would have to create on the spot spaces that did not exist on the originally created map in the Spanish Village to offer a space for those who paid for a booth.

Entrance and dance music would play until 2:30 p.m. where Reverend Pat Langlois would give the invocation followed by the National Anthem, Flag Raising Ceremony, introductions of the grand marshals, dignitaries and the master of ceremonies Ian

Gioseffi. Entertainment would start off with Randy Granger, followed by Exit 154, the Wilde Bunch, the NM Women's Chorus, Anna Wolfe, UNI recording artists Rachelle Karman and Karen Monty, the NM Pride Pageant performers, EMCC Choir, RISCLEE's Empress Athena Love and Princess Royal Brianna Deleon, concluding the band Third Hand. Many would leave prior to the performance of Third Hand as had happened at previous PrideFest's. The committee would need to address what would be the time that the event should end for future PrideFest's. This same concern had plagued so many committees previously.

The 1997's Pride event cost $5450. Each year the cost had an estimated increase of $2000. The Albuquerque Pride Committee started off with zero dollars in the bank because the year before all money over the expenses was donated to the Breast Cancer Coalition of New Mexico. PJ Sedillo, the President of Albuquerque Pride, had put $1500 on his credit card to pay for any incidentals accrued early on for putting on the event. He eventually was paid back when the event made a profit. The net income would be $772.47. In 1997 Albuquerque Pride had a very successful year with money in the bank, a non-profit status obtained and a community that would now back this newly formed organization/business that had successfully incorporated. On 8 August 1997, and as a Private limited company (Ltd.) company, ALBUQUERQUE PRIDE, INC began its operations and trading. ALBUQUERQUE PRIDE, INC would have 7 directors, and registration number: 1880699. The office would be located in 420 Central Ave SW, United States, Furthermore, ALBUQUERQUE PRIDE, INC.

Albuquerque Pride, 1998

After much debate, a segment of the community still wanted the Pride event to be moved from the Spanish Village to Downtown Civic Plaza because they had felt that Albuquerque Pride was hiding behind the walls of the New Mexico State Fairgrounds even though the parade went up Central Avenue for a three-mile route. Havens Levitt from WIMMIN led the charge to move the event to Civic Plaza. The Pride Board decided to sponsor a Political Rally at Civic Plaza on June 12, 1998, and offer this segment of the community who supported the Civic Plaza location "cart blanche" to present the event. Press releases were sent out to all major news outlets in Albuquerque, and the community would be inundated again with events scheduled for Pride '98, one being the rally. The event would cost $665 for a sound system and permits. It is estimated that only twenty individuals attended the event.

Many people who responded to surveys conducted during and after the Pride Celebration would respond why they were adamant against having the event at Civic Plaza and why they did not attend. The number one reason was that there was no shade (trees and grass) and that the concrete was uninviting. The second reason was that some individuals felt uncomfortable about the environment and those who responded to the survey said that the space was uninviting and did not feel welcoming. Overwhelmingly, those who responded to the survey stated that the Spanish Village felt like "home" and offered a place that they could call their own. This would be a relief to the Albuquerque Pride Board who stood by its decision to utilize the State Fair Grounds. This year marked the final debate pertaining to where the Pridefest would end and call "home." Other possibilities were being looked at for 1999. Considerations were being made to utilize the Spanish Village and rent the Indian Village (North) because the area was needed for the large number of attendees. It was predicted that attendance for Pride would increase 1000 people per year. Albuquerque Pride would envision the endless possibilities for the growth of Pride by locating the Pridefest at the NM State Fair.

The Albuquerque Gay & Lesbian Parade and PrideFest's (AGLPaP) Board Members PJ Sedillo and Tony Ross would attend the annual convention for International Gay & Lesbian Pride Coordinators (InterPride) in New York City in 1997 to gain ideas on how to improve the '98 Albuquerque Pride. PJ and Tony for many years would pay out of their "pocket" to attend the events to learn more and to be educated on how to make Albuquerque Pride a better event. Eighteen countries, including representatives from nearly every state in the US, would be in attendance. Many of the positive changes for Pride in Albuquerque would be obtained from the workshops that these two Board Members attended. At this convention the national theme would be voted upon for all Prides to utilize the selected theme for 1998.

The theme would be "Unity Through Diversity." A logo contest would take place in the community. The logo designed for Albuquerque would have a world unraveling by six individuals each in the representing the color of the rainbow. The globe would be surrounded by the words, "Unity Through Diversity." Another suggestion was to have gender parity for the Board of Directors. Albuquerque Pride would move in this direction. In 1998, pat baillie (no capital letter usage was her preference) and PJ Sedillo would become Co-presidents. However, PJ Sedillo was elected Empress of RISCLEE and their Board of Directors would not let him be part of both organizations/ incorporations. PJ Sedillo would resign as co-president, and Anthony McKinney as a "figurehead" would take his place. PJ Sedillo would be designated as a, "Consultant to the Board," so that the event would resume as expected. The other board members would be Tony Ross-Secretary/Treasurer, George Rombold-Accountant, Caroline-Parade Check-in, Elaine-Merchandising, Martinique-Pride Pageant Coordinator, and Will Wroda-Parade Line-Up (stand in for PJ Sedillo). The Mr. and Miss Gay Pride Pageant would take place in May, and Millennia would be crowned Miss NM Pride 1998. The Mr. NM Pride would not fulfill his duties, and Sid Fierro would step in as an escort and later be inducted into Pride history and given the honorary title of Mr. Gay Pride 1998. These individuals would make up the final members of the Board of Directors of Albuquerque Pride. The proposed budget for 1998 would be $9,550.

1998

Albuquerque's Gay and Lesbian celebration would be quoted by the *Albuquerque Journal* as "Pink Saturday" which would kick off with the 22nd Annual Gay and Lesbian Pridefest, undaunted by what appeared to be a hate crime against a lesbian couple on the Tuesday before the Pride Parade. Vandals broke the windows of a car and truck and damaged a motorcycle at their home in the NE Heights. APD detectives investigated the incident as a "hate crime." The phrase, "Don't Be Gay" was scrawled on the couple's car. Vandals also took a rainbow flag hanging at the home and tried to burn it.

Although the mood was festive, participants voiced concern about the recent act of vandalism. Various Gay and Lesbian advocacy and church groups joined the more than forty parade entries with floats and marchers with rainbow flags who would declare the '98 theme, "Unity Through Diversity." APD would decide to have non-uniformed police officers present during the parade who would also walk around the Pridefest event. The community members would be unaware of the concern for their safety.

The parade would again start with a press conference where representatives from several national and local Gay and Lesbian organizations would address the more than 200 people gathered at the start of the parade at Central and Richmond. A representative from Mayor Jim Baca's office proclaimed June as Gay and Lesbian Rights Month in Albuquerque. The representative also voiced the Mayor's regrets that he could not attend the event. Many were upset that the Mayor would be a no show especially because of the recent hate crimes that occurred days before the event.

The parade with Grand Marshal Jon Hull and Alan Stringer would follow the same route with thousands of spectators lining the parade route. The Nob Hill Area would become the place to view the parade. At times the number of spectators overflowed into the streets which stopped the entries from moving forward. This congestion would move the Pride Board to have parade monitors line the streets so that this did not happen in 1999.

Jon Hull, one of the parade's Grand Marshal, had been an active member of the Albuquerque Gay and Lesbian community since 1979. Having been discharged from the Air Force in 1980 for homosexuality, Jon learned early the importance of a stable and unified Gay and Lesbian community base. When he discovered the existing umbrella, organization had become cumbersome and ineffective, Jon brought together many of the people that had been disenfranchised by the old gay organizations and co-founded Common Bond to be a broadly based, highly structured, and highly visible umbrella organization. Common Bond served the Albuquerque Gay and Lesbian community from the early 1980's to1998 the same year that Jon Hull would become Grand Marshal.

During Common Bond's existence the organization would nourish and spawn many of the independent groups and services that exist today such as The New Mexico Gay Men's Chorus, NM AIDS Service, the NM Outdoors Group, The Wilde Bunch, The Duke City Professional Association, PFLAG Albuquerque, and Albuquerque Pride. Jon Hull was also the creator and producer of the famed, "Caught in the Act" variety show which would last for sixteen years and would raise over $40,000 for Common Bond and the greater Gay and Lesbian community.

Alan Stringer, Jon Hull's partner for life, was a native New Mexican from Albuquerque who was educated at UNM. He worked for twenty-five years as a teacher of English and creative writing at Manzano High School. At the same time he was an organist in the larger community. One of the founding members and an early president of Common Bond, he was a spokesperson for the Gay community on TV, in classrooms, churches, and as an educator for social workers and APS counselors. His primary contribution to the Gay community was in the founding of the New Mexico Gay Men's Chorus where he served as its accompanist and manager. He was director for the First Unitarian Church of Albuquerque, accompanist for Congregation Albert (reformed synagogue), president of the board of Opera Southwest, and a published composer with 175 works which had been performed nationally and internationally.

Honored dignitaries for the Pride Parade would be Kerry Lobel, Executive Director of the National Gay and Lesbian Task Force; Sonia Bettez, activist and founder of Lesbians for Change; Sandy Lane, chair of the New Mexico Coalition of Parents Friends and Lesbians & Gays; and the Reverend Pat Langlois, pastor of Emanuel Metropolitan Community Church. PJ Sedillo AKA Fontana DeVine (drag persona) current Empress VI of RISCLEE would conduct double duty. He/She would be responsible for the line-up of the parade despite that Will Rhoda was the committee chair for the line-up of the parade. PJ Sedillo in six-inch heels, red dress, and bouffant wig would ensure that the parade would be ready to go. PJ Sedillo had made sure to put his car, with his Emperor Ian Gioseffe, in the middle of the line-up. The parade would start, without a hitch. PJ Sedillo, Empress VI of all New Mexico, would jump into the convertible, attach the six-inch crown, and be ready to, "do the queens wave." He/She would jump out of the car when they reached the NM State Fairgrounds to ensure that all entries safely entered.

The success of Pride 1997 had Albuquerque Pride make no major significant changes for PrideFest at the Spanish Village in 1998. Booth selections, however, were added to support the increased request for participation. The only problem that Albuquerque Pride was worried about was that the Spanish Village could not support or hold the capacity of attendees and that the fire department might be called to limit the amount of people in attendance. Albuquerque Pride had a plan which was to move some of the individuals to the Indian Village if this situation would arise. A bar for liquor would be set up immediately with a makeshift stage for performers who were informed that they might have to perform twice during the day. Albuquerque Pride did not have to use the Indian Village, but they were prepared for any possible issues. This preventative action would be part of the future planning for Pridefest. The "what ifs" would help the event grow because some of these "what ifs" would end up becoming actualities.

Pride entertainment for 1998 was scheduled again from 1:00 p.m. to 6:00 p.m. starting with DJ Dealer. The opening, welcome and invocation were done by Reverend Pat Langlois (honored dignitary). PJ Sedillo-Consultant to Albuquerque Pride, a.k.a. Fontana DeVine Empress 6 of RISCLEE, sang the National Anthem. Highlights for entertainment were RaShaan Housten, Beverly DeMarco-Miss International Gay Rodeo Association, Bonnie Greathouse, and the ever popular, legendary Linda Cotton. The event would again end with Third Hand; however, Albuquerque Pride tried to make sure that many would stay until the end. Many would leave early, but 500 would stay to hear the final band. Albuquerque Pride stated in the booth registration that no one would be able to leave their booths until 6:30. This would stop the many booth proprietors from packing up and leaving prior to the events conclusion. About 200 individuals would dance to the music of DJ Dealer until 8:00 p.m. when the State Fair stated that it was time to end the event.

Albuquerque Pride would encounter another successful year. There would be two proposed Pride budgets for 1998 from 5/19/98 to 8/20/98. The event was expected to cost $9,550 for the year; however, it cost $11,214 for the event. In the end the event would have its costs coved and the group would profit $450.00 to put towards the next year.

Albuquerque Pride, 1999

The Albuquerque Gay & Lesbian Parade and Pridefest, Inc. (AG&LPaP) would meet December 13, 1998, to discuss the '99 event. Those present would be Pat Baillie (now used with capitals because the media would self-correct), Steve Perea, PJ Sedillo, Tony Ross, Veronica Roman, and George Rombold. These six individuals would meet to discuss the event in 1999 and take on board positions. The small number of individuals would be heavy on the hearts of those who were there. Each year Albuquerque would lose volunteers who would participate. Volunteers would be asked to be part of a year-long commitment, and many throughout the years would come and go because of the stressful demands put on each volunteer with the overwhelming duties. Many community members did not realize the extensive year-round commitment delivered by those who volunteered to produce a successful Pride event each year.

George Rombold gave his treasurers' report stating that an outstanding bill for the telephone was paid in the amount of $41.23 and that the State and Federal taxes would be paid. The proposed budget for 1999 would be $10,700. The 501(c) 3 packets were completed and ready to be submitted. Pat Baillie had been working with Steve Homer, Attorney at Law. The Board discussed to no longer put a date on the T-shirts as they could then be sold for future Prides. Discussion also took place to have a Youth or Teenager Pageant in conjunction with the current Pride Pageant. The Under 21 group and Lois Dickerman would be asked to assist in this endeavor.

Tony Ross, who had served many years on the Albuquerque Pride Board, would become President for a third of the year in 1999 taking PJ Sedillo's position. PJ Sedillo had stepped down for the year to assume the duties as Empress VI of RISCLEE. Pat Ballie finished Tony Ross's term for 1999. The Board of Directors of Pride agreed to take no nominations for the Grand Marshal of Pride who was currently serving on the Board.

PJ Sedillo, elected in 1999, would receive the honorary distinction of Grand Marshal because at the time of nomination he was not on the Board of Directors of Albuquerque Pride. At that time, he had served and dedicated his life to Pride in Albuquerque for ten years. From 1999 to 2010, it would become a standard procedure that no members on the Pride Board for that current year could become an Honored Dignitary or Grand Marshal of Pride.

Tony Ross would be instrumental in his brief tenure as co-president of Pride in getting changes to the application process. He would work closely with PJ Sedillo, his partner at that time of seven years, to change the Parade and Event Application process. This process of receiving permission from the City of Albuquerque became an overwhelming task. It would take up to three months to obtain permission from all of those who needed to sign off on the City of Albuquerque's Parade and Event Application. The packet needed to be taken to different agencies for approval. They were the Chief's Overtime, Park and Planning, City Barricades (the company providing the barricades), City Supervisor, Transit Services, the Nob Hill Association, the Area Commander, the Albuquerque Fire Department and the City of Albuquerque Special Events.

Albuquerque Pride would meet with Mayor Jim Baca of Albuquerque to present the difficulties in obtaining a parade permit. He said that he would work on the situation but still needed a closure for Central Avenue from the Chief Administrative Officer. Tony Ross would meet with Lawrence Rael and obtain a letter signed for the request to utilize Central Avenue east from Richmond to San Pedro for a parade in June. This letter became significant for making changes for the application process. Eventually Albuquerque Pride would assist in making drastic changes for all who would ask to produce a parade or event in Albuquerque. The City of Albuquerque would have two meetings per month to discuss parades and events where the key participants who needed to sign off on the paperwork would be present. This major change, brought on by Albuquerque Pride, would make it easier for all others to obtain a permit.

The 1999 Pride Theme would be "A Prideful Past A Powerful Future! Stonewall 30." The logo would have a cartoonlike earth with a rainbow streaming from a rocket that moved towards another planet that looked like Saturn. This would be Albuquerque's 23rd Annual Pridefest and a celebration honoring thirty years of Stonewall. This would also be the first year the shirt would be a tank top. The Albuquerque Pride Board didn't realize that "tanks" needed to be bought for both genders (male/female). This was a defining moment for clarity because "all" genders did not care if it was a male or female shirt, only that the cut fit well to each person's individual body. This would be a defining moment on what would be offered to the entire community in the future without literally "putting a label on it."

1999

May 22nd would be the annual Mr.-Miss-Ms. New Mexico Gay Pageant held at Foxes. The titleholders that evening was Mr. Rafael Lucas and Miss Sybil. June 5th would be the first Mr.-Miss-Ms. New Mexico Youth Pageant held at Emmanuel MCC located at 341 Dallas NE on the corner of Copper and Dallas. The first ever youth title holder selected was known as Geraldine. Unfortunately, she was not able to be located for her participation in the Pride Parade. She had given a phone number that was disconnected and an address that did not exist.

June 6th would be the Official Pride Week Kick Off Party hosted by the Albuquerque Lesbian and Gay Chamber of Commerce at the Albuquerque Social Club. June 12th was Pride Day. At 8:30 a.m. would be Pridefest check in at the Spanish Village for those who had booths. Check-in would take place for the parade would be conducted at 10:30 a.m.

at Richmond and Central Avenue. At 11:30 would be a community gathering/press orientation and dedication of a Hate Crimes Car. The parade would then step-off at noon.

The Honored Dignitary for Albuquerque Pride-Stonewall 30 would be Edward Clayton who had never set out to become a Gay Rights activist. He earned a degree in performing arts and embarked on a successful career as a country music singer and radio air personality. Then in 1983, he decided to forsake that line of work and enlisted in the United States Marine Corps. During his first years in the Marines, Clayton excelled not only in his academic training but in all aspects of military life as well. From top secret security clearances to Marine-of-the-Year for the First Marine Aircraft Wing in Lwakui, Japan, he showed his tireless efforts and enthusiasm to be an exemplary Marine. But in September of 1987 Clayton's world began to unravel. A fellow Marine turned Clayton in for being a homosexual. Clayton's Sergeant-Major fully expected the accusation to be proven false. Instead, the charges were proven to be true. Discharge proceedings were initiated, and Clayton was transferred to Camp Pendleton, California. While in the brig at Pendleton, Clayton was harassed, beaten daily, and forcibly raped by an HIV positive inmate. After his discharge, Clayton began to fight for his rights for all those who had been victimized even though they had honorably served their country.

The other Honored Dignitaries for 1999 would be the Gay, Lesbian Bisexual Veterans of America Color Guard (visiting from Phoenix, Arizona), the New Mexico Gay Pride Titleholders, and Victims of Hate Crimes. Albuquerque Pride would honor those who had experienced hate in their lives. A car would be designated specifically for hate crimes with a banner draped on the car in the parade. The banner was showcased to remember all those who had died or who had been beaten physically or emotionally. Individuals were able to add names to the banner for remembrance. Many names of those that had experienced a hate crime were added to the banner. Grand Marshals for the parade were Ann Frost, Mary Morell, and PJ Sedillo. Anne Frost and Mary Morell would be recognized for their years of service to the Women's Community at Full Circle Books. In 1998, it would be noted that this Albuquerque landmark marked its 25th anniversary.

Full Circle Books (FCB) was created to carry books of interest for women, for Lesbians, and for their friends, families and children. It was a whole different concept from just another book business. FCB also carried a large selection of beautiful, non-sexist, non-racist books for children of all ages and specialized in books for healing from abuse to violence. Women from the University of New Mexico could find books that mainline stores could not or would not carry. The bookstore would grow to become the community resource for the Albuquerque Gay community. They would eventually move onto the web so that other women who needed a place to find their voice could find them. By the time they got to 1998 and their 25th anniversary, FCB was one of the oldest and largest Feminist Bookstores in North America. Many women came to Albuquerque and found their way to FCB. There they found a welcome and supportive place to grow and connect. In 1999, Mary and Ann decided to search new horizons and had other paths to follow. They decided to close FCB. Nevertheless, they would participate and be honored as Grand Marshals for Pride 1999 because of their accomplishments and importance to the community.

PJ Sedillo would also be recognized as a Grand Marshal for his many years of service to Albuquerque Pride. As a native Albuquerquean, he received his BA in Elementary Education from Highlands University and began teaching for APS for ten years. He had created, started, and choreographed the first ever Gay and Lesbian Dance Troupe known as Albuquerque Beat. He performed for "Caught in the Act," and the Albuquerque Civic Light Opera, as the drag illusionist Fontana Divine, Empress 6, and raised over $50,000 which was given back to the community. PJ had been an advocate for Human Rights in Albuquerque. As mentioned earlier, he had worked with Neil Isbin in securing job protection for APS employees in the creation of a sexual orientation policy. He had served on the Board of Common Bond for several years where he began working on the Pride Parade in 1989/90. In 1996, he formed the Albuquerque Gay Parade and Pridefest. He had kept the dream of Pride alive during that stressful time, often working with only a few volunteers, never receiving compensation, and said to be sure that each June Albuquerque had a place to come together to celebrate.

PJ Sedillo would have a car designated for him to ride in the parade; however, he oversaw the 1999 parade line-up process. He needed to make sure that forty-two entries would successfully enter Central Avenue off of Richmond. The would be the second time that PJ ran five "or so" blocks up Central to catch up and jump into his car so that he could be part of the parade, this time not as an Empress of All New Mexico, but as Grand Marshal.

Pridefest at the Spanish Village would take place from 1:15-5:30 p.m. DJ JoJo assisted with bringing the upbeat sounds of Pride. He would become a fixture with the event. DJ JoJo started as Albuquerque Pride's official DJ in 1999 and would produce a CD as a keepsake for many people who attended Pridefest. Notably, Albuquerque Pride would also receive an Executive Order from Mayor Jim Baca as well as a letter of support from Vice President Al Gore.

Awards for entries in the parade would be presented on the mainstage as follows:

- Best Float/Performing - The Wilde Bunch
- Best Float/Community - tie between MCC Albuquerque and MPower
- Best Float/Business - Albuquerque Mining Company

- Best Classic Car/Group - Lambda Car Club
- Best VIP car - Annie and Mary's Grand Marshal Vehicle
- Best Motorcycle/Group was the Sirens which should be noted as an organization that was successfully led by Maria Bautista.

Maria Bautista would be instrumental in ensuring that the "dikes on bikes" contingency would lead future Pride events in Albuquerque. Not only did she ensure that this motorcycle group was represented, but she would also become an icon for preserving, supporting and fighting for future GLBT issues in our community and the grater Albuquerque area.

- Best Banner Group was awarded to Del Otro Lado.
- The overall best entry, the Judges Prize, was given to Emmanuel Metropolitan Community Church for best use of theme, color and crowd appeal.

The Albuquerque Pride Board would again successfully pull off another great Pride. The Pride Board, although small, would become a mighty force for the future, and planning would soon begin for 2000. The event had outgrown the Spanish Village, and talks were being held pertaining to future sites.

Chapter 8

Albuquerque Pride 2000 to 2005 (Enter the Twenty-First Century)

Albuquerque Pride would celebrate several great and honored milestones in the Twenty-first Century. They experienced and relished the 25th Anniversary in 2001, the 30th Anniversary in 2006, and the celebration of 40 years of Pride in 2016. Many great changes occurred for Albuquerque Pride in the 2000's. For many of the previous year's Albuquerque Pride had been seen worldwide as a small Pride, yet starting in 2000 the event would grow by leaps and bounds and would change its identity. In 2000, Albuquerque Pride had survived for twenty-four years and stood proud as one of the few Pride events that had been around for so many years. Only a few other Prides in the United States were older, some being in Chicago, San Francisco, and New York City. The first event here, in the desert of the Southwest, had occurred seven years after Stonewall which is a milestone that should be victoriously proclaimed.

Elected Co-presidents for 2000 would be Pat Baillie and PJ Sedillo. Pat Baillie would become the first female identified Co-president and PJ Sedillo the first male identified (the word "identified" would be used as a description for how one perceives their own gender identity; thus, this description was used to ensure that the transgender would not be discriminated for becoming a leader for Albuquerque Pride). This would be the trend to have a both genders identified as co-presidents. Similar problems of the animosity between Gays and Lesbians had also occurred in the community. Therefore this concept was introduced and supported by InterPride which would also occur in other cities as it did in Albuquerque. The annual Albuquerque Pride Corporate meeting would change the bylaws to reflect these new corporate officers' positions.

This team (Pat Baillie and PJ Sedillo) would become the "glue" in 2000 that would solidify the future growth of Albuquerque Pride. Unified, they would bring the community together. They would try and successfully resolve many of the past issues of unuttered divisive words spoken between the elder Gays and Lesbians that permeated throughout the community from 1970 to 2000. PJ Sedillo and Pat Baillie joined together to proclaim that the time had come to, "bury the hatchet" between identified males and females and move on. This proclamation would also be supported by the GLBT youth who became an integral part of Pride. The youth did not comprehend or relate to the reasoning why Gays and Lesbians in Albuquerque would have so much opposition.

The importance of Pat Baillie's leadership and her devotion to Albuquerque Pride should be recounted for historical purposes. It began in 1995 when Pat Baillie and her partner Reverend Pat Langloise arrived in Albuquerque. They would become the "new" force that would revitalize the Emmanuel Metropolitan Community Church. This church had separated from the Metropolitan Community Church of Albuquerque (MCCA). In years previous both churches which held different ideologies, competed for support from the GLBT community.

PJ Sedillo and his partner (Board Member) Tony Ross would be responsible at the conclusion of many Prides to ensure that the event location was left in "good standing" meaning that they had to leave the space as they had found it. This was specified in the contractual rental agreement and requirements from the NM State Fair. In 1999, one of these requirements from the NM State Fair Grounds was to have all rental property placed in its original location. This included the twenty-five, 50-pound picnic tables that were spread throughout the Spanish Village. All tables would have to be moved back to the location from where they had originally been acquired, with some tables placed one on top of the other. Albuquerque Pride had not paid for a forklift, so this had to be done manually. Also, the space needed to be free of trash so that Albuquerque Pride would get their cleaning deposit back.

All who had participated in the celebratory event of Pride 1999 had left the successful event. PJ Sedillo and Tony Ross were left alone to move the tables back and to clean up. This would be an occurring event after each Pride where the masses would leave and only a few would be left to put things in order. Those who participated and enjoyed Pride events did not realize that once the event concluded there was a massive amount of clean up. Essentially a "Pride City" was built for a brief period and then the entire city had to be cleaned, packed up, and returned to either the Pride Office or storage units. For future Albuquerque Pride's, this would occur on Sunday. The entire Board of Directors had worked intensively hard throughout the year and the weeks leading towards the scheduled Pride events, especially for the Saturday all day event which included the parade and PrideFest. All volunteers (most of them were the Board of Directors) would need to report early on Sunday to ensure that all was put back in order at the fairgrounds, and when completed all items needed to be taken back to storage or the Pride Office. Sadly, these few dedicated volunteers would complete this task, and throughout the years it would be estimated that about fifteen individuals would complete this duty for an event for thousands of individuals.

In 1999, after the event was done, Reverend Pat and Pat Baillie who were some of the last to leave were amazed that PJ Sedillo and Tony Ross were working so hard to get the Spanish Village in proper order. Pat Baillie had asked PJ and Tony where the final crew was for assistance. Both were awed and stated, "that it was them." Reverend

Pat and Pat Baillie who was from California and who had participated in many of Prides on the Westcoast were shocked by what they saw and experienced. They immediately called some members of the congregation from the EMCC who arrived to assist in the final clean-up and reorganization of the Pridefest grounds. Pat Baillie' saw first- hand the lack of volunteers for Albuquerque Pride that led her to become an active vocal member and important advocate for Pride in Albuquerque. She became co-chair for Albuquerque Pride starting in 2000 and would be instrumental in becoming the sounding board and positive voice to deter the mindset and temperament of all of those who were adamantly opposed to the incorporation process of Pride in 1996-1997. The unification between PJ Sedillo and Pat Baillie would also unify the GLBT community.

Albuquerque Pride, 2000

In 2000, Albuquerque Pride had a lot to celebrate. The community and political organizations in conjunction with Albuquerque Pride, who had become the "right arm" for the GLBT community, collectively would be a force to be reckoned with a quick "fist" of action to defeat a statewide definition of marriage. Celebrations would also transpire because Albuquerque's Mayor Baca would take a stand for human rights by signing an executive order providing domestic partnership benefits for city employees. Letters of support would also come from the Vice-President of the United States, Al Gore. He would write that he would be unable to attend the event but that he offered his best wishes for a memorable event. His letter stated the following:

> At the beginning of this new millennium, I hope that Americans will join in recognizing that the diversity of our people is the source of our strength. Our nation's success depends on our ability to value the positive contributions that every member of our society can make, regardless of any differences in race, religion, ethnic origin, economic background, or sexual orientation. You can be sure that I will continue to support the right of every American to succeed without the burden of prejudice, discrimination or persecution not only in government but in all walks of life.
>
> Tipper joins me in thanking you for your commitment to our nation and its fundamental values of inclusion, opportunity, and respect for every individual. Please accept our warmest regards,
>
> Sincerely,
> Al Gore

These victories would embody the Albuquerque Pride and International theme for 2000, "Take Pride! Take Joy! Take Action!" The t-shirt would be a simplistic design with a "waving" Pride Flag. The Board had decided to purchase tanks again for sale only in the color of ash gray. Half of the t-shirt's styles purchased for sale would be male and the other half female. No clear distinction would be made to the general public only stated at events, "buy the one that fits you best."

The event was also titled as the Albuquerque Gay, Lesbian, Bisexual, and Transgender Pride Day. This would be the first time in 2000 that the word, "transgender" was included on signs, some merchandise, in the Pride Program, and media articles.

2000

The Pride Board consisted of Co-presidents-Pat Baillie/PJ Sedillo, treasurer-George Rombold, Volunteer Coordinator-Veronica Roman, Entertainment-Dino Leyba, Permits-Tony Ross, Fund Raising-Steve Perea, and Business Representative-Beth Reynolds. The Board would declare that, "We come out 4000 strong on Pride Day but don't forget to use that power…we have just three choices this year: Take Pride, Take Joy, Take Action." Albuquerque Pride was well on its way to becoming one of the largest celebrated GLBT events in the state of New Mexico. It was evident by each year's growth that the Board and event needed to be insured. Casswood Insurance Company would become one of the first major insurance companies in the United States to provide insurance to Prides nationwide. They would become the official insurance provider for Albuquerque Pride.

The budget for 2000 was $8391.50. Notably, the event was paid for by selling shirts and other merchandise for Albuquerque Pride. Board members were required to set up a table, months and weeks before Albuquerque Pride. The tables would be set up at multiple Gay bars to provide information and to have sign-up sheets for volunteers. Shirts and "rainbow pride" ribbons would also be sold to bring in money to sustain the proposed budget. These "rainbow pride" ribbons, insignificantly made, would garner numerous amounts of donations for Pride ($1.00 at a time). Being at the Gay bars would become a "ritual" for the Board members. Months before the event they would be seen weekly at the bars putting up tables to promote Albuquerque Pride. This became the best way to get information out to the community. Information /sale tables were also set up at monthly/weekly GLBT organization meetings such as PFLAG, the Wilde Bunch, the NM Outdoors Group, and NMGRA.

Pride Week events would start Saturday, June 3rd, with the Mr., Miss, Ms. Pride Adult Title competition at The Ranch bar. On Sunday, June 4th, the Mr., Miss, Ms. Pride Youth title contest would be held at Emanuel MCC. The pageant winners crowned were Miss NM Gay Pride 1999-2000 Miss Sibyll, Mr. NM Gay Pride 1999-2000 Ralph Lucas, and Ms. NM Youth Gay Pride 1999-2000 Geraldine. The titleholders were obligated to raise a minimum of $750 individually for Albuquerque Pride. This would be a requirement for future Albuquerque Pride titleholders to fulfill.

On Tuesday, June 6th, a VIP Party was held at the Martini Grill. This event was offered to Albuquerque Pride's 2000 sponsors. The sponsors for that year were Premier Distributers (Bud Light), Albuquerque Gay and Lesbian Chamber of Commerce, Emmanuel MCC, NM Gay Men's Chorus, Pulse Nightclub, ID Lubricants (national sponsors secured from InterPride), Albuquerque Mining Company, Foxes Lounge, Frank Moschiano (CPA), New Mexico AIDS Services, MPower, The Ranch bar, and Tony Ross who would sponsor Mother Jose as 2000's Grand Marshal.

This would be the first year the Albuquerque Pride would have a, "window display" contest for the businesses located on Central Avenue in the Nob Hill area. The Nob Hill Business Association was contacted to work jointly with Albuquerque Pride. The night before the parade the Pride Board, volunteers, and the Grand Marshal Jose Sarria were all driven in classic cars by the Rainbow Roadrunners (GLBT car club) to vote on the window displays. Some of the businesses that participated were the A Store, Buffalo Exchange, Sisters and Brothers, Musical Theater Southwest, and Birdland. Birdland was awarded the winner. This event would solidify the importance of Gay Pride in Albuquerque on Central Avenue.

The Pride Day Parade started at noon at the corner of Richmond and Central and took the same three-mile uphill route heading east on Central Avenue making a left on San Pedro into Gate 4 at the New Mexico State Fair Grounds. The parade had forty-nine entries. Some of the entries were America Online, Gay Games VI, Native Pride (contingency of different tribes from NM), Mayor Jim Baca, Denny's, Intel, and the Dolls (a local drag troupe).

As part of their sponsorship agreement, Pulse Nightclub would be honored as the last entry for the Albuquerque Pride Parade which would re-occur for many years. Pulse Nightclub in 2000 returned as one of the oldest sponsors of Albuquerque Pride and was instrumental and vocal in support of the event ending at the Spanish Village, which had been a past controversy. Scott Gardner, the owner of Pulse, also hosted the Pride VIP Party and created an after-hour party located in a large, fenced area outside the Pulse bar at 4100 Central, SE. This would be the place to be seen and to go to after the conclusion of the Pride Parade and Pridefest. The judges for the parade were also located outside the Pulse.

Starting in 2000, Albuquerque Pride would select a nationally recognized person to be Grand Marshal of the parade. Contributions from the local community members would be recognized under the title, "Honored Dignitaries." The Grand Marshal for 2000 would be Jose Sarria, also known as Mother Jose or the Widow Norton. He was an American political activist from San Francisco, California. Known for his years of performing at the historic Black Cat Bar in that city from the 1950s and 1960s, Sarria entertained patrons with satirical versions of popular songs and operas while encouraging them to live their lives as openly as possible. He frequently dressed in drag. Sarria had served in the United States Army during World War II. Following his discharge, he studied to become a teacher and frequented the Black Cat. He appeared regularly at the Black Cat.

As an early GLBT activist, Sarria co-founded several homophile organizations, including the League for Civil Education, the Tavern Guild, and the Society for Individual

Rights. He became the first openly Gay candidate for public office in the United States when he ran for the San Francisco Board of Supervisors in 1961. In 1964 Sarria declared himself "Empress José I, The Widow Norton" and founded the Imperial Court System, which grew to become an international association of charitable organizations.

Following the closure of the Black Cat in 1964, Sarria went to work with restaurateur Pierre Parker. The pair operated French restaurants at World Fairs. Sarria worked at several more Fairs before retiring in 1974. After living with Parker in Phoenix, Arizona, for several years, Sarria returned to San Francisco and then moved to Palm Springs. He continued to reign over the Courts for forty-three years, before abdicating in 2007. For his lifetime of activism, the city of San Francisco renamed a section of 16th Street in Sarria's honor. Jose Sarria finally resided in Los Ranchos de Albuquerque, New Mexico where he passed away August 13, 2013.

Albuquerque Pride declared two Honored Dignitaries for 2000. They were Jerry Small and Havens Levitt. Jerry Small moved to Albuquerque in 1991 after living in Los Angeles, California, for sixteen years. Since finding his home in New Mexico, he had become a vital leader and fundraiser in the community. He had worked to develop AIDS awareness in the workplace and AIDS education from a religious perspective. He had also worked just as hard at raising money by organizing events such as the Albuquerque AIDS Walk and the Ticket to Travel for People Living through Cancer. His activism also extended to the Jewish community where he produced such events as The Chanukah Festival, the Jewish Art Festival, and Israel Independence Day for the Jewish Federation of Greater Albuquerque. He had also served as a Board member of Congregation Albert.

Havens Levitt would be the Albuquerque Pride's second Honored Dignitary. She was born in Los Alamos, NM, and moved to Albuquerque in 1954. Her first claim to fame was that she graduated from Sandia High School where she was valedictorian. She would recount that Gary Johnson, a future Governor of NM, was in her class and not valedictorian. She would work for the IRS in Houston when she came out and got involved in political work. Havens Levitt would come back to Albuquerque in 1980 and would be the founder of Women In Movement in 1981. This group would be dedicated to bringing quality events in NM for women and the community. In 1981, Havens began working with the Albuquerque Public Schools as a teacher. She would realize that she needed to work for the Gay, Lesbian, Bisexual and Transgender Youth in APS where she worked to create a safe space. She conducted full day workshops for the Gay Lesbian Education Network and PFLAG that trained APS counselors on how to work with GLBT youth. She would often state that, "Perception is 90% of the truth. If we perceive and act upon the perception that we do belong, we will."

Pridefest 2000 would be packed with "wall to wall" participants. There were over sixty booths at the event. Entertainment would be scheduled throughout the day which included Third Hand, Exit 154, UNI, Prysm, The Wilde Bunch, The Outsider, the United Court of the Sandia's Emperor and Empress, NMGRA's titleholder Brianna DeLeon, comedian Ellen Watson, and the NM Pride Titleholder. This would also be the first year that Pridefest would have a, "Continuous Dance Tent" that was placed directly north of the Spanish Village in order to support the massive number of attendees.

The year 2000 would also mark the last year that Pridefest was to be held at the Spanish Village, as the event had outgrown the space. The Pride Board realized that it was time to take the event on a grander scale. The 25th Anniversary of Albuquerque Pride would be moved to, "Main Street" in the heart of the New Mexico State Fair Grounds which would be a massive undertaking for the small but mighty Board of Albuquerque Pride. Notably, in 2000, Albuquerque Pride would become a 501c3 tax exempt organization, ending a long arduous process that finally came to fruition.

Albuquerque Pride, 2001 – 25 years

The year 2001 would require the most transformation and detailed planning for Albuquerque Pride to move from the status of a little Pride and enter the "big leagues" with the other Prides held in larger cities. The Albuquerque Pride Board would conduct the largest media campaign in its history to promote the Pride Parade and Pridefest. Posters were distributed and could be seen throughout Albuquerque, and over twenty businesses in the Nob Hill area had windows specifically decorated for Pride. The Pride Programs would be distributed throughout the community two weeks before the Pride Parade scheduled for June 9th, and the *Advocate Magazine* would include Albuquerque Pride in its Pride Guide 2001.

Planning began the following week after the conclusion of the 2000 event. The Pride Committee had sent four representatives to the annual InterPride Convention in Atlanta where Pride Organizations from the US and around the world convened. The convention would select the 2001 International Theme of, "Embrace Diversity." At the convention, PJ Sedillo was elected to the position of Regional Director. As Regional Director he was responsible for representing Pride events located in Texas, Oklahoma, Colorado, New Mexico and Kansas.

The Pride Board met with the NM State Fair Grounds planning committee to discuss moving from the Spanish Village to, "Main Street." It was discussed to pattern the event after the actual NM State Fair but on a smaller scale. The budget would increase immensely as this would be the first year that different buildings and spaces would be needed to be rented including Main Street. Because of this change, the budget for 2001 was $19,186.85 compared to the budget for Pride 2000 which had been $8,391.50. The budget had more than doubled from 2000. This increase in the budget was extremely, "scary, frightening, terrifying and petrifying" for the entire Pride Board, but it would be needed for the drastic move from the Spanish Village to Main Street. Money needed to support this extreme endeavor would need to be made through sponsors, t-shirt sales, vendor booths, and any donations from the community, and an awareness campaign was immediately started to let the community know about the plans for 2001. The community would need to be united to ensure that the 2001 event would occur.

The areas that were budgeted and secured for Pridefest 2001 were Main Street (Pride Vendors and Dance Tent), the Box Car (Pride Mainstage), the Fine Arts Building (Pride Office, Coffee House, and 1st Juried Art Show), Waterfall (Children's Area), and the Channel 4 KOB Broadcast Location (The Pink Triangle Café). Pride events would start on June 1, 2001. Some of the events planned were as follows:

June 1 - NM Gay Men's 20th Anniversary Concert at the Kimo

June 2 - Mr., Ms., Miss NM Youth Gay Pride 2001 Pageant and Stepdown for Miss. NM

- Youth Gay Pride 2000 - Fantasia at EMCC – 6:00 p.m. Stepdown Show for Miss NM Gay Pride 2000, Casandra & Andy Davis at Foxes - 10 p.m.

June 3 – Interfaith Pride Service at EMCC

June 7 – Nob Hill Window Display Contest Judging (winners announced at Pridefest) Disco Diva CeCe Peniston at AMC

June 8 – Noon submission deadline for first Pride Art Show at Fine Arts Bldg. VIP Reception and Art Show Preview hosted by The Pulse

On Saturday, June 9, 2001, the Gay, Lesbian, Bisexual, Transgender and Allied (ally added in 2001) community celebrated 25 years of Pride in Albuquerque. The year's theme was, "Embrace Diversity." The t-shirt was again offered in male and female styles in black. The logo had stars with a bigger star hugging the world. Albuquerque Pride had realized that the simplicity of the logo would be best for sales, and it was evident that t-shirt sales at this time were instrumental in ensuring that the Pride budget would be met.

Reiterating from the past, Albuquerque Pride celebrated the growth from a small gathering in 1976 to over 4,000 people who attended in 2000. The parade lineup took place from 10 am to 11:45 am starting off at the corner of Bryn Mawr and Central. Previous lineups would take place only on Richmond; however, because of the increased amount of interest of parade participation, the lineup would occur on Central in front of the businesses between Bryn Mawr and Richmond. Also, there would be entries lined up on Bryn Mawr and Richmond all facing north to make a right hand turn onto Central.

2001

Many entries that had registered that morning were located at the overflow parking lot of the Wells Fargo Bank on Richmond and Central. The Albuquerque Pride Board would realize that the line-up for the parade would have to be scrutinized and needed to be changed for 2002. However, before any future changes could be made an emergency meeting was scheduled with the City of Albuquerque to utilize Bryn Mawr for the parade's lineup. Southwest Safety would become the official barricade company that would be instrumental in supporting all requests required from the City of Albuquerque to meet all city requirements. This barricade company would be an advocate for the Pride Parade for many years.

JoAnne Ramponi, who volunteered to register entries, would become an "icon and fixture of Pride" for officially completing the registration process for the parade. Her no-nonsense attitude would ensure that the parade would leave on time. The Pride Parade would have over 85 entries (49 entries for 2000). The parade would step off at noon on time and proceed east on Central to San Pedro and then to the NM State Fairgrounds. Over 5000 spectators watched the parade especially individuals overflowing the streets in the Nob Hill business district to, "Embrace Diversity." This would solidify the transformation of the Albuquerque Pride Parade. It had become one of the most watched parades in the city of Albuquerque.

The Grand Marshal for Pride 25 was Deian McBryde a native New Mexican. Mr. Deian McBryde graduated from Rio Grande High School in 1982 and was the first male Rocky Raven. He served in the Air Force and moved to New York where he quickly became a popular solo performer on the nightclub and cabaret scene. He was named, "Out 2000 Entertainer of the Year" in New York. His debut CD, *Mollyboy*, was released in 1998. A national women's magazine *Girlfriends* selected Deian as one of, "America's Men We Love" along with other celebrities such as Antonio Banderas, Al Gore, and Oscar de la Joya. Following his 2000 tour in Australia, Deian completed his second CD, *Love & Other Distractions*, a beautiful collection of cabaret love songs from his live show. His cabaret performance was a highlight of Pridefest. He gave an encore performance at the Albuquerque Mining Company that evening at 9 p.m.

In 2001, Albuquerque Pride would create specific categories for the selected Honored Dignitaries. The three categories were Ally, Political, and Community Honored Dignitaries. Toots Obenshain would become Albuquerque Pride's Honored Dignitary-Ally. Toots and her family moved to Albuquerque with her husband Scott and lived in the South Valley. She had been a teacher most of her adult life and advocate for equal/civil rights for everyone. In 2001, she was president of PFLAG Albuquerque where she helped move the organization positively into the future.

Gloria Nieto was Pride's 2001 Honored Dignitary-Political. She was the Executive Director of the People of Color AIDS Foundation in Santa Fe and served on the Democratic National Committee as the vice chair of the Gay and Lesbian caucus. At the Democratic convention in 2000, she became the first Latina lesbian to address a Presidential convention. She also served on the board of National Stonewall Democrats and the Federation of States. Finally, working with the National Latino LGBT organization, she developed policy and provided testimony to a Congressional hearing on AIDS in minority communities.

Erika Novich would become Albuquerque Pride's 2001 Honored Dignitary-Community. She had become an important educator in the Albuquerque Public School

System; however, her devotion to the poor and less fortunate caused the Pride Board to honor her selfless acts of kindness whether working at the food bank, spearheading fundraisers for the less fortunate or assisting Albuquerque Pride with volunteering. Ms. Novich had played a major role in advocating for all. Within the Pride Program there was no picture or bio for Erika Novich because of her humbleness and modesty. Under her name and honored title, the words simply stated, "Not pictured, but certainly not forgotten."

Albuquerque Pride selected Mayor Jim Baca as an Honored Dignitary. Jim Baca rode in the 2001 Pride parade and read the city's proclamation on the Mainstage at Pridefest. He had been serving his first term as mayor of Albuquerque. As a native New Mexican, he graduated from St. Pius High School and the University of New Mexico. He was a veteran of the US Air Force and a former television news anchorman for KOAT-TV and KOB-TV. He sought out GLBT inputs early in his term and signed an executive order ensuring that city employees had domestic partner benefits (Amendment 4). He had opened dialogue about including sexual orientation in the city's Human Rights Ordinance. Mayor Baca would pay for a full page in the Pride Program. The advertisement stated the following: "The health of our community will be determined by how highly we value diversity. As Mayor, I have fought hard to ensure [that] this respect for diversity is reflected in your city government—this effort is now paying dividends. Join our fight for human rights!! Together we can make Albuquerque the best mid-sized city in the nation!! Best wishes for a successful Pride Parade and Pridefest. Thank you for continuing to raise awareness in the community– Jim Baca."

Albuquerque Pride highly publicized PrideFest's new location, Main Street at the NM State Fairgrounds from 1 to 5 p.m. It would be decided that the event would be free, and volunteers would be located at all entrance areas to collect a $5.00 donation. Some volunteers who collected and, "barked" for donations would experience words of scorn, disregard and disdain. Many who entered the gates would not realize the $19,000.00 price tag that needed to be raised for the event to happen. This would be a reoccurring factor that would plague future Albuquerque Pride's.

Pridefest 2001 had expanded and obtained over 60 vendors, an art show with over 75 entries, youth area, Triangle Café, dance tent, live stage, coffee house, dance lessons, beer garden, Dunk Tank, Moon Jump, Volleyball section, and car and bike show. On top of this, the NM State Fair division would also require Albuquerque Pride to have an official First Aid Station with a licensed doctor.

One of the biggest successes of Pride 2001 was the creation of the first Juried Art Show. In the past there had been art showings that were part of Pride; however, this was a first to honor and celebrate the great artists in the Gay community. Utilizing the Fine

Arts building offered a new exciting attraction for those who attended. Many would be thankful for the opportunity to enter a building with air-conditioning to escape the heat. Many would stay in the building to experience not only the art show but the coffee house and the Over 21 Room sponsored by the leather community who provided practices and styles of dress organized around sexual activities. Wearing leather garments was one way that participants in this culture self-consciously distinguished themselves from mainstream sexual cultures.

The Pride committee had decided to sell food for the event at the Pink Triangle Café which brought in $1700 from selling drinks, hotdogs and chips. However, selling food at the Pink Triangle Café limited the Board's availability throughout the day's events. Tony Ross, a member of the Board of Directors, would contact and recruit contractors from his business to help assist during that day. Without their assistance the Pink Triangle Café would have been a disaster.

There had been another vendor, Reed's, with a food cart at Pridefest. Reed's would be the first food vendor to participate. This is significant because mainstream food vendors who participated annually at the NM State Fair would become interested in participating in future PrideFests. Overwhelmingly, it was estimated that there were over 5000 individuals who showed up for PrideFest 2001. Pride 2001 Financial Analysis would report the following:

Opening balance	**$2,014.00**		
Receipts:			
Gate	$2462.00		
Pride Booth	$ 315.00		
Café	$1700.00		
Art Show	$ 300.00		
Auction	$ 339.00		
Parade	$1030.00		
Booths	$1927.00		
Ads	$1805.00		
Sponsor	$6365.00		
T-Shirts	$ 464.00		
Bank Div.	$ 29.00		
Shows	$2396.00		
Pageants	$ 340.00	**Total Receipts:**	**$21,486.00**

Note: Budget was overspent by $184.00. A huge budget increase from Pride 2000 to Pride 2001 necessitated hard work to provide needed funds for signed contracts. Even though the budget was slightly overspent, the closing balance

exceeded the opening balance by $101.00. – Respectfully submitted, George B. Rombold, Treasurer.

The year 2001 marked Albuquerque Pride's 25th Anniversary. The Board felt that the budget would reach well over $20,000 and that many would be willing to open their pocketbooks to donate to Pride if the event did not meet the final budget of $19,371. Surprisingly and revered by the Albuquerque Pride Board they were able to pay all costs of the enormously expensive event and celebrate with an opening balance of $2,115 for the following year after all expenses had been paid.

Albuquerque Pride, 2002

PJ Sedillo and Pat Baillie Pride Co-Presidents would state that Albuquerque Pride took a big step in 2001 by moving Albuquerque's Pridefest to a bigger venue at the NM State Fairgrounds. The move to Main Street brought out record crowds with over 5000 GLBT and supportive community members. Both had agreed that they had learned much from Pride 2001 by ensuring a bigger and better Pride for 2002.

The International Pride Theme and Albuquerque's theme was "Pride Worldwide." The t-shirts were not offered as a tank top as the community wanted t-shirts so that they could wear them throughout the year. This was a change that was made from surveys that were conducted at the end of each Pride for the community to add input to positive and negatives at the event. The logo designed had a three-dimensional world with a rainbow wrapped behind the earth with the scripted wording, "Pride Worldwide." The event was completely supported by the following volunteer Corporate Board Members: PJ Sedillo-Male Co-Chair, pat baillie-Female Co-Chair, George Rombold-Treasurer, and Joy Ehler-Secretary/Booth Coordinator. Because of the huge success of Pride 2001, many individuals from the community would step forward to volunteer for the event.

The Planning Committee consisted of Tony Ross-Permits/Pride Food Booth, Deb Conway-Art Show Coordinator, Reva Chapman-Assistant to Treasurer, Bill More-ALGCC Business Representative, Denise Edwards-Merchandising/Pride Booth Coordinator, Linda Davis-Art Show Assistant, Andy Davis-InterPride Representative/Region 3, Midnyte (aka Michael Tellez)-Mr. NM Gay Pride 2001, Serena (aka Michael Davis)-Miss NM Gay Pride 2001, Erin-Ms. NM Gay Pride 2001, and Karma-Miss NM Youth Gay Pride. Other key planning representatives were Lana Taylor Sinatra (Dino Leyba)-Pageant Coordinator, Kate Chapman-Personal Assistant to Co-President Pat Baillie, and Albert Cota-Main Stage Manager. The budget for 2002 would be $26,962.00.

2002

In 2002, Albuquerque Pride was disappointed with the result of the printing for the Annual Pride Guide. Many saw guide's print as not, "attractive" as the organization had wanted because newspaper print had been used. It was decided that the future Pride Guides would need to be of higher quality and quantity. Despite the quality of the Pride Program, over 3000 copies were to be distributed throughout the community weeks before the event and would be replenished throughout the week before the Pride Parade.

The Pride Board would make the decision to have the Pride Parade on the second Saturday in June and would continue this date for future Prides. This would make it easier to plan other Prides in New Mexico. It would also make it an easy way for the greater Albuquerque community to put the day of future Pride's in their calendars.

May 24th would be the Adult and Youth Pageant Interviews. On May 25th were the 2001 Mr. New Mexico Pride-Midnyte and Miss New Mexico Pride-Serena's step-down show at the Albuquerque Mining Company. On May 26th at 8 p.m. would be the Mr., Miss, Ms., and Youth Pageant at the Pulse Nightclub. The pageant was for all ages; there was a charge of $5.00 at the door. On June 1st was the Mr., Ms., Miss, NM Adult Pride Pageant (note the word Gay was removed from the title). The event was held at the Sunshine Theater located at 102 Central Avenue. Meet and great was at 5:30 p.m. The pageant would begin at 7:30 p.m. Tickets were available at Sister and Brother's for $10.00 in advance and $12.00 at the door. There was an after-hour's show at the Albuquerque Mining Company where the newly crowned Miss NM Pride Gia Del Rio, Mr. Ernie, and Ms. Andrea Quijada would have a time to savor in their victories and start their community service of raising money for Pride 2002-2003.

The title from the Pride Pageant had become in 2002 some of the most sought-after titles for the drag community. The show would also assist in becoming a crucial fundraising and promotional event for Albuquerque Pride. Sinatra DeVine Productions sponsored the Adult and Youth Titleholder pageants. The events would be produced and emceed by drag personas Lana Taylor Sinatra and Fontana DeVine, the creators of this not-for-profit organization. This pageant would serve as the foundation for future pageant competitions and would become the, "name say" for upcoming entrepreneurs who would begin to produce and take on the extensive pageantry in the future. For a couple of years Lana Taylor Sinatra would be part of this not-for-profit business but would ultimately retire. Fontana DeVine (AKA PJ Sedillo) for many years to come would take the lead for producing, emceeing, and finalizing the event with the support of the Board of Sinatra Devine and Albuquerque Pride. The Albuquerque Pride Pageants would become just as important as the past variety show, "Caught in the Act" which had been known for its monetary support and the promotion Pride.

June 6 was the Business Windows Display Judging which had become a huge event supported by the Nob Hill Business Association. On June 7th, the Albuquerque Pride Juried Art Show took place at the Fine Arts Building at the New Mexico State Fairgrounds. Entries needed to be turned in from 8 a.m. to 2 p.m. This event held during Pridefest had grown overwhelmingly. Up to three entries only would be allowed by an artist. The artist also had to pay a $5.00 price per piece entered. Artwork could be sold at the Pridefest where a portion of the sales would be donated to Pride.

Also, on June 7th from 5 p.m. to 6 p.m., was a book signing at Sisters' and Brothers' bookstore with Patricia Neil Warren, Albuquerque Pride's 2002 Grand Marshal. Patricia Nell Warren was the author of the most popular Gay novel of all time. She had written professionally since the age of seventeen. Over the years her literary subjects had ranged from women, human rights, gay life and mixed blood people, the earth, and wildlife. Warren had published eight novels with three published under her own imprint, Wildcat Press. The *Front Runner, Harlan's Race, and Billy's Boy* are a landmark series which followed an evolving family through twenty years of Gay life. These books have become essential Gay literature for bookstores worldwide.

Warren's best-known book, *The Front Runner*, was first published by William and Morrow in 1974 and became the first Gay novel to make *The New York Time's* Bestseller List and to be mass-marketed into chain stores and supermarkets across America. This landmark classic about the relationship between an ex-Marine track coach and his top male runner has sold over ten million copies worldwide and has been translated into ten languages. In a survey of Gay bookstores nationwide, it remains the number one bestselling Gay book in history.

Finally, on Friday, June 7, from 7 p.m. to 8:30 p.m. the VIP Wine & Cheese Reception and Art Show Preview took place. It was sponsored by The Pulse. Tickets for the event were $20 or two for $30. Artists, sponsors, honored dignitaries, and the Pride Board would be given a complementary ticket to attend. This would become the event that was known as the event to, "see and be seen" at for Pride. Individuals who attended this event could also view the introduction of the Pride Archives that also took place at the Indian Arts Building.

PJ Sedillo (Co-president of Pride) who had collected years of boxes full of past Pride memorabilia decided to catalogue and put in frames the historical perspective of Albuquerque Pride. This event would only showcase thirty-five panels from 1977 to 2002 (there are now in 2016 currently over 300 panels in the collection). T-shirts and merchandise from past events were also displayed from events sanctioned only for Pride in Albuquerque held during Pridefest. This would become the first ever display of the historical events for those who participated from 1976-2002. The formation of presenting these archives would lead PJ Sedillo to ensure that all historical artifacts for Pride in Albuquerque would be catalogued and honored. This display and collection of historic memorabilia ultimately led to the creation of the first book and now this sequel.

After the event was concluded on Friday, and for future Friday Pride events, Pride Co-president PJ Sedillo and Andy Davis, a strong advocate for the event, would walk the fairgrounds to ensure that all was secured and ready for Saturday. PJ, who rarely smoked cigarettes (or would admit that he never bought cigarettes), would ask Andy Davis for one, and they would walk together, "lit up" for inspection. This included checking or verifying the fencing, vendor booth set up, lighting and sound, decorations, and tables. They made sure that the waterfall was running, the beer stations were positioned, the dance tent was set up, the grass was mowed, and the ID Lube trash receptacles were in place. These were only a few of the areas that needed to be checked, inspected and approved for Pridefest.

This process would take up to three hours; however, it would be a time when both who had dedicated their devotion to Albuquerque Pride would relish in the beauty and serenity of the location. They would then realize that the next day would become a, "rainbow colored, glorified event, sparkled with glittered loudness, and Prideful splendor" for those who would attend and experience Pridefest 2002 in just few hours away. With the passing of Andy Davis, as a NM Pride Titleholder and Board Member, PJ Sedillo would continue this ritual until his tenure as President of Albuquerque Pride ended. He would light a cigarette in honor of Andy Davis and begin his sanctioned march of inspection.

June 8th was Pride Day. The Pride Parade would utilize 2001's lineup on Central Avenue, Richmond and Bryn Mawr. Check in was located on the corner of Richmond and Central between 9:00 a.m. and 10:30 a.m. with JoAnne Ramponi- Pride Check-In Volunteer at the helm. A total of forty–seven pre-registered groups were given a preassigned number. If registering on June 8th, individuals would first need to check in on Central to get a number for the lineup. This process would become problematic for the lineup because Pulse's Sponsorship put them last. Ultimately, there would be sixty-two entries for the event, with fifteen entries signing up that morning to participate. The Pride Board would need to analyze this reoccurring situation to make the Pride Day lineup more efficient.

Jo Kenny would be the Honored Political Dignitary. She had worked for social change since the late 1960's on a variety of fronts including support for United Farm Workers, for veterans of the Vietnam War, supporting for feminist and union issues, and of course for LGBT civil rights. Jo Kenny would state, "I am a progressive and an activist because of the values that are at the core of my heart: that everyone is entitled to equality and justice and to live their lives with dignity and respect. I believe in economic justice, our responsibility to be stewards of the planet, and the rights of women to have freedom over all aspects of their lives, including reproductive freedom." Jo Kenny's start to advocacy would begin in 1978 in California where the right-wing was trying to pass a statewide law that would make it illegal to be a lesbian or gay teacher or even a vocal L & G (lesbian/gay) ally in the public-school system.

John Fleming, Honored Community Dignitary, had moved to Albuquerque with a new and infused phase of his life. He had come out of the closet. He stated, "I became me and started learning how wonderful life can be." This is when he also learned how gratifying it would be to be involved in trying to create change. Common Bond would lead him to be instrumental in participating as a member, Board Member, and volunteer. Next, he would become active in the New Mexico Outdoors organization. His next steps would be the Secondary School Project, the Scholarship Committee for Common Bond, and Duke City Businesses and Professional Associations President. This association would become the ALGCC-Albuquerque Lesbian Gay Chamber of Commerce. He would become a crucial advocate for PFLAG Albuquerque, the Coalition for Equality in New Mexico and NMPower.

Joe and Jean Travis would be honored with the title of Honored Ally Dignitaries. Joe and Jean Travis had become familiar, beloved faces in the GLBT community. They supported various AIDS organizations in the state of New Mexico. Their work was launched after the death of their only son Michael. From making a panel for Michael to be included in the AIDS Memorial Quilt, they became involved in the NAMES Project New Mexico in 1995. Joe served as the Chairman of the New Mexico Chapter of the AIDS Memorial Quilt and worked tirelessly to bring the Quilt to the State of NM. He would eventually, through his endeavors, display the Quilt at some relevant events such as the AIDs Walk and the Friends for Life Dinner. Beginning in 1990, Joe Travis had a float of Quilt Panels entered in the Gay Pride Parade. Both Jean and Joe worked long hours to finally display a majority of the memorial quilt at the Albuquerque Convention Center for World's AIDS Day 2001. They would take sections of the Quilt panel and present them to students in the Albuquerque Public School System for prevention education.

This instrumental couple would also start the NMAS Food Bank that would become essential for many. For many years they gave, "their life's blood" to keeping this food bank open. Joe and Jean shared their personal story of caring for and losing a family member to AIDS which led to their life's work in the community. They would become honorary, "parents" to anyone who needed support. In their loving and parental way, Joe and Jean were the absolute best at holding hands and lending a shoulder to any who needed them. They had been frequently invited to attend drag shows. Despite their age and the smoky conditions of the bar where the shows occurred, they would state, " [the] Queens call us mom and dad, and how could we resist their performance." Jean and Joe would be honored for turning a crisis in their family into a way to make a difference in the world for all their time, energy and love of Albuquerque Pride. The community would say "Thank You."

As was previously done in 2001, the Board Albuquerque Pride—Pride Worldwide 2002 would denote the Mayor of Albuquerque as Honored Dignitary. As a native of Albuquerque, Mayor Martin Chavez began his first term as Mayor in 1993 and had become an important positive advocate for the GLBT community. Martin Chavez returned to Albuquerque public service as Mayor in 2001. He immediately rededicated himself to Albuquerque's diverse citizenry. He appointed a cultured, varied, and talented team that reflected the community's diversity. He would be committed to the youth, public safety and high lighting Albuquerque's bright future. As Mayor in 2002, he would state, "Throughout all the tough decision-making, I never lost sight of the underlying issues that affect a city's consciousness." He would be proud to sign legislation to end employment discrimination, enact a hate crime ordinance, and work closely with the various organizations to build a sense of community. He would provide yearly proclamations touting the Pride event. During his tenure he would participate by riding in an honored dignitary car provided by the Rainbow Riders' Car Club.

After attending numerous InterPride Conferences, the Board of Albuquerque Pride felt assured that the time had come to secure a, "Headliner" for the event. The mere logistics of having a nationally known performer would be an unsurmountable experience. The general population of those who attend Pride events may not know the logistics (sometimes ludicrous) that need to be fulfilled for obtaining and providing a "notable and iconic" performer for Pride. Besides the extreme expense for their performance, some of the other items that needed to be paid for were their travel expenses from their location to Albuquerque. If their arrival was at the airport, would a limo be required to the hotel? If the hotel was not a "star" appropriate location, what extra services would need to be obtained? What time would a sound check is done? Does the event have the proper equipment requested? What if they ask for red jellybeans in the "rider," and they are not in the dressing room? What if there are only two white lined towels instead of the five as they requested? These were only a few of the requirements that Albuquerque would have to deal with when bringing in nationally known headliners for Albuquerque Pride. Many did not realize the cost and the requests made each year by the headliner who would entertain and bring enjoyment for those who attend Pride.

Despite all these possible hindrances, Albuquerque Pride would contract Thelma Houston their first ever headliner and deem her as an Honorary Grand Marshal. Thelma Houston was a multi-talented singer, songwriter, actress, and international performer. She was noted as an accomplished entertainer whose credits were a testament to her desire to meet new challenges and create new opportunities.

Within her three decades (noted in 2002) as a recording artist to her credit, Thelma Houston proudly looked at a career rich in achievement. When the dance music era of the 70's was at its height, Thelma Houston's passionate, gospel-routed voice stood out memorably above the rest. *Don't Leave Me This Way*, her Grammy-winning gold single, was an outstanding example of the soulfulness she brought to the dance genre. It would be at this time that the Gay community would relish this song as a fight for independence.

Known as a humanitarian for her ongoing support for a variety of charitable causes and most specifically for her tireless efforts in the battle against AIDS, Thelma Houston would join all of those at the event closing as a headliner on the Pridefest Mainstage from

6 p.m.to 7 p.m. Albuquerque Pride would state on posters and to the media, "Come hear the woman who got us through the 70's and continues to call to us to grow, learn, and fly into 2002."

There would be eighty-one Pridefest Vendors for 2002; however, fifteen would register on the day of the event. This would be the last year that Albuquerque Pride would sell food. Food sales would be given to those food vendors who were able to meet all the specificities from the State Fair. Some of the food vendors were Funnel Cakes, Garduno's, The Ice Cream Man, and Reed Concessions. Albuquerque Pride would re-evaluate and analyze what would be the appropriate payment for a food vendor space for next year's Pride in 2003.

The Main Stage for Albuquerque Pride would have PJ and Pat emcee. This would be an undertaking for them because both would be, "stretched" in different directions ensuring that the event was on schedule. They had both agreed to come together at 11:44 a.m. to emcee and ignore any problems (which would be an extreme difficult decision). Despite any problems Pat and PJ were able to announce the first act UMOJA (a male acapella group). Umoja is a Swahili word meaning unity; however, in African American communities the word has become divisive as describing homosexual love which has deeply divided those who oppose homosexuality.

Many African families and congregations were unsure about supporting loved ones who came out as lesbian, gay, bisexual or transgender, especially when the Bible appears to teach otherwise. Certain factions could facilitate safe, non-threatening dialogue about the diversity of human sexuality, or others could create complete havoc and destruction. This tension existed within African American faith communities in relation to LGBT individuals. Albuquerque Pride felt that this population of the community needed to be validated, supported and honored. That was one of the major reasons why Pat Baillie and PJ Sedillo felt the necessity to introduce the first performers on the Mainstage.

The next emcees for the Main Stage were Martinique and Sid, past Pride titleholders who would introduce the NMGMC, the Sugar Kookies, Angelica del Rio, Laticia Lovato, and Ann Lincoln. The final emcees would be from the New Pride Titleholders-Miss Gia Del Rio and Mr. Ernie. They would introduce the performers Eric Chavez, Ronda Carlisle, and Randy Granger. Adan Branchal a "stellar" Mariachi member would get the crowd excited and open for Headliner Miss Thelma Houston at 6:00 p.m.

The budget for Pride 2002 was $26,942 and was secured. The event also needed to be gated because of liquor requirements. Volunteers, "pleaded" for a $2.00 donation at the gates where those who donated would receive special promotional items from the sponsors. Unfortunately, many individuals who came through the gates were outraged, rude, and refused to pay for the event. This would become a foremost issue for Albuquerque Pride to deal with. As a major Pride event in Albuquerque and destination for others in the Southwest, the event for 2003 might cost $30,000. Many who would attend did not realize that the few volunteers who worked the entire year to produce the event would be ultimately responsible for paying for the event.

Albuquerque Pride, 2003

In 1976, about twenty-five members of the Gay Community had walked down on the sidewalk of Central marking the first Gay rights march in Albuquerque which then gave, "birth" to a Pridefest that moved from Morningside Park to the Spanish Village and then overtook the New Mexico State Fairgrounds. The event in 2003 would have over 7,000 individuals attending the daylong event. More space would be needed for vendors, and more entertainment would be requested from the community for twenty-seven years of Pride.

Questions would be posed in 2003 as to why there was a Pride every year? Some would say that the event is just a big party. The Albuquerque Pride Board would agree that a Pride event was there to celebrate, but to continue to move ahead on the GLBT issues that were faced in New Mexico, a Pride event also needed to take place. In 2002 there had been a recent signing by the Governor for hate crimes and non-discrimination and gender identity. Being, "out," educating, networking, and finding the Gay community voices would be a focus. Mayor Chavez had proclaimed an Executive Order to protect Transgender city employees as a step to fulfill and complete protection under the laws of the State of New Mexico which was well ahead of its time for the nation. Board Members of Albuquerque Pride worked closely with the mayor on this task force. PJ Sedillo and Pat Baillie spearheaded this task force. Ultimately, this would lead to answering the question to the community as to why Pride should be alive in Albuquerque.

In July, the Albuquerque Pride Board decided to enter a float in the New Mexico State Fair Parade scheduled for September. This would be one of the "scariest" endeavors that the Board would face in 2003. Some of the Board Members would not participate, since they could be fired from their jobs, family members did not know, or they were not out. There would be twenty-four brave individuals (one shy of what had occurred in 1976) who would ride on an extravagant float built by different community organizations who had come together to support Pride's endeavors. The Board had decided to only have the wording ALBUQUERQUE PRIDE on the float. Most were unsure what would happen. All in all, participation in the largest parade in New Mexico would garner a first-place ribbon for participation. Those who were part of this groundbreaking statement that the Gay community was part of the greater Albuquerque community would be celebrated.

PJ & Pat, Co-presidents of Pride in 2003, would proclaim and remember that old song, "Let Peace Begin with Me," and decided to have the community come together to share, "Peace Through Pride." This was the theme selected from the International Pride organization of Pride Coordinators. Albuquerque Pride, as a member of this international organization, would decide in 2003 at their annual meeting, that future Prides each year would accept and honor the selected theme from InterPride. Themes from InterPride were selected a year in advance which made it easy to plan for upcoming Prides in Albuquerque.

2003

2003's t-shirt design has been one of the best-selling t-shirts to date. It won in 2023 at Pridefest best overall t-shirt, the "People's Choice." This was one of the most difficult t-shirts to produce. The rainbow colors had to be added together so when screened through the process to get the rainbow affect. However, a very little amount of red could be seen. To solve this problem the Pride Board showed up one evening at Black Duck Printing Company (which became the official t-shirt printers) and with red magic marker Sharpies added the color on over 500 t-shirts. All in all, this has been a crowd favorite for years.

The Corporate Pride Board would include PJ Sedillo and Pat Baillie -Co-presidents, Andy Davis-Secretary, and Reva Chapman-Treasure. The Planning Committee would be Tony Ross-Booth Coordinator, Andrea Quijada-Ms. NM Gay Pride 2003, Ernie Martinez-Mr. NM Gay Pride 2003, Crystal Torres-Youth Area and Dance Coordinator, Midnyte (Michael Tellez)-InterPride Region 3 Alternate Director, Bill Moore-Representative from ALGCC, Committee Volunteers-Karma/Mario Uzzel and Armando Moreno. Other key Planning Representatives were Lana Taylor Sinatra (Dino)-Pageant Coordinator, Kate Chapman-Pridefest Facility Coordinator, Albert Cota-Stage Manager, Michael Madlener-Car Club Coordinator, Veronica Roman-Hispanic Arts Coordinator, and Ruth Jimenez-Literary Salon Coordinator. The amount of needed committee members and volunteers was extremely evident in 2003.

Notably, Co-presidents Pat Baillie and PJ Sedillo would be honored as Grand Marshals in 2003 from the New Mexico Gay Rodeo Association and during the ceremony the Co-presidents, when they received the award would ensure that the entire Board was introduced to the crowd for those present would see all of those who had made the event happen. The budget for Pride 2003 would be $37,232.47.

Of upmost importance for this historical account of Pride, it must be reiterated that when a, "budget" is released to the public or presented to the Pride Board at its Annual Corporate Meeting, most assume that the amount of that proposed budget is money that is, "available;" however, these are not available funds to produce Albuquerque Pride. It is the money that needs to be obtained and secured to put on the event. These funds are not in, "hand" but are needed to be acquired to meet what is budgeted to produce the event. If the budget is not obtained, then areas requested or certain items are reviewed to see if there is a need for them or not.

Each year this becomes a difficult and stressful situation for those on the Board to decide what must be included in the budget or not. When the budget is not met, the Pride Board must work on revising. This might increase multiple questions being asked, or it might be as simple as removing one "porto-pottie." Other questions asked for revising the budget might be about removing one police officer from the parade, purchasing no crowns for the titleholders, or decreasing the number of decorations.

Many who attend Pride events do not realize the amount of work needed to put on an event whether it is a small event, a medium sized event like Albuquerque Pride or an event attended by one million participants. All Prides, in order to happen, need to obtain funds through fundraising, sponsors, and donation from supporters.

Pride Day would be scheduled for June 14, 2003. The theme would be announced to the community as, “Peace Through Pride.” The year before in 2002, Albuquerque Pride’s program was deemed, “unacceptable.” In 2003 Albuquerque Pride would showcase the event in a program that would be well received by the community. The program would cost $3,157, and this was a significant increase that would have to be budgeted for. Additional fundraising would need to take place to pay for the program.

May 30th would be the 2002 NM Pride Titleholder Step Down Show at the Wool Warehouse at 7:00. May 31st would be the NM Pride Pageant. Youth and Adult Interviews and Pridewear Preliminaries were at 2:00 p.m., and the Pageant was at 7 p.m. June 7th would be an event to meet the Honored Dignitaries from the community at Sister and Brothers’ Bookstore. Abraham Placencio, The United Court of the Sandias, and Jean and Jim Genasci would also be at the event to be congratulated for the work that they had done for the community. June 12th would be the annual Business Window Display Judging conducted on a Thursday night. The voting panel viewed window displays by all the supportive businesses. The winners selected would be determined as a tie between Buffalo Exchange (3005 Central) and Birdland (3213 Central). Friday, June 13th, would be the Juried Art Show with the VIP Wine and Cheese Reception that evening. The event sponsored by the Pulse would include meeting all the VIP’s including the Grand Marshal Miss Gay America 2003-Dominique Sanchez and the headliner Thea Austin.

In 2002, Albuquerque Pride would have to turn off the music for those who still wanted to stay, dance, talk and just, “be” after the event. Hundreds were upset that Pride would be shut down. Albuquerque Pride was aware that the event must end at a certain time to meet the requirements from the New Mexico State Fairgrounds. How would Pride now provide a proper closure for the few who were still celebrating after the event had ended? Some venue changes were made for those who would need some type of finalization, a closure. Importantly, those who stayed after the event did not realize that multiple contracts would be signed and would require many logistics to be included to put on Pride. These required paying for and keeping the sound system past the contractual agreement, negotiated contracts with security, negotiated and paid use of appropriate space at the NM State Fairgrounds, and the availability of Board Members and volunteers to be in attendance. These would become only a few of the many reasons for Pride to be extended, but could the budget sustain this request?

Many Albuquerque Pride vendors, Board Members or those who attend the event do not realize that the contractual times enacted by the NM State Fairgrounds are signed and set, “in stone.” Many of these contractual agreements are budgeted to the minute one begins using the space to when we leave. Therefore, because of the unknown they make it difficult to pay for any extension of the event or prior use of each space. This would make it extremely difficult to figure out the times for Pridefest to begin and end. The act of keeping the event for even just an hour longer could have devastating effects on the budget. Trying to figure this out would become an ongoing issue for future Prides in Albuquerque.

However, due to this problem in 2002, upon listening to the community and reviewing impromptu survey answers and suggestions, the Board Members heeded a need for change. Below are adjustments in 2003 that were then provided from the Pride Board:

- The parade lineup has changed. Do not look for us on Richmond and Central Avenue as we've outgrown the side streets. This year [2003], thanks to the UNM Women's Resource Center, we'll be lining up at UNM. Entries need to turn north on Girard from Central, past the fire station and pull in the parking lot behind Ortega Hall where we will all be in one place for the lineup.
- We [Albuquerque Pride] will also be doing pre-judging of all floats and VIP cars at UNM at 10:30 (be sure that your group is there by then). The parade starts at 11:00 a.m. [new time]. Once we turn onto Central from Girard, the parade route hasn't changed and will proceed up Central turn left on San Pedro and enter the State Fair. This will be a new exciting process as we are extending the parade route. It is suggested that your group make a float as the walk will be longer and uphill.
- The Pridefest Celebration times have gone back from noon to 5:00 p.m. with the headliner Thea Austin performing at 5:00. The dance tent will stay open for those who want to continue partying with Pride after 5:00. The dance tent will end at 6:00.

The reasoning that the dance tent would end at 6:00 would be that at 7:00 p.m. a Youth Dance (no alcohol) would take place, thus providing a reason for those still dancing to leave for the youth (this simplistic response, but crucial, would give an explanation to those adults who still wanted to dance to leave the NM State Fairgrounds). A Youth Dance was not created because of the need for those to exist who were still present after the event had concluded. Numerous requests from the youth and the community would ask what is provided for the youth from Albuquerque Pride. The sound company's contract would be obtained until 12:00 p.m. that evening. Since the sound system's contract was still, "active," the Albuquerque Pride Board agreed that it would be easy to set up a Youth Dance. It was decided to then move to the Hispanic Arts Building. With the leadership of the Albuquerque Pride Youth Titleholders, the youth gathered to decorate the building. The Adult Titleholders, who had shown up in the evening to perform, also provided their support.

The Hispanic Arts Building would be a new acquired location for Pride 2003 that would provide private weddings, dance lessons, and a meet and greet for Thea Austin. An increase of 100 panels for the Pride Archives would be placed among the walls for attendees to view the history. The panels would be an integral part of educating the community about the importance of Pride in Albuquerque. Because of these important changes made for 2003, Albuquerque Pride would conduct its first official survey to gain information and data to assist Albuquerque Pride with their future growth. Some of the survey questions asked for demographic information was the following:

- Age
- Home Zip Code
- Live in (city, small/medium town, pueblo/reservation, rural)
- Lived in NM for how many years?
- Year of first Albuquerque Pride you attended
- Sex (Male, Female, Transgender, Not Identify, Other)
- Sexual Orientation (Gay, Lesbian, Bisexual, Queer, Straight, Not Identified, Other
- Community Group (Political, Social, Drag, Leather, Spiritual Organization/Practice, Other
- Racial Group (select all that apply): Asian, Black, Hispanic, Indian/Native American, White, Other
- Highest Education Level (6th grade, 9th grade, High School/GED, Some College, BA/BS, Master's, Doctorate
- Family Income [you define family] (Less than $20,000, $20,000-$40,000, $40,00-$75,000, $100,000-$150,000, Over $150,000.
- Are you registered to vote? Yes No
- Did you vote in the November 2002 election? Yes No
- Have you ever contacted an official about GLBT issues? Yes No

This would be a first for the Albuquerque GLBT community to obtain crucial data from the community in terms of demographics. A Give-A-Way for filling out the survey would be given to a lucky individual. The winner of the Albuquerque Pride Survey Drawing of two Roundtrip Tickets on Southwest Airlines (Sponsor for Pride 2003) was Holly Lindsay and her partner. The Pride survey results were reviewed, reassessed, and presented in October 2003 at the National Coming Out Month Celebration.

As written previously, 2003 marked another change for the Pride Parade. For years the staging area was held on Richmond and Central. Previous growth had required the event to utilize Richmond, Silver, Central and Bryn Mawr for staging. In 2003, the event outgrew the area and was moved to UNM. The staging area would be able to have over seventy entries. This new staging area would push to the limit the amount of space needed. The location would be reviewed for next year's Pride Parade and revamped if needed.

As in past parades Albuquerque Pride would congratulate the 2003 Grand Marshal and Honored Dignitaries. Cars to ride in were provided by the Rainbow Roadrunners Car Club. Dominique Sanchez, Miss Gay America 2003, would be Albuquerque Pride's 2003 Grand Marshal. For thirty years, female impersonators had been, "camping it up," capturing many imaginations and being out in front of the GLBT movement. In 1973, a contest was created to crown the most glamourous of those female impersonators and provide them an opportunity to network across the country, build a stronger community, and continue to be a visible sign that all could be what they dream. Dominique Sanchez competed at the 30th Annual National Pageant held October 2002 in Little Rock, Arkansas. The categories for the event were Male Interview, Creative Costume, Evening Gown, On Stage Interview, and Talent. This 27-year-old Leo came through a field of contestants from all over the country as the best and the brightest. Based in Little Rock, Arkansas, Dominique enjoyed dancing, cheer leading, reading, and fashion designing. When on the road promoting the Miss Gay America event, she was raising the standard for female impersonators all over the country. Grand Marshal Dominique Sanchez and all the other, "drag queens" (female impersonators who have made Prides occur all over the world) would be saluted!

The United Court of the Sandias (UCS) was honored as the Community Honored Dignitary. Their support was backed and remembered by those who were at Stonewall, those drag queens that pushed the edge. UCS did shows in the gay bars to entertain and try to make the community a better place by the tips they would collect from those individuals in the audience who would graciously honor their performance by tipping, "and raising one dollar at a time." This is what UCS continued to do, honor, strive for, and sometimes weekly, tirelessly and unmentioned conduct a show to raise money for those less fortunate.

This institutional belief system would come forth from Mother Jose (Grand Marshal in 2000) the founder of the Court System. In the late 1960's she began the court for those who were put down in society to feel better about themselves. She created titles based on a monarchy such as Emperor, Empress, Prince and Duchess. Over the years, this court system grew and became a major fundraising organization in their local communities. UCS was no exception.

The Albuquerque Pride Board would recognize the difference UCS had made for the community for the 2003 year in Pride. It must be remembered that in 1996, the Common Bond Community Center which assisted individuals to put on a yearly Parade and Pridefest was having financial and internal problems. That year, subsequently, Albuquerque Pride left Common Bond to become its own entity. The event was sponsored by RISCLEE (The Royal Imperial Sovereign Court of the Land of Enchantment Empire) which eventually became UCS (the United Court of the Sandias) which was instrumental in ensuring financially that the Albuquerque Pride event in 1996 would transpire and therefore produce subsequent Albuquerque Prides to occur.

Albuquerque Pride would honor UCS in 2003 as a major fundraising organization in the community and would salute them for the many, "drag shows," carwashes, raffles, and other fundraisers that they had almost every weekend. They had benefited many groups and individuals. These drag queens and entertainers had collected thousands of dollars while voicing their motto, "one dollar at a time." UCS consists of many who have come and gone and those who are now being, "born" as new court members and drag queens. All must be honored that have raised awareness and money for Albuquerque Pride. There are those who have yet arrived who are ready to fulfill the dream of making the community a little bit better.

Abraham Placencio (AKA Angelica Del Rio) would be Albuquerque Pride's 2003 Political Honored Dignitary. Some of his/her accolades include being Co-President of the Coalition for Equality in New Mexico, the first Miss Gay New Mexico performer in the community, and TV show producer for Community Cable Channel 27. Under all this glamour was the hard work of Abraham as he moved to build bridges and understanding throughout the State. In 2003, Abraham and the work of the Coalition and many others brought about the passage of the hate crime and anti-discrimination laws at the State level. His devotion took years of educating, networking, and talking to others who might not understand the GLBT community.

Jim and Jean Genasci (AKA "Mom" and "Dad") would be 2003's Ally Honored Dignitaries. They had both been long time activists for minority causes and the GLBT and Ally Communities. Both had been involved in PFLAG in Massachusetts and New Mexico. Jean served for six years on the National Board of PFLAG (Parents, Friends, Lesbians and Gays) and served as both Chair of the Regional Directors and national Vice President. She also represented the national PFLAG in the Freedom to Marry Coalition. Jim co-founded a chapter of PFLAG in Massachusetts and co-led a second one. Jean was a retired public-school educator. Jim was a leader in his professional field of physical education, athletics, and sports. Since moving to New Mexico, they had worked on the Albuquerque Scholarship Fund Committee and the PFLAG Albuquerque Speaker's Bureau. Jean worked on the Human Rights Advisory Committee to Mayor Baca; APS

Superintendent's Community Council on Equality and Community Advisory Board, PFLAG Albuquerque Community Liaison and was a founding member of NM Gender Advocacy Information Network. Jim was a volunteer teacher at the Palo Duro Senior Center where he assisted both beginner computer users and those who wanted to construct their own web sites. Jim and Jean had spent countless hours working at the legislature and in the community. Both were committed to working to bring visibility to GLBT issues.

Honored Dignitary Mayor Martin J. Chavez would also be highly regarded. As a native of Albuquerque, Mayor Chavez earned a bachelor's degree from UNM and a law degree from Georgetown University in Washington, D.C. Martin Chavez served as the first Director of NM's State Worker's Compensation Administration in 1986 and in the NM State Senate from 1989 to 1993. On December 1, 1993, Martin Chavez began his first term as Mayor of Albuquerque. He was proud to sign legislation to end employment discrimination, enact a hate crime ordinance, and work closely with different groups including GLBT leaders to build a sense of community. Martin Chavez returned to Albuquerque public service as Mayor in December 2001, and he immediately rededicated himself to Albuquerque's diverse citizenry. He appointed a cultured, varied and talented team that reflected the community's diversity. Mayor Chavez would understand the need for strong public safety initiative and a continuing revitalization and redevelopment in the city. He continued to support the executive order providing city employees with domestic partner benefits.

Pridefest 2003 would be from noon to 5 p.m. There were over seventy vendors, mainstage, youth area and stage, dance lessons, art show, dance tent, literary salon, and six food vendors. Located at the Pride Mainstage at 12:35 would be a, "Getting Our Rights" celebration to thank the many elected/appointed officials who had supported the GLBT community. Some of these elected/appointed officials in attendance were Governor Bill Richardson, Lieutenant Governor Diane Denish, Attorney General Patricia Madrid, Senator Dede Feldman, and Representative Mimi Stewart. Other officials Stuart Bluestone, Liz Stephanics, Pam Hine, and Ken Martinez would also be in attendance.

Some of the entertainment on the Mainstage included the Debi Graham Band at 1:00 p.m., Blayne Bell at 2:35 at 4:15, Nobody'z Bizniz would open for Thea Austin, Pride's Headliner who would close Pridefest 2003. Thea Austin, International Pop/Dance Artist, was the original lead singer of SOULSEARCHER and the original vocalist of SNAP. She became famous for her emotionally powerful and potent contralto vocal delivery and her creative songwriting talents which were best known for the international multi-million selling hit, "Rhythm Is A Dancer," which scored a #1 hit on the Billboard Hot 100 Singles Charts for 54 weeks, peaking at number 3. The single written by Austin went on to become a universal dance anthem. She also co-wrote several other international hits for

SNAP including, "Color of Love," "See the Light," and "Believe In It." She also, opened for Michael Jackson's, "Dangerous Tour" and HBO Special. Thea Austin would take the mainstage at 4:45 and sing well past 5:30. Those who attended Albuquerque Pride in 2003 fell in love with Thea.

Albuquerque Pride ended at 6:00; however, the free Youth Dance located in the Hispanic Arts Building was scheduled from 7:00 to 10:00 pm. The NM Pride Titleholders would attend and provide entertainment. The building was transformed with decorations by the Youth Dance Committee. There would also be food and drinks free to those who attended. This event would grow to about 85 youth. Many appreciative parents would drop off their children at the event which would be the highlight for 2003.

Albuquerque Pride, 2004

Gay Marriage became the hottest issue in 2004 in the State of New Mexico. Sandoval County experienced the first ever same sex marriage licenses issued from a Republican County Clerk, Victoria Dunlap. The county clerk had examined New Mexico's marriage laws and decided that she was bound by their language to issue marriage licenses to same-sex couples. February 20th, amid a firestorm of controversy, the Republican issued licenses to gay and lesbian couples who raced to get their marriage licenses in Sandoval County. Reverend David Gant from EMCC and Reverend Judith Maynard were at the courthouse ready to immediately marry those who were in line.

Sixty-four licenses were handed out. This was abruptly stopped by the State Attorney General Patricia Madrid (Democrat) who intervened that same day. She would write to local officials an advisory statement. It said, "No county clerk should issue a marriage license to same-sex couples because those licenses would be invalid under current law." Albuquerque Pride, as well as the community, was stunned by her actions. Patricia Madrid had been honored the previous year in 2003 on the Pridefest Mainstage Legislative Celebration for her part in contributing to the many human rights legislation that took place that year. She would refuse to meet with leaders from the community from Albuquerque Pride, The Coalition for Equality, and EMCC and MCCA to discuss her actions. New Mexico's state legislature would consider a constitutional amendment limiting marriage to one man and one woman, but the measure would die in committee, leaving State law silent on Gay marriage.

These brave couples who were married were known as the "Sandoval 64." They would take on this controversy in New Mexico and bring it to the forefront. Mainstage at Pridefest celebrated the marriages that were conducted in Canada, Vermont, Massachusetts, and New Mexico's own Sandoval County.

The Executive Pride Board of 2004 would consist of PJ Sedillo-Male Co-chair; pat baillie-female Co-chair, Andy Davis-Secretary, and Reva Chapman-Treasurer. The Planning Committee would consist of Tony Ross-Facilities, Ernie Martinez-Member at Large, Steve Benoit-Business Representative, Veronica Roman-Volunteer Coordinator, New Mexico Pride Mr., Miss, MsTer, and Mr. Youth 2004 titleholders Tony, Raquel, Jesse and Aries, Andrew, Crystal, and Frida. Other Key Coordinators would be Dino Leyba-Art Show and Pride Pageant, Kate Chapman-Facilities (Pridefest), Albert Cota-Mainstage Manager, Michael Madlener-Car Club Coordinator, Ken Neukhemper-Pavilion Stage/Drag Coordinator, Laticia Lovato-Pavilion Stage/Karaoke Coordinator and Midnyte (Michael Tellez)-Bar Representative/Region 3 InterPride Director.

2004

Midnyte introduced a possible international theme at the InterPride Conference. There was an extensive process held each year at InterPride to choose the International Pride Theme. Most importantly each theme had to be able to be translated in every language in attendance at the conference. Notably, the word, "out" or "coming out" does not translate easily and was not considered for many years. The theme that Midnyte submitted was *Viva La Differencia, Viva La Pride* which was voted upon by the entire delegation, accepted and approved as the International 2004 Pride Theme.

In 2004, community artists submitted logo designs to be decided what would be the best t-shirt design for that year. The Pride Board had a difficult time selecting a logo as there were many great submissions. It was decided that year to produce a t-shirt and an official Pride Pin to be sold that year for merchandise.

Pride planning meetings were scheduled for March 18, April 7 and 20, May 6, 13 and 25. They were located at 1525 Girard in the Amigo Case Management Office. Amigo Case Management would provide meeting space and be a sponsor for Albuquerque Pride for many years. April 20th would be Albuquerque Pride's Pageant Application Deadline and Meeting. On April 30, there was a deadline for a 10% discount on parade and booth registrations and all ads to be put in the Pride Program. This discount was introduced to try to avoid the numerous parade and booth entries that would occur the day of the event making it difficult to start the parade on time and the logistic changes needed to be made at Pridefest for booth set up. Booths were required to set up starting at 6:30 a.m. and needed to be in place no later than10:30. The early payment would also assist in ensuring that the budget would be reached.

This year marked another first for Albuquerque Pride. After years of debate the Pride Board would vote unanimously to have an entrance fee into the Pridefest gates for the continued growth of the event. Adult admission would be $3.00. Children under 10 would be $1.00. A massive media campaign would take place to ensure that the community would be aware of this change. A few members were opposed to the charge, stating that Pride was for all and that there should not be a fee to participate. The Pride Board's campaign to educate the community about the cost of the event worked and over 8,000 people would pay the $3.00 at the event gates. The budget (as of April 30, 2004) would be $52,741.

Expenses:

Fairgrounds Rentals & Facilities	$12,650.00
Pride Shows/Pageants	$ 3,960.00
Parade Costs	$16,000.00
Promotional Costs	$12,600.00
Administrative/Other Costs	$ 4,601.00
TOTAL BUDGET	$49,811.00

Income (estimated incomes as of April 30, 2004)

Parade Registrations	$ 1,200.00
Pridefest Booths	$ 3,500.00
Pride Program Ads	$ 2,300.00
Sponsorship	$13,000.00
Barter: $10,000.00 (not included in total)	
Titleholder Fundraising	$ 3,500.00
Pageant Income (projected)	$ 3,500.00
Pridefest Art Show (projected)	$ 700.00
Merchandise Sales	$ 1,000.00
Pridefest Gate (projected)	$19,000.00
TOTAL INCOME	$47,700.00

(within $5000.00 of budget + need 2005 seed money)

The campaign to educate the community about the budget for Pride would be successful. Many did not realize the amount that it cost to put on the event including the parade. It was assumed that the use of Central Avenue was free and that the Albuquerque Police Department was also required to work without payment because it was their job. This would be one of many falsehoods pertaining to the expenses needed to produce Albuquerque Pride. For many years, and some to this day even assume that PJ Sedillo, President of Albuquerque Pride, got paid for assisting with Pride. For his entire tenure he was only a volunteer and never received any payment for the jobs he performed. Duly noted if he did receive any payment, it would have to be reported to the "feds" because of the non-profit status and public knowledge.

The only real fear that the Albuquerque Pride Board had that year was that the budget was dependent upon obtaining sponsors and upon those who attended the event paying the $3.00 to enter Pridefest. It was projected that $19,000 would be obtained from sponsorship. The Albuquerque Pride Board had all agreed that they would donate funds from their own personal accounts if the budget was not reached. Despite this fear the community came together to support this new change. The incoming amount surpassed was projected. Having an entrance fee for future Albuquerque Prides would continually be debated by a segment of the GLBT community who felt that the event should be free. Interesting enough, many of these proponents against Pride never became an Albuquerque Pride Board member.

Sponsors for the event would play a major role in assuring the existence of Pride in Albuquerque. Albuquerque Pride Sponsors for 2004 would be Miller Lite (Albuquerque Beverage Co.), Sinatra DeVine Productions Inc., Pulse/Blu Nightclub, New Mexico Aids Services, AMC, Out in Albuquerque, Double Tree Hotel, Pride Gym, MCCA, EMMC, Maddox & Co., Frank Maschiano-CPA, Amigo Case Management, Abraham Placencio, United Court of the Sandias, Sisters & Brothers (The Alternative Store), the Albuquerque Convention and Visitor's Bureau (ACVB), and Basic Rights NM.

In 2003, a survey was conducted by Albuquerque Pride. The results and data collected would show and reveal the amount of revenue Albuquerque would receive from sponsors for the annual event. June 13, 2004, there would be an article in the *Albuquerque Journal* highlighting the census data from the survey that would pinpoint NM for companies that sold to gay and lesbian households. The survey data collected at Pride 2004 and the Journal article would provide crucial statistical data for future reasoning to investment in the event. This would lead to a partnership with the ACVB which would highlight the event in, "The Official Visitors and Vacation Planner" magazine distributed throughout New Mexico and the United States. The ACVB would now be able to promote the event to those from other states who would contact the bureau about what was available for the GLBT community in Albuquerque.

May 7th, the 2003 Titleholders Step-Down would be at the Wool Warehouse with a reception and 7 p.m. show. May 8th was the 2004 Pride Pageant with contestant interviews held from 12:00 to 4:00 p.m. There was a band at 5:30 p.m., and the NM Pride Pageant would start at 7:00 p.m. to crown a Mr., Miss, Ms., and MsTer Adult, and Youth titleholders. This would be the first year that the MsTer category would be introduced. Definitions for each category would also be introduced to the community as follows:

Mr. - Self-identified male (gay)
Miss- Drag Queen/Female Impersonator
Ms. – Self-identified female (lesbian)
MsTer – Drag King

That evening the titleholders crowned would be Mr. NM Gay Pride Tony Carson, Miss NM Gay Pride Raquel del Rio, MsTer NM Gay Pride (the first year of our drag king title) Jesse, and Mr. NM Youth Gay Pride Ariel Le Chat. They in a combined effort would raise almost $4000 for Albuquerque Pride.

Scheduled for June 10-13 would be the performance of Howard Crabtree's *When Pigs Fly.* This was a comic revue about a unique young man's dreams of life upon the stage, based upon a book by Mark Waldrop, directed by Zane Barker, presented by Musical Theater Southwest (MTS) also a sponsor of Albuquerque Pride 2004. Shows benefiting the AIDS Emergency Relief Fund and Albuquerque Pride would be Thursday, Friday and Saturday at 8 p.m. The 2004 Albuquerque GLBT Pride Business Window Display Contest would grow again with the number of participants. There would be judging conducted by the Pride Board. The community could vote by picking up a ballot at the business and submitting it on Friday, June 11th, from 8:00 a.m. to 9:00 p.m. Voting also took place online at www.abqpride.com. This would be the first time for Albuquerque Pride to utilize its website for voting. There was an increase interest in participating in 2004. The following businesses participated in the contest:

Addicted to Comics and Hobbies-4008 Central SE
Albuquerque Mining Company-7209 Central NE
Alphaville Video-3408 Central SE
A-store-3500 Central Ave SE Beyond
Borders-111 Carlisle Blvd. SE
Birdland-3213 Central Ave. NE
Buffalo Exchange-3005 Central Ave. NE
Buster's 66 Coffeeshow-3624 Central Ave. SE
Café Next Door-4013 Silver SE
El Paso Import Co/Mariposa Gallery (2 windows)-3500 Central Ave. SE,
Evolution/Crush-4517 Central Ave. NE
Flying Star-3416 Central Ave. SE
Hey Johnny-3418 Central Ave. SE
Martha's Body Bueno-3105 Central Ave. NE
Morningside Antiques-4001 Central Ave. NE
Musical Theater Soutwest-4804 Central Ave. SE
Off Broadway-3110 Central Ave. SE
Peacecraft-3215 Central Av. SE
Two Serious Ladies-3901 Central Ave. NE
Unique Plaza-4716 Central Ave. SE

The winners of the 2004 Albuquerque Pride Business Window Display Contest were First Place-Café Next Door, Second Place-Buffalo Exchange, and Honorable Mention-Unique Plaza.

On June 11th, Albuquerque Pride's Art Show at the Fine Arts Building at EXPO NM would open from noon to 7 p.m. The NM State Fair would change its name to EXPO NM in 2004. That Friday evening there would also be a Names Quilt Viewing, Marriage Collage display, VIP Reception, and the first viewing of the Albuquerque Pride Archives in the Indian Arts Building from 12:00-9:00 p.m. PJ Sedillo had volunteered for Albuquerque Pride since 1989 and had collected numerous of boxes filled with meeting agendas, newspaper articles, pictures, trophies, etc. all recording 27 years of Pride in Albuquerque. PJ Sedillo decided that it was time to organize and frame panels to record the history so that it would not be lost. That year over 30 panels of Pride memorabilia was displayed that became the "birth" of The Albuquerque Pride Archives. Many who entered the exhibition were awed by the past artifacts that had been so well preserved for future generations to experience. Some who saw the archives for the first time would also contribute their own Pride memorabilia to be part of the Albuquerque Pride Archives. In 2016, there are over 250 panels of history pertaining to Pride in Albuquerque. These panels have contributed to much of the content within this book and some are highlighted after each chapter.

Albuquerque's 28th Annual GLBT Pride Parade was scheduled for June 12, 2004, with its step-off at 10:30 a.m. from Central and Girard to Expo NM. The parade would highlight 2004's Grand Marshals Reverend Dr. Mel White, Legislative Allies, and Honored Dignitaries Steve Helmreich-Political, George Rombold-Community, and Christy Carbon-Gaul-Ally.

Grand Marshal, Reverend Dr. Mel White was the author of *Stranger at the Gate: To Be Gay and Christian In America* and the Justice Minister of the Universal Fellowship of Metropolitan Community Churches (UFMCC). For thirty-five years of Rev. Mel White's life, he struggled to, "overcome" his homosexual orientation through prayer, fasting, various aversive therapies, exorcism, and even electric shock therapy. A victim of misinformation and biblical misuse, Mel thought his same-sex orientation was a sickness and a sin. During those, "closet years" Mel served the Christian church as a prize-winning television producer and filmmaker, a best-selling author, a pastor, seminary professor, and ghost writer to religious leaders including Billy Graham, Pat Robertson, and Jerry Falwell. After a time of terrible depression, Mel White finally reconciled his Christian faith and his sexual orientation.

In his autobiography, *Stranger at the Gate: To Be Gay and Christian in America*, Mel announced, "I'm gay, I'm proud. And God loves me without reservation." Reverend White and his partner, Gary Nixon, have traveled across the country as the UFMCC Minister of Justice seeking equality and understanding for God's lesbian, gay, bisexual and transgender children. In 1997, Mel and Gary received the ACLU's National Civil Liberties Award in Atlanta, Georgia, for their efforts at applying the "soul force" principles of Gandhi and Martin Luther King to the struggle for justice for sexual minorities. At Pridefest Reverend Mel White spoke to the crowd and asked, "for all to continue to fight and live your life completely out, in all aspects of your life. Each one of us has the gift to change the world."

Steve Helmreich would be Albuquerque Pride's 2004 Honored Dignitary-Political. Steve moved to Las Cruces in 1988 to work at the Computing Research Lab at New Mexico State University. In the years preceding the move, he had been in the process of coming out and decided that the move was a good opportunity to start everything out on an open footing. The AIDS crisis was an impetus for his coming out. Steve continues to be involved with that issue. He had served on the Governor's HIV/AIDS Task Force. At first, he found it difficult to get connected to the Gay community in Las Cruces, which resulted in the formation of a Gay men's group (SGMA-Southwest Gay Men's Association) and a newsletter (The Normal Heart). Out of those experiences Steve met his partner, Guy Wolffarth. Pushing for domestic partner benefits at New Mexico State University and inclusion of sexual orientation in Human Rights Ordinance has added a political slant to Steve's activities. He also is a church organist at Peace Lutheran Church in Las Cruces and believes that drawing the spiritual connection between sexuality, theology, and religion is an important task for the times.

George B. Rombold was selected as Albuquerque Pride's 2004 Honored Dignitary-Community. He was born in 1930 and is the father of two, grandfather of seven and great-grandfather of five. After the death of his grandson in a house fire, George introduced to the Albuquerque City Council and spearheaded the passage of the Allan C. Pfeiffer Smoke Detector Ordinance. For six decades, George had experienced the actual formation and progress of the GLBT community in Albuquerque. He was an advocate and supporter of equal rights and social justice for all people and a participant in efforts toward self-acceptance within the Gay community and understanding in the community at-large.

George was the founder and administrator of The Littlest Angels, an organization providing funerals and burials for abandoned infants. He was also active in participating with the AIDS Emergency Fund, author of *Through a Glass Darkly* an autobiography, and former Treasurer of Albuquerque Pride Board of Directors. Additionally, George Rombold was a member and former vice-moderator of Emmanuel Metropolitan Community Church, and recipient of the United Court of the Sandia's Humanitarian of the Year award, as well as being recognized in Marquis', "*Who's Who in America.*"

Christy Carbon-Gaul was Albuquerque Pride's 2004 Honored Dignitary-Ally. Christy was a shareholder with the firm of Sutin, Thayer & Browne and now the owner of her own law firm. Christy practiced primarily in the areas of Estate Planning and Probate,

Corporate, Non-Profit and Real Estate law. Christy received her B. S. degree in accounting from Trinity University and her J.D. degree, *cum laude*, from Creighton University School of Law. Christy served as President of the New Mexico Women's Bar Association and as past-president of its Mid-State Chapter. Christy, also, served on the Board of Directors of the NM Wildlife Association which operates Wildlife West Nature Park in Edgewood, New Mexico. She and her husband, Dan, have two children. Christy Carbon-Gaul has provided legal advice and counsel for Albuquerque Pride, "pro-bono" for numerous years and is a strong advocate for marriage equality. Many of her clients are GLBT whom she assists in writing wills and domestic partner agreements.

The legislative Allies honored this year were Governor Bill Richardson, Lieutenant Governor Diane Denish, Albuquerque Mayor Marin Chavez, Senator Cisco McSorely, and Representative Gail Beam. All would be present on the Pridefest stage to receive a plaque and recognition for their positive support of GLBT New Mexicans. Mayor Martin Chavez would read the Executive Order proclaiming Gay, Lesbian, Bisexual and Transgender Pride Week. Albuquerque Pride 2004 would be dedicated to all those who had worked hard to ensure equality was being granted to all GLBT New Mexicans and citizens of the United States including the Sandoval 64, Albuquerque Pride's 2004 Honored Dignitaries, Grand Marshal and those in NM State government. Pridefest celebrated the many brave individuals who stood up for full marriage rights. *Crosswinds Weekly* (Newspaper) would present its *Profiles of Commitment* that was released during Pride Week. The newspaper would highlight activists, women, men, and teens committed to fighting for the nation-wide struggles for GLBT rights.

PJ Sedillo, Male Co-chair of Albuquerque Pride and Board Member Tony Ross would be highlighted in the newspaper. While they had always been active in the Gay community, legal events surrounding their marriage have added new importance to their political activism. Sedillo, an Albuquerque Public School teacher, led the fight for domestic partnership benefits for years and was denied. In 2003, Governor Richardson signed a bill amending the State's Human Rights Act to include a prohibition on discrimination based on sexual orientation. The couple jumped on the new provision and filed a lawsuit against the district. In October of 2003, Tony Ross and PJ Sedillo would represent Albuquerque Pride at the annual InterPride Conference held in Montreal, Canada in Ottawa, Canada in 2003. This would give them the opportunity to actually "tie-the-knot" and get legally married.

During open enrollment another round of insurance changes or additions for APS, PJ Sedillo would do his annual trudge to APS's Central Office; however, this time was different. He had a marriage certificate in hand. This would be the first time that he took the forms because PJ Sedillo was not asking for domestic partnership benefits but this time for full spousal benefits. The couple would experience a whirlwind of news stories in papers and on television. The couple would be the first same-sex couple in the nation to get full spousal benefits from a public school system. Their marriage along with others would be honored by Albuquerque Pride.

It was expected that over 10,000 individuals would watch the parade or participate, attend the multiple events prior to the parade and attend Pridefest. There were over 100 booths and many food vendors as well as a Karaoke Stage, a Drag Stage, the annual art show, archives, youth dance in the evening, car show and coffee house/poetry slam. The Pridefest Mainstage would showcase many local Albuquerque performers who were given a standard fee of $20 for their performance. Albuquerque Pride had grown over the years and made a name for being one of the largest, most hospitable GLBT events in the Southwest.

The group Shitting Glitter would be one of the first groups/bands to contact Albuquerque Pride from West Hollywood, California, to play on the Mainstage at Pride for free. They agreed to pay their own way and receive the standard $20.00 fee paid to entertainers. This alternative rock band would be described as, "angst meets kitsch in a colorful sonic landscape where new wave and indie rock are combined with queer sensibilities, a dash of political activism, and a twist of surrealism." Shitting Glitter had performed at large events from Los Angeles to Reykjavik, Iceland and would grace the Albuquerque Pride 2004 Pridefest Mainstage and become a "hit" with the crowd. Many new Shitting Glitter fans would be made that afternoon.

Pridefest would have three major performers in 2004. Nationally known comedian Dana Goldberg would be on the Mainstage at 1:30 p.m. The noted Headliner would be Pepper MaShay (Sponsored by Pulse) at 3:00 p.m. The Featured Performer Paul Lekakis (Sponsored by AMC) would perform at 4:35 p.m. The Board of Directors and Planning Committee decided to have the major performers perform early in the day because of the large number of attendees who would leave the event by 5:00. This would become a dilemma for future Albuquerque Pride Board Members to solve.

Dana Goldberg would state that she was, "raised by a wild pack of Jews, otherwise known as her mother and siblings." Dana Goldberg was a force of nature on stage. She set the standard for smart comedy. Her timing and tongue-in-cheek edginess was why she continued to collect loyal fans in cities all over the world. Goldberg's quick wit and playful stage presence was spreading like wildfire! Voted one of the "Top Five Funniest Lesbians in America," CURVE Magazine raves, "She's smart, cute, and seriously funny!" The *Irish Post* wrote, "Dana's sharp, insightful observations are concealed behind an easy-going chatty style. This makes her one of a handful of comics able to transfer their work across the Atlantic." Goldberg started her comedy career in 2003 in front of 650 people in a sold-out theater in Albuquerque, New Mexico. Seven months into her career she was invited to Scotland by Emmy Award Winning writer Paul Wagner to perform with thirteen other American comedians as part of the US Comedy Invasion at the Fringe Festival in Edinburgh. After returning to the states, Goldberg began competing in festivals and competitions all over the country. She was one of five national finalists to perform in the "Wendy's Good Taste Comedy Challenge" produced by HBO and TBS in Las Vegas, Nevada as part of The Comedy Festival.

Pepper Mashay was 2004's Albuquerque Pride headliner. Perhaps nobody is more surprised by Dance Diva Pepper Mashay's esteemed status among the gay masses than the humble Ms. Jean McClain, the real person living within Pepper's persona. With three billboard chart-topping dance anthems in the past two years, her voice had continually connected with the audience that seemed to admire her strength, her fierce presence, her ability to feel real. Fame was a long time coming for McClain. The Muncie, Indiana-born army brat moved to Los Angeles and spent decades as a studio singer, eventually backing the biggest voices in the business such as Cher, Tina Turner, Whitney Houston, Mick Jagger, Michael Boston, Lenny Kravitz, and countless others. Wife, mother, and part-time breadwinner, she paid her dues singing mostly rock, R & B, until the mid-90's when a short European tour with a female vocal trio landed her in the middle of one of Europe's largest dance clubs.

After returning stateside, McClain joined ranks with various dance producers, one of whom pitched a stage name Pepper, because of her freckles, and MaShay, a "rip-off" of the word paper-mâché. Her hits included *Dive in the Pool* (Showtime series Queer as Folk lead single in 2001), *I Got My Pride* (featured on Sex and the City), *You and Me [Feels So Good]* (No. 6 on Billboard Charts), and *I Pledge* (a spoken-word Pledge of Allegiance). MaShay's brand of house was mighty, maternal, and materially gay. Even with her star on the rise, but she was firmly grounded, earthy, and unstoppable.

The Featured Performer for Albuquerque Pride 2004 was Paul Lekakis. Paul was a native New Yorker and currently resides in Los Angeles. He is an internationally acclaimed record artist who is best known for his top ten MEGAHIT, "*Boom Boom Boom – Let's go Back to my Room*" and "*Come on Over to My House.*" Paul would be Albuquerque Pride's closing act on the Pridefest Mainstage at 4:35 p.m.

The year 2004 would be a year of many changes and growth. The budget of $52,741 would be obtained with "seed" money for 2005 in hand. The Pride Board exhausted and enthused after the event, would plan for the Annual Corporate Meeting in August and discuss Albuquerque Pride 2005. Preparations would also begin for 2006, which would be 30 years of Pride in Albuquerque. September 2004, marked the second year that Albuquerque Pride participated in the New Mexico State Fair Parade to let the greater community know about the wonderful event held every June in Albuquerque. The Pride Board created their own entry and took second place honors.

Albuquerque Pride, 2005

In 2004, three months after the success of Albuquerque Pride 2004, the organization would again participate in the NM State Fair Parade. In previous years of participation Albuquerque Pride had received "top" awards with many spectators in awe of the extravagant floats. This September, the Pride Committee decided to "spell out" Gay, Lesbian, Bisexual, and Transgender. The floats actual wording was as follows:

Albuquerque Gay, Lesbian, Bisexual Transgender Pride
Hearts & Heritage-
Ready to Party!
10 % of Albuquerque History,
Always 10% of the City!
Pride 30th Anniversary
June 8-10, 2006

The float was decorated with a garden of beautiful flowers, colorful butterflies, and many multicolor hearts each having a year from 1976 to 2006 located in middle of the heart. The float was created based on the NM State Fair's Theme "Hearts and Heritage." The City of Albuquerque would be celebrating 300 years. Albuquerque Pride would announce on its float that they were celebrating 30 years which is 10% of Albuquerque's history and 10% of the population who were GLBT. The Pride Board felt that this would be a great opportunity to promote the 30th Anniversary of Albuquerque Pride scheduled for 2006.

As mentioned above, Albuquerque Pride floats had won prizes before; however, this year would be different. PJ Sedillo, Co- president of Pride, would state, "We're not "GIBLETS" [pertaining to the acronym GLBT] anymore: we are gay, lesbian, bisexual, and transgender; and this is who we are." Yet, the change in signage brought forth more negative reactions from the crowds of watchers lining the parade route than in previous years. There were many moments of booing, hissing, as well as silence and the negative shaking of people's heads in reaction to the float. PJ Sedillo would state, "It was like a coming out moment; it was like our Stonewall." Thirteen individuals, some dressed in "normal" attire with one in leather and one in drag, walked or rode on the float. Individuals who walked would remember the first Pride March in Albuquerque where twenty-five walkers boldly marched down the sidewalk on Central Avenue celebrating the right to live and love as they choose. In 2005, thirteen people would have to deal with that lack of acceptance from the greater New Mexican community which was disheartening. Kate

Chapman, the Facilities Coordinator of Albuquerque Pride, would write a letter which was given to each one of the thirteen individuals who participated. This is the account of the event:

Stepping Out of the Bubble

September 10, 2005, clear and sunny. The New Mexico State Fair Parade steps off and with it, the 3rd annual Albuquerque Pride float entry. As in the previous two years, the Pride float was bright and cheerful, with the riders in various costumes, many rainbows, and huge colorful butterflies. Basically, the same high-quality, high-energy float—but this year, there was a difference

Rather than just "Albuquerque Pride" (the banner in 2003), or the slightly more daring "Albuquerque GLBT Pride" (2004), the banner on the side of the float boldly spelled out the truth of who we are—"Albuquerque Gay, Lesbian, Bisexual, Transgender Pride."

I wasn't on the float that day. However, towards the end of the day, the phone calls started coming in, the reports came back from the float riders, in tones of outrage, fear, shock, and stunned amazement.

- "They booed us…they BOOED us."
- "It was fine, they loved the front of the float, they were clapping and cheering until they saw the words on the side…then they turned their backs on us."
- "He covered his little girl's eyes!!"
- "I was afraid…I thought Albuquerque was different."
- "I have never been so ashamed of being straight in my entire life. I went home and cried."
- "I was in the front, and everybody was cheering…I didn't realize how bad it was for the people in the back of the float until I saw their faces.
- "They turned their backs on us."
- "I was afraid to walk away from the float at the line up."
- "There was this group of people...they were still cheering us even though the people around them were glaring…I was afraid for them."

I was afraid. I was afraid. I was afraid. This is the theme I heard over and over—almost unbelieving in their shock. I sent a letter to all 13 riders on the float, thanking them for their courage, and inviting them to write their experiences to include in this accounting. Here are some excerpts from their letters back to me (Kate Chapman):

- "I've been in many parades in my day, Fourth of July's and Cinco de Mayo in Texas, two Gay Prides here, two in Santa Fe, and I've never had an experience like this. We had cheers for our brightly colored float, butterflies and some fun 'costumes,' but we also had many 'boos' and more significantly, some silent protest. A grandmother moved her umbrella over her eyes as the children waved. A couple, years younger than I, dressed as I used to dress, stared as we passed. The boyfriend tried to wave but the blond girlfriend grabbed his hand, and she forced it back into the closed, crossed position, but I kept eye contact with him" – J.W.
- "I don't feel like a hero. I felt like a blot. I don't think I can remember a time when I was so hated and ashamed. Hated by the people who stopped their child from clapping, by the lady who was my gramma's age who booed at me. Ashamed because this is the 'tolerant' world I live in. Last year when my best friend bailed on me, after 15 years, because I came out, didn't hurt or shock me near as much as the parade did. In what felt like forever, but what was probably about 30 minutes, I felt reduced to tears. All I could say to anyone on the float was "Just keep smiling and waving. It is all we can do, and don't be ashamed, it is what they want."—H.L.
- "As we started off, I was completely excited! Wow to be on a float that was me being proud of who I am, and with my friends!!! At first I noticed a few 'boos', and that was ok, I understand that there is still some ignorance in this land but I never thought it was going to be from people in my hometown. Then I saw lots of people clapping as we went by, and as they saw us under an open banner of 'Gay Lesbian Bisexual and Transgender', the ugliness I saw shocked me. They stopped clapping, and suddenly I thought I was in a death march."—N.J.
- "I was embarrassed because of their actions and to be 'Straight'...I was sad and upset with peoples actions because I wasn't raised that way. When I got home that day I did call my Mom and Dad and thanked them for raising us to be so open-minded and non-judgmental. I was there to support my friends. I didn't think it would affect me SO much until all I could do was cry and cry."—L.M.

This is the timbre and tone of the letters I (Kate Chapman) received. What I think is even more telling, is what I didn't receive. Although I spoke with all 13 people who were on the float, and all of them were extremely distressed by their experience and adamantly in support of me writing about it so the story would be told—only 4 of 13 were willing to write about their experiences for me so I could better understand and convey the story. This experience was so profoundly upsetting to the people on the float that weeks later, when I sent a third request for letters, I was met with the same sickened responses. "I just don't know….I can't think about it…I don't want to relive it….I'm sorry…I'll try."

I've thought about that for quite a while now…the people who were on that float. We have our bars, our dancing groups, our concerts, our churches…even the Pride Day parade is well tolerated in Albuquerque—very little harassment except from the predictable frothing religious zealots on the corner, and no one takes them too seriously, so long as they don't get in the way. We can pretty much live inside our culture, with a few excursions outward, safely and anonymously, if we choose. But there is no anonymity when one is riding on Central in a rainbow float with the words "Gay, Lesbian, Bisexual, Transgender" taped in huge letters to the side.

It seems that so long as we "stay in our place, and don't get uppity" it's okay to be queer in Albuquerque. But when we step into 'their space' by being openly queer in a public 'family' event, the retribution is instant. The hatred and distain suddenly become real and palpable. It's okay to be queer…but do it in your own time, and in your own space. Or else. The sudden silence, the turned backs, the covered eyes, the vulgar gestures, and the hisses say 'you are not welcome here, Faggot, Dyke, Abomination, Sicko. Stay out of our space.' Well, news flash, Albuquerque—the public space IS our space. We live here. We have houses and families here. We work, commute, go to school, pay taxes, buy groceries, mow our lawns, raise our children, and go to church here. Many of us were born here, many of us grew up here, and many of us will grow old and die here. There is a thriving queer community in New Mexico, and like the other communities represented in the State Fair Parade, the GLBT community has the right to ride and be seen—UNDER A BANNER OF TRUTH about who we are and what our float represents.

The following is excerpted from my letter (Kate Chapman) to the riders on the Albuquerque Gay, Lesbian, Bisexual, and Transgender Pride Float, State Fair Parade, September 10, 2005:

- "I wish I had been there this time with you. I rode the last two-years, but not under an open banner of 'Gay Lesbian Bisexual and Transgender.'
- What has become crystalline in my mind is that we've had a very clear demonstration that our work to establish our place in the larger society, and to protect our future, is not over—we cannot and must not back down.
- What I can say is that I will not back down-that I will continue to stand up for our right to live as free and open citizens of this city, this state, this nation, and this world. I will be on that float next year. God willing. I urge you to commit to the same-don't let them frighten you into the shadows-you don't have to live there.
- More than anything else I had to say in this letter. I wanted to make sure that I said, loud and clear. I consider each and every one of you to be a hero. Heroism is not necessarily flashy or loud or even publicized-but when ordinary people stand courageously for what they believe is right, flying in the face of adversity-that is heroism at its very finest. And you are heroes to me."

Kate Chapman- Facilities Coordinator, Albuquerque Pride

After all was said and done, the experience at the New Mexico State Fair Parade would make Albuquerque Pride stronger. The Board of Albuquerque Pride would schedule a meeting with the parade marshals and the NM State Fair Parade committee because it had been mentioned that they had received calls from the greater Albuquerque community that the Pride float was vulgar, inappropriate, and that some of the participants were "fornicating" on the parade float. This meeting did not go well; however, the Albuquerque Pride Board decided and would come to consensus that education of the greater "straight" Albuquerque community would be the focus for 2005. This had been attempted for previous Prides in Albuquerque, but now there would be more intensity. Instead of having an entry in the parade in 2006, Albuquerque Pride with the assistance of the GLBT community would have a booth in the Manuel Lujan Building for the entire thirteen days of the New Mexico State Fair. This huge undertaking would put the GLBT in the forefront of educating the entire State of New Mexico that GLBT individuals existed in "The Land of Enchantment."

To make a forceful and positive statement, Albuquerque Pride would utilize the InterPride theme for 2005 which was "Equal Rights-No More- No Less." The winner of the 2005 Pride logo contest was Joseph L. Martinez whose design would be seen on all Pride banners, advertisements, cover of the Pride Program and on all 2005 Pride T-shirts.

The theme showcased was drawn in bold black letters with the oversized lettering of NO which was stressed. This wording would be on top of an electrified, flaming rainbow.

2005

Starting in 2004, Albuquerque Pride began designing a commemorative pin for each year. In 2005, Teresa Ewers of Graphicbliss Graphic Design created the design for the pin which would become part of Albuquerque Pride's merchandising campaign. Most of Albuquerque Pride's merchandise would be sold at The Café Next Door, New Mexico's Only GLBT Bookstore.

This was the last GLBT bookstore in the state of New Mexico and would close its doors at 6 p.m. on Saturday, March 5, 2005. With the increasing amount of gay and lesbian books being bought over the internet and with sales at large bookstores that now carried GLBT books, music and DVD's, the bookstore was unable to compete and had to close. The Café Next Door provided meeting space for the Albuquerque Pride Parade and Pridefest. The Café Next Door would sponsor the event; one of the owners, Ruth Jimenez, would serve on Pride's Board as the Community Business Representative. Notably, the site of the establishment was where Common Bond's Community Center had been located.

Twenty-nine years of Pride had seen some remarkable changes. The Pride Parade had gone from a sidewalk march to the longest running parade on Central Avenue in Albuquerque. Pridefest was once held in Morningside Park and now was a major event at EXPO New Mexico welcoming almost 10,000 attendees in 2004. The year 2006 would mark the 30th Anniversary of Pride and would become the largest GLBT event in New Mexico. The Albuquerque Pride Board would consist of Co-presidents Pat Baillie and PJ Sedillo, Tony Ross, Reva Chapman, and Kate Chapman. The Pride Pageant would take place May 6-7 and on Friday would be the stepdown for the 2004 NM Pride Titleholders (*get rid of special guests Raquel Del Rio and Throb Dance Crew*) Miss Frida Roxx, MsTer Jayson DaBoi, Ms. Ticia Lovato, and Mr. Youth Tony Carillo.

Saturday Interviews were held at 12:00 p.m. and the Pageant at 7 p.m. The crowned titleholders would become part of the Board. They included Ruiz Phoenix /Carol Montoya-MsTer NM Youth Pride, Alazay Serenity DeVine-Miss NM Youth Pride, LE-Miss NM Pride, Carmen Miss NM Pride and Ro Velasco Mr. NM Pride 2005. Notably, in 2005, Co-presidents Pat Baillie and PJ Sedillo would be honored by Common Bond as the recipients of the Russel Gray Lifetime Service Award. This would be a great honor because of Russel Gray's previous prestigious dedication to ensuring that Pride had existed in the 1980's. As noted, before, Russel Gray would be given the title as New Mexico's Harvey Milk; however, until this book was written many had forgotten about his noteworthy contributions to New Mexico.

The team of the Albuquerque Pride Board would graciously thank the forty plus Sponsors that made the event happen in 2005, and a VIP Sponsor Lounge was started in 2005. All sponsors were given the "royal" treatment. A space to sit, relax, eat, drink and be merry was only accessible to Sponsors. It was located in the Hispanic Arts Building where the sponsors received gifts, beverages, and food. The 2005 Albuquerque Pride Sponsors were Sinatra DeVine Production, Sheraton Hotels, Miller Lite, Pulse//blu, AMC, Amigo Case Management, Pride & Equality Magazine, Karla Ludi, NM Voice, Pride Gym, Balancing Point Acupuncture, Julian's Tafoya's House of Portraits, Café Next Door, abq ARTS, NM AIDS Services, Guys & Dolls, Maddox & Co., MTS, EMCC, Frank Maschiano-CPA, Steve Benoit/Realtor, Black Duck Tees, ID Lubricants, Gay Fuel, Exhale, Comcast/Showtime, IMM Inc., Image Makers, Common Bond Inc., WIMIN, Albuquerque King Club, and Mayor Martin J. Chavez.

One of the sponsors of the event had been the ever-popular drag team known as Sinatra-DeVine. Fontana Devine, Lana Taylor Sinatra, and Tony Ross put on an annual show featuring premier female impersonators. As a 501c3 non-profit organization monies raised would go to put on Albuquerque Pride. Also, this organization was influential in producing and promoting the Albuquerque Pride Pageants.

The Pride Board had been working all year to ensure that the event would reach all ages, interests, and the diversity of the community. The Albuquerque Pride Board would thank the many volunteers who gave up part of their Pride Day to make the vision a reality but would also thank all those who would come out, bring friends and family, support the vendors and make new connections. The Pride Budget for 2005 was over $60,000. Throughout the years, Pride had always made its budget; however, each year in order to present the largest Pride event in the State of NM Albuquerque Pride had increased the working budget. Since 1990 the budget, on the average, had seen a $20,000 increase per year. It was projected that by the year 2007 the Albuquerque Pride budget would be over $100,000. Below is the Albuquerque Pride budget that was set at $60,711. The actual amount spent for 2005 would be $61,405 with $5,474.21 cash in the bank, putting Albuquerque Pride in the "black" with funds to support moving forward for 2006, to 30 years of Pride in Albuquerque. The next list revealed the projected Pride Budget presented at the Annual Pride Meeting in August for 2004 for Pride 2005.

PRIDE BUDGET

Budget Area	Budget Amount	% of Total
Fairgrounds-rent, facilities, security, insurance	$16,800.00	28%
Pageant- production, show, costs, regalia	$4,900.00	8%
Parade- barricades, police, permits	$4,100.00	7%
Pridefest-Children's Area, stages, sound entertainers, tents, awards, interpreters	$19,250.00	32%
Promotional-merchandise, advertising, program web site, community events and memberships	$13,250.00	22%
Administrative-storage, phone, PO Box, accounting	$201.00	13%
Other-conferences, miscellaneous	$40.00	1%
Total	**$60,711.00**	**100%**

**Noted the actual budget amount was $58,541 and was not known that it was incorrect until this book was written*

Albuquerque Pride in 2005 would concentrate on promoting the event to other states. This would be a priority and at the top of the list for the Pride Board. In 2005, Albuquerque Pride would attend and have an entry in Phoenix's Gay Pride Parade. Thousands of flyers would be distributed along the Pride route with information about attending Pride in Albuquerque. Advertisements were also put in GLBT Magazines/ Newspapers in Phoenix, Arizona, Denver, Colorado and El Paso, Texas.

June 1st the 2005 Window Display Application was due, and from June 4-8 judging for the Window Displays would take place. Twenty-seven businesses would participate. The winners would be First Place Image Makers, Second Place Birdland and Honorable Mention Gates Apartments, & the A Store.

June 7th and 8th was the Uncensored Art Show drop-off at the Fine Arts Building. Notably, in 2003 a few entries included nudity, and some claimed that it was pornographic. In 2004 the art was separated and put in a separate room that the Art Show committee chair deemed as "adult content." There were posters outside the room stating that there was nudity and adult content located in the room. Many of the artists were offended by this separation of their art, and the majority of the community felt that this was unacceptable because the community should be honoring and celebrating all of the artistic contributions from the GLBT community. It must be remembered that in the 1980's this similar situation would be posed and confronted by individuals between the Lesbian and Gay community; however, this time would be different because of the strength of the artists. The Pride Board would proclaim 2005's art show as the Uncensored Art Show because of the controversy brought up in 2003. All art was showcased together, cooperatively based on its form, artistry, and not on its "adult content." Because of this issue, ultimately, the 2005 Albuquerque Pride Board would select a gay and lesbian artist as Pride's Grand Marshals. These noted individuals would be Delmas Howe and Harmony Hammond.

The Pride Office located at the Natural Resource Building, would be open on June 9, 2005. Many people who attended the Albuquerque Pridefest did not know how much prior set up had gone into putting on this two-day event. Essentially, an "entire city" is being built in one day to be ready for Friday and Saturday. Tents needed to be set up, with fencing put up, ticket booths put in place, art collected, and archives set up. Main Street and other venues were decorated, beer stations secured, children's area set up, dance tent and sound systems checked, and the setting up of the Albuquerque Pride Office which essentially became the headquarters for the event. The Pride Office was the first location set up to immediately begin registration and to have a central location for all of those multiple questions asked by many. All needed materials and equipment were brought into this office so that the event could run smoothly. A computer and printer, and all other supplies even paperclips had to be obtained, moved to the Expo NM and organized so that the event could go off without a "hitch." June 9th would also be a Dinner/Art Show reception at the Hispanic Arts Building showcasing the instrumental artwork of Delmas Howe who would give a keynote address.

On June 10th, a faction of the Lesbian community expressed their feelings that women's issues were not represented by Albuquerque Pride and that Albuquerque Pride had "sold out" to commercialism. An event was advertised in *Crosswinds Weekly*, and the *Alibi* with a distribution of flyers in numerous locations. The event's theme was Fire Pride Weekend, and the location where it was to be held at the Silver Moon Lodge. This event would promote Pride discounts with a $49 room rate or $130 for three nights which would become misleading for "Pride Goers" because this event was not sanctioned or associated with Albuquerque Pride. The event was stated as Womyn Only, Non-Smoking and OVER 21 ONLY.

A Dyke March was planned for Friday to begin at University and Central with congregating at 5:30 p.m. Step-off would be at 6 p.m. A handful of individuals would attend this event because many lesbians would be at Expo NM setting up or waiting to meet Harmony Hammond, Albuquerque Pride's Grand Marshal. Marchers for this event were not given a specific plan on what direction they were to march. The march would proceed west on Central with participants sometimes walking in the streets and stopping traffic, due to the lack of leadership for how to proceed the Dyke March would eventually disperse. After the march there was a Dyke March After Party with a DJ and a special performance by the ABQ Kings Club (Drag King Troupe) from 9 p.m. to 2 a.m. with an entrance fee of $5.00 for 21+ only.

Fire Pride Weekend would have on Saturday June 11th a Disco Party after the Parade. The Fire Pride Weekend would cost $10 to experience the entire events planned. Sunday June 12th was a Pride Champagne Brunch at 11:00 a.m. with the cost of $5 for the day or $3 per meal.

Albuquerque Pride would only promote these events due to possible liability issues. Individuals who had planned to attend Fire Pride Weekend did not realize the huge expense involved with putting on a Pride event. It must be noted that some of the individuals who produced this event were instrumental in arguing about the entrance fee for Pridefest, and yet they had produced an event with numerous entrance fees. The Fire Pride Weekend would not take place in 2006. Although important as this event was, the tone of the community was changing. The factions that had separated the community in the past for separation between the sexes would become almost a past memory with some questioning about the separation. Many who attended the event thought that it was sanctioned and produced by Albuquerque Pride, though it was not.

Ultimately, Albuquerque Pride would have to deal in the future with the unending problem of those who would want to ride on the "coattails of Pride." There would be those who would profit from the event yet would not assist in providing volunteers, becoming a sponsor, or collaborating or acknowledging the importance of the event.

Friday, June 10th, at Expo NM all Indoor Venues would be open. These included the GLBT Art Show and the Pride Archives from 12:00 pm to 6:00 p.m. The event was free. This would give an opportunity for those to participate who could not afford the $3 fee for adults and $1 fee for children on Saturday. Booths had the option to be open on Friday. From 6:00 p.m. to 10:00 p.m. was held the Meet the VIP's Delmas Howe and Harmony Hammond-Grand Marshals and Ultra Naté 2005 Headliner. Announced as the Uncensored Art Show Opening the cost was $10 to attend. Grand Marshal Harmony Hammond would be available for book signing. The events also included the showing of the film *Truth or Consequences of Delmas*. Winners of Pride 2005 in the Pride Juried Art Show were the following:

- Best of Show- Ashley Bonal
- Painting- 1st/Hosano, 2nd/Ronnie Chavez, 3rd/Janie La Berge
- Sculpture- 1st/Tina Garcia, 2nd/Justin Lehman, 3rd/Raymond Sandoval
- Pastel- 1st/Ron Picco, 2nd/Marian Berg, 3rd/Max Woltman
- Prints-1st/Ron Picco
- Photography- 1st/Rob Thalman, 2nd/Thompson Chichalvello, 3rd/Deanna Nichols
- Water Color- 1st/Jerry Small, 2nd/Miles Beway, 3rd/Jerry Rodriguez
- Drawing- 1st/Alan Martinez, 2nd/Teresa Lopez, 3rd/Blas Sanchez
- Mixed Media- 1st/Ashley Bonal, 2nd/Susanna La Luz, 3rd/Blas Sanchez

June 11th was Pride Day! Because booths were open on Friday, some materials and merchandise were left out; therefore, a security officer had to be hired for the entire night. Also, a camper trailer was brought into Expo New Mexico because PJ Sedillo and some of the volunteers for the parade would spend the night at the State Fair Grounds. The parade line up would go through another transition. This was a new line up they would experience. They all needed to wake up at 4:00 a.m. to make it to UNM by 5:00 a.m. to prepare, set-up and be ready for those entries that might arrive at 6:00 a.m.

Set-up would be in the parking lot directly south of Johnson Field. The space had prepared for fifty-five entries; however, sixty-nine entries were registered and participated. PJ Sedillo and the well-practiced team of volunteers had logistically worked on the parade line and would be prepared for this. Line-up for the parade began at 7:00 a.m. As expected, there were floats that began to arrive at 6:30 a.m. Gardner and Little, who were spectators at the Pride Parade, felt safe and comfortable enough to celebrate their Gay Pride and just be themselves. They felt that "the whole event promotes diversity, originality and lets us express ourselves safely...and we don't feel threatened here because there are so many other gays here. And there's solidarity and strength in numbers."

Pat Baillie estimated that 10,000 attended the parade and festival on Saturday as compared to an estimated 1,500 in 1996. The Albuquerque Police Department; however, could not confirm that estimate as it only did crowd control outside the fairgrounds. The Albuquerque Police Department would also not give an estimate pertaining to those in the crowd. The Parade Winners were as follows:

- Float Business-Thai Orchid Cuisine
- Float Community-MPOWER
- Motorcycle-Mary Korch
- Motorcycle Group-Vroom/Vroom
- Performing Group-MCC Albuquerque
- Car Group-Rainbow Roadrunners Car Club
- Mounted Unit-NM Gay Rodeo Association
- Walking Banner-Duke City Derby
- Judges Trophy-MPOWER (In order to get this award, it is the best "bribe" category)
- Honorable Mention
  - Best Use of Body Paint and Nipple Rings-Pulse/Blu
  - Best Use of Children- Different Kids All Kinds of Families

One of the most exhilarating experiences for participating in Albuquerque Pride was being selected as a Grand Marshal or Honored Dignitary with the opportunity to ride in a classic car down the center of Albuquerque and to be greeted by thousands of cheering individuals. The Albuquerque Pride Board realized the importance of the selection process of these individuals who would best represent the event. The selections were based on current events, GLBTQ individuals that had not been represented as a previous Grand Marshal or Honored Dignitary, or those who deserved to be recognized for their contributions to the GLBT community and their positive support of Pride in Albuquerque.

Because of their involvement in the controversy the year before about whether "art is art," Delmas Howe and Harmony Hammond would be honored as Albuquerque Pride's 2005 Grand Marshals. Delmas Howe, a recognizable artist who lived in Truth or Consequences (Tor C), New Mexico, was born in El Paso, Texas in 1935. He was raised in Hot Springs, New Mexico (now known as Tor C) and graduated from high school in

1953. He received a bachelor's degree from Wichita State University in 1957 and then went immediately into the Air Force for four years where he played the bassoon in the US Air Force Academy Band at the Academy in Colorado Springs, Colorado. In 1961 after the Air Force, he went to New York City to study bassoon, with the first bassoonist of the NYC philharmonic.

Delmas Howe then received a scholarship to do graduate work at Yale University. In 1962, he started at the Arts Students League in NYC. He spent the next ten years studying art and music in NYC. Heading west back in 1975, he accepted a position designing fabric in Amarillo, Texas. In 1979 he had opened a studio in Amarillo for designing art for public space. He had his first one man show in 1979 in NYC called the *Panhandle Pantheon* featuring his first series of Rodeo images. Those images would be showcased in the Hispanic Arts Building. Also showcased would be his controversial series known as the *Stations: A Gay Passion.* This artwork portrays the AIDS crisis from the perspective of gay individuals being subjected to the Catholic Church and how this congregation of gay men would encounter persecution subjected at the New York City Piers in the timeline of the 1980's. The artwork would be linked ultimately to the "Catholic Stations of the Cross." Delmas Howe would become a controversial figure for 2005, both from the mainstream media and the religious community; however, Delmas Howe would provide the opportunity to bring forth issues whether positive or negative for the GLBT Community. Ultimately, this discussion of these issues would assist with a positive media campaign.

Harmony Hammond, also, would be acknowledged as Albuquerque's 2005 Grand Marshal. Harmony was honored as an artist, art writer, independent curator, volunteer firefighter, and martial artist who lived and worked in Galisteo, New Mexico. Considered a pioneer of the feminist art movement, she had lectured, written and published extensively on feminist art, lesbian art, and the cultural representation of "difference." She was a tenured Professor at the University of Arizona where she taught painting and combined media and was a member of the executive committee for LGBT Studies. Harmony attended the University of Minnesota from 1963-1967 (B.A., 1967). In 1969, she moved to Manhattan where she was co-founder of A.I.R., the first women's co-operative art gallery in New York (1973), and co-editor of *Heresies: A Feminist Publication on Art & Politics* (1976),

In 1983 she moved to Santa Fe, New Mexico. Her groundbreaking book *Lesbian Art in America: A Contemporary History* received a Lambda Literary Award for Lesbian Studies in 2001. It must be noted that earlier in 1987, Kate Clinton, a lesbian/feminist comedian, was the guest speaker at the Gay Pride Fiesta, and Harmony Hammond as an artist would be deemed as Co-honored Dignitary for Pride; however, this title would not be announced or proclaimed until the day of the event. Harmony would sign copies of her book Friday night at the VIP party and on Saturday during Pridefest her opus would be showcased at Pride reflecting the "Queer Reader" which is a nationwide project to restore or to create new art out of books that had been vandalized at the San Francisco Public Library because of the perceived GLBT content.

Each year the Pride Board selected New Mexico individuals who work tirelessly for GLBT causes and present a positive image of the community to others. Albuquerque Pride's 2005 honorees were Hal Simons, Midnyte, Lynn Perls, and NAMBE. Honored Dignitary/Community would be given to Midnyte a.k.a. Michael Tellez, the manager of the Albuquerque Mining Company. Midnyte moved to Albuquerque from Gallup after attending Eastern New Mexico University in 1971. He found the doorway and came out "forced" by his friend and fellow bar manager Sid at Foxes. Since then, he would become an active member and participant in the Gay scene in New Mexico. As a gay advocate his start would occur as an individual who by chance stumbled across the first twenty-five brave individuals in 1976 who were attempting a Gay Pride March. He would be heading up Central Avenue to find a location to get lunch when he encountered the group at its end. Because he was intrigued, he would follow, join and reflect on what was experienced at Morningside Park and not knowing that what was attempted was significant. He would recount his experience that he was just looking for a place to eat, but what he had heard was a new concept that was incomprehensible. Needless to say, he would be intrigued by what was happening, and he would collect his thoughts and sit with the few who successfully completed the first Gay Pride March in Albuquerque. It would be years later that Midnyte (Michael Tellez) would realize and recount the significance of what he was a part of, which would be associated with Stonewall and ultimately Albuquerque's own Stonewall. He would dedicate his life to ensure this remembrance.

Lynn Perls, an attorney would be Albuquerque Pride's Honored Dignitary-Political. Lynn Perls, a domestic relations attorney in Albuquerque, New Mexico, represented individuals who are same sex and opposite sex couples in matters of family creation, protection and dissolution. She had become a frequent local and significant speaker who addressed issues pertaining to domestic relationships and estate planning for lesbians and gay men. She received her BA degree from Pitzer College and in 1989 graduated magna cum laude from the UNM School of Law. Lynn was a founding member of the New Mexico Lesbian and Gay Lawyers Association, member of both the New Mexico State Bar Association and American Bar Association Family Law Sections and served on the Board of Directors of Equality New Mexico. Lynn was a National Center for Lesbian Rights cooperating attorney for the marriage equality cases in New Mexico.

In May of 2004, when the state of Massachusetts legalized same-sex marriage, Nambé a New Mexico company, decided to recognize the dedication of these couples. Nambé which means "Design Your Life" had manufactured serve ware, barware, home décor and gift items. The company was founded in the village of Nambé, a small town outside Santa Fe, New Mexico, in 1951. Their signature eight-metal alloy whose major component is aluminum was developed in 1953 by Martin Eden, a former metallurgist at the Los Alamos National Laboratory. Nambé presented each couple with a wedding gifted from their extensive collection. Albuquerque Pride would salute their endeavors by having them as an Honored Dignitary-Ally.

A new category for Honored Dignitary would occur in 2005. Hal Simons would become the first Albuquerque Pride Honored Dignitary-Arts. Hal Simons was the Artistic Director for Musical Theater Southwest. At the time of the award, he was in production with *A Man of No Importance*, a GLBT-themed production, which would run during Pride Month. Hal was a graduate student at UNM working toward a Master of Arts in Directing. He had appeared as Charlotte Von Mahlsdorf in *I Am My Own Wife* and directed *Mr. Charles, Currently of Palm Beach.* Other MTS directing/choreography credits included *Grease, The Rocky Horror Show* and *Ain't Misbehavin'.* Other performing credits included Mercedes in *La Cage aux Folles*, Ebenezer Scrooge in *A Christmas Carol*, and his MAC-nominated turn as Ann Miller in MGM Society. Originally from New York, Hall choreographed the Off-Broadway hit, *Tony n' Tina's Wedding* and directed and choreographed the Off-Broadway Revival of *Berlin to Broadway*. He actively supported the LGBT community by creating venues where the mainline community could see positive images of GLBT performance art.

Pridefest 2005 would have over 110 vendors, food areas, Children's Area, Art Show, Pride Archives, Indoor Car Show, Dance Tent, Drag Stage, Karaoke Stage, and Main Stage. New for Pride this year was a Pie Baking Contest. Albuquerque Pride would evaluate different activities that were similar to successful NM State Fair activities. Many individuals would bring their desserts to be judged. The contest was determined to be a huge success.

Parking was $2, admission $3 for adults, $1 for children under ten. These fees would again be challenged by a segment of the GLBT community. A few protestors would be outside the gates with signs stating that the event should be free. The Albuquerque Pride Board would again work on this issue. In 2006 they would offer a solution for those who wanted free entrance. They could volunteer prior to the event or on the day of the event. Those who volunteered would get free access to all the events.

In 2005, Jody Watley was asked to become Albuquerque Pride's 29th Anniversary Headliner. The talent agency that Pride employs had stated that she would be available in June. Albuquerque Pride announced in numerous flyers and advertisements that she would be headlining. Jody Watley declined the date for Albuquerque Pride after she was asked to perform on VH 1 scheduled for the same day. Therefore, Jody Watley would become the headliner who did not headline. Albuquerque Pride would then secure another known entertainer to grace the Pride Mainstage. This headliner for 2005 would be Ultra Naté. The Featured Performer would be Gioia Bruno, the lead singer from Exposé.

The Pride Headliner, Ultra Naté, was known as being "daringly eclectic." Ultra Naté on the "Pride Circuit" would be described as never being your typical dance music diva. Throughout her illustrious 15-year career, the internationally acclaimed singer/songwriter and performer had always been a musical chart maker who strived to challenge herself artistically without rules. She had boldly erased the borders between pop, rhythm-and-blues, and dance with a flamboyant flair confidently incorporating various musical mediums into her repertoire (including house, soul, future jazz, drum 'n' bass, electronic and rock-pop), which included some of the most infectious, urgent and daringly eclectic music.

Record producers, fans, and Albuquerqueans would revel in her first release, *Brass In Pocket*, boldly transformed The Pretenders' seminal 1980 hit into a haunting and brazen tripped-out electro-dub confection, claiming it as her own. Her live version of her classic 1989 hit *It's Over No*w was a certifiable hit for the enduring veteran. Over the past years, Ultra Naté had been quite prolific collaborating with an impressive list of artists and producers at a dizzying pace. Ultra Naté had added the title of DJ to her long list of credits, and she could often be seen manning the decks at her own weekly Baltimore soiree "Sugar." Ultra Naté would perform on the Pridefest Main Stage at 1:00 p.m. and would be signing autographs in the Fine Arts Building after her performance.

Gioia Bruno would be honored as 2005's Featured Performer at Albuquerque Pride. Gioia Bruno would make her mark on the music scene as the lead singer of the Arista Records pop group Exposé. The group's double-platinum albums were titled *Exposure* and *What You Don't Know*, with numerous chart-topping singles such as *Come Go With Me, Point Of No Return,* and *Let Me Be the One*. Her releases included the very popular "circuit" dance song *From the Inside*, a "dance smash" with her self-penned anthem song called, *Free to Be*. Her newest recording was a cover of the Kenny Loggins hit, called *This is It*. In August of 2004 Gioia released her debut song *Incredible* from her new album on Koch Records. Gioia would perform on the Pridefest Main Stage at 3:00 p.m. and would sign autographs in the Fine Arts Building after her performance.

Albuquerque Pride would successfully produce another year's event and would successfully obtain the funds to meet the budget with "seed" money for 2006 which would be a celebration of thirty years of Pride in Albuquerque. The 2005 event would end with its Youth Dance from 8:00 p.m. to 11:00 p.m.

This free event would have over 100 youth from Albuquerque and surrounding cities attend. Some parents would drop off their children so that they could experience the event. They then would wait in their cars until the end of the event, as they would for any "straight" dance school function. This year, the Albuquerque Pride Board spent time meeting with the parents of the youth who attended this event. The parents were grateful that this "Pride Youth Dance" occurred. Interestingly enough, the parents would state that their children would talk incessantly about the event months, weeks, and days before it occurred sometimes trying on many different outfits to make sure that they had the right one. Some of the youth's parents would describe this event as if they were going to "Prom" unassured, excited and overjoyed. Parents of those who attended would wait to hear from their children as if this would be their first dance experience.... somewhat normal but now normalized for those who attended. Although tired, exhausted and drained, the Albuquerque Pride Board members and volunteers would go in and out of the Youth Dance to see the excited faces...those boys on one side and the girls on the other (but now different) because each identity was infused. The situation normalized and became exciting because it was normal. The dance, ultimately, would reveal why Pride was so important.

Every year individuals of the Albuquerque Pride Parade and Pridefest who volunteered or were part of the staff or Board of Directors for the entire year had meaningful experiences. These shared experiences recounted at the annual meeting are the reasons why people volunteer countless hours for Pride. The following experience and account are from Kate Chapman, ABQ *Pride-Facilities Coordinator:*

> It was about 10:00 on a sunny June 11th – Pride Day, 2005. The parade was ready to kick off, so I took advantage of a chance to look at the entries, because as a parade monitor on the back of a motorcycle, I usually don't get much of a chance to really see the parade. I was wandering through the balloons, flags, music, roller-skaters, drag queens, convertibles...greeting friends and taking pictures...when I saw her.
>
> Standing immobile in the flurry of colors, she was a woman of indeterminate age, but certainly almost 60. Her long, grey, ragged hair was caught back in a careless ponytail, and her clothing was dull and worn. She loosely held a pretty bouquet, obviously collected from the UNM landscaping and was gazing around her at the cheerful bedlam of 300-some queer folk and their supporters jousting their way towards a roaring good parade and Pridefest. Although I don't usually approach street people, something told me I needed to go up and speak to her. So, I walked up, carefully furling my rainbow flag behind me.

“Hello-my name is Kate-may I help you? Are you looking for someone?” The woman, weathered and probably old enough to be my grandmother, looked at me, startled, then smiled sweetly and said, “Oh no…I’m waiting for my parents…they’ll be here soon.”

‘Oh boy’. I thought, ‘Someone isn’t quite all here mentally…’ – I would have moved on, but again, something encouraged me to stay, so I did. A pause, then she asked me…what is all this…? I dutifully (and, I must confess, somewhat proudly) explained that this was the Gay, Lesbian, Bisexual, Transgender Pride Parade, and that is was going to kick off soon, go up Central, and go to the State Fair Grounds, where there would be a big party all day. She took this information in silently, looking from me to the young man zipping on his rollerblades, then to a group of PFLAG parents talking to a set of lesbian moms with a toddler in a rainbow-decorated stroller. She looked back at me and started to talk.

The story was more than a little disjointed…but I could follow her tale of years on the streets…years on the streets as a queer woman. The places she’d slept and the missions that had turned her away, the ministries that had given her clothing and a warm meal. She told me about being harassed and about being cold. There was something about police, and something about her family…maybe she spoke of the parents that never did come for her, the parents for whom she still waited. Perhaps they were the ones who’d sent their rebellious, unconventional daughter to the streets. And as a constant threat through all of this, again and again, she references to her “sweetheart”, a sweetheart who was unmistakably a “she”. I listened in awe to this weathered, worn, and slightly addled woman tell me her story pitying her hardships and admiring her strength to survive.

Soon, though, I knew I had to get on the motorcycle and go—when she stopped talking, I extended my hand to her and said, “Thank you for sharing your story with me—I really have to go now—I hope you enjoy the parade.” She took my hand in hers—her grip was surprisingly strong and said “wait…don’t go yet”. I paused, thinking…oh man I am never going to be able to gracefully get away…. but I waited. Still holding my hand, she reached into some secret fold in her faded clothing and pulled out a carefully folded dollar. A treasure—maybe the most money she’d had in a week, maybe the money for today’s single meal. She pressed it into my hand and said, “Please…please take this and make sure it goes to help this” and she gestured around to the parade line up. Then she looked directly into my eyes-I could see her spirit so clearly, speaking directly to mine— "I want you to know that you are doing the right thing—you are making a difference."

Stunned, my eyes blurring with tears, I thanked her for her contributions, and assured her that I would make sure that her dollar got to the right place, that I would make sure that her story was told, and that we would strive to make sure Pride continued to make a safe place for GLBT people to live out loud and out proud. I squeezed her hand as a farewell and walked away. I watched for her as the parade moved out…but I didn't see her again. However, I'll never forget her face.

Kate Chapman, ABQ Pride, Facilities Coordinator

Chapter 9

Albuquerque Pride 2006 – 30 Years of Pride

Thirty years ago, Albuquerque was a very different place for the gay, lesbian, bisexual, and transgender community. Only a few places to gather existed. One Saturday in June, that changed as individuals walked along the sidewalks not knowing what was to happen or occur. The result would be Albuquerque's own Stonewall. Few marched unnoticed, and even less would end up at Morningside Park to rest and talk about what had just happened. In due course, these individuals wanted to be more visible to begin to claim their civil rights. That was the start of Gay Pride in Albuquerque.

Albuquerque Pride in 2006 entered its 30th year. The Pride Committee would proclaim that they would be committed to increasing GLBT visibility, educating the general community and helping to network the ever-growing and diverse community. The Board would state that, collectively, they needed to come together to obtain their civil rights and that more remained to be done. The Co-presidents would state, "This weekend, take some time to look back on where we have been and thank those who kept the struggle going and believed in our lives. Look ahead at where we may go and where our youth will lead us. [We] Thank all of you for all your contributions and the Pride Planning Committee for all of their hard work this year as we come together as a community to celebrate a world of *Pride not Prejudice*."

The 2006 Albuquerque Pride Board would consisted of Co- presidents PJ Sedillo and Pat Ballie; Heather Larkin/Incoming Treasurer; Andy Davis-Secretary; Le McKeller/Volunteer Coordinator; Midnyte/Business Representative; Tony Ross/Booth Coordinator; Brian Johnson/Parade Coordinator; Tyler McCormic/Registration; Maria-Jayson DaBoi/Assistant Facilities Coordinator; Kate Chapman/Facilities Coordinator; Elizabeth/Pride Photographer; Lori Ellison/Member at Large. The 2006 Albuquerque Pride Key Coordinators consisted of Michael Madlener/Car Show; JoJo Peanue/DJs; Richard and Dino/Art Show; Ticia Lovato/Karaoke Stage; Virginia/Mainstage-Stage Manager; Shoshona/Interpreters; Havens Levitt/Queer Bake Off. Also, on the Albuquerque Pride Board would be the 2005 Pride Titleholders: Alazay-Paul/Miss Youth Pride 2005; Ruiz-Carol/MsTer NM Youth Pride 2005; Carmen-Nick/Miss NM Pride 2005; Ro Mr. NM Gay Pride 2005; LE, Ms. NM Gay Pride 2005. To keep their title and crown, they would be responsible for raising $1500 as an adult and $1,000 as a youth titleholder.

There had been confusion in the past as to how many years Albuquerque Pride has had titleholders. The 2006 Pride Program would proclaim ten years. Technically, in 1997 Martinique Bouvier was the first Albuquerque Pride titleholder (again later changed to New Mexico Pride titleholder); however, in 1996 a pageant was held for Miss, Mr. Ms. NM Pride under the auspices of The Royal Imperial Sovereign Court of the Land of Enchantment Empire (RISCLEE), now known as the United Court of the Sandias (UCS), who owned the title. In 1997, on Pride Day, RISCLEE produced a pageant that would crown Mr. Gay Pride-Gabriel Duncan (did not complete his reign), Ms. Gay Pride-Diana Johnson, and Miss Gay Pride-Victoria Vale. Diana Johnson and Victoria Vale would be the first title holders who reigned for an entire year.

The noted titles under RISCLEE would be handed over to Albuquerque Pride as well as the title ownership to put on future pageants. For that reason, titleholders have been noted as New Mexico Gay Pride titleholders and not Albuquerque Pride Titleholders because at the time they represented the entire state because there were no other viable Prides in the State of New Mexico. At the time of the creation of this title, there were no other Prides in New Mexico able to support a pageant. This would be the reason why they would continue to represent the entire state.

Confusion for dates of years crowned versus years served also created another problem. Past pageants were held close to the date of Pride or on the day of the event. In 2000, the pageant would be held in March or April which would be two months before the event would happen. Therefore, each year Pride would have titleholders that would be outgoing and incoming. The 2005 Pride Titleholders were crowned in 2005; however, because of their title responsibilities, their term and step-down would be the next year in 2006. They would be noted as 2005-2006 New Mexico Pride Titleholders and this would become the standard from then on.

In 2006, the *ALIBI* newspaper would highlight some Albuquerque Pride Titleholders. On the cover were Miss Anastasia- the current Miss NM Pride 2006-2007, a past MsTer NM Pride Jayson DaBoi, and a past Mr. NM Pride Adan Branchal/Ariana (in drag). Within the newspaper their experiences were spotlighted as “drag” performers. The newspaper would also have at timeline of the past 30 years and promote the Albuquerque Pride schedule.

Albuquerque Pride for many years had their meetings always open to the public at many different locations in the city. Some past locations have been at the Common Bond Community Center, MCCA, Emmanuel MCC, The UNM Law Center, Foxes Lounge, The Albuquerque Mining Company, and Amigo Case Management. The year 2006 was the first year that Albuquerque Pride would have the opportunity to have an office. In the past, Pride would meet at a determined location that would be made available for meeting space. A storage unit was also purchased those years to "house" all the needed materials to produce the event.

The Pride Office would have an Open House and officially open its office doors to the community on Saturday, January 14, 2006, from 12:00 to 3:00 p.m. The office was located at 2610 San Mateo NE, Suite C (Just north of Menaul). The Open House was free for all to attend. Sponsors would get a free BBQ while others were asked to make a $3 donation. A Pride gift was given to the first 100 who dropped by, and the event was a huge success. Other Prides from around the United States sent letters of support. A "new home" greeting card was handwritten stating, "Dear Albuquerque Pride-Much health, happiness and success in your new home!! Keep up the great work! Together in Pride, The Pittsburgh Three Rivers Pride Committee."

The proposed Pride budget for 2006 would be $90,845. This amount was voted upon at the Annual Corporate Albuquerque Pride Meeting held on Monday, January 9, 2006, at the new office. The budget proposed was as follows:

Expenses:

Budget Area	Amount	Percent of Total
Fairgrounds Rentals & Facilities	$27,960.00	33%
Pride Shows/Pageants	$ 5,120.00	6%
Parade Costs	$ 4,660.00	6%
Pridefest	$23,950.00	28%
Promotional Costs	$19,290.00	23%
Administrative	$ 2,465.00	3%
Other(conference, retreat, misc.)	$ 7,400.00	1%
TOTAL BUDGET	$ 90,845.00	100%

Projected Income (estimated based on an attendance of 10,000):

Income Area	Projected Income
Parade Registrations	$ 2,000.00
Booth Registrations	$ 5,500.00
Pride Program Ads	$ 5,000.00
Sponsorship	$28,000.00
Merchandise Sales	$ 3,000.00
Titleholder Fundraising	$ 3,600.00
Pride Pageant	$ 5,000.00
Gate Ticket Sales (estimated)	$25,000.00
Event Entries/Other Fundraising	$ 1,500.00

Other Pride Day Fundraising	$ 1,000.00
TOTAL INCOME	$79,600.00
Barter (not included in budget)	$ 11,000.00
Shortfall (excess will go to Pride 2007)	$ 10,245.00

2006

Albuquerque Pride would use the InterPride Theme for 2006, *Pride Not Prejudice*. The controversy of the year would occur because of Albuquerque Pride's annual logo contest. Each year logos would be submitted to the Pride Board and then narrowed down for appropriate use of the theme. These suggested and approved logos in 2006 would be presented to the community so that they could vote on them and have a community voice that expressed their views pertaining to each logo presented that represented the theme *Pride Not Prejudice*. One logo utilized a Native American symbol (created by someone who was not Native American). The community expressed their views to not use the logo because it might offend certain segments of the community. Another segment of the community felt that another submitted logo was also offensive, but it would win with votes overwhelmingly from the GLBT community.

The logo would have two hands raised with the words "Pride Not Prejudice" in the center. The hands would have shackles with the chains broken underneath the theme. Some individuals were offended by the color of the hands and felt that it looked as if the community were "slaves," and it would ultimately offend the GLBT African American Community. Many changes were made to the logo (a few noted as rainbow color hands or outlined hands with no color, or white hands shackled). Eventually, the hands would be removed, and the pair of shackles without the hands would become the 2006 Pride logo.

The official pin, which was not controversial, would be the design of a triangle with a rainbow-colored checkmark in the middle, the word PRIDE in bold was located on top and similarly on the bottom of the triangle was the wording NOT PREJUDICE. Surrounding the artwork (circularly) was the wording Albuquerque Gay, Lesbian, Bisexual, Transgender Pride 2006, and on the bottom of the circle 30th Anniversary. The winner of both the designs including the transformation of the logo for 2006 t-shirts, cover of the program, Pride banners and all advertisements was Teresa Ewers of Graphicbliss Graphic Design. T-shirts and pins from 2006 would be sold to meet the budget as well as previous pins and t-shirts. Albuquerque Pride would also mark up the price of past t-shirts to promote the collectability of the merchandise.

Another secondary theme utilized was PRIDE 2006 – 30 DAYS TO 30 YEARS. Albuquerque Pride would start its celebration on May 11 and end on June 10 (which was 31 days of events). The *Normal Heart* newspaper and other print media would state that, "Beginning on May 11, 2006, Albuquerque Pride will be at events hosted by different community groups and businesses. This is called '30 days to 30 Years' where we celebrate the community and invite others to attend and check out what's out there in

Albuquerque. At each event, you can come by and learn about GLBT and ally organizations and pick up your collector Pride Card (one card will be produced for each of our 30 years with all the highlights of our Pride history). Also stop by and find out about Pride or purchase other Pride merchandise. If the event is a 21+venue, Pride will set up outside the door so that you can come by and keep your collection going. Get ready for an incredible year and see what else is going on in Albuquerque!

On each date in the calendar, you will find: Date of Event; Pride History Card Year that will be issued at the event (year tied into when the organization/ business/event was founded); Location/Host Group for Event; and Start Time. Also, a day to wear a color a pride color would be part of the 30 days; Pink (to represent the pink triangle), red, orange yellow, green, blue, purple, and black (to represent all those we have lost in the GLBT community)." The following table shows the different events throughout the month.

MONDAY	TUESDAY	WEDS	THURSDAY	FRIDAY	SATURDAY	SUNDAY
Come Out in the Albuquerque GLBT Community!	**Come out to all 30 days!**	**Pick up a Pride Card, get info, buy merchandise**	**May 11 1993** Foxes/UCS 10:00 pm	**May 12 2003** Sheraton Kareoke/ EQNM 8:00 pm	**May 13 1977** Ironic Horse/ Book Signing 3:00 pm	**May 14 1978** Pride Office/Book Sales 1:00pm
May 15 1979 Pride Office/ Meet the New Titleholders 5:00 pm	**May 16 1980** Race Matters UNM 8:30 am AND 1st Cong./Family Night/PFLAG 7:00 pm	**May 17 1982** Pride Office 7:00 pm National Day Against Homophobia- Moment of Silence 8:00 pm	**May 18 2005** UNM Law School- RM 2402/ Drops of Rain Kickoff Meeting 7:00 pm	**May 19 2004** Wyndam/ Common Bond- Under 21 6:00 pm & AMC Show- Jayson DaBoi 10pm	**May 20 2002** St. John's/ NM Gay Men's Chorus 8:00 pm	**May 21 1984** Pride Office/ Drop In Hours 12:00 pm
May 22 1997 Pride Gym 7:00 pm Rainbow Wk- wear the color & get a gift! WEAR PINK	**May 23 1986** Sweet Tomato Restaurant- Dinner for Pride 5:00 pm WEAR RED	**May 24 1987** The Candy Lady/Old Town- Stroll 6:00 pm WEAR ORANGE	**MAY 25 1988** Sidewinders/ CW Dance Lesson Night 8:00 pm WEAR YELLOW	**MAY 26 1989** Pride Office/Drop in Hours 5:00 pm WEAR GREEN	**MAY 27 1991** Guild Theater *Maiden Fest* 1:00 pm AMC/Title holder Show- 10:00 pm WEAR BLUE	**MAY 28 1990** Black Box Theater, Las Cruses/ Randy Granger & TNH WEAR PURPLE
May 29 1992 Pride Office/ Buy tickets 12:00 pm WEAR BLACK!	**May 30 1994** Rio Grande Botanical Gardens 3:00pm	**May 31 1995** Exhale Bar/ Karaoke 8:00 pm	**June 1 1999** OutYonda/ Kuir Productions 7:00 pm	**June 2 1996** Pulse/Dance Night Club 8:00 pm	**June 3 1981** Guild Theater WIMIN & Crone Productions 1:00 pm	**June 4 1976** MCC Alb. 10:00 am
June 5 1985 Foxes Bar/ STOMP 8:00 pm	**June 6 1998** Primary Voting! Stop by the Pride Office 3:00 pm	**June 7 2000** Fine Arts Bldg. at EXPO NM/ Pride 5:00 pm	**June 8 1983** Morningside Park/ Pride 8:00 pm	**June 9 2001** Expanded Pridefest/ Pride 12:00-10:00 pm	**June 10 2006** Pride Parade & Pridefest- 11:00 am -10:00 pm	**THANKS TO ALL FOR A GREAT 30TH!**

Some of the events would be highlighted in numerous newspapers throughout New Mexico. Equality New Mexico and Emcee Eric Griego (City Council) along with Ms. NM Gay Pride 2004, Ticia Lovato would produce "Pride In Our Voices" Karaoke Night at the Sheraton Uptown. The event would state that it would be, "an excuse to get *out* of your car and up on stage to sing at the top of your lungs!" PFLAG would start its "Family and Friends Night." Instead of their normal monthly PFLAG meeting, they held a Families Friends Night potluck on May 16th. Community organizations and businesses were asked to attend. Eat, drink, and be gay was proclaimed, and after the meal each organization and business was given the opportunity to promote their event.

The New Mexico Gay Men's Chorus would be celebrating 25 years with a special anniversary concert in Albuquerque on May 20 and 21 and in Santa Fe on May 23. The group was conducted by Paul Barrientos who had originally conducted the choir known as The Brash Ensemble. Music for the evening included Mozart and past music selected from previous conductors including the songs *Sometime I Wish, Shenandoah, Make Them Hear You, Mythic New Mexico,* and *Don't Fence Me In.* The event also included

The Longest Time from Billy Joe's and other pop songs. The chorus concluded the event with the *Rhythm of Life* from the musical "Sweet Charity."

Foxes would have a SMOKE FREE event for One Night Only promoted by STOMP (Stop Tobacco On My People), Equality New Mexico, the NM Department of Health, and Foxes Lounge. The event was proclaimed as the GAY American Smoke Out...Take Your Last Drag. Needless to say, this event did not go well. With all who showed up for the night, including the drag queens who were asked to perform, most of those who were at the bar would be offended by STOMP members promoting, asking, and even demanding the patrons not smoke. Those from STOMP who were given a chance to present their event were booed off during the stage and would be eventually asked to "pack up and leave." In the end, money was raised from the drag queens who performed at the event in the amount of $250 which was given to STOMP.

The Guild Cinema located at 3405 Central; NE in the Nob Hill would present the movie *Maiden Fest* at 1:00 p.m. which was an Award-Winning Documentary directed by Betsy Kailin. The movie showcased an empowering journey of self-discovery. There would be a workshop to discuss the viewed documentary. It would be, "a feast for the senses of mind and spirit." The movie would also be proclaimed as a women's search for the connection between spirituality, self-knowledge, and romance. A DVD signing party would also follow the screening. These are only a few descriptions of the events that would occur during the 30-year celebration.

In 30 years, Albuquerque Pride had grown to reflect the size and diversity of the area's queer community. Several businesses participated in the window contest. They were Image Makers, Planned Parenthood, Peacecraft, Birdland, Martha's Body Bueno, Immanuel Church, Buffalo Exchange, and A Store. Based on online voting, the overall winner was Image Makers, first runner up was Planned Parenthood, and second runner up was Peacecraft. Additionally, the Pride Board selected Buffalo Exchange for the Board Award for Best Use of Theme.

On the opening night of Thursday, June 8th, about 300 attended a moving Candle Night Vigil (many name changes would occur i.e. Candle Night, Candle Light, Candlelight) which originated in 2006. This evening would also highlight the dedication to celebrate the eventual construction of a GLBT memorial at Morningside Park. Set-up for the 8:00 p.m. event started at 4:00 p.m. to 7:00 p.m. Stations would need to be draped, lights fashioned, and sound system, speakers and mics set in place. The park would also need to be cleaned, as this was one of the parks known for its prostitution, drugs, and crime. The park had also been known as the "cruise" where some Gay men would meet for sex.

The Candlelight Vigil would be a new and extra budgeted event produced by Albuquerque Pride. They would work with the Social Club to promote this event where they would provide secured parking and offer an after event with food and drink specials. This would be one of the most spectacular events held during the 30 days for 30 years' events. This event was conducted to commemorate those brave individuals who participated in Pride's first parade held in 1976. The event also honored the past, present and future participants of Albuquerque Pride. The City of Albuquerque, along with the assistance of AJ Carian (Admin/Culture Services at City of Albuquerque, would dedicate a future, proposed memorial-art sculpture at Morningside Park to be proclaimed as the birthplace of Albuquerque's GLBT civil rights movement.

The location would become Albuquerque's own "Stonewall." The memorial would have two pedestals with trees located on the top (from a local artist). On each tree a plaque would delineate information about Pride in Albuquerque. The first pedestal would state the following:

> Dedicated to those gay, lesbian, bisexual and transgender (GLBT) community members who were here to create the roots of our community at the first Albuquerque Pride in June 1976. Coming out at the event began the work to raise awareness, educate the larger community and join the nationwide movement for GLBT civil rights. "We do not ask for our rights on bended knee. We demand them, standing tall, as dignified human beings. We will not go away (The Advocate, October 1967)"

The second pedestal would state the following:

> Dedicated to those who continue to show the diverse branches of the lesbian, gay bisexual and transgender community, this memorial stands in memory of those who time after time have stood up, come out, fought, and sometimes died for our civil rights. It is also dedicated to those who will walk this path as our future. May they draw strength from these roots and blossom into a world we can only imagine?

This proclamation of a dedicated art sculpture from the mayor would be proclaimed; however, it would take the Co-President PJ Sedillo to ensure that this would take place (the final verbiage would combine both proclamations and be put on a plaque on one of the pedestals).

During the Candlelight Vigil, previous facts pertaining to Albuquerque Pride's history were presented. Collector Cards would be given out at Pride events, and some information would be shared; however, many of the questions about that first Pride event would be somewhat of a puzzle and answers to unanswered questions needed to be put together.

After extensive research was gathered for the 30-year celebration of Pride in Albuquerque and through the archival process, data collected had been sifted through and compiled by head archivist PJ Sedillo. Most of the information uncovered would become integral for completion of this book. The multiple data collected would reveal new information about those few individuals who participated in the first march who started at different locations. PJ Sedillo had discovered different accounts and perspectives about the first Pride in Albuquerque. He would try to honor all those past heroes by ensuring that the stories of those brave walkers, who began the march from the many various starting places, would be respected. PJ Sedillo began to "connect the dots" about where the first Pride event in 1976 started and ended. Notably, because of this archival process, it would not be revealed until 2016 of where, how, and who first started the event. The next section provides an account of what occurred forty years ago.

Facts collected for this book revealed the many discrepancies of where the first Pride March took place whether on the north side or south side of the sidewalk on Central Avenue. Because of data collected the assumption would be made that it was on the south (east to west) sidewalk. It must also be noted that some past 1976 marchers stated that it was somewhere between Washington and Aliso. Some also recounted that it started on San Mateo Boulevard where they marched down Central to UNM.

George Meade, who was part of the planning committee, would provide credible, uncovered information about the first attempted march in 1975. Because the event did not occur in 1975, the processes outlined, would become the framework for the first actual attempted march in 1976. Using 1975's attempt for a march would suggest that the start of the event would be at the MCC church. The MCC church had not been located on the corner of Morningside and Copper and then would have started there in 1977; therefore, the first Pride had people meeting at a bar and proceeded east on Central to UNM to finalize a rally with the UNM gay organization known as Juniper. Following the same plans and utilizing them for 1976, would support all these scenarios which has been validated and supported by the few participants; however, some who were not part of the original plans in 1975, would choose to start their march at different locations. Therefore, many would march from various locations and directions on Central Avenue. In the end, the marchers would encounter others walking on Central Avenue not knowing that the event was occurring or had taken place.

The following accounts are based on the archivist's assumptions after the immense data collecting, sifting through the archives, and meeting and interviewing the few individuals present at the original event. Accounts would reveal that Juniper and

MCC produced the first event that would start at the location known as the Warehouse, an "after hours" bar just off Central also known as Kapps located on Alvarado for coffee and donuts. Some members of MCC would meet on the corner of Morningside Park and Copper which was designated the official start off point and wait for others to join for the rationalization, reasoning, and clarification of what would take place.

A few others started at other locations that would proceed with the intent to meet at UNM. Some started from Foxes Lounge on Central and Wyoming and marched to UNM (the furthest location) where Juniper [first Gay organization located at UNM] had its office. Because of the low turn-out, some would march to UNM unnoticed by the media and others. These twenty-five individuals who participated, walking up Central Avenue would produce an event not knowing what was happening.

After making it to UNM a few people would congregate. There had been no substantiated information collected that there was a rally at the end of the march; however, it was expected that one took place. Some had said that there was someone who spoke when they arrived, but no formal rally occurred because the marchers had reached UNM at different times. Eventually, those who walked to UNM would head back to where they had started or left their cars. That is where some would meet others who were unaware of the March and join in, after the fact. Some of the individuals would end their journey at Morningside Park to rest from the heat to reflect.

Those who had completed the march would walk back still chanting to where they started and stumble upon others who were part of the Gay community unaware of what just had happened. Those who marched would try to educate those who they encountered. Michael (Midnyte) Telles remembers walking with friends on Central Avenue and stumbling across the marchers. He knew some of the individuals marching and decided to join them in their courageous chants. When it was over, the protestors separated in different directions, but Midnite and a few decided to pick something up to eat and go to Morningside Park. Midnyte remembers that what they had just experienced did not have any resonance at the time and figured it would not have any future significance. This is similarly how many of the protestors who participated in the Stonewall Riots had felt. These few brave individuals did not realize the significance and power of their voice. Their chorus of voices would start off meek and would eventually become one mighty voice, part of history and the start of Albuquerque's own historical Stonewall Riots.

In 2006, many more brave individuals would march collectively to the Candlelight Vigil at Morningside Park. Individuals would march from the locations where people had met in 1976. Others would also start walking from the various locations that Pride in Albuquerque had been started or where the rally/Pridefest had taken place for the past

30 years. Participants were asked to meet at Morningside Park at 6:30 p.m. and were shuttled to the walking location. Two walkers were suggested to walk from each location; however, there would be many more that would participate. The walkers were asked to locate a small rock found at the area where they started large enough to write the location on it. They would walk to Morningside and Central and wait for all to arrive. At 7:55, all walkers would turn the corner and walk down Morningside collectively following the VIP car to Morningside Park. These were the times and places that the marchers would start from:

Location	Start Time	Distance
Foxes Lounge	6:30 p.m.	4.6
Texas/Central	6:45 p.m.	3.0
Expo NM (Spanish Village)	7:05 p.m.	2.0
Expo NM (Main Street)	7:05 p.m.	2.0
4001 Silver	7:50 p.m.	0.2
Copper/Morningside	7:50 p.m.	0.2
Tulane/Central	7:35 p.m.	0.7
Bryn Mawr/Central	7:30 p.m.	0.8
Richmond/Central	7:25 p.m.	1.0
Girard/Central (Lot E)	7:20 p.m.	1.1
Girard/Central (KUNM Lot)	7:15 p.m.	1.2
Yale Park (Stanford/Central)	7:10 p.m.	1.3
UNM (Johnson Field)	7:10 p.m.	1.3
University/Central	7:00 p.m.	1.7
Albuquerque Civic Plaza	6:30 p.m.	3.6

Hundreds of participants met at the corner of Morningside and Central, and they collectively marched and placed the rock on the proposed Pride Memorial at Morningside Park. Music blared at the park playing Maxine Nightingale's (who would perform at Pridefest) 1976 hit *Right Back Where We Started From*. VIP's were introduced, and the mayor would dedicate the future art sculpture by reading and unveiling the plaques. The sidewalk was lined with 30 candles with a year from 1976 to 2006 written on it. Candles would be passed out to the participants, and each collector card starting from 1976 would be read proclaiming the facts for that year. Individuals were asked to come forward and light their candle from the first year that they had participated with Pride. The final card was read for 2006, and those participants who had never attended a Pride event were asked to come forward. The crowd roared and applauded. When all candles were lit, the song *I know Where I've Been* from *Hairspray* the musical was played.

There's a light in the darkness
Though the night is black as my skin
There's a light burning bright showing me the way
But I know where I've been

There's a cry in the distance
It's a voice that comes from deep within
There's a cry asking why
I pray the answer's up ahead
'Cause I know where I've been

There's a road we've been travelin'
Lost so many on the way
But the riches will be plenty
Worth the price the price we had to pay

There's a dream in the future
There's a struggle that we have yet to win
And there's pride in my heart
'Cause I know where I'm going
Yes I do ! And I know where I've been

The success of having events planned at EXPO NM on Friday in 2006 would have Albuquerque Pride try to promote this free event to the greater community. Scheduled for Friday Night Pridefest on the Main Stage was the group Joni & Johnny, the Pride Titleholders, April Ball, The Wilde Bunch, and Randy Granger who closed the event. Other happenings were the dance tent which opened with music provided by DJ JoJo. Openings would also occur at 8:00 p.m. with the Art Show Awards, Drag and Karaoke Stages, the Pride History Archives and VIP/Sponsor Party. The Friday night events were admission free. Also, during the evening was the first ever Pet Parade with awards. There were snakes, dogs, cats, and ferrets all dressed in Pride Costumes. Three thousand people showed up for the Friday Night Pride.

Saturday, June 10, would be the 30th year of marching proudly on Central Avenue. Line-up for the parade would be in the east lot of UNM on the northwest corner of Central Avenue and Girard. Motorized units would exit and drive through Campus Road to Redondo then onto Girard heading south to Central. Walkers and animals would join the parade on the corner of Girard and Central. Judges would be located at the Starbucks in Nob Hill. A few past marches had a ribbon cutting ceremony. Albuquerque Pride in 2006 would state that this was its first ever Ribbon Cutting Ceremony to start the Parade. What was different was the Albuquerque Chamber of Commerce sponsored this event. The ribbon was held by Albuquerque Pride's Titleholders across Girard and Central Avenue. In attendance were, Mayor Martin Chavez, Governor Bill Richardson, Lieutenant Governor Diane Denish, Reverend Judy Maynard (MCCA)-Community Dignitary, Virginia Stephenson-Political Honored Dignitary, Raymond Sandoval-Art Honored Dignitary, Marth Doster-Ally Honored Dignitary, and Grand Marshal David Kopay.

The winners of the 2006 Pride Parade were Business Float-AMC, Community Float-Rio Rancho High School/Gay-Straight Alliance (Best Use of Theme), Performing Group/Walking-Wilde Bunch, Performing Group/Motorized-MCCA, Motorized Car/Truck (Group)-Native Pride, Motorcycle /Single-Teddy Bear Scooter, Horse Mounted –NMGRA, Walking Banner Group-Gay Red Hat Society, Judges Prize- Friends of Sappho, Honorable Mention-Diane Denish and Her Leather Boys. The judges were Wendy and Zane Barker, Robb Sisneros, and Johnny (Q) Quintana. The awards were presented on the Mainstage at 12:30 p.m.

Martha Doster would be Albuquerque Pride's 2006 Ally Honored Dignitary. In 1976, Martha Doster opened Martha's Body Bueno and was located at 3901 Central Ave. NE, three blocks east of Carlisle. The shop was known for its Body Bueno products, Romance Products, gifts, and cards. Martha's Body Bueno was the first "straight" store in the Nob Hill area to sell products specifically designed for the GLBT community. Martha Doster had originally suggested that there should be a window display contest in the Nob Hill area because at the time she was the only business decorating her windows for Pride. For many years, the store would sell Pride T-shirts and other merchandise where 100% of sales would go directly to Albuquerque Pride. For her continued support with the GLBT community, she was an ally that would be honored in 2006.

Raymond Sandoval was Albuquerque Pride's 2006 Arts Honored Dignitary. He lived in Jemez Springs, New Mexico, population 364. Surrounded by the Santa Fe National Forest nestled in the walls of San Diego Canyon; Raymond made his home where his great grandfather settled. Sandoval says, "I wanted to see the stars at night and hear the crickets again." Sandoval, a graduate of the Pennsylvania Academy of Fine Arts, received numerous awards and commissions. His artwork ranged from small bronzes to colossal monuments. Sandoval's most well-known work is the colossal bronze of TAMANEND in Philadelphia, Pennsylvania, located on Penn's Landing along the Delaware River. TAMANEND commemorates the contributions of Native Americans Indians. As an artist, Sandoval uses the figure as language. The art becomes the messenger. Sandoval would be invited to be a part of Dia de Los Muertos ~ Erotica exhibit, where he used that idea for his art incorporating a clean simplicity using traditional methods, with a twist.

He continued to work and was accepted into juried shows and was noticed by Albuquerque Pride for his submissions in the Albuquerque Pride Art Show. Raymond Sandoval had also designed numerous floats for the Albuquerque Mining Company, thus pushing others to create breathtaking floats for the Parade. Raymond Sandoval truly embodied the title of Albuquerque Pride's 2006 Arts Honored Dignitary.

Albuquerque Pride would also honor MCCA for assisting in the first Pride event that occurred 30 years ago by awarding them as Pride's Honored Dignitary-Community. The Metropolitan Community Church of Albuquerque began in 1975 as a part of the Universal Fellowship of Metropolitan Community Churches, a Christian church with an outreach to the gay, lesbian, bisexual, transgender communities, and allies. Throughout their history they have remained focused and excited about sharing the message of God's love and diversity for all of creation. In the fall of 2000, MCCA would purchase its own building located at 1103 Texas Street, NE. In 2002, Reverend Judy Maynard would come to Albuquerque, New Mexico, to lead the congregation to a new level and phase of ministry.

Because of her contributions, Virginia Stephenson would be Albuquerque Pride's 2006 Political Honored Dignitary. Virginia Stephenson was a successful manager in electrical wholesale distribution for twenty years before transitioning from male to female in 2001. She had been active in the GLBT advocacy for some years, having served as a facilitator of the Transgender Support Group of NM; a founder and director of NMGAIN, a political advocacy group for gender variant persons; a director and secretary for PFLAG Albuquerque; and a director of Soulfource-Albuquerque. She was also director of the Equality New Mexico Foundation, the GLBT rights group of NM. In 2003, as a lobbyist for the Coalition for Equality in NM, she was a part of the team that was instrumental in the passing of the Human Rights and Hate Crimes laws, which included protections for sexual orientation and gender identity.

David Kopay was honored as Albuquerque Pride's 30th Anniversary Grand Marshal. This would be the second time that Mr. David Kopay was asked to be part of Albuquerque Pride. On, Tuesday, December 9, 1975, David a six-foot one-inch tall, 205-pound football player was in top physical shape. Born in 1942, David Kopay had been co-captain of the University of Washington Rose Bowl football team and then went on to an impressive professional football career. He was however coming to grips in 1975 with the fact that he was a gay man and had come out in the *Washington Star* that morning with a headline that read, "Homosexuals in Sports/Why They Have Everything to Lose."

Kopay has come a long way since his days as a pro from 1964-72. He tells his story in his coming-out-autobiography, *The David Kopay Story*, which was a New York Times bestseller. His story is told with an obvious sadness about the isolation and self-loathing he felt when he was coming to grips with his homosexuality. He had tried it all—psychotherapy, hypnotherapy, family confrontations, and then, surprisingly, acceptance from former teammates and coaches. For more than 25 years, Kopay had been fighting the good fight on behalf of gay rights and showed "no strings attached" of slowing down. His nickname was Psych. Kopay was still very opinionated and a forceful advocate for Gay rights. Fairness was a common theme with Kopay. He never felt he was fairly treated by football once he came out. He was angry that, “there never was a shot for me” in coaching, and that the, “NFL has totally run away from me,” because they never acknowledged the positive contributions, he had made for Gay rights.

David Kopay jumped at the chance to be a diversity speaker for the league. Instead of coaching, Kopay forged a successful career for the past 20 years at Linoleum City in Hollywood, owned by his Uncle Bill, where the ex-player is the principal buyer for TV and movie studios. Kopay was single and lamented that his image, “got in the way of my romantic life.” Kopay was seven pounds below his playing weight and was working with a screenwriter on a film treatment of the *David Kopay Story*. The film will center on his relationship with tight-end Jerry Smith while both played for the Washington Redskins in 1969 and 1970. Smith died of AIDS in 1987 while never publicly admitting his homosexuality. To honor Smith’s desire for privacy, Kopay never mentioned him by name in his book, though it was a catalyst in Kopay’s coming out. David’s extraordinary self-revelation has long inspired gays who struggle with their sexuality.

David Kopay still active as a speaker lives in Los Angeles and was ambassador to the Gay Games in Chicago in 2006. Mr. Kopay was Grand Marshal for Pride in Albuquerque in 1983 and returned to add his stories to Pride’s history. He was amazed at the growth of the event and would speak at the Pride History Archives at 2 p.m. in the Hispanic Arts Building to share his return to Albuquerque and share his stories of Pride’s past, his experience in the present and his view of the future. Albuquerque Pride was honored for the return of this great man as the 2006 Grand Marshal.

Pridefest 2006 would start at 11:00 am with DJ Stich “spinning” his music. The opening of the event would start at 12:00 p.m. on the Mainstage with a welcome from the Co-presidents Pat Baillie and PJ Sedillo. Sponsors, Honored Dignitaries, Grand Marshal and VIPs would be introduced. The proclamation would be read by Mayor Martin Chavez; Governor Bill Richardson and Lieutenant Governor Diane Denish would also speak. The dignitaries would be on stage to help with the presentation of awards for the parade. Diane Denish was pleased when she was announced with an Honorable Mention award.

Also, at 12:00 p.m., DJ JoJo would open the ever-successful Dance Tent; the Karaoke Stage would begin, and the Drag Stage would have special appearances from Miss Gay Carnival At Large 2006, Fantasia Isabella Devine, MsTer Youth NM Pride Ruiz Phoenix and Icee L’atee. The stage would be opened for any drag performer who wanted to perform. The event this year was in the Indian Arts Building. Pridefest 2006 had many other events scheduled throughout the day. Some of the official events were the Fine Arts Show, the Pride Archive, Rainbow Roadrunners Car Show, and the Queer Bake Off/Bake Sale. Winners from the Albuquerque Pride Fine Arts Juried Exhibition and Sale Show and Queer Bake Off were as follows:

Art Show		Queer Bake Off
Mixed Media	Blass Sanchez	Cake Joan Lamunyon Sanford – Love Goddess Cake
Best of Show	Marian Berg	
Peoples' Choice	Dino	Pie Lisa Wisdom – Missouri Pecan Pie
Painting	George Hayes	
Watercolor	Jo Schunan	
Photography	Diane Alire	Cookies Havens Levitt – Marianne Loves Ginger Snaps
Pastels	Marian Berg	
Sculpture	Max Early	Bars/Brownies Katie Councilor & Megham O'Brien- The sleepover! Biscotti
Drawing	Roberta Begaye	
Prints	Ron Picco	Anything Else Brian Herrera – Fudgepacker's Delight

At 1:30 p.m. the UCS Monarchs performed and would emcee the show. They would announce the Pride Idol Competition for 2006 based on the TV show *American Idol*. Numerous events were held months before at local bars to narrow down the top three candidates who won. Each performed on stage and through audience applause the winner was announced. These shows at the bar served as fundraisers for Albuquerque Pride. At 2:45 p.m. the 2006 Pride Titleholders performed and would emcee the rest of the show on the Mainstage. Local entertainment including Throb Dance Troupe, the ABQ Kings Club, Vertigo Venus (Punk Rock Band), Helena Drive Jason & The Argonauts, and Sarah Bettens would perform.

At 2:15 on the Pride Mainstage would be the pop/rock group The Trampolines. The group consisted of Chris Stake-Vocals/Guitar, Mark Sundermeir-Vocals/Guitar, Brian LaRue-Drums/Vocals, Nick Ehlers-Guitar, and Brain Chambliss-Bass. The group from Denver, Colorado, had heard about Albuquerque Pride because of Denver's and Albuquerque's connections with InterPride. RaShaan Houston a gifted vocalist, songwriter and live performer who has garnered much praise as a rising star in dance music who combines equal parts gospel roots, jazz sensibility, and 70's soul with just a dash of rock influence performed on the Mainstage at 4:00 p.m. Shittin' Glitter would grace the Pride Mainstage at 6:30. They had been a huge hit the year before.

Albuquerque would have two major performers gracing the Mainstage for 2006. They would be the Featured Performer Maxine Nightingale at 3:00 p.m. and Headliner Tiffany at 7:00 p.m. who would also make an appearance at the Pulse Nightclub at 11:30 p.m. Maxine Nightingale became Pride's Featured Performer for 2006. Born, November 2, 1952, in the west London suburb of Wembley, England, Maxine was a mere sixteen years old when she began singing in her school band. She recorded four singles including *Don't Push Me Baby* and *Love on Borrowed Time* by 1971.

Theater attracted Maxine in the early 70's, and she appeared in the hottest musicals-*Jesus Crist Superstar, Hair, Godspell,* and *Savages.* In 1976, she signed with United Artists and debuted with *Right Back Where We Started From*. The most interesting

Pride Fact is that Maxine's multi-platinum pop single, "Right Back Where We Started From" hit the #1 position in 24 countries around the world, including the U.S. This was in 1976, the first year that Albuquerque had a march. They would celebrate 30 years of song with 30 years of Pride which had really signified that Albuquerque Pride was, "right back where they had started from."

Like many successful performers, Tiffany's career began when she was very young. Born on October 2, 1971, in Norwalk, a quiet suburb in Southern California, Tiffany was performing nationwide at fairs, special events and on talent shows such as Star Search by the time she was five. By the time Tiffany was thirteen years old, her voice and determination landed her an audience with producers George Tobin and Brad Schmidt. Soon after, she was offered a contract with MCA Records and began work on her first album-the self-titled debut, Tiffany. To promote the album to her target audience, a plan was hatched to have Tiffany perform nationwide at shopping malls. Within weeks she was singing to over 5,000 screaming fans in Salt Lake City, Utah.

Tiffany would become Albuquerque Pride's 2006 Headliner. Overnight, Tiffany had become a pop culture and teen icon featured in magazines, newspapers, and even on *The Tonight Show*. Both *I Think We're Alone Now* and *Could've Been* were US #1 Billboard singles. *I Saw Him Standing There*, which hit the Top Ten, was also included on her 1987 debut album. By the 1990's, Tiffany decided to take a break, but she devoted herself to writing lyrics resulting in the album *The Color of Silence*. Albuquerque Pride was honored that Tiffany would grace the Pride Mainstage in 2006.

Tiffany would end Pridefest when she performed at the Boxcar Stage at the New Mexico State Fair Grounds. The stage was only two steps away from the audience. The audience grew to over 8,000 spectators who wanted to see Tiffany. The Pride Board felt that Tiffany's safety was at stake, as the spectators could rush the stage. The entire Albuquerque Pride Board and volunteers (consisting of about twenty) sat and linked arms in front of the stage to provide a "human barricade." Tiffany came out to perform, and the crowd went wild. The Pride Board pushed back and forth ensuring that no one would get on stage to cause havoc with the performance. After the 45-minute performance, the audience left giving the Albuquerque Pride Board and volunteers a chance to meet personally with Tiffany. She and her husband (manager) were very happy for the provided protection. This event would lead The Albuquerque Pride Board to realize that the stage needed to be built up so that the audience could not grab at the performer in the future.

In 2006, Albuquerque Pride Board tried to get the word about the event out all over. Albuquerque Pride participated in three Pride Parades in the United States. The organization would have a parade entry at Denver Pride, Phoenix Pride, and Santa Fe

Pride. Albuquerque Pride also joined the Consolidated Association of Pride, Inc. (CAPI). Pride events occur and are celebrated somewhere, each month of the year, throughout the world. InterPride would establish different regions throughout the world. CAPI's region consists of states from Arizona, California, Nevada, Washington, Hawaii, Utah and Oregon. Albuquerque Pride would send delegates yearly to this region conference as well as members who would attend the annual International Pride conference known as InterPride.

Albuquerque Pride would also continue the celebration of Pride by supporting Southern New Mexico Pride in Las Cruces by assisting them to create 2006 Pride events. The Southern New Mexico Pride Pageant scheduled for June 17, 2006, would be located at The Underground on the NMSU Campus at 7:00 p.m. Saturday, June 17th, would be the first Southern New Mexico Pride Parade at 9:00 am. The location of the event would be at the old SOLO parking lot. Following the parade was a picnic at Pioneer Women's Park from 10:00 a.m. to 3:00 p.m. Albuquerque Pride's region director, Tony Ross, would ensure and assist that Prides were supported at each event, which was one of the major missions of InterPride. From 8:00 p.m. to 12:00 a.m., would be an even entitled *Not Your Mom's Prom*. This event would be open to all who had not experienced the "perfect" prom. The event was located at the Fulton Center on the NMSU Campus. Events like this were promoted by Albuquerque Pride. Board Members or titleholders would attend to promote and support Pride events throughout New Mexico.

In 2006, after Albuquerque Pride had concluded in June, the Board would work to obtain the "First-Ever GLBT Booth" for the community at the NM State Fair. This came about because of the experience with the float entered in 2005 for the third year at the New Mexico State Fair. Albuquerque Pride would schedule a meeting with the parade marshals from the NM State Fair Parade because they had been mentioned they had received calls from the greater Albuquerque community that the Pride float was vulgar, inappropriate, and that some of the participants were "fornicating." Some of the Parade Monitors would write on their report "Disgusting-YUK!", "Vulgar!!! Never Again!" This is the response that was sent to the Albuquerque Pride Board from the NM State Fair Parade:

> AFTER THE 2005 PARADE, THERERE HAVE BEEN MANY PHONE CALLS EACH DAY CONCERNING A FLOAT ENTRY IN THE PARADE. UNLIKE THE NORMAL FEW PROBLEMS ENCOUNTERED, THESE CALLS HAVE BEEN VERY ADAMENT ABOUT THE "ALBUQUERUQE PRIDE" ENTRY #182.
>
> THIS ENTRY WAS ACCEPTED 2 YEARS AGO WITH AN ACNOWLEDGEMENT OF THE RULES WHEN THEY ENTERED. THEY PRESENTED A NICELY DECORATED FLOAT BOTH YEARS WITHOUT ANY CONTROVERSIAL ADVERTISING OR ADVERSE REPRESENTATION. THE ENTRY WAS AGAIN ACCEPTED FOR THE 2005

> YEAR......HOWEVER, AS IT PASSED THE JUDGES STAND, I MARKED MY NUMERIC SHEET WITH THE COMMENT – DO NOT ACCEPT AGAIN NEXT YEAR. THE NUMEROUS PHONE CALLS HAVE BEEN VERY EXPLICT ABOUT THE CONDUCT FURTHER DOWN THE ROUTE.
>
> THE AUTO TRADER ENTRY WAS WAITING NEXT TO THIS #182 ENTRY IN THE LINE UP AREA AND [was] EXTREMLY UPSET CONCERNING THE FOUL LANGUAGE AND VULGARITY USED BY THE ENTRANTS. THEY WERE FURTHER CONCERNED WITH THE CONTINUAL LOUD PROFANITY BECAUSE OF AN ADJANCENT FLOAT OF YOUNG WOMEN WAITING ALSO TO GO ONTO THE PARADE ROUTE.
>
> THE WORDS USED BY THOSE WHO PHONED WERE: VULGAR; OBSCENE; OFFENSIVE; GROSS PERVERSE; RADICAL; UNREASONABLE; PROFANE; SUGGESTIVE; FOUL LANGUAGE; CORRUPT; DEBASED; SEXUALLY PERVERSE; REPULSIVE; DISGUSTING; AND DISTASTFUL. I WAS TOLD BY MY MONITORS THAT THOSE ON THE FLOAT WERE SHOUTING PROFANITIES TO THE CROWD; DISGUSTING HAND MOTIONS; DANCING SEXUALLY PERVERSE; DISROBING TO THE ALMOST POINT OF NUDITY; ETC. ETC. (THERE ARE 4-5 MONITORS THROUGHTOUT THE ROUTE EACH YEAR).

(I'm sorry for the crowd "taunts" – please do not respond to them.) Have a good Parade. [Handwritten response at the end of the letter from the Parade Marshal]

This meeting did not go well; however, the Albuquerque Pride Board decided and would come to consensus that education of the greater "straight" Albuquerque community would be the focus for next year's Pride in 2007. This had been attempted for previous Prides in Albuquerque, but now there would be a more intense attempt. It was decided that instead of having a parade entry in the parade, Albuquerque Pride with the assistance of the GLBT community would have a booth in the Manuel Lujan Building for the entire thirteen days of the New Mexico State Fair. This huge undertaking would put the GLBT in the forefront of educating the entire State of New Mexico that GLBT individuals existed in "The Land of Enchantment."

On a final note, a major change that took place in Albuquerque was the dissolution of Emmanuel Metropolitan Community Church of Albuquerque (EMMC). In 1997, because of a disagreement of ideology the church separated, and two churches were created. This would be a rarity in many states to have two MCC churches. However, finally after years of being disjointed, in 2006, both churches would again join together. A special ceremony would be conducted to dissolve EMMC and then join collectively with the Metropolitan Community Church who had originally started the first Pride event in 1976.

Chapter 10

Albuquerque Pride 2007 to 2009

Marketing the event would become a priority for Albuquerque Pride in 2007. This would become a novel idea from the Albuquerque Pride Board to expand the message of Albuquerque Pride. The idea had been germinated from the seeds planted with obtaining and having a Pride booth at the New Mexico State Fair in the fall because of what had occurred the year before.

Although the booth was staffed with a majority of Albuquerque Pride Board Members and volunteers, those who had come forward initially had some trepidation about being accosted by homophobic types at the fair, which was only one of the many fears of staffing the booth. The experience was far more reassuring and warmer than anyone had expected. So many people at the State Fair booth had an incredible experience. Individuals who were almost afraid to sit at the booth would come back charged up. Staffers had come to the table, having a positive experience, and wanting to tell their stories. There were tales about one's cousin who had just come out, friends who were gay, neighbors who were gay and had lent them their lawnmower, and family members who they thought might be gay and what should they do. All in all, the participation with this event would prove that the greater New Mexico community was glad to see that Pride was there at the fair.

The booth at the fair brought together many organizations and volunteers. Over 3000 New Mexicans were positively educated by the Gay, Lesbian, Bi-sexual, and Transgender Community. Those who participated were the NM Gay and Lesbian Lawyers, PFLAG ABQ, the Human Rights Alliance, Equality NM, ABQ Pride, Inc., Pride Gym, Common Bond, Metropolitan Community Churches, Women In Movement in NM, the NM Leather League, the Sandia Out Professional Association, the Ranch, the Pulse, Foxes/ACM, the Albuquerque Social Club, NMGRA, the NM Gay Men's Chorus, the Gay and Lesbian Chamber of Commerce, Maddox Reality, Steve Benoit Reality, Tallia Freedman Realtor, Primetimers, and NMAS. Many individuals volunteered from our allied community who also participated. Two such brave individuals were JoAnne Ramponi and Janet Espinosa.

The booth would be staffed for two hours with three volunteers (for safety) instead of the required two from the NM State Fair. This staffing needed to occur throughout the entire 13-day event from 8:00 am to 9:30 pm. It was a great undertaking to make sure that the booth was staffed throughout the entire State Fair. The NM State Fair representatives told Albuquerque Pride and its volunteers that if at any time there was no one at the booth, they would be asked to pack up and leave. Despite all the roadblocks encountered to obtain a booth, the community would keep it "up and running." Pat Baillie and PJ Sedillo would show up daily, sometimes hourly, to make sure that the booth was staffed.

Thousands of New Mexicans stopped by the booth and asked to take a "quiz" (GLBT Challenge). The "quiz" would ask them to pick who was GLBT among the list of famous GLBT people in history. Out of the twenty individuals on the list all were gay, lesbian, bisexual or transgender. Their entry form was included in a drawing noted as the GLBT CHALLENGE DRAWING. Winners would receive a Toshiba DVD Player and a handmaid rainbow afghan donated from Johnny Valencia.

Despite all the resistance from the NM State Fair representatives, the New Mexico GLBT Community at large was successfully able to educate the many groups and individuals who stopped at the booth. To make sure that the GLBT community continued to have a presence at important events in the State of New Mexico, Pat Baillie would become instrumental in ensuring the GLBT State Fair Booth, would happen. Pat Baillie would recount that there was a woman who was dead set on reaching the booth and aftertime stumbling through a sea of cowboy hats she would spot the rainbow flag. Once she arrived at the haven, Pat Baillie would respond, "Hello! Yes, you did indeed find the gay table." In due course, the success of this endeavor would bring the community together with Albuquerque Pride leading the helm. Securing a booth at one of the largest attended events in the state known as the New Mexico State Fair would move Albuquerque Pride to be noted by the GLBT community as the leading and most influential organization in the state of New Mexico.

After the successful conclusion of staffing a booth at the State Fair, Albuquerque Pride would take a brief month off and then begin in October to plan the 31st Annual Albuquerque Pride Parade and Pridefest. The Pride Board consisted of Co-president, Male-PJ Sedillo, Co-president, Female-Pat Baillie, Secretary-Kate Chapman, and Treasurer-Heather Larkin. The Planning Committee included Sophia-Business Representative, Tony Ross, Maria Johnson, AJ Carian, Brian, Tony Carson, LE, Nate, JoJo, and Ken. The Board would also include the 2006 Pride Titleholders Adan, Mr. NM Pride who had upon completing his title year opened a new Salon named TEAZE with Leannette Lucero at Menage a Spa. Anastasia, Miss NM Pride would be noted as a founding member of the performing group Façade. Prince Julian, Ms. NM Pride would declare that she came out in 1999 and had been loud and proud in both the GLBTQ and Leather Communities. Clarrissa Danger was Miss NM Youth Pride. She would become Albuquerque Pride's first deaf title holder representing the youth in the community.

Volunteers for the 2007 event would be Virginia Cleary-Stage Manager, Kelly Clark and BJ Felter-Family/Children's Area, Raven Rykers-Pet Parade, Richard Osmess/Justin Tanis-Art Show, Rainbow Roadrunners Car Club-Car/Bike Show and VIP Cars, DJ Stich-Creative Arts Venue DJ, and John Hull-Pride Theater. Also, because of the transition created by the change for electing titleholders, the 2007 Pride Titleholders would also participate at Board meetings, but they had no voting privileges until the Annual Corporate Board Meeting held in August of each year. The 2007 Pride Titleholders were Angelica Del Rio-Miss NM Pride, Joaquin Del Rio-Mr. NM Pride, Lil Dreamer-Ms. NM Pride, Veronica-Miss NM Youth Pride, and Vincent Chavez-Mr. NM Youth Pride.

The budget for 2007 was expected to be $97,730. Albuquerque Pride had adjusted the budget because of the previous years located at Mainstreet at Expo NM. There would be a projected shortfall of $5730 because it was estimated that $92,000 would come in as income. The Pride Board would have to work diligently to obtain this shortfall or cut certain expenses for all the events. In the end, the final expenses for 2007 exceeded $127,000, but the Pride Board would be able to obtain the funds.

In 2007, it would be an expectation for those on the Board to donate financially (Notably, this is not a new concept as it is a regular request for many who participate in the multiple non-for-profits within the United States.). The Board Members of Albuquerque Pride would contribute money based on what they could contribute in addition to their volunteerism for the year to make sure the event would occur. Contributions donated to Albuquerque Pride from the Pride Board would range from $100 to $5000. Much of the GLBT community did not realize the amount of time and money provided by the Board members to ensure that the event would take place. It must be noted that the amount spent just to utilize Expo New Mexico was $16,724.89. The community would not be aware of the amount of money needed to put on this event, and some individuals continued to be adamant that the event should be free. This would become an ongoing problem for the existence of Pride.

Albuquerque Pride had always partnered with national and local businesses that had become proud sponsors of Albuquerque Pride. Each year the sponsors have assisted with monetary funds to help produce Albuquerque Pride. Evolution, "a bar in progress," made flyers stating, "Evolution Presents Gay Pride." This statement caused confusion in the community concerning where and when the actual Pride event was to take place. Albuquerque Pride met with Evolution to discuss the controversy. Even though no money was given to Pride for sponsorship, Albuquerque Pride graciously noted Evolution as a sponsor to ease the confusion in the community. One of the agreements between Albuquerque Pride and the bar was that they would create a special drink with half of the proceeds to be given to Albuquerque Pride. Unfortunately, any money collected was never given to Albuquerque Pride.

The year 2007 would see the celebration of 31 years of Pride. The organization would look at the possibilities for the GLBTQQIA (Gay, Lesbian, Bisexual, Transgender, Queer, Questioning, Intersex, Ally (*a term first mentioned and used for marketing*) community. New Mexicans were protected with hate crimes and non-discrimination laws for both sexual orientation and gender identity; however, in 2006, the community missed by one vote in obtaining domestic partner benefits for all New Mexicans.

The community had been enquiring about why its event was not as large as those in Phoenix, Denver, or Dallas with bringing in "named" headliners. This would be an ongoing problem for future events. However, the community at large did not know how much "named" entertainment would cost. Ultimately, the community would be adamant about paying for the entertainers because they believed that the event should be free and open to all. Again, this would plague Albuquerque Pride in the future on how to obtain sponsorship dollars with offering them exclusivity in naming rights and branding.

The theme for 2007 was "United for Equality" which was also the International Pride theme. The logo had six interlocking gender symbols. Each gender symbol was a color of the rainbow. These interlocking gender symbols would show the intertwined unity among the different relationships that exist in the culture (gay, bisexual, lesbian, etc.) on top of the symbols was the wording "Albuquerque Pride 2007," and below was the theme "United for Equality." Tia Terchila Valerie Brazis designed the logo. This logo would be on all t-shirts and print materials.

The annual commemorative pin was designed by Graphic Bliss Design. On the top of the design were five "paper-doll" cut outs connected at their hands. The individual colors were red, white, black, and yellow. The final "paper-doll" color was a rainbow which was place in the center of the other two colors. Underneath was the bold lettering of the word "UNITED." Under the word united was the wording "For Equality." Below that was "Albuquerque Pride 2007."

"O Pride! How do we celebrate thee? Let us count the ways! In fact, the many ways to celebrate Pride in Albuquerque may be all but innumerable" was quoted from the major GLBT newspaper in the state known as the *New Mexico Voice*. Pat Baillie, Pride's Co-Chair, gave *New Mexico Voice* a brief guide to the many ways to celebrate this year's 31st Pride. "There are events, together called 'Countdown to Pride', almost every day between now and Pride on June 9, and details are available at the Pride website at www.ABQpride.com."

2007

After the 30th Pride, the Board Members and regular volunteers wanted to extend to the community the opportunity to get to know other organizations better. The "Countdown" was a chance for the community to meet other groups. In addition, the many smaller organizational meetings, receptions and plays held in the community would give people an opportunity to try some smaller scaled events that they might not have access to promote. This "Countdown" was created so that the community would become involved and be aware of the many different diverse community events held throughout the year with the intention to have all come together even before the June 8-9 Albuquerque Pride events.

Some of the events with this "Countdown" would publicize that even 'newbies' could learn square dancing from The Wilde Bunch, and then they could participate at the dancing exhibition at PrideFest. Other events would be for those who knew little of Albuquerque's history as a GLBT community and would showcase the founders and shapers in 2007. One could have attended Common Bond's recognition ceremony and benefit, "Just Desserts," honoring Bennet Hammer, Ann Nihlen, Lisa Wisdom, and Tyler McCormick.

May 15th, PFLAG would have a meeting where Pride would present the 30-day event. This would be a potluck, and PFLAG Albuquerque would continue this potluck and event sharing each year. May 16th was the Albuquerque Convention and Visitor Bureau's Annual Luncheon. Because the Albuquerque Convention and Visitor's Bureau were a sponsor of Albuquerque Pride, the Board would attend this luncheon to present the 2007 Countdown to Pride events.

The Hyperfest Music Festival would begin May 17th. The festival would run from Thursday to Saturday with numerous venues throughout the Albuquerque Area featuring performers from across the U.S. and the world. Many of the performers were GLBT or GLBT friendly. Metropolitan Community Church had services at 9 a.m. and 10:30 a.m. each Sunday starting June 2 until Pride Day. MCCA had become home to many of the leaders in the GLBT community and had been a major source of emotional, spiritual and community support during the 30 years of Pride in Albuquerque. May 18th was the Common Bond's Fourth Annual Community Service Awards. On May 19th a Pride Reception was held at the Holocaust Museum and on May 20th there would be a Pride Beer Bust at Sidewinders. These beer busts would be an opportunity to make funds to pay for Albuquerque Pride. May 22nd would be the Wilde Bunch Dance Night. The Leather League, people interested in Kink or Bondage Discipline, or Sadomasochism, held a special welcome event at 7 p.m., Tuesday, May 22nd, to encourage those not already involved to learn more about the five or six groups within the umbrella organization.

The "Race Matters" conference was set for Wednesday, May 30th from 8 a.m. to 3:30 p.m. at the New Mexico Continuing Education Complex. The conference, sponsored by the New Mexico Voices for Children, was an intentional look at policies that perpetuated the racial divide and was aimed at focusing on official policy looking through a racial lens. The Albuquerque Pride Board would staff a booth at the event to provide valuable information and awareness about the June event. May 30th and 31st, Sidewinders Bar would host a country-western event that included two special events for the GLBT community. One could take country western dance lessons at 7 p.m. and then attend a beer bust benefiting Albuquerque Pride and The Wilde Bunch. These were only a few of the many organizational meetings planned for the GLBT community. This

“Countdown” would be heavily promoted by the *New Mexico Voice* and the ACVB (Albuquerque Convention Visitors Bureau). The Pride committee joined the ACVB in 2006 to assist in marketing through their campaign “Destination Albuquerque” as a fact that Albuquerque was a Gay-friendly destination.

Pride’s 2007 Grand Marshal was the National Organizers for the “Nazi Persecution of Homosexuals, 1933-1945” from the US Holocaust Memorial Museum in Washington, DC, which was on display in Albuquerque at the New Mexico Holocaust and Intolerance Museum on Central, next to the Kimo Theater. The display was open from 11:00 a.m. to 3:00 p.m., Tuesday to Saturday until June 16. The powerful exhibit was an important piece of history and culture for the community.

Two years previously, a group of local community members would come together to bring to Albuquerque this powerful exhibit on the impact of the Holocaust to the homosexual community. The Holocaust is the name that refers to the systematic, bureaucratic, and state-sponsored campaign of persecution and murder. In addition to creating racially discriminatory laws that led to the mass murder of all European Jews, many other groups were targeted because of their perceived “racial inferiority.” Among those were Roma (Gypsies), people with disabilities, and some of the Slavic peoples (Poles, Russians, and others). Other groups were persecuted on political and behavioral grounds such as Communists, Socialists, Jehovah’s Witnesses, and homosexuals.

The “Nazi Persecution of Homosexuals, 1933-1945” exhibit would take participants through the years before and during the World War II. It would show how quickly homosexuals in Germany went from a thriving community to prisoners in concentration camps. Even after the camps were liberated, homosexuals were kept in prison because in Germany, Paragraph 175 still made homosexuality illegal. The exhibit was a chance to learn from history and realize that protecting Gay rights is a continuing effort. The exhibit also highlighted the local contemporary GLBT history. It was a chance to honor those who sacrificed in some way and to vow “never to forget.” In addition to the exhibit, Sol Arts Theater, presented “Bent” on June 1. The play formed a perfect complement to the holocaust exhibit because the play centered on two homosexual lovers in a concentration camp in Nazi Germany.

As June began, the activities for Pride began to heat up as well. On June 2, it was Gay Day from 11:00 a.m. to 3 p.m. at Cliff’s Amusement Park. Participants were asked to wear red to show support for the GLBT community for the First Annual Gay Day at Cliff’s Amusement Park located at 4800 Osuna Road. The event was from 11:00 a.m. to 10:00 p.m. Neil Macernie was the coordinator for this event. On June 2nd would also be the Inaugural Pride Interfaith Service held at the First Unitarian Church of Albuquerque at 7:00 p.m. This event entitled “Keepers of the Vision” featured music by the NM Gay

Men's/Women's Chorus. Sponsoring faith communities were Church of the Good Shepherd, United Church of Christ, Congregation Albert, First Congregational Church, First Unitarian Church of Albuquerque, La Mesa Presbyterian Church, Metropolitan Community Church, St. Michaels and All Angels, and the Westside Unitarian Universalist.

Wednesday, June 6th, the Albuquerque Independent Business Association hosted a mixer at Aurora Publishing while Old Town hosted a stroll through the plaza. Both events likely helped the community to mix with new friends. Thursday, June 7th, was the annual memorial known as the Candlelight Vigil at 7:30 p.m.at Morningside Park. Also, the Buffalo Exchange (clothing store) gave $5off coupons to those dressed in their Pride best where there was a DJ and yummy treats.

June 8th to 9th was the actual Pride celebration. According to Pat Baillie, the celebration of Pride had burgeoned since the event moved from the Spanish Village at Expo New Mexico onto the fairgrounds during its 25th celebration. Prior to that year, attendance had been at approximately four to six thousand persons. In 2007 there were over ten thousand people who would attend and celebrate.

Friday night there was a scheduled headliner at the fairgrounds. In other years, such a production would have been a risk perhaps not worth taking since the celebration of Pride was close to an event known as Wimminfest. The headliner was "BETTY" who performed the main theme song for the series *The L Word.* BETTY is a five-piece pop rock band fronted by Elizabeth Ziff, Alyson Palmer, and Amy Ziff. Albuquerque Pride would exalt this band's unique sound as a blend of tight harmonies layered over rocking guitars and solid rhythm section. According to their fans, since 1986, BETTY has performed their memorable live show, full of exciting, hook-laden songs, clever word play, and manic energy in clubs, theaters, and arenas all over the world.

Admission for both Friday and Saturday events, including parking were made available online for only $15. Tickets bought for only the Friday events were $8. The Friday event drew approximately two thousand persons, which was more than the previous year. Besides the headliner, the pet parade began at 6 p.m. Altogether, the Friday event was much quieter, more upscale, and generally, quite a bit cooler. It was encouraged for individuals to bring their pets on Friday night to have some food and beer and to celebrate with their four-legged friends and family who would not be allowed on Saturday. The Saturday event would be too chaotic in nature for the animals to be in attendance. The successful annual Pride Art Show and entertainment began at 7 p.m. At 7:30 p.m. there was a VIP/Sponsor reception at the Hispanic Arts building, and at 8 p.m. BETTY performed. After BETTY's performance was the "Pride Idol" competition. Individuals who had competed the month prior in clubs and other venues for Pride were selected to perform karaoke-style to win the Pride Idol title. Among clubs selecting their entrants were Pulse, Exhale, and Sidewinders. BenJammin' would win the coveted Pride Idol title for 2007.

Big improvements were made on Saturday, the actual day of the Pride Parade and Pridefest. One of these improvements was a solution to the myriad parking and walking challenges that occurred for previous years. Parking would be available at the Expo grounds beginning at 7:30 a.m. on the morning of the parade. The Pride organizers arranged for a shuttle service along Central Avenue to start before the parade began and to end by 3:30 p.m. It would run between Expo New Mexico and the main campus of the University of New Mexico, making stops at PeaceCraft, Kelly's, and O'Neils. The shuttle cost $1 for the day. Using the shuttle gave those who liked to watch the parade a great viewing spot along the parade route. A separate shuttle service would be provided for those who wanted to party and avoid driving. This service would be $10 per person and would end at 7:00 p.m.

Line up for the parade was at UNM at Girard and Central from 8 a.m. to 10 a.m. A ribbon cutting ceremony and certificate presentation was conducted at 10:00 a.m. by the Albuquerque Chamber of Commerce. The annual ribbon cutting ceremony would officially start the Pride Parade. Grand Marshal, Honored Dignitaries, Mayor Martin Chavez, and Lieutenant Governor Denish would cut the ribbon announcing that the Parade and Pridefest celebrations had begun. The Dykes on Bikes would lead the parade and proceed east on Central, north on San Pedro and into Expo New Mexico where everyone gathered for Pridefest beginning about 11:00 a.m. As with previous parades, the Rainbow Roadrunners car club would provide classic vehicles for the Grand Marshal, Honored Dignitaries and any other VIP's.

The 2007 Grand Marshal was the Local Organizing Committee coordinating the "Nazi Persecution of Homosexuals, 1933-1945" exhibit from The United States Holocaust Museum (April 29-June 16 at the New Mexico Holocaust and Intolerance Museum) along with Honored Dignitaries for their activism in New Mexico. Albuquerque Pride would select Mary Oishi (Under 21, Poetry Slam, KUNM)-Community Honored Dignitary, Bob White (City Attorney)-Political Honored Dignitary, Marshal Martinez- Emerging Leader Honored Dignitary, The NM Gay Men's Chorus-Arts Honored Dignitary, and Lieutenant Governor Diane Denish-Ally Honored Dignitary a title newly created in 2007.

Albuquerque Pride would include "In Memoria" recognition for those who in the community had passed away in previous years. The list for the previous year would include Gordan Church, Nancy Parker Davidson, Linda Gilkey, and Stacey Wadley. Geneva Convention (Matthew Thomas Bubb), famed and legendary performer would pass away leaving behind her honored legacy. A performer and founder of the drag troupe known as The Dolls, she assisted with giving positive support to Albuquerque Pride for many years. Also, Barbara Gittings, Gay activist would pass away in 2007. Gittings first came to the public spotlight in 1965 when she and a handful of gay men and lesbians held demonstrations outside the White House and Independence Hall seeking equal rights for homosexuals. These were the first such demonstrations in American history and began an era of gays coming out of the closet. Finally, The Albuquerque Human Rights Board would mark the tenth anniversary of the passing of human rights activist Neil Isbin. Neil Isbin assisted with producing the Pride Parade/March for many years. He would be remembered for his hard work and dedication to making our community a better place.

The 2007 Parade winners were Dykes on Bikes-Motorcycle, Tommy's Furniture Repair-Float Business, NM Burn-Float Community, 2007 Pride Titleholders-VIP Group, City of Albuquerque/Mayor Chavez-VIP Individual, NM Gay Rodeo Association-Walking Group, Southwestern Indian Polytechnic Institute GSA-Judges Choice, and Mariachi Orgullo de Nuevo Mexico-Performing Group. This mariachi group would become the first "out" gay and lesbian mariachi group in the United States. Their coming out was a brave statement made within the inner circle of this "machismo" performance community.

Pridefest 2007 had over 100 vendors/groups, food areas, Family and Children's area, Art Show, Pride History Archives, Indoor Car Show, Queer Bake-Off, Dance Tent, Indoor Drag and Karaoke Stage, and Mainstage. Throb, a local dance troupe, had become an important part of Albuquerque Pride's entertainment on the Mainstage at Pridefest. As extraordinary performers, this group had produced amazing routines and had enormous supporters who specifically attended Pridefest to watch them perform. Parking at Expo NM was $3.00, admission was $10 for adults and $2 for children under ten.

As what had occurred in the past for many Pride marches/parades, there would be either a rally or Pridefest to conclude the event. This would be a time for the crowd to come together as a family and in essence become one. VIP's would give their passionate speeches and awards were presented. Introductions of the Pride committee was made plus welcomes and honors were given to those from government who had supported the Gay community by marching, speaking at events, and riding in the parade or by signing laws protecting the rights for the GLBT community. Some Albuquerque Mayors would be proud to give a proclamation for the event. One of the proclamations from Mayor Martin J. Chavez for 2007 is as follows:

Executive Order

From the desk of
Mayor Martin J. Chavez

Whereas, the City of Albuquerque prides itself on finding ways to bring people and cultures together to grow and share in diversity and strengths: and

Whereas, the City of Albuquerque is determined to continue recognizing and uniting with the Gay, Lesbian, Bisexual and Transgender community: and

Whereas, the City of Albuquerque strives to create an environment of acceptance and opportunity for it GLBT residents and families: and

Whereas, the City of Albuquerque supports equal rights, strong families in any form and the creative, free expression of identity, love and community: and

Whereas, the City of Albuquerque understands the importance of diversity awareness, education and visibility: and

Whereas, the City of Albuquerque believes in this year's theme "United for Equality", realize that despite bigotry and intolerance, GLBTQ individuals have contributed significantly and productively to our collective past and will be, without doubt, constructive participants in our city's bright future: and Now, Therefore, I Martin J. Chavez, Mayor of the City of Albuquerque, New Mexico, do hereby proclaim June 4th to 10^{tth}, 2007as:

"**Gay Lesbian, Bisexual and Transgender Pride Week"**

Throughout the City of Albuquerque and I encourage everyone to help me celebrate our city's colorful citizenry and endeavor to never let prejudice pale our pride.

Events continued throughout the afternoon at the fairgrounds and at 7 p.m., Saturday night headliner Kimberley Locke would perform on the Mainstage. Kimberly Locke would be the "biggest" known celebrity hired to perform as the Featured Performer on the Mainstage for Albuquerque Pride. Kimberly Locke was the 1,580th person to audition in Nashville for American Idol. She had made it through cut after cut and was eventually flown to Los Angeles to be narrowed down with the other hopefuls. Week after week, Locke survived, until she found herself in the final three, and the last female contestant standing. Ruben Studdard went on to win the title, but Lock left an unforgettable impression on the public. It was that impression that ensured the success of her debut album, *One Love*. When Locke's first single *8th World Wonder* shot to number one on the Billboard chart, she was taken by surprise. She had noticed that her first album's success was attributed to her massive Gay fan base. Locke believed that Gay fans were not only attracted to her music, but identified with her music. Locke in 2007 returned her love to her Gay fans by playing Gay Pride events. She had performed at Pride festivities in Cleveland, San Francisco, Kansas, City, Orlando, and in Albuquerque for Pridefest.

Kimberly Locke would also give a second concert at Sidewinders Bar who sponsored the Featured Performer. Albuquerque Pride would attend the concert at 11:00 p.m. to make sure that all aspects of the rider were being followed. The Albuquerque Pride Board had a major concern. The bar had only provided an 8' x 8' stage that was 13 inches off the ground. The Albuquerque Pride Board found this unacceptable; however, it was too late to rectify the situation. As was done before to protect Tiffany from the fans, the Albuquerque Pride Board would do it again. They linked arms and sat on the edge of the stage ensuring the safety of Kimberly Locke. If fans were getting too close to Kimberly Locke, they were asked to move back.

There would be one other event at Expo NM. A youth dance was held at the creative Arts Building until 11 p.m. Kimberly Locke would stop by to say hello to the youth and give the participants some advice and words of wisdom. She would sing a few bars acapella ant then state, "to stay true to their hearts and don't let anyone ever make you feel unworthy of the true person you are." The youth "went wild" when she arrived, as it was not announced that she would be able to show up at the dance. The DJ played one of Kimberly Locke's songs, and she danced with them for a while and then had to leave to prepare for her next performance at The Ranch.

Albuquerque Pride had worked hard on promoting Pride 365 days a year. Albuquerque Pride was the first organization to have a float and community information table at the State Fair. The first years were very difficult because participating with these community events trembled the very hearts of the Pride Board who dared to be "open" and take that risk to be proud to the greater community. In 2007, with the assistance of other GLBT organizations, and after four years of having a presence with an information booth at the Manuel Lujan Building located in the NM State Fairgrounds, many citizens from New Mexico had come to the knowledge that the GLBT community was a permanent fixture, just like the Spanish Village, cotton candy, the Midway, and green chile corndog.

The year 2007 also marked an important milestone for Albuquerque Pride. According to the *New Mexico Business Journal* article entitled "Annual Festivals & Cultural Event," Albuquerque Pride/Pridefest was ranked number twenty in attendance for all annual festivals and events in the State of New Mexico with over 10,000 participants. The number one most attended event was The Albuquerque International Balloon Festival and second was the NM State Fair.

Albuquerque Pride as the leading Pride organization in New Mexico would assist other Prides with their events. This is one of the primary responsibilities as a member of InterPride. Other Prides in the state that Albuquerque Pride would assist would be held in Santa Fe, Las Cruces, Socorro, Gallup, and Farmington. Albuquerque Pride would also have parade entries for Pride on The Plaza and the 11th Annual Phoenix Pride Parade.

The Albuquerque Mining Company became a major sponsor and supporter for many years. The bar celebrated their 20th anniversary; however, this premature celebration would come to an end. The bar would close its doors in 2007 within the following months of its 20th anniversary. The former manager, Midnyte, (Michael Telles), would state that the AMC was, "one of the greatest sources for Pride in addition to being a popular social destination, all will be missed." The community wanted to know why this fixture was closing its doors. Midnyte explained, "The city had been trying to buy up that area for quite a while, and we weren't given an explanation. They just told us the land and property had been sold." Midnyte also noted that DWI crackdowns had taken a toll on bars and other nighttime venues throughout Albuquerque in the attempts to clean up Central. The Albuquerque Mining Company would close its doors and become a passing memory of the countless support that the bar provided to the Gay community and Albuquerque Pride.

Albuquerque Pride 2008

Celebrating 32 years of incredible Pride history in Albuquerque, the Pride Board began to look at the great positive possibilities for the GLBT community and allies. In the State of New Mexico Albuquerque Pride would become instrumental in the protection for hate crimes and non-discrimination laws for both sexual orientation and gender identity. Albuquerque Pride and Equality New Mexico with the support of other GLBT Allies, individuals, and groups would experience positive legislation that was so close in 2008 of receiving full and deserved domestic partnership benefits voted at the 2008 legislative session. Yet, despite this downfall of not receiving these benefits, the fight would continue and provide an opportunity for the community to come together and work harder than ever as a cohesive group. It was evident that Pat Baillie and PJ Sedillo's partnership had mended the rift between the Gay and Lesbian community that existed for many years.

Despite this legislative defeat, Albuquerque had so much to celebrate in 2008. The event had grown year by year and rivaled many of the "big" Prides that happened all year long. Many Prides around the country would look to what Albuquerque Pride had achieved, and in New Mexico similar events would be patterned after the Albuquerque Parade and Pridefest.

For many years, Pat Baillie had served Albuquerque Pride as the Female Co-chair and had become a valued leader in the Albuquerque community and the State of New Mexico. In January of 2008, Pat Baillie embarked on a new and wonderful journey. She had left Albuquerque and moved to California to pursue great and awesome endeavors. She would become the Director of Training and Professional Development for Out and Equal Advocates which is the world's premiere nonprofit organization dedicated to achieving lesbian, gay, bisexual, and transgender workplace equality. Out & Equal collaborates with Fortune 1000 companies and government agencies to provide a safe, welcoming and supportive environment for LGBT employees. The Executive Board of Albuquerque Pride and the community would miss her expertise, friendship, and knowledge. Albuquerque Pride was pleased to announce and have Pat Baillie as the Pride Honored Dignitary for 2008, a title well deserved.

A campaign started in 2008 tried to emphasize how much the event cost and the extensive amount of time the dedicated Board spent in volunteering. Albuquerque Pride stressed to the community that they must collectively remember all of those who volunteer for Pride who made a difference. Unbeknownst to the community, many did not realize that the Board from the President on down had all been volunteers and had not been paid for their services. The community had misconceptions that past Presidents, Co-Presidents, and Board Members of Pride were getting paid for their services, and this erroneous belief still exists, 50 years later.

The 2008 Pride Board's emphasis was for those who had not experienced Pride. The Board would seek out those declaring that this would be their first Pride and tried to capture their voices about experiencing the exhilarations of Albuquerque Pride. Albuquerque Pride would have meet and great at the Radisson Hotel and invited anyone new to Pride, with an interest in Pride, who was looking to find information, or wanting to become a future volunteer. There were 52 individuals that showed up. The Pride Board had felt that it was a success.

In the official Pride Program, it was stated that, "Maybe you might be the next Pat Baillie who will assist with the future growth of Albuquerque Pride. As you meet and greet others, rekindle past relationships, learn about the community and embody the 2008 theme 'Live*Love*Be,' let us all honor our history and celebrate 32 years of Pride as we look to a bright prosperous future."

PJ Sedillo in 2008 would again become the solitary President for Albuquerque Pride. In 2000, the organization would follow the recommended course from InterPride to have a female and male co-chair; however, by 2008 this practice had also been changed and dissolved for Albuquerque Pride. Ultimately, having two Co-chairs, both female and male, would heal the community from the decisiveness that had existed between Lesbians and Gays. In 1983, the theme for unification of the Gay and Lesbian community was "Galesbian," which would become a laughing matter from both genders; however, the Co-presidencies of Pat Baillie and PJ Sedillo had unified both sexes. Despite the unsightly entertaining, amusing theme from 1983, the unification from these two individuals would start the healing process. In their own unique way, they were able to celebrate and honor the theme "Galesbian" 25 years later. Unbeknownst to many from the community, both would play "good cop, bad cop." Of course, PJ would be play the good cop, and Pat Baillie would be the bad cop; however, Pat Baillie ultimately would ensure that all individuals would be heard and honored and let PJ Sedillo become the "bad cop" when deemed necessary.

The Executive Albuquerque Pride Board for 2008 would include PJ Sedillo-President, Heather Larkin-Treasurer, Tony Ross-Facilities, Maria Johnson-Pride Representative, and Brian Johnson-Secretary. Next, the Committee Chairs for Albuquerque Pride would be Virginia-Stage Manager, JoJo-Dance Stage, BJ/Taylin and Kelly-Family and Children's Area. Finally, for 2008, the rest of the Board would include Jeremy-Volunteer Coordinator, Nate-Volunteer, Rea Chapman-Hospitality, Raven Rykers-Pet Parade and the Candlelight Vigil Coordinator-Will Finch and Dan Boxrund.

The New Mexico Titleholders for 2007 were Joaquin Del Rio-Mr. NM Pride who was a member of the fantastic dance troupe known at Throb. He would have a wonderful title year and then embark on a new and exciting life in California. He would be missed by all his fans and the Board of Albuquerque Pride. Angelica Del Rio-Miss NM Pride, a legend in the Drag Community (AKA Abraham Placencio-Honored Dignitary 2003), represented her title year well as an ambassador (a new title created by Pride to explain their duties) of Albuquerque Pride. She had made new contacts and fulfilled her duties well above her yearly requirements. She had also become a sponsor of Pride for 2008 and would be remembered for years to come.

Lil' Dreamer-Ms. NM Pride would start out as a meek and shy individual who would eventually become a beacon for others in the GLBT community. With a soft-spoken attitude, she helped the community come together to succeed. Veronica Lopez-Miss NM Pride Youth had entered the competition starting on a journey of transformation. Unaware of the intense needs as a female impersonator, which included the extreme make-up transformation and costuming she would be hindered at her beginnings as a performer; however, her metamorphosis would be transpired by the many "seasoned drag queens" that would provide the knowledge, strength, and courage for her to proceed to be empowered as Miss NM Pride Youth.

The NM Pride pageant would be held in April. The 2007-2008 Pride Titleholders elected prior to the actual event would perform June 14th on the Mainstage at Pridefest for Albuquerque Pride. These winners would be Latina Del Rio-Miss NM Pride, Johnny Q.-Mr. NM Pride, Jay-MsTer NM Pride, and Alize Serenity Mistique-Miss NM Youth Pride. These individuals would quickly become involved in attending weekly Pride meetings and a titleholder retreat. They also had the responsibility of making a float or getting vehicles for the parade. It would become a fast-paced event for those who were a 2008 titleholder.

The Pridefest responsibilities for these titleholders would become a priority; however, they were still all responsible for fundraising and meeting their financial responsibilities to keep their crown. This would assist in obtaining the Pride budget. The Pride budget for 2008 was $120,900; however, the expected projected income was $117,000 which the Albuquerque Pride Board would have to work diligently to obtain, or certain budget items would have to be eliminated. Notably, the Pride budget would be obtained even though Latina Del Rio would not complete her title year. The first runner up, Aleah Rico, would assume the title to fulfill her reign. Aleah Rico would successfully obtain the financial responsibilities tied to the budget and surpass the amount needed. She would be given "Honored Dignitary" status by the Albuquerque Pride Board.

The 2008 International and Albuquerque Pride theme was **Live *Love *Be*. The community was again asked to submit logos for the T-shirt and official Pride Pin. The winner would have their picture and bio in the program and have the honor of showcasing their design on all Pride merchandise and advertisements.

After working many years together with Black Duck (the official Pride t-shirt printing company) they would begin to submit numerous logos from their art department. In the past, logos that were selected needed to be redrawn for printing purposes, whether they were in the proper format or hand drawn. Black Duck entered numerous designs so that it would become easier step for production of the T-shirts. The winning logo design for the T-Shirt chosen for 2008 would be selected from Black Duck Printing.

The logo would have a group of people celebrating in various poses. Each one would be colored in one of the rainbow colors. On the top of the individuals was the wording Live* Love* Be*. Below the phrasing was Albuquerque Pride 32nd Anniversary, 2008. The background incorporated silhouettes in black which were a concert stage and lights. This year would have the “biggest” number of t-shirts sold in Albuquerque Pride’s history. 500 t-shirts were sold out in a week, and a new order of 250 t-shirts had to be made to have shirts available for Pride 2008. This was also the first time that pre-orders were made so that individuals could secure a t-shirt in the right size. This t-shirt also had been selected at the yearly archives display as the winner of “People’s Choice” for best logo at the 2021, 2022 Pridefest.

2008

The Official Pride pin was circular with the wording Live, Love, Be on the top and Albuquerque Pride 2008 on the bottom. In the middle was a flower with eight colors of the rainbow and located in the middle was the peace sign. This simple design would be the first time that the Official Pride Pin would be sold out before Pride Day. An overnight order would be shipped for those who wanted a 2008 Official Pride Pin.

New to 2008 was an advertisement on the back of six Albuquerque City buses. Albuquerque Pride was a sponsor of the *Albuquerque Clean Air Campaign* and was provided placards on the back of City buses. This would be the first time that Albuquerque Pride would advertise on such a grand scale. All buses were located on the Central and San Pedro routes. The response from the community was overwhelming which in turn increased the number of participants, spectators and volunteers in 2008.

The *Alibi* magazine, known as "Albuquerque's Only Alternative," had become a "staple" for producing their yearly issue focusing on Pride in Albuquerque. In 2008, the *Alibi's* issue the "Best of Burque" would award Albuquerque Pride as the Best Outdoor Festival/Parade. The newspaper would write, "Honey, nothing's gayer than a parade, but only ABQ Pride comes out swinging every June (June 13 and 14 this year) with an unbeatable parade/festival combo that's purely in the name of love. Awww." Second place would be awarded to the Albuquerque Balloon Fiesta. Albuquerque Pride had come a long way from when eggs and shouts of hate were hurled at the participants in 1977 to be awarded the Best Outdoor Festival/Parade in Albuquerque. Times had changed.

Albuquerque Pride had received many honors as one of the most successful GLBT events in the state of New Mexico; however, with this success it is of the upmost importance for this Pride history to share the many 2008 unsanctioned events held that year. Others in the past had been, "riding on the coattails of Pride" using the organization to gain dollars to support their business/organizations. In 2008 this would become more evident than what had been experienced in the past. Albuquerque Pride would have to deal with this issue head on with no clear direction on how to handle it. The next June dates mentioned will reveal the extensive number of events held in 2008 that did not assist Albuquerque Pride's budget to produce the event. Letters were sent to all the businesses and no responses were received.

Albuquerque Pride had requested individual meetings with the following businesses asking them about their "Pride Event." These meetings would be, "all talk and no action." They would reveal events produced by these different factions with no monetary support for Albuquerque Pride. In the past, many of the gay bars in the community would honor Pride and had become instrumental in assisting monetarily with producing the Pride event in Albuquerque; however, in 2008 the "tides had changed." The next dates of these unsanctioned Pride events held in Albuquerque revealed that each affair would occur based on indications that the GLBT community believed that they were supported and associated with Albuquerque Pride. These predicaments would have Albuquerque Pride deal "head on" with these factions who wanted to ride on Albuquerque Pride's coattails without providing any monetary support.

Other organizations, as in the past, did not understand or realize the budgetary concerns that Pride in Albuquerque would have to deal with yearly. In 2008, Albuquerque Pride would cost $120,900 and every dollar would count for the organization to produce the event and obtain needed seed money to exist in 2009. The Pride Board had made some conclusions and assumptions pertaining to why the community did not understand what the fundamental cost was to produce Albuquerque Pride. These conclusions and assumptions made by the Albuquerque Pride Board were that the community believed that money expressed in "budgeted form" had been already obtained and that these funds would easily be made available to produce the event. These assumptions from Albuquerque Pride and the community would be an ongoing problem for years to follow. Despite the pleas from Albuquerque Pride and ongoing meetings held to assist monetarily with businesses, bars, and other organizations many events would still be produced whether officially or unofficially stating publicly no funds deemed to Albuquerque Pride. Albuquerque Pride would try to ensure and show that unity existed; however, unity did not pay the bills. The following are unauthorized or somewhat supported events for Albuquerque Pride 2008:

Unsanctioned Events-Thursday, June 12

Evolution Downtown would promote "Time Warp Thursdays" with DJ Devin, hosted by Sabryna Williams and featuring a special performance by Robin S ("It Must be Love," "Love for Love," "Show Me Love") at 9:30 p.m. Evolution Downtown would promote this event as a Pride event. Lotus Nightclub and VIP Ultralounge sponsored "Come Out, Come Out, Wherever You Are Beach Party" noted as a Pre-Party with a charge of $10 for 18+, $5 for 21+ with doors opening at 10 p.m. A percentage of the proceeds would go to the NM AIDS Services. Sidewinders would have country dance lessons with Bill and Denny with music provided by DJ JoJo. Finally, at UNM Keller Hall the NM Gay Men's Chorus at 7:30 p.m. presented "Why We Sing" featuring Mariachi Orgullo de Nuevo Mexico. The price was $10 in advance from UNM or $12at the door. Albuquerque Pride would not receive any monies from these events.

Unsanctioned Events-Friday, June 13

Evolution Downtown proclaimed "Camp Fridays" at 9 p.m. with DJ Stitch and a special live performance by LOGO TV Top 10 artist Cazwell. Exhale Bar and Grille would have a Variety Show featuring Micha, the UNM Theater Department, and DJ Boop. The Fairfield Marriot Hotel would have – Tribal Pride – "Video Foam Party" featuring DJ Irene from 9 p.m. to 2 a.m.DJ Leo Matthew would also spin. Individual tickets were $20 for 21+ and $25 for ages 18 to 20. Finally, Sidewinders would have an event with music provided by DJ JoJo starting at 8:00 p.m.

Unsanctioned Events-Saturday, June 14

Albuquerque Pride's main celebration was on Saturday, June 14th; however, Evolution Downtown (Bar) held a Block Party on the Fourth Street Mall starting at 8:00 p.m. featuring sets by CuriousSoul (Las Vegas), the Wonder Twins, DJ PJ, DJ Joey Canez (Phoenix), and headliners DJ Corey D. and DJ Eddie X. There would be live performances from Pepper MaShay and hotel packages available at the Hyatt Downtown. It must be noted that Evolution Downtown did not provide any other financial support for producing the event. Exhale Bar and Grille would promote DJ Mike T who would be spinning R&B, hip-hop, and country and did not provide sponsorship. Exhale Bar did let Albuquerque Pride sell merchandise at their bar and they did pay for an entry in the parade. Admission for this event would start at $15 and entertainment began at 6:00 p.m. which was well before the conclusion of the Albuquerque Pridefest and was looked upon as a "slam" to the Pridefest.

Sidewinders would promote "Pride Celebration" with music from DJ JoJo with no money given to Albuquerque Pride. Again, at the Fairfield Marriot at 9 p.m. would be "Tribal Pride" with a main event featuring DJ Kimberly S. and Frenchie Davis who would perform at Albuquerque Pride earlier in the day. Again, Tribal Pride would become a sponsor for $1,000; however, it would cost Albuquerque Pride more to bring Frenchie Davis in to perform. Ultimately, Tribal Pride would generate a lot of money from their event, and Albuquerque Pride would not recoup the amount that was spent to bring her in.

Notably, each headliner that is brought in to perform for Pride events requires travel/airfare, hotel accommodations (usually 5 star), performer riders, miscellaneous expenses, limo service, food expenses, manager or sales representative, and backstage dancers/singers (also requiring the same items above), and extra expenses to provide a "meet and greet." Contracts would need to be obtained for each performer, and the assistance of legal advice would be needed from Albuquerque Pride to ensure that they would "not lose their shirt" in the process of obtaining performers for Pride.

At the end of the day, Albuquerque Pride would sanction and "bless" all these events within the official Pride Program and within the *Alibi* hoping that the budget would be made. The Board of Directors felt that any negative actions taken against the bars or organizations who did not provide sponsorship would be an unworthy problem to take on; however, Albuquerque Pride would need to rectify this situation pertaining to the many produced events that jumped "on the coattails of Pride" without assisting and ensuring that Albuquerque Pride would exist. Many felt that community had come to take Albuquerque Pride for granted because the event had grown by leaps and bounds. Little did the community know that each year it was getting increasingly difficult to obtain the funds to produce such a huge event. Interesting enough, many individuals would be willing to pay upwards to $25 for an unsanctioned event, but voiced dissent for having to pay $15 to enter the gates of Pridefest.

Sanctioned Albuquerque Pride Events

New to this year was the introduction of a Pocket Pride Guide. This 8 ½" x 11" sheet had a map of Pridefest on one side of the entire page which had the names and locations of booths and each venue. It also had the scheduled events for Friday and Saturday. This Pocket Pride Guide once folded into four sections would also have the logo on the front and would include advertisements from key sponsors for 2008. This document was well received by the community as they would not have to carry the Pride Program booklet for the entire event. They would have all the information needed for the event on an item that was easy to carry. The official Pride Program could be taken home when the attendees had left Pridefest.

At 7:30 p.m. was the Candlelight Vigil held at Morningside Park. This annual celebration would have over 1000 participants who would come out to get their annual collector's card and to experience this moving event. The Albuquerque Social Club would sponsor an event after the Candlelight Vigil for those who would want to meet and discuss the event that just took place and plan out the weekend of Pride events. There would be no cover charge, and food would be made available for those who attended. A special Pride drink would be made with some of the proceeds going to Albuquerque Pride. The Board would thank the Albuquerque Social Club for their partnership in working together and would give the club special access to all Albuquerque Pride events. Because the club could not receive any advertisement due to State laws about membership clubs, the ASC would be given a multitude of free passes to give to their members for their gracious sponsorship.

Friday, June 13th, would be the Albuquerque Pride Celebration from 5:30 to 10:00 p.m. at EXPO NM. It would again be a free event and open to the public. At 6:00 would be the Pet Parade. Registration would open at 5:30 at the Pride Office, and prizes would be awarded to the whole family. The Pet Policy for Friday welcomed all pets of all kinds. It was suggested to not, "let the dogs rule again!" It was stressed to make sure that all pets be leashed and that they are able to get along with the many people and other animals attending the Friday night event. The policy for Saturday at the parade would be to welcome pets, but participants would remind that it was a 2.7-mile, uphill route in the June heat. Water and a plan would be asked from the participants if their pet could not make the entire route.

For Saturday at Pridefest the policy was "NO PETS ALLOWED" except for working/service animals. It was also stressed to "PLEASE DO NOT LEAVE YOUR PET IN A CAR AT EXPO NM." The Board wished that they could allow pets on Saturday, but due to the large crowds and numbers of children present, it simply would not be safe for either the animals or humans. If a pet was brought to the fairgrounds the attendee would be asked to remove it. The year before the Pride Board had encountered many animals that had been left in cars and were close to dying. The police had been contacted to assist with the problems. Windows were cracked to give the animals left in the hot cars some cool air to survive. This is one of the reasons why these drastic changes had been made in 2008.

Beginning Thursday, artists of all ages, all sexual orientations, and gender identities in all mediums were invited to display their works of art at the 2008 Pride Art Show. Art could be submitted on Thursday, June 12th, from 3:00 p.m. to 8:00 p.m. and on Friday, June 13th, from 9:00 a.m. to 2:00 p.m. It was reiterated that the Art submitted did not have to depict GLBT themes as this would be a chance to show off one's creative side. There were professional and amateur artist divisions for the juried art show and a non-juried show for those who just wanted to display their Pride. Friday, June 13th, at 6:30 p.m. at the Fine Arts Building at EXPO NM was the opening for the 2008 Pride Art Show along with Mainstage entertainment. Awards were presented at that time. Many of the artists were there to discuss their work, and many pieces were made available for sale. The Art Show hours were from 6:00 p.m. to 10:00 p.m. on Friday and 11:00 a.m. to 6:00 p.m. on Saturday.

Also, at 6:30 a new venue in the Pride Archives would open. This would be the "Caught in the Act" Theater which would open in the Hispanic Arts Building at EXPO NM. Jon Hull who had been instrumental in the past as an advocate for GLBT rights, founder of Common Bond, supporter of Pride in Albuquerque, and the creator and producer of the famed variety show "Caught in the Act" would create an intimate theater that showcased past performers from the variety show, parade videos, and also Pridefest Mainstage entertainment. This would be a great addition to the Albuquerque Pride Archives as these venues were showcased together. Remarkably, the Pride Archives in 2008 had grown to over 200 frames and was out growing the space needed to show the archived frames. Also, in 2008 was the introduction of archived frames that showcased the Albuquerque Pride Pageants with frames dedicated to the title year with individual frames honoring each titleholder.

Albuquerque Pride had responded to requests made from the community who could not afford the event on Saturday. Therefore, Albuquerque Pride would provide a Friday Night Pride Event for those individuals and others who came from other states and countries to experience more than one day of Pride. The Friday Night Pride Event on the

Mainstage would be spectacular and one that should not be missed. Albuquerque Pride also tried to capitalize on an evening event which had not been possible for Saturday because many of the attendees on Saturday would leave between 4:00 p.m. and 6:00 p.m. to rest and get ready to go out to the many gay bar events held in the evenings. Pride would become a "ghost town" by 7:00 p.m. with the only individuals left being the under aged attendees who attended the Pride Youth Dance.

The Mainstage entertainment would start at 6:30 p.m. Starting at 7:00 p.m. would be performances by Deep Dickollective-progressive rap artists and God-des and She-two groundbreaking female hip-hop artists, legends in the lesbian community. This was the first year that two main performers would grace the Pride Mainstage, and they would "bring the house down."

God-des and She before their career started would state, "Well, we're going to pack up our U-Haul and move to the city of dreams!" This move would take them in March of 2004 from Madison, Wisconsin, to Brooklyn, New York. They took New York city by storm and played sold out shows at the famed Knitting Factory. They opened for MC LYTE and Slick Rick, performed at the Supper Club for the Showtime/ GO NYC magazine L WORD party, and performed countless other high-profile gigs. These women were magnetic on stage, lighting up the faces of the Albuquerque Pride audience. GOD-DES had been rhyming for over ten years. She started out as a percussionist; a marching band geek turned rapper. She spent her school bus rides home rapping for her friends- a natural performer from the start. She was also an "out" gay and stated that she was a "white dyke Jewish rapper from Wisconsin, didn't think that they existed, huh?" According to multiple press releases, SHE, the other part of the duo, "can sing her ass off." She added another female layer rarely heard in Hip Hop today. Furthermore, SHE's contribution elevated the music to a whole new level. Their chemistry on and off the stage was undeniable.

Deep Dickollective would be the act with the most unusual name that Albuquerque Pride had contracted with to perform on the Mainstage. Little did the Board know that the group had its own following who went from state to state just to hear them perform. These "groupies" would show up on Friday night raring to hear them perform. Albuquerque Pride would hear raves from the community. Others would spread the word about the awesome concert that was missed if one was not there for Friday Night PrideFest. Deep Dickollective (D/DC), since their release of their demo "Bourgie-n-Ghetto," in 2000 had been a creative and cultural force driving popular and academic discourse around race, class, queerness, and masculinity as reflected in the burgeoning hip-hop subculture according to the GLBT music industry.

Appearing in countless features, essays, and articles in the LGBT and mainstream media, D/DC had toured colleges and festivals around the U.S. and Canada since mid 2001winning the Best Hip Hop Group award in the 2003 San Francisco Gay Guardian readership poll. They came to more recent mainstream attention through their central presence in Alex Hinton's documentary *Pick Up The Mic.* Premiering at the 2005 Toronto International Film Festival, the documentary had since screened in 50+ film festivals internationally and was broadcasted on the LOGO network with the DVD release in 2008. Another release known as *On Some Other* (Sugartruck Recordings, 2007) would be the group's fifth overall release and first studio recording since 2004. The D/DC was known for *The Famous Outlaw League Of Proto Negroes*, which was a 2005 Outmusic Award double nominee and a Top Ten Album of the 2004 selection from *Out Magazine*. Albuquerque Pride would be thrilled by the performances that both God-des and She and Deep Dickollective gave for the Friday Night PrideFest event. This event would be talked about "again and again" on Saturday the actual day of Pride.

Finally, with the crowd thrilled and excited the Pride Mainstage event would end with the 2nd Annual Pride Idol competition. God-des and She and Deep Dickollective would judge the competitions. The following were the winners: 3rd Place-Anthony Montano, 2nd Place-Holly LaBeau, and the 1st Place/Pride Idol-BenJammin. The Friday night events would end by 10:00 p.m. giving the Pride Board a few hours after closing the event to be ready for Saturday, the 32nd Annual Parade and Pridefest held in Albuquerque.

Spectators crowded Central Avenue on Saturday to behold the Albuquerque Pride Parade. The event was held in conjunction with Pridefest noted by the *Albuquerque Journal* as, "an annual celebration of lesbian, gay, bisexual and transgender communities." Pridefest after the parade would include an art show, bake-off, and "hair bowl" that would have hair and makeup artists compete for top prizes. Albuquerque Pride would salute the sanctioned sponsors for 2016 by extending a gracious thank you for sponsoring the event. On Saturday, sponsors were provided the opportunity to go to the VIP Lounge from 12:00 p.m. to 5:00 p.m. Once there they would receive a plaque and a "sponsor goodie's pail" with many promotional items given from Albuquerque Pride and sponsors. There were complimentary drinks (both alcoholic and non), food, and a calming environment with bar service located at the "heart" of Pridefest. Sponsors were also given free parking passes, tickets for the event on Friday and Saturday and many complementary drink tickets. Official sanctioned sponsors for 2008 in were:

PRIDE BENEFACTOR

Miller Lite (Premier Distributors)
QBliss
IN THE LIFE (Documentary)
Southwest LGBT Press
Gardunos

PRIDE DONOR

Steve Benoit (Realtor)	Sidewinders
Century 21-Unica Realty / Jim Sutton	Sinatra DeVine Productions
ID LUBRICANTS	ONiell's Pub
Maria Johnson AKA Jayson DaBoi	EQNM
ALIBI	Amigo Case Management
MADDOX & CO. (Realtors)	MCCA
QVEGAS	City of Albq.-Cultural Services Dept.
Marriot Albuquerque	93.3 kob.fm
abqARTS	New Mexico VOICE
WELLS FARGO	COMCAST
SOPA	ACVB
Black Duck Tees	PRIDE & EQUALITY (magazine)
NM AIDS Service	IMM Inc.

PRIDE PRODUCER

Angelica Del Rio	Tribal Pride
KUNM	WIMIN
NM Leather League	Animal Welfare Dept.-City of Albuquerque

The Pride Parade would start at the corner of Central and Girard at 10:30 a.m. sharp. Current Pride Titleholders, Grand Marshal -Mara Keisling, Honored Dignitaries, and the Albuquerque Chamber of Commerce conducted the annual ribbon cutting ceremony. Albuquerque Pride would again provide a free bus shuttle starting at 7:00 a.m. at EXPO NM and ending at 1:00 p.m. The parade proceeded east on Central Avenue. Judges were located at the Starbucks in Nob Hill. Trophies would be awarded to the "best of" categories. The parade entered EXPO NM (NM State Fair) at gate 3 located on Copper and San Pedro. The winners for the pride parade were:

Best Motorcycle- Ian/Beads U& Fabulousness
Best Motorcycle Group- Jessica A. Vallez & Francia Gray
Best Motorized Vehicle-The Old Fire Truck
Best Motorized Group-Democrats of NM
Best Motorized Performance-57 Raging Trannies (Teresa Johansen & Partner)
Best Horse/Mounted Unit-Tandem Bike
Best Walking Performace-Wilde Bunch
Best Walking/Banner Group-THE PLANET
Best Business Float-Sidewinders
Best Community Float-Navajo AIDS Network
Judges Prize-NMPower
Honorable Mention-Albufurque (Best use of Faux Fur)

The 2008 Grand Marshal was Mara Keisling who would be honored as Albuquerque Pride's first transgender Grand Marshal. She was the founding Executive Director of the National Center for Transgender Equality (NCTE). As a Pennsylvania native, Mara went to Washington after co-chairing the Pennsylvania Gender Rights Coalition. Mara, a transgender-identified woman, also acknowledged that she was a parent and Pennsylvanian. She graduated from Penn State University and did her graduate work at Harvard University in American Government. She served on the Board of Directors of Common Roads, an LGTBQ Youth Group, and on the steering committee of the Statewide Pennsylvania Rights Coalition. In 2008 Mara had over twenty-five years of professional experience in social marketing and opinion research.

A.J. Carian was Albuquerque Pride's 2008 Honored Dignitary-Political. He was a lifelong, proud Albuquerquean who was completely thrilled to be acknowledged by Albuquerque Pride in this extraordinary way. A.J. was a member of his high school GSA (Gay/Straight Alliance), worked on the Clothesline Project and Outfest 200, acted in local plays and films, and received a certificate of distinction for his service to UCLA's queer community by wearing "pink" for his graduation ceremony. A.J. had worked as an Assistant to Albuquerque's Mayor Martin Chavez on outreach projects with Albuquerque Pride, youth groups, theater companies, New Mexico Aids Services, the Gay and Lesbian Chamber (both local and national) and many other GLBT organizations. A.J. was appointed the Deputy Director of Cultural Services in 2005. He had also worked at DW Turner Strategic Communications. Outside work, A.J. continued to devote his time and talents to the Dolls (Albuquerque's premier drag troupe), Closet Cinema, local theater, and deserving political campaigns.

Pride on the Plaza-Santa Fe Pride, would be given the acclamations as Albuquerque Pride's Honored Dignitary-Community. The annual Pride parade and Festival would be held Saturday, June 28. Pride In The Plaza was one of the activities of the Human Rights Alliance. The Human Rights Alliance was founded in 1993 in response to the defeat of Senate Bill 91, civil rights legislation for lesbians and gay men. Rallying around the enthusiasm of their grassroots crusade, local activists joined together to create the non-profit organization whose primary goal was to end discrimination of all kinds. The Alliance sought to build coalitions with groups who would work for civil rights for all New Mexicans. Activities of the Human Rights Alliance included the Annual Gay-La fundraisers, Pride on the Plaza-Santa Fe's annual Gay Pride celebration, lobbying day at the State Legislature, periodic newsletters, Candidates/Legislators Forums, coalitions with Unidos, Equality New Mexico, and others.

Honored Dignitary-Arts would be The Wilde Bunch. Kent de Jong, who was president, would write his autograph in the Official Pride Guide for their participation.

Notably, Kent de Jong had been instrumental in the 80's with finances for Common Bond and had assisted with the development of the parade in Albuquerque.

The Wilde Bunch, a gay square dance group started by Don Durham and Teddy Garvin, held their first public performance at "Caught in the Act" at the Kimo Theatre in June of 1983. Over the years, nearly 300 people had been through the Basics of Gay Square Dancing in Albuquerque. The Wilde Bunch, as a charter member of the International Association of Gay Square Dance Clubs, was one of the first clubs in the country to reach parity early on with the number of men and women in the club which has continued all these years to have an all-inclusive policy for dancers. Both Bill Eyler (1983) and Kris Jenzen (1989) had become internationally recognized callers both in the Gay and straight communities. The Wilde Bunch was honored with the Golden Boot Award.

Honored Dignitary-Ally would be Black Duck Tees. It must be noted that in the past it was difficult locating a printing company who would be open and offer to print t-shirts for this Gay event. Black Duck Tees would become the most welcoming business supporting the Pride event. Black Duck was the creative venture of the two brothers Doug and Dana Bird. Black Duck has received awards both nationally and internationally for both quality and creativity in their industry. From a one room shop with a single manual press in 1989, Black Duck had flourished, becoming a production powerhouse with three manual and four automatic presses, giving them the capabilities to produce over 24,000 shirts a day. In addition, they have embroidery machines with a total of 64 sewing heads. Notably, the artists for Black Duck would submit logos for Pride which would be selected for consecutive years.

Pride Honored Dignitary/Grand Marshal would be given to Pat Baillie who had been Co-president with PJ Sedillo and a Board Member of Albuquerque Pride. She had moved to Albuquerque and was very active in Emmanuel MCC. She then found her way to Albuquerque Pride. Starting out as the Media Contact for Albuquerque Pride in 1997, Pat in 1998 became female Co-president of Albuquerque Pride and served in that position for nine years. Pat's community work did not stop with Pride Day. She stayed active and involved in the leather community, traveling to events all over the country during that year. Her message had always been one of positive sex which has kept her actively involved with workshops and speaking events. She would be given a job with Out & Equal in California and would be missed in the community. PJ Sedillo would now have to ensure that all voices from the community would be heard. This would be his awakening to make sure that no matter what was presented for the Pride Event, PJ Sedillo would listen, honor and respect all those who wished that their voices be heard.

Pat Baillie (originally expressed and written as pat baillie) would become instrumental in bringing the gay and lesbian community together in her tenure. For a brief period of time, those wounds would be healed; however, within four years after her departure some individuals from the past would re-open the wounds to declare their own pride event that would become a mask for the separation between gays, lesbians, the rich, and the poor in the community pertaining to Pride.

Despite the wonderful event of the Albuquerque Pride Parade, the Board and President would have to deal with one of the first major lawsuits for the event. During the annual Gay Pride Parade a former Albuquerque Police spokeswoman who had been promoted to sergeant, accidentally moved her vehicle and while backing up knocked over a baby stroller. The two-year old girl in the stroller was not injured, and aid from the police was given immediately. The incident occurred about 1 p.m. at Carlisle and Central Avenue where the parade was taking place. According to an *Albuquerque Journal* reporter who witnessed the accident and gave an account to the police, the woman with the stroller was starting to cross the crosswalk. The rear driver's side of the SUV struck the stroller which kind of bounced. The woman should not have been crossing the street because all access to the road was closed. Ultimately, the woman was blamed for not following proper procedures and no legalities occurred; however, this would be the first time that the parade had grown to over 10,000 spectators. The Nob Hill area would be a saturated mass of parade enthusiasts, and Albuquerque Pride would be made aware of a situation to deal with in 2009.

Albuquerque Pride for 2008 would begin selling online tickets for the event. This would be a first that wrist bands would be made available for volunteers, staff and vendors. Also, individuals who purchased a ticket online were able to print their tickets. This would be new for Albuquerque Pride which now would need scanners. Albuquerque Pride would have a specific entrance for those who purchased tickets online which assisted in the participants getting into the festival quickly. However, many would wait to the day of the event to purchase tickets making lines long and those entering aggravated. Pride volunteers had to deal with the rude and inappropriate responses for those entering Pridefest 2008. PJ Sedillo, Tony Ross, and Andy Davis would head to the gates with garbage bags in hand and take only cash for them to enter Pridefest. A volunteer followed who was there to assist with making change. Once all was calm, the garbage bags full of money were taken to the treasure who was shocked by what had occurred and the intense need to focus and begin counting the money.

Events would begin at 11:00 a.m. Scheduled for that day was an Indoor Car Show, Pride Archives, Mainstage Entertainment, "Caught in the Act" Theater, Adult Area, Drag Stage, Queer Bake Off, Family and Youth Area, Poetry Reading, Karaoke, and over 150 booths. The Mainstage entertainers featured Josh Zuckerman, Amber, and Frenchie Davis. Pridefest would conclude with the Youth Dance in the Hispanic Arts building from 8:00 p.m. to 11:00 p.m. New for this year was the Hair Bowl. This event would be sanctioned by Albuquerque Pride and the Haircare Center Salon. It was open to any salon with a design team of five. The team would compete for the best up and coming hair and make-up artists that Albuquerque had to offer. There was a coveted trophy for the Grand Prize winner, Most Creative Hair, and Most Creative Make-Up. Along with other prizes in the hair and beauty industry this would be a chance for those to "Bring It" and be part of the First Annual Hair Bowl. Johnny Melendez and Brenda Schultz were the coordinators for the Hair Bowl.

Albuquerque Pride would have three accomplished performers for the Mainstage this year. Josh Zuckerman was an American performer, musician, singer, songwriter and recording artist who would perform for the spectators and open for Amber and Frenchie Davis. As an Independent Recording Artist, Josh had some of his original music featured on TV shows. The Josh Zuckerman discography included 5 CDs performing with Background Static of Perpetual Discontent, Mr. Z, and the Shashka Frashkas. This included tracks *From A to Mr. Z, Got Love?*, *Out From Under*, *A Totally New Sensation,* and the single *All I Want For Christmas* with the former band 'China White' which included friend and drummer, Paul Galiszewski. His music was distributed nationally throughout the U.S.A. and was also bought worldwide.

Josh Zuckerman wrote, recorded and performed original music. He played the guitar, violin, and some piano and performed nationally with original music and some cover songs by other musicians, per the credits on his five album liner notes. He had released eleven music videos, some featured on MTV-Beta and VH1 Online, Logo, Youtube.com, and his website. Zuckerman's albums contained original music compositions and original lyrics, while some of his early work featured his talent musically where he fiddled with the violin while fusing the country music and rock/pop sound. Opening up for Amber, Josh would have the crowd wanting more. He would continue his performance at Sidewinders that evening with a huge following who knew nothing about him prior to his performance. Johnny Q, Mr. New Mexico Pride who was part of "Up With People" knew Josh Zuckerman from their connections at past performances. Johnny Q would make him feel like a welcomed member of the Albuquerque Pride family.

Amber would be designated as a Pride Performer for 2008. This was because each performer had an "equal star status" and the term Featured Performer of Headline was discontinued in 2008. Amber was born in the Netherlands and partially raised in Germany by a mother who was a songwriter and piano teacher. Her father was an opera singer whose gift of singing would be passed to Amber. She amassed an impassioned army of fans with a string of worldwide hits that included: *Sexual (li da di), Above the Clouds, The Need to be Naked.*

According to the music industry, these songs were described as smarter, bolder, and more infectious than the average, paint-by-numbers pop tunes, with sterling gems like "Yes" from the Studio 54 soundtrack with Ultra Nate and Jocelyn Enriquez. Her "One More Night" release would be marked as an impressive song garnering a seven consecutive number one dance single in addition to a number one dance chart hit, eventually making the song into the official Top 40 Billboard Charts. Amber would state, "I am in a happy place now and there is nothing like owning your own music and masters and running your own show and destiny. No longer do I have to live in anyone else's world or dance to someone else's beat." She would be one of the first who would sue and outright own all her rights to her music. That night Amber would become one with the Albuquerque Pride spectators.

In 2008, Albuquerque Pride's final Mainstage Pride Performer would be Frenchie Davis. She had famously been booted as an American Idol contestant. At the time Frenchie Davies was outraged that the contestant, David Hernandez, would be allowed to continue Idol after it had been revealed that he was a stripper at a Phoenix area club. Davis had been kicked off the show after it had been revealed that she once modeled for an adult Web site.

Frenchie Davis was born in Los Angeles, California. She began as a theater student at Washington, D.C.'s Howard University. While studying there, she got her first acting/singing job playing one of the street urchins in a production of *Little Shop of Horrors* and then in a production of *Jesus Christ Superstar* the following year. She then auditioned for American Idol and turned out to be a huge favorite with America to win the show. Frenchie then worked for *Entertainment Tonight* and performed the song "And I Am Telling You." Later, she was cast in the Broadway show *RENT*, and in the role of Effie White in *Dream Girls* which played for four years. When she left the show, she said, "I know that I will look back at these times as some of the best of my life…thank you so much."

In August, Frenchie stepped into the shoes of Jennifer Holiday and starred in a one women stage play based on the legendary gospel great Mahalia Jackson called "Sing, Mahalia, Sing." In 2008, famed DJ/Remixer Tony Moran would release Frenchie's new dance single called "You Are" which would be a number one song on the charts. In November 2008, Frenchie would be starting her 30th Anniversary tour of the show *Ain't Misbehavin* with Ruben Studdard (2003 *American Idol* Winner).

Albuquerque, and the world, would experience many newsworthy events this year. There was an attack that sent a gay man to the hospital. Six people had been charged in the February 27th beating of a gay man outside a Santa Fe hotel. Those charged had been indicted on a Thursday. All six men were charged in the beating that put 21-year-old James Maestas in the intensive care unit at St. Vincent Hospital for more than a week. Those who were part of the vicious crime were prosecuted under the New Mexico Hate Crimes statute. The Attorney General's Office would announce that because it was a hate crime, they could add one year in prison for each count if the suspects were convicted. They were eventually convicted.

Another Hate Crime conducted in the State of New Mexico was a crime that the police in Albuquerque theorized as a prostitute that was killed for being a man. The individual was Ryan Shey Hookie who was found in an alley in the 1600 block of Ridgecrest. When the police found her, she/he was partially clothed in women's attire. The motive had been unclear. Although it was suspected that it was indeed a hate crime, and the case would be never solved. Albuquerque Pride would honor these two victims during Pridefest which would proclaim and account for the many victims left silent from the senseless crimes done to them.

In 2008, America had the opportunity to select a President who would champion the Rights of the Gay, Lesbian, Bisexual, and Transgender Community, and President Obama was elected. During his acceptance speech, he would mention that he and the United States must come together as a cohesive group, which included individuals who were gay. Hillary Clinton, who ran against Obama, would become Secretary of State under the Obama Administration. This would be the first time that a former 'First Lady' would assume such a high duty within the government. This year, three great individuals would also be lost. First, Patrick "Patricia" Murphy would be murdered, and the murder noted as a hate crime. Patricia was Miss NM Gay Rodeo Association 2008 and be a candidate for Miss New Mexico Pride in 2005. She was noted for her "spot on" performances of the iconic Diana Ross. Her friends would know her as Patricia. Dana Madsen would be arrested for her crime. Police had said that he admitted to killing Murphy at the Brandywood Park Apartments after an argument. He had said that it was in self-defense. This killing would "shock" the community as most knew that it was not a hate crime, but a "crime of passion." There were no laws on the books for same-sex couples to be identified. Friends and co-workers were concerned with Patricia spending time with Madsen; they had stated that 'she' was killed because Madsen was uncomfortable with her sexuality because it questioned his.

Next, Lois Dickerman, who had been given the title has an Honored Dignitary in 1998 for Albuquerque Pride because of her outstanding work as a counselor in the Albuquerque Public School System and her contributions to the Common Bond Under 21 Group, would pass in 2008. Her legacy of supporting the youth would live on.

Lastly, Andy Davis, Mr. New Mexico Pride 2000, who had served Albuquerque Pride for many years passed away. One of his dreams had been for the Albuquerque

Pride to purchase Rainbow Flags that would be flown each year at the entrance of PrideFest at EXPO New Mexico. Individuals who stood by him to purchase those first flags from Andy's endeavors would graciously be given the honor to raise the rainbow flag at the entry walkway. People would say that the experience was Andy's legacy. He had pushed hard for a year or two with the cost of the flags often being mumbled at Board meetings. It was in 2007 that Andy Davis would be able to raise the first flag. It was in that moment that Albuquerque Pride would see that Andy's dream had come true. This was only one of the many contributions that Andy Davis made towards moving Albuquerque Pride forward. Many times, Andy Davis would assist PJ Sedillo making sure that PJ stayed focused on the true and real meaning of Pride in Albuquerque. Davis had also become a "daddy" to many new NM Pride Titleholders as he would offer the same father figure mentality to titleholders from the United Court of the Sandias, the Leather Community or the NM Gay Rodeo. He reached out, taught, offered help or a swift kick in the butt to those who took on the sash or the crown. He would pass in 2008 and would be missed.

Albuquerque Pride as a member of the International of Pride Associations (InterPride) and CAPI (Consolidated Associations of Pride) would have Pride Board members attend conferences in Vancouver and Long Beach to better the organization. Also, throughout the year Albuquerque Pride would participate in many other Prides in the Unites States. Some of these were Santa Fe Pride, Las Cruces Pride, El Paso Pride, Flagstaff Pride, Phoenix Pride, and Las Vegas Pride. There were a few Prides that Albuquerque Pride would attend or assist with their production. It would sponsor many events throughout the year. There would include Equality New Mexico, the AIDS Walk, NM Gay Rodeo Association, and Rio Grande Leather. Pat Baillie would step down this year as Co-President of Albuquerque Pride and would be awarded the *Vincent R. Johnson Model of Hope* sponsored by *Pride and Equality Magazine*.

Finally, in 2008, Albuquerque Pride would again sponsor the GLBT information booth at the NM State Fair grounds. This had been done for the past four years along with various community groups. The first and second year of staffing was extremely difficult. Many angry slurs, and hateful statements were made to those who staffed the booth. However, all the love from those who needed information would outweigh any problems encountered. Albuquerque Pride would thank the many brave individuals who had staffed the booth in the past which had become a 'fixture" at the NM State Fair in the Manuel Lujan Building.

It would be time for the booth to close its doors. An article from the *Normal Heart* would state in its headlines, "Thousands At Fair LGBT Community No Big Deal." During the 17-day event the LGBT Community and allies were visible at the fair. As the days went by, there were fewer negative comments and more positive interactions for 2008. It was evident that the booth that had been created from hate would come into fruition as positively educating New Mexicans about the GLBT community. From the ashes of the horrible experience of the parade entry in 2006 Albuquerque Pride's booth would rise as in Greek mythology, a Phoenix, reborn and regenerated. Because of this experience, a new metamorphosis had taken place within the Board of Albuquerque Pride. The community renewed the organization to become a 'powerhouse' as a business, philanthropic entity and educational institution that would not be reckoned with by others in Albuquerque, New Mexico; the US; and the world.

Albuquerque Pride 2009

Thirty-three years of incredible Pride history in Albuquerque would look at all the possibilities for the community and allies. New Mexicans would be protected with a hate crime and non-discrimination law for both sexual orientation and gender identity. Despite these gains, Equality New Mexico, with the support of many individuals and groups, would be no closer to receiving the deserved domestic partner benefits. During the 2008 legislative session, the benefits would not occur, so the "fight" would continue.

The event had grown year by year and had rivaled any of the "big" Prides that occurred all year long. Many Pride events around the country would look at Albuquerque Pride's achievements because Albuquerque Pride's achievements had been recorded, noticed and declared at the many InterPride conferences that Albuquerque Pride had attended. Many Prides would pattern their events after Albuquerque's Pridefest. Albuquerque Pride was noted as the ninth most attended event in the State of New Mexico by *New Mexico Business Magazine*. Albuquerque Pride, for the second year in a row, received "Best of Burques" Best Festival and Parade from the *Alibi* beating even the International Balloon Festival.

Albuquerque Pride would also state how important it was to remember that each person who came to Pride made a difference. If this was a person's first Pride he or she was asked to be open to see his or her future of positiveness. It was expressed that as one's first Pride this might set the person on a path as an individual who would be part of or one of the producers of Albuquerque Pride, or as a future member of the Board of Directors. It was also expressed that as one met and greeted others, he or she could rekindle past relationships and learn about the community to embody the 2009 Pride Theme "Your Rights, Our Rights, Human Rights."

The logo for the 2009 Pride t-shirt would be won and designed by Black Duck Tees who would also choose the color of the tee (ash gray). The logo was a coat of armor with rainbow flares in all directions. On top of the coat of arms was the wording "Your Rights."

On the bottom was "Our Rights, Human Rights." This shirt would win the "Best People's Choice" during the Albuquerque Pridefest 2021 archival showing.

2009

The 2009 Pride Pin would be designed by Graphic Bliss Design. It had 'Lady Justice' draped in the rainbow colors. On the left was the wording of the theme and on the bottom was the date. This would be the final Albuquerque Pride Pin created for merchandise until 2023 and 2024.

The Executive Board for 2009 consisted of PJ Sedillo-President; Christopher Biles-Treasurer; Virginia Cleary-Secretary; Brian Johnson-Vice President; and Johnny Q-Titleholder Representative. The Board of Directors consisted of Tony Ross-Director of Pridefest/Pride bookkeeper; Jay Quiles-Office Manager; Sarah Barbee-Director of Special Events; Jesse Lopez-

Director of Marketing; and Danny Hernandez-Director of Media/Communications. The 2009 Pride budget was projected at $140,300 with an expected income of $131,000. Pride would work extremely hard to obtain the budget and would succeed again not in the 'red' for 2010. Christopher Biles/Treasurer and Tony Ross/Bookkeeper would work tirelessly so that the budget would be obtained to produce the event. Ultimately, the community at large would not realize the stress that would be placed on all the individuals who produced Albuquerque Pride. That is why this chapter highlighted all unsanctioned Pride events that markedly made self-financial gains while making no contributions to the actual Albuquerque Pride evet.

The Planning Committee and Pride Volunteers consisted of Marshal Martinez-Proclamations/Media Training; Gwen Cannova-Kinzie-Pride Performance Stage/Vodka Lounge; Nate Brown-Pride Booth/Merchandise; Dan Boxrund-Office Assistant/ Volunteer; Kelly Clark-Children's Area; Jen Crowe-Art Show; WIMIN-Queer Bake Off/Poetry Slam; Dan Boxrund and Will Finch-Headliner Hospitality; Car Club-Car Show Rainbow Roadrunners; Virginia Cleary-Manager and Mainstage; Angelica Del Rio and Raven Rykers-Pet Parade; Flo Fader-Dance Tent; Dan Boxrund and Will Finch-Candle Light Vigil; Kay Castillo and Dusty Calhan-VIP area and Debbie Martinez/Tony Ponce-Pridefest coordinators. Notably many volunteers would perform "double duty" as a volunteer.

The Albuquerque Pride Board worked countless volunteer hours to put on Pride each year. In November of 2008, the first Albuquerque Pride Board Retreat was held to prepare for 2009. The mission and vision of Pride was reviewed and revised. During this weekend retreat the Board would produce an Albuquerque Pride Procedures Manual and Volunteer Welcome Packet for future Board Members to use.

The 2008-2009 NM Pride Titleholders had gone well beyond their responsibilities and become legends in the community. Johnny Q-Mr. NM Pride had an exciting and memorable title year. As a goodwill ambassador of Albuquerque Pride, he would represent his title and the community at the many events he attended across the City of Albuquerque, the State of New Mexico, and the United States. The Board of Albuquerque Pride and the community would be so proud of his positive endeavors and would recognize him for all his hard work and dedication as a 2008 titleholder. He would be long remembered for his accomplishments.

Jay-MsTer NM Pride would have an enjoyable and wonderful title year that would become a shining light for those in the GLBT community. Throughout his year with his fine-tuned performance skills and hard work he was empowered to speak publicly to many organizations about the significance of Pride. Albuquerque and the community would thank Jay for all his crowning achievements and a job well done.

Aleah Rico would be given the title for Miss NM Pride as a first runner up because Latina del Rio did not fulfill her duties. Although Aleah only held the tile for a short time, she would represent it proudly. She had always worked hard at standing up for her community in every possible way with every organization in which she was involved. Aleah Rico truly embodied the spirit of commitment and bringing the community together even though she was first runner up. She would be honored as the true victor for the title.

As the titleholders ended their year of success as Ambassadors of Pride, the 2009-2010 NM Pride Titleholders would be crowned to lead during their reign. The titleholders this year were Miss NM Pride-Sabryna Willams, Mr. NM Pride-Tony Medina, Mr. Youth NM Pride-Marcos Jay, and Miss Youth NM Pride-Simone Segovia.

Thursday, June 11th, would be the Fourth Annual Candlelight Vigil. The year 2009 also brought forth the final stage for the completion of the Albuquerque Pride GLBT Memorial at Morningside Park. The final official meeting was held Wednesday, May 13, 2009, at 4:00 p.m. On the agenda was the Art Selection Committee Recommendation for relocation of Trees (art sculptures) at Morningside Park.

With the assistance of the City of Albuquerque, Mayor Martin Chavez, the foundation known as *1% for the Arts Division*, the Albuquerque Arts Board, Albuquerque Pride, and its President PJ Sedillo, they would establish a permanent Memorial Art Sculpture that was dedicated to the GLBT community. This would occur at the Candlelight Vigil on June 11, at Morningside Park at 6:30 p.m. Two bronze trees, known as the Fernandez Trees, were placed on eight-foot pillars that graciously mark the entrance to the park. Notably, the Memorial Art Sculpture would be the second GLBT Memorial in the nation next only to the city of New York's memorial commemorating the Stonewall Riots. The unveiling ceremony of the Pride Memorial at Morningside Park would be remembered as a celebration that honored members of the GLBT community.

The unveiling ceremony would be emceed by Jon and the Pop Tarts from 93.3 KOB FM. The opening ceremony would have the presentation of colors by the Bataan Chapter AVER. The National Anthem was sung by Pride Board Media Director-Jesse Lopez. After these reflections were given by Mayor Martin J. Chavez, Sherri Brueggeman-Public Arts Program Manager, Ray Garduno-District 6 Representative, and PJ Sedillo-President of Albuquerque Pride. PJ Sedillo would read the plaques that would eventually be put on the foot of each column (it must be noted that eventually only one plaque would be secured with all the wording combined):

Plaque 1

Dedicated to those gay, lesbian, bisexual and transgender (GLBT) community members who were here to create the roots of our community at the first Albuquerque Pride in June 1976. Coming out at that event began the work to raise awareness, educate the larger community and join the nationwide movement for GLBT civil rights.

We do not ask for our rights on bended knee.
We demand them, standing tall,
as dignified human beings.
We will not go away.

-The Advocate, October 1967

Plaque 2

Dedicated to those who continue to show the diverse branches of the lesbian, gay, bisexual and transgender community, this memorial stands in memory of those who time after time have stood up, came out, fought, and sometimes died for our civil rights. May they draw strength from these roots and blossom into a world we can only imagine.

-June 11, 2009

The ceremony would continue with a blessing from Pride Interfaith Representatives followed by a Ribbon Cutting Ceremony. The Albuquerque Pride Board and 2009-2010 NM Pride Titleholders would pass out the candles. Facts were read from 1976 to 2009, and the participants were asked to come forward and light their candle on the year that they first attended Albuquerque Pride. Those who would light their candle for 2009 would get a burst of applause. After all the cards were read, a song was played. Those in attendance were asked to please be silent for personal reflections and then asked to leave as they desired. After the Candlelight Vigil was over, there was a reception held at the Albuquerque Social Club. Going to the ASC after the vigil would become a tradition for years to come for those who wanted to de-escalate from the intense event and be welcomed to enter a safe and happy space.

Friday, June 12th, was the Friday Night PrideFest and Concert at EXPO NM from 5 p.m. to 10 p.m. Albuquerque Pride would continually have to re-evaluate the Friday Night and Saturday events. Many of those who would go to Pridefest on Saturday would begin to leave the event about 4:00 p.m. to rest, get refreshed, and head out to the bars to celebrate Pride. Albuquerque Pride would spend a large portion of their budget trying to get performers for the Mainstage. These headliners were usually put at the end of the event; however, no matter how "big" the performer was, Albuquerque Pride would have a difficult time keeping most of the crowds after 5:00 p.m. The Friday Night event in 2008 was a huge success and had been free; however, in 2009 there would be an entrance fee because the "name" headliner would perform Friday Night instead of Saturday. The Headliner was Taylor Dayne who would perform at 8:00 p.m.

The event on Friday would still have its pet parade, dance tent, art show, Pride Archives; however, the mainstage would be a fast-paced show to keep the crowd until the venue closed at 10:00 p.m. This was the schedule of performers:

6:00 p.m.	Jay-MsTer NM Pride
6:05 p.m.	Aleah Rico
6:10 p.m.	Ya Ya Boom
6:45 p.m.	Freddy Prinz Charming
7:45 p.m.	Ashely Seywut
7:50 p.m.	Joseph & Company
8:00 p.m.	TAYLOR DAYNE
8:45 p.m.	ABQ Kings
9:00 p.m.	Eric Himan
10:00 p.m.	Venue Closes

Albuquerque Pride's Headliner Taylor Dayne would be a huge hit. Taylor Dayne came to prominence in the late 1980's and continued to appear at the top of the charts through the 1990s. Dayne's first seven singles hit the US Top Ten. She had topped the US Hot Dance Club Play chart three times. Overall, she had seventeen individual Top Ten's on Billboard Charts, including her most recent Billboard Dance #1 "Beautiful" in May of 2008. She remained a pop favorite in America and abroad. She had signed with Arista Records, and her first song to reach the Top Ten was the dance-pop hit "Tell It to My Heart" in 1988. Hits that followed included, "Prove Your Love," "I'll Always Love You," "Don't Rush Me," "With Every Beat of My Heart," "Love Will Lead You Back," "I'll Be Your Shelter," and countless others. CMT had announced in 2009 that Taylor Dayne would be a contestant on the third season of the reality television series *Gone Country*. Friday night Taylor Dayne performed for 10,000 spectators which was the largest crowd ever for a Friday Night PrideFest.

Eric Himan would perform last on Friday. He had a following and was a featured performer who had played often at the Albuquerque Social Club. Although born in South Carolina, Eric Himan, singer-songwriter, had a hard time explaining where he was from. He said, "My father was in the Air Force, so we moved all around from New York and New Jersey to Hawaii and Florida." For his eighth birthday, Eric was given an electric guitar, though he was drawn instead to the sound of his sister's acoustic guitar and began lessons under the teachings of his father, a New York City jazz musician of thirty years. Eric found influence from musical artists such as jazz greats Charlie Parker and Billie Holiday, rock and roll legends the Beatles and Janis Joplin, and most of all folk impresarios, Ani DiFranco, Tracy Chapman, and Cat Stevens. He began writing songs when he was only twelve, playing in talent shows and at neighborhood recitals. Within these early years, he discovered that he had a unique and rather powerful voice that echoed down the halls of his Fort Walton Beach, Florida home.

In his first year of college at Pennsylvania State University, Eric recorded his debut EP INVINCIBLE and received much attention for his strong voice, lyrics and unique guitar work especially for the yearning love song, "Cold." He later sought out a band in need of a new singer by sneaking into a local bar and auditioning for them. Once they heard his voice, they called him at 4 a.m. with their offer. The band, Dunston Ashe, recorded *Permanent Record*, selling over 1000 CD's and opening for bands such as Fuel, Jimmie's Chicken Shack, and Pittsburgh's The Gathering Field. After three years the group disbanded to pursue different goals. Eric was now more resolved to become an independent musician. Press reviews note that Eric has a commanding stage presence, both melodic and intense which make his live performances impactful and impressive. His tattoo-filled arms cradle his guitar making it sing with quick percussive strokes. Singer-songwriter Eric Himan would take the audiences of Albuquerque Pride Friday night through an emotional and rewarding journey. He would creatively express himself through his sound, his passion for lyrics and his performance.

Despite the success of the event, the Albuquerque Pride Board would be responsible for getting the space back in working order for Pridefest. Some would leave EXPO NM at 12:00 a.m. Though this would be also the first year that a camper/trailer was brought to the fairgrounds for those who were responsible for the setup of the parade. These key volunteers could sleep in it and then to awake early to set up EXPO NM.

Golf carts would be driven from the fairgrounds to UNM to get the line up at 5:00 a.m. Typically, participants, especially the larger floats, would begin showing up at 6:30 a.m. The Parade Directors would be Brian Johnson and PJ Sedillo. The parade started at the Corner of Girard and Central at 10:30 sharp. Current Pride Titleholders, VIP's, Grand Marshal Gilbert Baker, Honored Dignitaries and the Albuquerque Chamber of Commerce conducted the annual ribbon cutting ceremony. The Parade proceeded east on Central Avenue. Judges were located at the Starbucks in Nob Hill. Trophies were awarded to the "best of" categories. The parade proceeded east on Central, took a left on San Pedro and entered EXPO NM at Gate 3 located on Copper and San Pedro.

The Pride Parade, with over 200 entries, would draw over 20,000 spectators who lined Central Avenue to support the city's Gay community. This is one of the reasons why the *Alibi* would don the parade with the title "Best of Burque" thus honoring Albuquerque Pride as the best parade and festival while second place was given to the International Balloon Festival. A little-known fact is that the Albuquerque Pride Parade is the oldest continuing parade that has been celebrated on Historic Route 66 (Central Avenue). The *Albuquerque Journal* would note the following: "Heavily decorated floats careened through a melee comprised of AIDS awareness walkers, feather-boa wearing cyclists, and cars with crepe paper taped to the windows and bumpers. Almost every person wore a mixture of rainbow colors to represent the connection they felt to one another."

Gilbert Baker who created the Rainbow Pride Flag in 1978 was the Grand Marshal. He would state, "The diverse colors of the flag represent the diverse Gay community. A rainbow is a beautiful symbol from nature. It's one of the most wonderful things, and we're beautiful, too." Baker had served in the U.S. Army from 1970 until 1972. After an honorable discharge, he taught himself to sew. He began making banners and ultimately the Rainbow Flag for his friend Harvey Milk, who was later assassinated on November 27, 1978. After the assassination of openly gay San Francisco Supervisor Harvey Milk, demand for the Rainbow Flag greatly increased. To meet demands, the Paramount Flag Company began selling a version of the flag using stock rainbow fabric consisting of seven stripes of red, orange, yellow, green, turquoise, blue, and violet. As Baker ramped up production of his version of the flag, he too dropped the hot pink stripe because of the unavailability of hot pink fabrics. Also, San Francisco-based Paramount Flag Co. began selling a surplus stock of Rainbow flags from its Polk Street retail store.

The original Gay Pride Flag was hand-dyed by Gilbert Baker. It flew in the San Francisco Gay Freedom Day Parade on June 25, 1978. It has been suggested that Baker was inspired by Judy Garland's singing "Over the Rainbow." The flag consisted of eight stripes. Baker assigned specific meaning to each of the colors: hot pink-sexuality, red-life, orange-healing, yellow-sunlight, green-nature, turquoise-magic/art, indigo-serenity/harmony, and violet-spirit. Since flags are public domain, Gilbert Baker has not made any money from Pride flag sales.

Today many LGBT individuals and straight allies often put Rainbow Flags in their front yards and/or on their front doors. Also, the simple act of placing a rainbow bumper sticker on one's vehicle is an outward symbol of his or her identity or support. The Rainbow Flag, in a LBGT context, has found wide application on all manner of products including jewelry, clothing and other personal items. The rainbow flag colors are routinely used as a show of LGBT identity and solidarity.

There would be six Honored Dignitaries for the 2009 Albuquerque Pride Parade. Pride Honored Dignitary-Political was Alexis Blizman. Alexis grew up in Farmington Hills, Michigan. While earning her BA in Political Science at Wayne State University in Detroit, she reinvigorated and became President of the Wayne State Young Democrats. Through that work she became active in paid and volunteer work on local, state, and national campaigns. In 1993, she helped to found the GLBT Caucus of the Young Democrats of America. In 1994, she also, helped the caucus get full voting rights.

After serving the Young Democrats of America in several capacities, in 1999 she became the first openly gay Democratic National Committee woman elected by the Young Democrats of America. Alexis received her JD degree at the George Washington University Law School in Washington, D.C. in May of 2003. While in law school, she served as the Director of Graduate Affairs of the Student Bar Association and the Chair of the Law School's chapter of Lambda Law. While in law school, she maintained her connections with the Young Democrats and the Democratic Party. In August of 2003, Blizman joined the Law Offices of Brian J. Moran in Alexandria, Virginia, as an Associate Attorney where she worked in the fields of Domestic Relations, Civil Litigation, Criminal and Business Law. During that time, Blizman remained committed to the political process, volunteering on several campaigns, working with GAY-LAW, and continuing to serve the Young Democrats of America as their General Counsel.

Alexis moved to Albuquerque in August of 2005 to take on the position of Executive Director of Equality New Mexico. During her tenure as Executive Director, Alexis increased Equality New Mexico's visibility in the LGBT community. She increased their list of statewide supporters, led LGBT Get Out the Vote programs during the elections, and helped to write and lobby for the passage of comprehensive domestic partnership legislation in the NM Legislature. Working with the LGBT and ally community to organize constituents and lobby in the Roundhouse, Alexis helped bring the Domestic Partner legislation within one vote of passage. Alexis left her position with Equality New Mexico in September of 2008. Alexis and her partner of fifteen years would move to Chicago, Illinois.

Pride Honored Dignitary- Business was Sidewinders. Sidewinders Albuquerque was once known as The Ranch which opened in 1990. The current owner, Mike Spencer, worked at The Ranch when it opened and stayed for a year working for JC, the original owner, as the first head bartender. He then returned home to California where he worked in several bars in San Francisco until 1999. He opened the first Sidewinders in Palm Springs in 2001 and sold it in 2005 when he took over The Ranch and renamed it Sidewinders. Sidewinders has had its soul rooted in Country Western, Leather/Levi, but it is open to all. Sidewinders prides itself as a supporter of the GLBT community, opening its doors to all who want to enter. Sidewinders believes in supporting all the organizations which make up the Albuquerque GLBT community. Its aim is to be a place where the GLBT Community can come and be comfortable and enjoy a friendly atmosphere, meet new friends, dance to favorite tunes and even learn how to two-step or maybe a line dance or two. Albuquerque Pride would thank Mikey (owner) and Dan (general manager) for all their dedication to making Albuquerque Pride a successful event.

Pride Honored Dignitary-Emerging leader would be Adan Branchal. He had been an active member of the Gay community for ten years and local performer for nine years as both a vocalist and in drag as Arianna. In addition, he held the title of Mr. NM Pride 2006-2007 along with his husband of eight years Joey (Anastasia) as Miss NM Pride 2006-2007. They became the first couple to hold the title in the same year. Shortly after 2007, he became a founding member of Mariachi Orgullo de Nuevo Mexico, the first all-gay mariachi. In 2008, he and Joey (the love of his life) were legally wed in San Francisco. Adan was a strong supporter of all aspects of the GLBT community and is happy to have been able to help them throughout the years.

Pride Honored Dignitary-Arts would be Ruben Gallegos. Ruben, a native New Mexican, was born in the Chimayo Valley in Northern New Mexico. He studied art at New Mexico Highlands University, where he completed his BA in Art Education. He is an accomplished Santero, carrying on the tradition of Hispanic folk art of Northern New Mexico. His work has been displayed at the Santa Fe Spanish Market for the past twenty years, and he has also been a featured artist at the Heard Museum in Phoenix. Ruben first achieved national recognition in the 1980's for his exquisite miniature paintings on eggshells. He won numerous local and national awards, and his eggshell paintings have been featured in national and international exhibitions. He has shown his work at the

New Mexico Governor's Gallery for two former governors. His art has been collected by President Clinton, First Lady Laura Bush, and actor Dennis Weaver.

In 2008, one of Ruben's pieces was chosen to be in the permanent State collection in Santa Fe. Ruben recently, has been recognized for his "Day of the Dead" painting, in which he often depicts scenes of everyday life from his childhood in Northern New Mexico. Ruben has been active as a leader and fundraiser in the Gay community. He represented the leather community as Mr. Rio Grande leather 2004 and competed at the International Mr. Leather contest in Chicago in 2005. He was also co-founder of the New Mexico Leather Wolves and is known for his support of charitable events, where he can be found doing some leather fantasy on stage to help raise money for a charitable cause.

Pride Honored Dignitary-Community would be The Rainbow Roadrunner Car Club. This group was formed in 1999 by a group of Albuquerque and Northern New Mexico gay car fanatics. They joined the Lambda Car Club International (LCCI) to be connected to people with similar interests throughout the country and beyond. The club has steadily grown and has made itself recognized throughout the GLBT community as well as respected by the national LCCI community. The club prides itself on being an organization with great camaraderie for anyone interested in hanging out with car crazy people.

The club has activities throughout Albuquerque and Northern New Mexico. Main activities include the first weekend in October hosting an annual Regional LCCI Invitational in conjunction with the Albuquerque Balloon Fiesta. This event lets the club showcase to LCCI members from throughout the USA. The club offers the Pride dignitary transportation every year for the Pride Parade in June and has a car show at Pride. Throughout the year there are fundraising activities such as yard sales, 5th Sunday of the Month Blasts at Sidewinders, and an annual Variety Show. The Car Club also participates in car shows in surrounding areas that are not connected to the GLBT community. There, they were welcomed and visible and took home quite a few awards. Fund raising activities assist with needed funds for club functions. Extra funds are donated to organizations in the community. The Rainbow Roadrunner Car Club understands the importance of community. Its goal is to be recognized and respected as a club with community pride.

Pride Honored Dignitary-Ally was the Nob Hill Merchants' Association. Albuquerque Pride was thrilled to have the Nob Hill Merchants Association accept this year's award. For many years, the merchants in the Nob Hill District had opened their arms to the GLBT community. Although Albuquerque does not have a "Gay Ghetto," many GLBT individuals have claimed that Nob Hill has become and has been "home" for them. For that, Albuquerque Pride honored them for letting the gay community members be who they are by opening their Nob Hill doors to let the community in.

Saturday, June 13th, would be PrideFest 2009. There would be over 150 booths. A "Pocket Pride Guide" would again be produced to highlight tall of the booth's vendors, organizations, and businesses with a map of the various venues and times for the events on Thursday, Friday, and Saturday. PrideFest would again have their Children and Youth Area, Indoor Car Show, Dance Tent, Hair Bowl, and Mainstage. The Mainstage would have two prominent performers, Lovari and Ryan Minz.

Lovari, born and raised in New York, reached number one on both the iTunes and Amazon R&B New Releases Chart with the single "Still In Love" (feat. Anny Jules) from his album "No Holding Back," featuring production from J. Staffz (Wiz Khalifa, G Unit). "No Holding Back" had been certified on DatPiff.Com for over 25,000 downloads. It was the follow-up to his award-winning album "The Statement." The preview single and music video "Foolish Beat" was featured on PerezHilton.com, and the lead single "Keep It Movin'" reached Amazon.Com's Top 40 R&B Singles Chart and Top 30 Digital DJ U.S. R&B Chart. In addition to his music, Lovari was an actor, appearing in the films "Salt" (with Angelina Jolie) and in the NY International Independent Film Festival award winning short film "Shore Thing," which he also co-directed.

Ryan Mintz would "close down" PrideFest as the last performer. He had been noted from his website as heartfelt, genuine, and quirky. That's what people say about Ryan's music. Armed with an acoustic guitar and a penchant for honesty, this San Francisco singer/songwriter had touched listeners at coffee houses, pride festivals, and folk gatherings across the country. With a unique voice that many liken to Cat Stevens, Ryan brought a gentle vulnerability to his raw lyrics. Aching heart one minute, and wry smile the next, Ryan has the unique ability to make audiences laugh and cry… sometimes within the same song. His debut record, *Monkeys & Ice Cream*, earned critical acclaim. "The real draw of this album is the absolute honest nature with which each song was written," wrote EDGE. The album charted on the OutVoice Top 40 and the Susanne Millsaps Performing Songwriter Showcase named Ryan a finalist in 2009. Ryan was a "green musician," releasing his CDs in eco-friendly packaging and advocating for more green practices in the music industry. "For me, music is emotion," Ryan says. "If I can help someone feel something, then I've done my job."

Finally, new for 2009 were the Pride Performance Stage and VIP Area which were Produced and Directed by Gwen-CK. The Pride Performance Stage would have its own stage crew. Emcees would be Chaz Malibu and Mauro Montoya. This new attraction would be jammed packed all day with numerous performers.

In the past, beer was the only alcoholic beverage allowed at PrideFest. In 2009, this would change because of a meeting that took place between Premier Distributors (Miller Lite), EXPO NM, the Bureau of Alcohol Tobacco and Firearms, Southern Wine and Spirits, and Albuquerque Pride. Absolut Vodka came on as sponsor. Since "hard" liquor sales would take place a lot of parameters were required. All Vodka sales needed to be sold indoors and needed to be consumed in the designated space(s). No children would be allowed in the venue, and security would need to be at the entrance and exit doors. Even though PrideFest started at 11:00 a.m., vodka sales could not begin until 2:00 p.m. and end at 5:30 p.m.

PJ Sedillo had volunteered for many years and served as President for Albuquerque Pride. He had two dreams that he wanted to accomplish during his tenure. Those dreams were to obtain amusement park rides and a fireworks show. During his tenure, he was unable to get the fireworks; however, there were five amusement park rides at this Pridefest. President-PJ Sedillo and Vice President-Brian Johnson would be the first to ride the Ferris wheel.

Changes for parking would also occur in 2009. It was suggested that for fast and easy parking and to avoid the parade congestion on San Pedro, vehicles should enter the Fairgrounds off Louisiana (Gate 8) and park in the infield (in the middle of the racetrack). Once parked, individuals could walk west through the tunnel and head for the ticket gate by Tingley Colosseum. This new change would have individuals directly pass the amusement park rides. There was so much that one could do and see at this Pridefest that set the event apart from other PrideFests held throughout the world. The event had been modeled after the New Mexico State Fair held in September and was becoming just as large. Albuquerque Pride would be the third largest event held on the fairgrounds with EXPO NM being first. The following are some of the events and performances scheduled for Pridefest 2009:

PrideFest Schedule – 11:00-6:30

11:00-5:00	Family and Youth Area (1:00 The Bird Lady)
11:00-6:00	Car Show, Pride Archives, Art Show, Pride Theater, Food, Rides, Booths
11:00	Queer Bake-Off Registration
1:30	Pride Dance Lessons / Square Dancing-Wilde Bunch
2:00	Queer Bake-Off Awards
2:30	Pride Dance Lessons / Salsa –Emotion in Motion
3:00	Poetry Slam
3:30	Pride Dance Lessons / Line Dancing – Desert Heat
4:30	Pride Dance Lessons / Hip Hop
2:00-5:40	Absolut Lounge
7:00-10:00	Youth Dance in Hispanic Arts Building

Main Stage Entertainment – 11:00-5:00

11:00	Music
11:45	Belly Dancers
12:15	Opening
12:45	Simone Segovia
12:50	Valentino
1:00	Wilde Bunch
1:10	Social Stigmata
1:30	Emotions In Motion
1:45	Sabryna Williams
1:50	Desert Heat
2:30	Roma Cupid
2:45	Art Show Winners
2:50	THROB Dance Troupe
3:00	Parade Winners
3:05	Full Moon Dance Crew
3:15	Femolition Derby
3:45	Blackout Theater
4:15	Marcos Jay
4:20	Entourage Dance Troupe
4:30	Lovari
4:35	Ryan Mintz

Pride Performance Stage / Vodka Lounge & VIP Area– 2:00-5:40

2:00	Jazzmin
2:20	Aleah Rico
2:30	Jayson DaBoi
2:40	Martinique Bouvier
2:50	Judy Lenzner
3:30	Sarah Wolf (Michele CK)
3:30	Adan Branchal
3:35	Cassie Dawn
3:45	Montana
3:50	UNM GSA
4:20	Mauro-Gay Erotica
4:30	Nick Love
4:35	Lynda Ross
4:40	April Ball and Jonte
4:40	Eve
5:15	Rashan
5:40	Vertical Expressions

In 2009, Albuquerque Pride would support and attend many sanctioned and not sanctioned events. There would be a showing of the movie *Trinidad: The Sex Change*

Capital of the World, LGBT Pride Interfaith Service, MCCA Pride Month Worship and Celebration, EQNM's Concert with the NM Gay Men's Chorus, Self-Serve: Sexuality Resource Center Courses, *The Producers* (Musical Theater Southwest Production), Albuquerque Gay Day at Cliffs, FIREWOMYN Pride, and the Dyke March on Friday, June 12th starting at 4:30 to 6:00. This march would occur without any permits would take over the streets closing intersections. Albuquerque Pride would support the event but would not sanction the event for legal reasons.

Albuquerque Pride would also assist with the First Annual LGBT Gallup Pride Fest; attend InterPride in St. Petersburg and Florida; CAPI in Las Vegas; have a float and assist putting on Pride at the Railyard in Santa Fe; help produce the first ever Pride in Madrid and New Mexico; and attend Las Cruces' Pride. Johnny Q, Tony Ross, and PJ Sedillo would volunteer and work at El Paso Pride and Flagstaff Pride and put an entry in the thirteenth Annual Phoenix Pride Parade. No longer was Albuquerque a little Pride. Smaller Prides were asking for assistance and looking towards Albuquerque Pride to provide leadership and guidance about how to improve their event or how to start one in their city. Albuquerque Pride was on the cusp of becoming the largest Pride event in the Southwest; however, that would change in 2010.

Chapter 11

Albuquerque Pride- 2010 –Transition of Solidarity

In 2010, Albuquerque Pride was on the cusp of becoming the largest Pride event in the Southwest. However, 2010 would be a year of change and controversial risk that would have the ideology of solidarity through Gay Pride stretched to its limits.

Albuquerque Pride had become the largest LGBT organization in New Mexico and had a surplus of money that assisted in adding and highlighting something new each year at the parade or PrideFest. In 2010, the Board of Directors agreed that it was time to use the surplus to hire an administrative assistant because the event was too immense for an all-volunteer event that took the entire year to plan, promote and present. The community at large had thought that PJ Sedillo was getting paid for his services for years; however, it must be recorded that he volunteered countless hours on top of sponsoring the event monetarily. He never received payment for his services. Albuquerque Pride as an incorporated business, especially a non-profit organization, had to reveal its loss and profits yearly because of the Public Information Act. For that reason, Albuquerque Pride had kept pristine financial records since 1996 when Albuquerque Pride became incorporated to obtain and sustain their non-profit status.

In August, Albuquerque Pride began a search for an administrative assistant. The salary for the person hired would be $27,750. This would be a huge commitment for the board to take on because that amount of money would need to be raised to hire the administrative assistant as well as the money needed to put on the event. With the administrative assistance's salary, the budget for 2010 would be $192,280.

September of 2010, Albuquerque Pride would hire Scott Turner as the first paid employee for Albuquerque Pride. This hiring process was arduous; however, with the guidance of Tony Ross, past treasure and bookkeeper for Albuquerque Pride, the experience would become "drama free." Scott Turner would work closely with the President, PJ Sedillo. Scott Turner's first training was on fundraising and how to obtain sponsors and keep the ones that Albuquerque Pride already had. With the help of this administrative assistant, PJ Sedillo (organizer/president for over 20 years), could now concentrate on obtaining his Ph.D. which had become his third job next to producing the Pride event and as his day job as a special education facilitator.

Despite the awesome job for Pride that Scott was doing, he had to take another job that offered more pay. Thus, in October of 2010, the Albuquerque Pride Board would again begin looking for an administrative assistant. This would be a faster process because how to proceed was known. The search would focus on college students who needed the salary and had the time to offer, and Albuquerque Pride would work around his/her school schedule. In October, James Reese was hired as Albuquerque Pride's administrative assistant.

Each year the Albuquerque Pride Board would have a difficult time choosing who would be an Honored Dignitary for the various categories (art, ally, political, youth, and community). It was decided that the community would make the decision for 2010; therefore, because of this decision the OUTstanding Awards would be created. This idea, brought forth by PJ Sedillo, would present another event and opportunity to fundraise for Albuquerque Pride. The idea was initiated from the *Alibi* newspaper that would promote and present its "Best of Burque" competition/contest which would declare the best food, hair stylists, bars, events (to name a few categories) voted by Albuquerqueans. Albuquerque Pride would be granted the title "Best of Events" for many years.

The Albuquerque Pride Board decided to work collaboratively with the *Alibi* (already experienced in this process) in 2010 to have the first ever OUTstanding Awards ceremony for the LGBT community voted by Albuquerqueans similarly like the "Best of Burque." The community and *Alibi* readership loved voting for the "Best of GLBT", and the response was overwhelmingly positive. This, in turn, assisted in advertisement sales for the *Alibi* newspaper. After the selection process was made and voted, the inaugural event was held at the Sheraton Waterpark. This event was a huge success and showcased as the "Gay Oscars," a red carpet, black-tie event. These are the following winners noted as the "CLASS OF 2010 Inaugural OUTstanding Award Winners":

2010 OUTstanding Award Winners

OUTstanding Bar or Nightclub	Albuquerque Social Club
OUTstanding Bartender	Ryan Wilkinson (Albuquerque Social Club)
OUTstanding Restaurant	Scalo Northern Italian Grill
OUTstanding Drag Queen	Aleah Rico
OUTstanding Drag King	Rocco Steele
OUTstanding Dance Troupe	Throb
OUTstanding GLBT Organization	UNM Queer Straight Alliance
OUTstanding GLBT Leader	Jordon Johnson (EQNM)
OUTstanding Straight Ally	Jim & Jean Genasci (PFLAG ABQ)
OUTstanding Civil Servant	Mimi Stewart (Representative)
OUTstanding Hair Salon	Swank
OUTstanding Stylist	Ryan Perrigo (Swank)
OUTstanding Massage Therapist	Gabe Torres
OUTstanding Real Estate Agent	Talia Freedman
OUTstanding Performance Artist	Madison Eriks
OUTstanding DJ	DJ Stitch
OUTstanding Store to Shop	Buffalo Exchange
OUTstanding Place to Meet	Albuquerque Social Club
OUTstanding Adult Store	Self-Serve Sexuality Resource Center
OUTstanding Gym	Sports and Wellness
OUTstanding Local Vocalist	Adan Branchal
OUTstanding Artist	Ruben Gallegos
OUTstanding Place to Worship	Metropolitan Community Church of Albuquerque

The success of this event was essential because having another profitable fundraising event like the annual Pride Pageant would be needed to assist in meeting the budget for 2010. The OutStanding Awards was a risk, but it turned out to be an overwhelming profitable success and would be continued in future years. Building on the events original foundation the OUTstanding Awards would become equally important for fundraising as the NM Pride Pageants.

The NM Pride Titleholders for 2009-2010 would be Mr. NM Pride-Tony Medina, Miss NM Pride-Sabryna Williams, Miss Youth NM Pride-Simone Segovia, and Mr. Youth NM Pride-Marcos Jay.

Unfortunately, the Pride Pageant would encounter controversies this year. One of which would be that Miss Sabryna Williams would have her title removed. Despite substantially raising funds for many other GLBT organizations, Sabryna's financial responsibilities for Albuquerque Pride were not obtained. This controversy would ultimately be one of the decisions made by the Albuquerque Pride Board of Directors that would become one of the many reasons for discord between Board members.

At the Board meeting addressing the issue, Vice-President, Jesse Lopez, pushed to have Sabryna William's (Anthony Montano) title removed. Other members reiterated the fact that Sabryna Williams should be removed according to the "Pageant Contract" she signed. Sabrina Williams's positive contributions to Albuquerque Pride did not outweigh her monetary responsibilities according to the Board of Directors. This contentious Board meeting would end with the Board of Directors voting for the tile to be removed. After the vote, Sabryna Williams would leave upset, and PJ Sedillo would follow her outside and console her. As a point of record, PJ Sedillo did not have a vote (according to the bylaws the President could only vote to break a tie).

By March of 2010, it was clear that tensions were high on the Board. Yet, despite the tensions that existed, and not talked about in the open, in April of 2010, PJ Sedillo-President, Tony Ross-Book-keeper, Johnny Q.-Titleholder Representative, James Reese-Administrative Assistant, and Jesse Lopez-Vice President would attend Phoenix Pride with an entry in the parade, which had been done in previous years. They would promote Tribal Splash and Albuquerque Pride with thousands of flyers along the Phoenix Parade Route.

By April, two months before the parade and PrideFest would take place, tensions were on an all-time high between Board members and even staff. After subsequent events and altercations, PJ Sedillo, President of Pride, volunteer since 1989 and official President starting in 1996, would come to the realization that it was time to let go of the event. Uncomfortable with what was occurring on the Board, as well as needing to focus on completing his Ph.D., PJ Sedillo, resigned as Board President, and Tony Ross would also leave.

Within a week after PJ Sedillo's declaration, Jesse A. Lopez would become President of Albuquerque Pride. The Executive Board would also to be re-aligned and would consist of Secretary-Dan Boxrud, Treasurer-Joell Ackerman, Titleholder Representative-Tony Medina and Staff-James Reese/Administrative Assistant. The Board of Directors would consist of Web Master-Neil Macernie (who would be voted as Vice-President within a month of the meeting), Parade Director-Danny Hernandez, PrideFest Director-Tony Ross, Volunteer Coordinator-Angie Poss, and Director of Development-Graham Thomson. PJ Sedillo would become a consultant and stay on the Board to offer his expertise so that the Pride 2010 would occur.

Mentioned previously in this historical account, Albuquerque Pride would encounter other organizations that would produce unsanctioned events and raise money without supporting Albuquerque Pride financially, and this year another organization/event would be the focus of a great deal of tension. Tribal Pride, also known as Tribal Splash, would end up sponsoring Albuquerque Pride in a limited capacity, but would end up posing a lot of problems. Much time was spend working with this organizer to provide financial support as a sponsor. In the end, PJ Sedillo would get Tribal Splash to donate $1000 (a miniscule amount compared to the budget) to offer their Tribal Pride/Splash event. It was all-night parties that secured "named" DJ's and entertainment. Held at the Radisson Hotel (where there was a waterpark), their events were scheduled for Friday/Saturday Nights and Sunday afternoon. Albuquerque Pride had successfully had events on Friday evenings for the past few years; however, events like Tribal Pride would take sponsors, attendees, and volunteers away from other Albuquerque Pride events. Not only was Albuquerque Pride concerned, but also were several the local bars because of the amount of lost revenue from those not going to the bars after PrideFest on Friday and especially Saturday.

In 2010, Vice-President Jesse Lopez (before he had assumed the presidency) had suggested an event similar to Tribal Pride/Splash. The Board would have him proceed, but they needed a cost analysis and how the event would affect the budget. The event would be a proposed budgeted item of $12,000 and would be known as Pride Fusion. This was a cost that had not been voted on at the annual August meeting for Albuquerque Pride. The Board would take a vote to proceed with this event; however, it must be noted that Tony Ross had passionately opposed the event because of the money needed for the newly hired administrative assistant. Tony Ross's concerns would be over-ridden, and the Board would vote to proceed.

In May, Jesse Lopez would sever ties with the producers of Tribal Pride/Splash, despite the fact that Past-president PJ Sedillo had signed a 2010 sponsorship agreement between both businesses. Tensions would rise between both camps and some members of the GLBT community would become aware of this feud. Two competing events would proceed and compete for attendees.

Albuquerque Pride's Friday and Saturday Night event named "Pride FUSION," was deemed as the "Only Official Albuquerque Pride Nightlife Event!" and the "Summers' Sexiest GLBT Nightlife Experience." It was scheduled for Saturday, June 12th, from 9 p.m. to 2 a.m. and was located at the Hyatt Regency Hotel. There would be different venues in the hotel which included "World Pride: ULTRA LOUNGE," "SPECTRUM NIGHT CLUB" (with DJ Flo Fader), and "CLUB ESCANDALO" (with DJ Quico). The event had $81 room rates with an all-access pass. Morgan McMichaels from RuPaul's Drag Race would perform at Pride Fusion; however, it was not clear where she would perform or at what time.

Tribal Splash, the competing, semi-unsanctioned event (because they had provided a $1000 sponsorship to Pride) was held at the Radisson Water Park and would tout being "BIGGER, BETTER, WETTER." There were three incredible parties for only $40 with hotel rooms that ranged from $100 with unlimited access to the waterpark. Tribal Splash had already been designated "as the place to be," so Albuquerque Pride would have an uphill climb getting individuals to attend their event. Albuquerque Pride had not finalized contracts until the end of May, and many faithful Tribal Splash participants had already purchased their tickets for Tribal Splash months in advanced due to their marketing campaign and email list. Albuquerque Pride had also passed out numerous Tribal Splash flyers in April when they attended Phoenix Pride.

This would be the first time that Albuquerque Pride would compete for the rights to Saturday night. Many bars, which were official sponsors, were also concerned about Tribal Splash and Albuquerque Pride putting on a rival event. Albuquerque Pride would obtain a bus for people who stayed at the Hyatt to get a free shuttle service to all the bars. The bus would also be going back and forth to Tribal Splash as a way of an "olive branch" between the two organizations. The outcome of this event will be presented later in this chapter.

June 2, the Albuquerque Pride Board of Directors would have a Retirement Party honoring PJ Sedillo, President of Albuquerque Pride and Tony Ross Director (Past President) of ABQ PrideFest at the Hotel Andaluz at 7:00 p.m. They would be honored that evening with a Lifetime Achievement Award. PJ Sedillo's and Tony Ross's biographies that were in the official Pride program and would be highlighted in the *NM Pride Guide* would read as follows:

PJ Sedillo in 1988 went to his first Gay Pride parade. The event was held at "Yale Park" where the UNM Book Store is currently located. At the Pride, he hid behind a building desperately not wanting to make the evening news because he wasn't out. The next day PJ as many do, had a "positive transformation." He was fed up and tired of hiding from the world because he was gay. The next day he decided to devote his life to speaking up for those who still hid behind those buildings. That week after his "coming out" he went to Common Bond (then Albuquerque's GLBT Community Center) and assisted with the parade. Within a year he was volunteering and would eventually become President of the organization for multiple years.

In 1996, PJ decided that Albuquerque Pride should become its own entity, business and event. Many community members were outraged, but he persevered despite the vicious taunts from some leaders of the GLBT community and the local gay newspaper. His "moral courage" set him on a path that would see Albuquerque Pride become the largest GLBT event in the State and have *NM Business Weekly* rank Albuquerque Pride's PrideFest as the 9th most attended event in NM. He often remarks that when he first started the event, it cost $1500.00. He would put the event on his credit card and get reimbursed after the event was done.

This year (2010) Pride's budget is $150,000.00 with an expected attendance of 50,000 for the 3-day event. PJ Sedillo also with the assistance of his mentor Neil Isbin secured non-discrimination for sexual orientation within the APS negotiated contracts for all APS school teachers. With the assistance of his "true love" Tony Ross, they have fought hard and won the right for all GLBT teachers to receive full spousal benefits. PJ Sedillo has worked tirelessly to put on the Pride Parade and PrideFest for the past 21 years. His dreams have come true by assisting the GLBT community to finally have a powerful voice. PJ Sedillo is ready for retirement as he pursues his Ph.D. He will be missed for many years, but the time has come for you to become that voice.

Tony Ross has assisted with Albuquerque Pride for the past 17 years. When he met PJ Sedillo, little did he know that he would take a journey that would enable Albuquerque Pride to become the largest GLBT event in the State of New Mexico. He has held the positions as treasurer, bookkeeper, and as PrideFest Director and has seen the event grow from a picnic at Morningside Park to a two-day PrideFest event at EXPO NM. As Tony coordinated the vendors/community boots, he saw the number grow from 20 to last year's record of 150+ booths. He was instrumental with Albuquerque Pride Inc. to obtain its 501 (c) (3) tax-exempt status.

This simple act has helped with the immense growth of the organization. As the financial bookkeeper of Albuquerque Pride, Tony has ensured the community that all monies obtained by the organization have been ethically and legally distributed and accounted for. Tony's unspoken honesty and integrity will be missed. Many have said that Tony Ross is the "backbone" of Albuquerque Pride, a statement that is well deserved. He will be missed by all, but as he retires from Pride, all is not lost. He will continue to support Albuquerque Pride and InterPride as a Region Director.

Friday, June 4th, was the annual Pride Idol competition from 5:00 p.m. to 9:00 p.m. It was located at the Banana Republic at Coronado Mall with the assistance of Johnny Q. This would be the first time that the competition would take place in such a "mainstream" location. Hundreds of people showed up to cheer the competitors, and the winner would perform on the Mainstage at Pridefest 2010. Besides viewing the competition, people could shop at the Banana Republic, and if they spent $100 they would get a 25% discount. On June 5th, the Fourth Annual Cliff's Amusement Park's Albuquerque Gay Day occurred with discount passes, with some of the proceeds going to Albuquerque Pride.

Thursday, June 10th, would be the Annual Candlelight Vigil at Morningside Park at 6:00 p.m. Albuquerque Pride would have a reception with NMAS at the Hyatt at 9:00 p.m. The Albuquerque Social Club (ASC) had in the past held a reception after the conclusion of the Candlelight Vigil and had been assured that this would continue in 2010 as their sponsorship. The ASC had scheduled entertainment, a buffet, no cover, and drink specials; however, the Board of Directors failed to contact the Albuquerque Social Club about the event. PJ Sedillo and Tony Ross attended the reception at the Social Club where they were met by the ASC Board and club manager who were concerned by the small crowd this year. Having two events at once, proved to be a problem. A reception was also taking place at the Hyatt this night. One of the reasons for moving the reception to the Hyatt was because of the contractual agreement that Albuquerque Pride had made with the Hyatt. Albuquerque Pride had to have so many "cash bars" throughout the entire three-day event that needed to make a certain quota in exchange for the ballroom space offered. A room quota of 50 which was also part of the agreement, needed to be reached by Albuquerque Pride.

The reception at the Hyatt was entitled "A Night with Mike Ruiz." Mike Ruiz was a celebrity fashion photographer and reality TV star. He would also be given the recognition as Albuquerque Pride's Grand Marshal. That evening he would set up and take photos of those who showed up at the reception and offer the opportunity to pay for the photos that were taken. Also, at the reception, guests would meet Tyra Sanchez, AKA James Ross, who was noted as a special guest. She was the winner of Season 2' RuPaul's Drag Race and had been a frequent drag impersonator of pop star Beyoncé Knowles. However, that evening she would not be dressed in drag and was there only to meet and greet for an hour because Tyra Sanchez would perform that evening at one of the sponsored bars. Albuquerque Pride would see none of the revenue collected at that Friday night event; even though Albuquerque Pride had graciously offered Tyra Banks a suite at the Hyatt for her one hour meet and greet.

The Friday Night Albuquerque Pride Celebration would be from 5:00 p.m. to 9:00 p.m. at Expo New Mexico. The venue would open with the Art Show and Pride Archives. Mainstage Entertainment would begin at 5:30 p.m. with the annual Pet Parade. Registration would start at 5:00 p.m. at the Pride Office or the Pet Parade. Prizes were awarded for "best of" categories. Lizards, iguanas, snakes, fish in bowls, and birds in cages were welcomed. Dogs and cats could come too. Awards would be given in the following categories: Best use of Rainbow, Most Unique, Largest, Smallest, Youngest Handler, Oldest Handler, Cutes, Most Butch, Most Gay, Best Pet Costume, Best Pet/Owner Costume Match, Best Pet/Owner Look-a-Like, Best Trick, Best of Parade, and Judges' Favorite.

At 8:00 p.m. the featured Performers would be BeBe Zaharas Benet and Headliner Martha Wash. The venue would end at 9:30 p.m. to continue the festivities at the Inaugural Albuquerque Pride Foam Party at the Hyatt, which was new for 2010. The Friday Night performances which Pride had started in previous years would present named entertainment to capitalize on Friday night instead of Saturday when in years past the community would go out to the bars that evening and leave PrideFest by 6:00 p.m. The featured Performer BeBe Zaharas Benet was a winner on RuPaul's Drag Race. She appeared on RuPaul's album and video on the track "Covergirl." BeBe had currently performed around the country booking shows. BeBe Zaharas Benet would make her debut on the Albuquerque Pride Main Stage that Friday Night of June 11th. The Pride Program would state "Don't Sashay Away...be ready to lip sync for your life."

Martha Wash would be Albuquerque Pride's 2010 Headliner. She was known for her 1992 release of "It's Raining Men" which still receives regular play in dance clubs and R&B radio to this day. She sang lead vocal on all three of Black Box's U.S. top forty hits, including the top ten smashes "Everybody, Everybody" and "Strike It Up," and the C & C Music Factory's "Gonna Make You Seat (Everybody Dance Now)," which hit #1 on the

Billboard Hot 100 in 1991. Martha Wash had been seen as a guest judge on RuPaul's Drag Race (2nd Season). She made her debut on the Mainstage for Albuquerque Pride that Friday night of June 12th. It was recommended for all to, "come see the sights and sounds of a Grammy nominated star." The crowds would be larger than expected for Friday Night, and the Board of Directors felt sure that the other events would be a success.

Also, June 11th, would be the Albuquerque Pride Friday Night Foam Party partnered with LIVEVERGE.com. The event was scheduled from 9:30 p.m. to 2:30 a.m. at the Hyatt, the official hotel for Albuquerque Pride, located at 330 Tijeras Avenue. This was a 21+ with identification event. The Foam Party highlighted DJ Chris De-Jesus who "spun his magic." A foam party, usually held in a nightclub, has guests dance and play in foam or soap suds. The event located on the west side of the hotel was fenced off. Tickets for the event needed to be purchased for $15 unless one had an all-access pass. There were issues with the foam machine, but Neil Macernie, who was a member of the Board of Directors, was able to rectify the situation.

Over 500 people attended the event which filled the space to capacity. Unfortunately, even with 500 in attendance, people were lined up outside the gates and were upset trying to get in. More tickets had been sold than the amount of people who could enter the Foam Party. Fortunately, Jesse Lopez had anticipated this, and he had fencing available to increase the space. Although it took time to reconfigure the space, all those who were in line were eventually able to come in to experience the Albuquerque Pride Friday Night Foam Party. The success of this event would produce high hopes for Saturday night's Pride Fusion noted as "Your ONLY Official Albuquerque Pride Nightlife Event!"

Other competing events held during Friday night were at the bar Exhale which had Tyra from RuPaul's Drag Race. She had briefly met people at a meet and greet on Thursday at the Hyatt reception after the Candlelight Vigil. Others who performed that evening at Exhale were Seymore Johnson, Sabryna Williams, Martinique Bouvier, Dawnyele, Madison Eriks, Extacy, and Latina del Rio. Sidewinders bar would have dancing and a drag show highlighting DJ "JoJo." Tribal Splash the competing event, did not have anything scheduled for Friday night according to the official Albuquerque Pride Guide; however, flyers were distributed throughout the Gay community about named DJ's and special entertainment specifically deemed for Friday night. Most of the performers who were at the Exhale bar did "double duty" by performing at both locations.

Saturday, June 12th was the 34th Annual Pride Parade located at Girard and Central. From 7:30 a.m. to 10:00 a.m. the parade line-up took place at UNM. Participants were asked to enter from Stanford. The Ribbon Cutting Ceremony on the corner of Girard and Central was at 10:30 a.m. which would announce the start of the Pride Parade what then traveled east on Central and then north on San Pedro into EXPO New Mexico.

2010

The theme for the 34th Albuquerque Pride was "One Heart, One World, One Pride." This was also the winning International Pride theme submitted by PJ Sedillo. The logo designed by Jesse Lopez produced a globe image of the earth that was tilted in the shape of heart. Among the continents was North America where there was a Zia symbol locating Albuquerque. The Zia symbol has sacred meaning to Native Americans. Four is a sacred number which symbolizes the Circle of Life with the four directions, the four times of day, the four stages of life, and the four seasons. The circle binds the elements of four together. The Zia Symbol, which is usually colored red, is comprised of a circle with four lines placed on the top, bottom, and each side of the circle. To the right side of the globe shaped heart was the phrasing of the 2010 theme. Underneath the heart was the wording "ALBUQUERQUE PRIDE 2010." Official Pride Pins would be discontinued.

The 2010 Grand Marshal was Mike Ruiz. As a New York-based photographer Mike Ruiz was best known for his high-impact, surreal brand of celebrity and fashion photography. He had worked with everyone from Betty White, Dolly Parton, Dennis Hopper, Lindsay Lohan, to the Jonas Brothers, and Zac Effron. His work had appeared in countless American and international magazines such *as Vanity Fair, Conde Nast Traveler, Interview, Paper, Citizen K. Dazed and Confused, Arena, Italian Elle, Spanish, and Brazilian Vogue*. He was a contributor to Dolce and Gabbana's "Hollywood" book and Iman's "The Beauty of Color" beauty book. Mike made his feature film directorial debut with RuPaul's uproarious comedy *Starbooty,* which was a film festival favorite in 2007. He had also directed several music videos for such artists as Kelly Rowland, Kristine W. and Traci Lords, Jody Watley, and the new pop sensation in 2010, Shontelle. Mike Ruiz was a founding partner of Miauhaus Studios, the elite Los Angeles photography complex featuring four full-service photo studios.

There would be no designated Honored Dignitaries for 2010 because of the inception of the Albuquerque Pride OutStanding Awards. The closest to Honored Dignitaries for 2010 would be Tony Ross and PJ Sedillo who rode in the parade as Lifetime Achievement honorees for Albuquerque Pride. Jo Anne Ramponi, who peacefully entered eternal life on Wednesday, April 14, 2010, would also be acknowledged for her honored contributions which were mentioned in "Your Ultimate Pride Program," the official program for Albuquerque Pride. The heading would state "In Memoriam-JoAnne Ramponi." She had served Albuquerque Pride for fifteen years and was usually the first person that one met during check-in at the Pride Parade and the pageants. She was responsible for checking in the multitude of parade entries. Always ready with her quick wit she made everyone feel welcomed at each event. Her warm hugs and explosive and exuberant laughter would be missed by all New Mexicans who would grieve the great loss of a "straight" ally who spoke up against any injustices made toward the GLBT community.

Albuquerque PrideFest at EXPO NM would be scheduled from 11:00 a.m. to 6:00 p.m. The following times are from the 2010 Pride Schedule:

11:00 a.m. to 5:00 p.m.	Albuquerque Pride Archives
11:00 a.m. to 6:00 p.m.	Family and Youth Area (1:00 The Bird Lady)
11:00 a.m. to 6:00 p.m.	Car Show / Archives / Art Show
11:00 a.m. to 6:00 p.m.	Mainstage Entertainment
12:00 a.m. to 5:00 p.m.	Absolut Lounge / Performance Stage / VIP Area
1:00 p.m. to 3:00 p.m.	Queer Bake Off
1:00 p.m. to 4:00 p.m.	Dance Tent (DJ Flo Fader)
1:00 p.m. to 3:00 p.m.	Pride Dance Lessons
3:00 p.m.	Poetry Slam
7:30 p.m. to 10:30 p.m.	Youth Dance (Must be under 21)

There would be no Featured Performers or Headliners scheduled for Saturday's Mainstage line-up. However, some of the best entertainers in Albuquerque would "step up" to perform. These stellar performers would be Flynnt, XTC, Shannon Haynes, Ro & Entourage, Mike Ruiz (Grand Marshal), April Ball, Throb, Full Moon Dance Crew, Becky Alter, Cassie, and the ABQ Kings Club. The Absolut Vodka Lounge performance schedule would include the following: Jazzie, Eve, Shannon, Becky Alter, Flynnt, Adan Branchal and Tish Lovato, Cassie, ABQ Kings Club, Lala, Rocco Steele, Michele, Bradd, Ruby, Shannon H, Alexis Taylor, Nikki and Rashon. Some performers would be responsible for being on the Mainstage and at the Absolut Vodka Lounge. This would give the opportunity for those in attendance at Pridefest to see performers they may have missed during a scheduled performance.

The Albuquerque Pride Parade and Pridefest would be well attended, reaching numbers that had not been seen in the past. From Thursday to Saturday, it was estimated that over 30,000 individuals had participated in the three-day event. Pride Fusion noted as "Your ONLY Official Albuquerque Pride Nightlife Event!" was getting ready to see how many would attend. Despite the awesome Friday night Foam Party, "All-Access" ticket sales were disappointing, and the Board of Directors were hoping that the mantra of Albuquerqueans living in "manana town" would hopefully transform the event into a success.

The event was considered a "bomb" despite the extravagant party/dance rooms created. There was an *ULTRA LOUNGE* with a guest DJ, *SPECTRUM NIGHT CLUB* with DJ Flo Fader, and *CLUB ESCANDALO* with DJ Quico. All rooms were well set up and ready to go; however, there were only about 100 individuals roaming throughout the rooms in search of more attendees. By 10:00 p.m. some people who had bought the All-

Access Pass, were demanding a refund and wanted the free shuttle that would take them to the bars and Tribal Splash.

Jesse Lopez would need the Board's assistance to pay "out-of-pocket" for the DJ's as money had not been made available that evening for payment. Some members of the Board would pay without ever being reimbursed. Morgan McMichaels would perform for about 150 individuals, and the crowd was even less for Goddess and She. The Pride Board would go room to room knocking on doors for those who might be in their room to announce the performers.

Tribal Splash would also encounter difficulties because they had over-extended the amount of capacity for their event. Some participants were extremely intoxicated and had caused problems at the hotel. Certain venues would be closed, including the water park for certain "lewd" behavior that took place. The Albuquerque Police Department would be contacted.

Some of the individuals who were staying at the Hyatt and had gone to Tribal Splash would be upset because the shuttle stopped at 12:00 a.m. Some individuals would go back to the Hyatt experiencing a party; however, since it had been so "dead" most of the evening the cash-bars had been closed, and the DJ's had left. Pride had concluded for 2010, 34 years of Pride in Albuquerque.

Reiterating for 2010, in August, Albuquerque Pride began a search for an administrative assistant. The salary for the person hired would be $27,750 with James Reese being offered the position after Scott Turner left. This would be a huge commitment for the Board to take on because of the amount of money needed to be raised to keep the individual hired in addition to the money needed to put on the event. This made the 2010 budget a grand total of was $192,285. The ultimate question now would be would the budget be obtained, and what would happen in 2011?

PJ Sedillo and Tony Ross, now retired, would be able to let others in the Gay community know from their point of view (without having to be "politically correct") about their own personal experience. They now were able to talk about the many dedicated years of service producing Albuquerque Pride with the assistance of their many dedicated volunteers and strong Board of Directors which made the event such a huge feat of accomplishment.

All of these key individuals from 1996 (when Albuquerque Pride was Incorporated) to 2010, through trial and error, pain and success, were able to produce a procedures manual, efficient corporate documents, sponsorship data, an extensive volunteer data base, a *Quick Book* accounting system with over 10 years of accountability, Community

Annual Membership Meetings, official/on time submission of By-laws and a non-profit corporation form-fillings. They had also participated nationwide as Region Pride Directors, supporting and assisting other Prides in Farmington/Socorro/Las Cruces/Gallup/ Taos/Flagstaff/Phoenix/El Paso, had sustained an official Pride Office location with a paid administrative assistant, and had seen to fruition an event that began with 1,500 individuals in attendance to over 50,000 individuals for a three day event. This tenured group would also see a budget increase from $1500 to over $192,000.

Each year the budget would be obtained; however, it must be noted that when the budget was not attained, PJ Sedillo and especially Tony Ross would donate funds “out of their own pockets” so that Albuquerque Pride would be in the “black and not in the red.” Many Board Members knew of these deeds but were asked not to let the Gay community know, and many of the Gay community still did not know that this transpired until now. Each August, two months after Albuquerque Pride had occurred, the Annual Corporate meeting would take place. At this meeting the Executive Board would be voted in which consisted of President, Vice-President, Treasurer and Secretary. For legal purposes a vice-president is not needed for the executive/corporate board.

An addendum in the By-laws in 2009 established an Emeritus Board of Directors. This definition was entered into the By-laws as patterned from Long Beach Pride’s By-laws which historically honored past presidents and parade chairs. The purpose of this Emeritus Board of Directors would be for them to offer input, guidance, and assurance to make sure that Albuquerque Pride would continue to exist whether monetarily or through volunteering. Some of the members of the Emeritus Board of Directors would be PJ Sedillo, Pat Baillie, Tony Ross, Tony Bucci, John Hull, Vangie Chavez, Steve Lopez, and any other Pride Chairs since 1976. Honorary Emeritus Board of Directors in Memoriam would be Anthony McKinney, Neil Isbin, Steve Slusher, and Russel Gray.

PJ Sedillo and Tony Ross were not notified about when the annual meeting was going to take place. The GLBT community had also not been notified about the meeting which through due diligence needs to be announced two weeks prior to the meeting. They had heard about the scheduled meeting from some of the Board Members who asked them if they were going to attend. Unaware that they had not been notified, Tony Ross and PJ Sedillo would attend the annual corporate meeting held in August at the Albuquerque Pride Office located at 2610 San Mateo Blvd.

When they arrived, one could feel the tension that filled the room. The Albuquerque Pride Inc. Board of Directors, Staff and Coordinators had all been secured, voted on, and selected prior to the annual meeting. These Board of Directors included the following: Jesse Lopez-President, Vice/President of Public Relations-Neil Macernie, Vice/President of Operations-J.R. LaBerge-Esparaza, Treasurer-Ricardo Cruz,

Volunteers-Alicia Billy, Family Area-Miranda Haynes, Pride Parade-Tony Carson, Dance Tent-Tom Rice, Pride AIDS Walk-Bunnie Fluffy Cruse and Aleah Rico, HIV/AIDS Food Bank-Joe and Jean Travis, OUTSpoken Poetry Slam-Erin Northern, Official Photographer-D'Asha Zelena Stephens, Special Events-Marcos Jay, Art Gallery-Stephanie Hainsfurther, Car Show-the Rainbow Roadrunner Car Club, and hired staff/Coordinator of Pridefest-James Reese. All those participants had been brought to the board or had previously worked closely with PJ and Tony.

PJ Sedillo and Tony Ross were bewildered upon reviewing the Albuquerque Pride By-laws which had been drastically altered. Any mention to an Emeritus Board of Directors had been slashed and removed. Voting took place fast and calculated to approve the By-laws which were similarly done when Jesse removed Sabryna Williams as a NM Pride Titleholder. Since there was no section in the By-laws pertaining to Pride Emeritus, there was now no voice sanctioned to those who had put in over 25 years of devotion to Pride in Albuquerque. PJ Sedillo and Tony Ross would leave the meeting perturbed and bewildered by what had been done. A few of the newly elected Board of Directors who had worked with PJ and Tony would go outside of the office to talk to them when they were preparing to leave. It is only then that some of the Board members realized what had just occurred. Some would resign, and some would stay on the Board not knowing or realizing the historical mishap that just occurred. It was at that moment that all those past individuals who had given their life to Pride would be swept away in an afternoon.

This was probably best for PJ and Tony's futures. PJ Sedillo and Tony Ross had become and were considered permanent fixtures of Pride in Albuquerque. In essence PJ Sedillo had become the "poster boy" of Gay Pride. Finally, at last, PJ Sedillo and Tony Ross would be free from the many years of Pride. PJ now would be able to continue working on his Ph.D., and Tony would be able to concentrate on his business and future retirement. They would view this upsetting experience as a blessing.

"Time heals all wounds," and there would be some "healing" that would need to take place for Albuquerque Pride. Most of the new Board Members did not know about the history of Albuquerque Pride and for the first time had encountered PJ Sedillo and Tony Ross who attended a meeting and left in a "fit of rage." Many years would take place before those Board of Directors and volunteers would come to the realization of what actually had occurred at that meeting. They would then understand how PJ Sedillo and Tony Ross had made many positive contributions for many years. However, before this realization occurred, tensions would reach an all-time high when in March of 2011 Albuquerque Pride would have to deal with a bid that had been put in to produce and hold a Consolidated Associations of Pride Inc. (CAPI) Conference which was to take place primarily in Albuquerque with an event planned in Santa Fe.

PJ Sedillo was designated as the Chairperson for this event. Albuquerque Pride had been members of InterPride and had sent representatives from 1984 to 2010 and as well to CAPI from 1996 to 2010. During that time regional distribution for InterPride had been a controversial issue for what region would best meet the needs of New Mexico. New Mexico had been part of Region 3 which consisted of Texas, Kansas, Oklahoma, and Colorado. Region 1 (CAPI) was California, Arizona, Mexico and Nevada. Albuquerque Pride had a close relationship with Phoenix, Tucson, and Flagstaff Pride, and it made more sense to be part of the Consolidated Associations of Pride Incorporations (CAPI). Region 3 had always had a difficult time in establishing its existence because of the massive amount of distance between each Pride event. It must be noted that Denver Pride is 444 miles away from Albuquerque Pride, and Pride Houston is even further. Therefore, Albuquerque Pride would become members of CAPI. Each year InterPride would hold a yearly international conference. The regions would hold a smaller conference to reach those smaller Prides that might not be able to attend InterPride.

In 2008, Albuquerque Pride attended the annual CAPI Conference in San Francisco. Albuquerque Pride and Santa Fe Pride had been closely working together as a team because of the professional relationship between PJ Sedillo-President and Doña Hatch President of Santa Fe Pride. This collaboration had been established by the many years of both presidents attending together the international level of Pride and promoting New Mexico Prides throughout the State and throughout the world. For years, each Pride organization would share volunteers, ideas and support which made each event a success. It was decided in 2008 that Albuquerque Pride and Santa Fe Pride would take that next step to produce a Region Conference for CAPI. This would be a huge undertaking. It meant that along with putting on their own Pride events for the year, they would need to obtain money, volunteers, and chairpersons to orchestrate a Region Conference.

Under the direction of Johnny Q., PJ Sedillo, and Doña Hatch a bid for the conference to be held in Albuquerque in 2009 would be presented in San Diego. The membership would vote no; however, they would give a yes for 2010, to give both organizations two years to prepare. This would be best for the organizations involved. Both Albuquerque Pride and Santa Fe Pride would work diligently to produce the event. Johnny Q. would have to step-down as Committee Chair because he had a prior commitment as a Board Member with *Up With People*, and Doña Hatch having surgery for her hip would have to step down; therefore, PJ Sedillo would assume the duties as Chairperson for the CAPI Conference.

Assuming the duties of Chairperson for the CAPI Conference, PJ Sedillo's first move was to meet with the host hotel that had originally been part of the bid and sign a contract. Needless to say, under the advisement of the Board of Directors of Albuquerque Pride, Jesse Lopez, the current President, had already gone to the hotel and said that the event would no longer take place and that the contract needed to be dissolved. PJ Sedillo, the newly appointed chair for CAPI, would work diligently to make sure that the event would proceed. Upon his meeting with the host hotel, he would come to learn what had happened. Fortunately, he was able to have contract resumed and honored. (The Albuquerque Pride Board had no authority to suspend the contract because PJ Sedillo had made the agreements with the hotel and signed his name.)

Santa Fe Pride would become the sole producer of the conference, and even with the rocky start, the event would end up as a huge success. There were over nineteen Pride Organizations from six different states. The CAPI conference would primarily take place in Albuquerque but was tied into Santa Fe Pride's Annual GAYLA fundraiser. The event would cost over $10,000 to produce, and the budget would be reached with a surplus of $650 that would go to Santa Fe Pride.

To this day, PJ Sedillo and Tony Ross continue helping and providing consultation with other Pride events in the State of New Mexico and nationwide to assist with their positive growth. In 2010, they decided to start the first ever Los Ranchos de Albuquerque Pride where they currently reside. For years, the two had wanted to have a free event on Sunday with a church service after the Parade and PrideFest on Saturday; however, because they were usually too exhausted, this event did not occur. This idea came to fruition in 2010.

Los Ranchos Pride was scheduled the first Sunday in June where MCCA had a church service that began at 10:30 a.m. At 11:00 a.m. there were about 300 attendees. There was a car show provided by the Rainbow Roadrunner's Car Club, food, and entertainment. The event took on the feel of an "old time" country fair. There were many games and contests, including a tamale eating contest. The event was not publicized and was only shared through Facebook and "word of mouth." In 2016, Los Ranchos Pride celebrated its sixth anniversary. The volunteers have continued to similarly run this event to keep the event small and family friendly.

Chapter 12

Albuquerque Pride- A New Direction 2011 and 2012

PJ Sedillo and Tony Ross, who had a combined 37 years of Pride expertise, would not participate in producing Albuquerque Pride in 2011. Because of their non-involvement in 2011, Albuquerque Pride would encounter change which was infused with new declarations, decisions, and directives to produce an Albuquerque Pride Parade and PrideFest. This would be attempted by creating new missions and visions for Albuquerque Pride, which would be conducted without any contributions from the past.

Furthermore, the 2011 Albuquerque Pride Board would not have access and information to what had been attempted and conducted at past Pride events that either resulted in a total loss of monetary funds or as a huge success supported by the intended mission of past Pride's in Albuquerque. In hindsight for this reason, PJ Sedillo had set up in the By-Laws for past Presidents, Vice –presidents a Board Members who would become "Emeriti." This idea had been consistently accepted and proclaimed by other older Pride organizations in the United States.

This new Board would produce, in the long run, for the community to experience a new formation and harmony of the LGBTQI (note the "L" had been put in front of the "G" in 2011) community in Albuquerque; however, this new, unique, different Albuquerque Pride Board would see a time of new growth and new ideas. Many of these changes would assist in a positive future growth for Albuquerque Pride. However, with this new direction for Albuquerque Pride, those who were on the Board would have to meet the 2011 budget request. They would have to deal head on with the financial losses from 2010 much of which was caused by the event known as Pride Fusion.

The Hyatt Regency hotel that held the Pride Fusion event would be the first business to not continue working with Albuquerque Pride after "breaking" and not fulfilling the contractual agreements. Liquor sales were dismal and the "quotas" which were needed in exchange for using the ballrooms were not met. Eventually, no legal actions were taken against Albuquerque Pride because the Bernalillo County was a major sponsor and supporter of Pride Fusion. Selected Bernalillo County Commissioners, Jesse Lopez- President of Albuquerque Pride, PJ Sedillo/Tony Ross Consultants of Albuquerque Pride, and the executive directors for the Hyatt Regency Hotels had all been part of the initial negotiations and eventual signing of contracts. The hotel would look at the event as a "wash." Besides the possible lawsuit, the 2011 Albuquerque Pride Board of Directors would also face many new challenges.

Albuquerque Pride 2011

The Board elected for 2011was President-Jesse A. Lopez, Vice President of Public Relations-Neil Macernie, Vice President of Operations-J.R LaBerge-Esparza, Treasurer-Ricardo Cruz, Volunteers-Alicia Billy, Family Area-Miranda Haynes, Pride Parade-Tony Carson, Pride AIDS Walk-Bunny Fluffy Cruse and Aleah Rico, Dance Tent/Foam Party-Tom Rice, HIV/AIDS Food Bank-Joe and Jean Travis, OUTSpoken Poetry Slam-Erin Northern, Official Photographer-D'Asha Zelena Stephens, Special Event-Marcos Jay, Art Gallery-Stephani Hainsfurther, Car Show-Rainbow Roadrunner Car Club and Coordinator of Pridefest-James Reese who was also the hired administrative assistant for Albuquerque Pride. Also, on the Board were the 2011 New Mexico Pride Title Holders who were MsTer NM Gay Pride Rocco Steele, Mr. NM Pride Raydon Hawk, Ms. NM Pride Tiffany Mariah De Marco and Miss NM Pride LaRhya Daniels.

MsTer NM Gay Pride 2011, Rocco Steele had been performing throughout NM and the US since 2002. He was one of the original members of the Albuquerque Kings Club (a drag king troupe). He also was honored as the first OUTStanding Drag King Award winner for 2010 and was crowned Mr. Merry Christmas 2009. As a member of the Transgender community, he raised awareness of issues faced by the Trans community throughout his titleholder year. Notably, he was the First Self-identified Trans Man as Titleholder.

In November 2010, Nic Sedillo aka Rocco Steele ran as MsTer New Mexico Pride and won the title for 2011. The following year, Nic ran again, but this time for Mr. New Mexico Pride identifying as a transgender man. He won the title for 2012 and became the first transgender man to win a title and the first person to hold two different titles.

Mr. NM Pride, Raydon Hawk worked many years to put Albuquerque on the map as an entertainment capital. He had produced many shows at Effex, Exhale Bar, the Albuquerque Social Club (now referred to as the SOCH). He was able to bring in celebrity performers to these venues. His platform for 2011 was the Trevor Project founded in 1998 is the leading national organization that provides crisis intervention and suicide prevention for the LGBTQ youth. Because of that, he understood the need of support for the personal struggles the youth of the Gay community faced and wanted to seek an end to the rash of suicides and abuse.

Ms. NM Pride, Tiffany Mariah Di Marco was a strong and proud transgender woman who believed in advocating a positive image of the GLBT community to all New Mexicans. She felt that by embracing her own difference she could become an activist to the public at large who would allow her to not only widen her sphere of empathy, education and optimism, but also to create the ability to enhance the blessings in her life by leaving a positive impression and impact on the lives of others.

Miss New Mexico Pride, LaRhya Daniels, for many years had been fundraising and advocating in New Mexico. She had focused on Women's issues as well as GLBT issues, drawing the connections between the similarities of each minority. She was born and raised in New Mexico. She was also a Board Member of the SOCH. Also, known as Marshal Martinez in 2007 he would be noted as an Honored Dignitary-Emerging Leader. He had truly come full circle by obtaining the title of Miss NM Pride in 2011.

In 2011, Sabryna Williams, a past Miss NM Pride whose title was removed in 2010 by the Albuquerque Pride Board, would become a "powerhouse" in the GLBTQI community. Jesse Lopez would recognize this. The Albuquerque Pride Board, who had originally removed her and taken away her title, would proclaim and reinstate her with all honors under the direction of the new Board of Directors. Despite that Sabryna Williams had been stripped of her title she had become a beacon of hope for those less fortunate, a fantastic advocate, and positive voice for the community. She would win numerous awards for her positive contributions.

Sabryna Williams would also be noted for her outstanding emceeing capabilities and would have to be "paid, hired and contracted" by Albuquerque Pride to emcee the 2011 NM Pride Pageant. In the past all emcees had volunteered and donated their time to emcee the Pride Pageants. On stage, during the competition, Jesse Lopez, President of Albuquerque Pride, would reinstate Sabryna Williams as Miss NM Pride 2010 and present her a six-foot trophy that had been made from numerous trophies pieced together. Sabryna Williams and others would laugh at this "comical" attempt at an award presentation. This would be a first time in Albuquerque Pride's history that a titleholder would be given his/her title back after having it removed.

In 2011, Bunnie Benton Cruse and Gilbert Bustillos, aka Aleah Rico (Miss New Mexico Pride 2008-2009 and 2013), would join the 2011 Albuquerque Pride Board. They asked Albuquerque Pride's help to bring back the AIDS Walk which was last held in 2005. The event was re-branded as the Michael Kink Memorial AIDS Walk and was held on April 30th at Highland High School. To help celebrate the event Cleve Jones, the founder and creator of the AIDS Quilt, was guest speaker. The walk benefited the Albuquerque Pride, Inc. and the Joe and Jean Travis Food Bank. To emphasize the need for outreach to people living with HIV, the event was re-branded as the New Mexico HIV/AIDS Walk benefiting HIV and AIDS resource organizations in 2012. Albuquerque Pride took a hiatus in 2015 to regroup and restructure the event. In 2016, Albuquerque

Pride entered a partnership with UNM Truman Health Services and re-branded the event the HIV Walk New Mexico.

2011

For many years, PJ Sedillo and Tony Ross's LLC known as Rainbow Spectrum would offer office space for Albuquerque Pride in exchange for Sponsorship. Office space was located at 2610 San Mateo Blvd. by the corner of San Mateo and Menaul which is a major "hub" within the City of Albuquerque. This year, the Albuquerque Pride Board would vote unanimously to discontinue the rental agreement between Rainbow Spectrum LLC and Albuquerque Pride. Albuquerque Pride was able to successfully move to another location because they were provided free office space located at 5th and Central in the "heart" of downtown Albuquerque at Effex Nightclub. This would be an exciting move for the Albuquerque Pride Board. They would have an office within one of the most attended gay clubs in the state of New Mexico. The office would now be available and open to many who would have never gone to the office located on San Mateo. The space was dedicated as the Pride Resource Center.

The Albuquerque Pride Board would be excited for 2011. James Reese, Administrative Assistant and Coordinator of Pridefest, would state verbatim in the *Pride and Equality* magazine, "Albuquerque Pride celebrates 35 years of consistent community involvement." This year's theme was driven by the constant mention from community members feeling divided. Feeling as if we lived in a fractured community; therefore, *Power, the Unity of Pride* was born. This theme was utilized to show hope in every step forward, and confidence in the fact that together we become stronger every day!" This would also be the first year since Albuquerque Pride was incorporated that the Pride Committee would choose a different theme than the selected International Pride Theme noted as "Pride Around the World."

A Message for the President would be in the Official Pride Program. This would be the first time the acronym GLBTQ (Q for Queer) also LGBTQ would be utilized. The message (*copied exactly from the 2011 Official Pride Program in its entirety*) is as follows:

> Friends, Family, and Supporters,
> STOP! CELEBRATE! THINK! Acknowledge! It's BEEN 35 Years since the first Pride march took place. All too often we don't take the time to reflect and value of our past as much as we fall to be more active to secure a stronger future. Albuquerque Pride was not always a celebration, a party, or even a time to get together in public. 35 years ago, was a time of turmoil, hate, ignorant individuals that stood strongly against homosexuals, and yes there were those that were forced to stay in the closet, some committed suicide.
>
> Today we still face these same challenges. Are they as strong? Are they prominent? Well, that depends on who you ask. See it's all subjective to the individual facing the crisis. To the teen that sees no outlet, to the mother or rather that lives in fear of coming out to their kids or family, to those that fear the rejection of their faith-based community, or for many other reason, they all see being Gay one way.
>
> As a community we cannot forget these challenges! We must not forget these that have come before us, those that fought for the right to hold their partners hands, that fought to say it was not a psychological disorder. 35 years ago, it may have been a celebration, but in the same right, it was a major struggle.

Stonewall happened and sent a wave across America. It hit New Mexico loud and clear we are homosexuals! We are people! We love who we are, and will no longer, stand for intolerance of hate! The Pride friends, I reflect on where we have come and acknowledging that as a community we have much more to do.

This past year Albuquerque Pride, Inc. and the Board of Directors went through a transition process. During this transition we faced many challenges and trials. We reached out to the community, answered some tough questions, had our ups and downs. I did not take this position thinking everything would be easy, I did it because the end result, for me, it is worth it. Every rumor and faced many negative comments. I, along with the Board of Directors and the staff, have worked hard to make sure the stability, accountability, and image of Albuquerque Pride is head on, and we have done it together!

In the coming year we are moving the Pride Resource center from the Spectrum Building on San Mateo and Menaul to the top floor of EFFEX nigh club. This offers us more space for the Joe and Jean Travis HIV/AIDS Food Bank, GLBT Library, Coffee Center, Counseling Services, and exclusive GLBTQ Organizations workspace and phone line and more. We look forward to the possibilities of giving out Pride Scholarships, and GLBTQ Organizations Grants. Albuquerque Pride has been changing in a positive way! Together we will work with you to fight for marriage equality, end discrimination, take care of our youth, and most of all each other.

In closing, thank you to each of you that buys a ticket, your dollars help to support the HIV/AIDS food bank, the Aids Walk, the Resource center, and staff. Thank you to James Reese, our Pride Coordinator and staff, the Albuquerque Pride Board of Directors, Committee Chairs, vendors, sponsors, and of course the hundreds of volunteers.

Together in Pride,
Jesses A. Lopez
President, Albuquerque Pride Board of Directors

Pride & Equality magazine, not directly associated or part of the corporation would be given permission from Albuquerque Pride Inc. to permit on its cover the statement

"THE ONLY GLBTQ PUBLICATION ENDORSED BY ABQ PRIDE, INC." Also, on the cover was a picture of Dario who would be a performer at Albuquerque Pride 2011. One of the featured stories was an interview with Jesse Lopez "The new face of ABQ Pride." The following are a few excerpts from the interview:

> ***Pride & Equality* (*P & E*): First, congratulations on your new post. You have some big shoes to fill. What was the moment like when you found out you were voted in as the new President?** Jesse Lopez: I was fortunate enough to fill PJ Sedillo's shoes as ABQ Pride President upon his retirement. It was a proud moment because I realized the positive impact a position like this holds in the community.
>
> ***P & E*: I don't think it's a surprise to know that many felt that you did not deserve this post. So, let's clear the air here. Why do you feel that some people in the community didn't feel you deserve this position and what do you plan to do to prove them wrong?** Jesse Lopez: Wow! That's a loaded question. I came in after a long standing and very accomplished President. PJ took pride from a small park to Expo New Mexico, growing it to be the largest GLBTQ event and organization in the state, so, of course, there would be apprehensive individuals in the community to someone new taking over. I believe the post is deserving of anyone willing to give of their time, commitment, and most of all their passion. Am I deserving? For me, it is a call to action. A true moment I found where I could make a difference. But I alone am nothing without a dedicated board, staff, and a community that believes in what ABQ Pride's mission is. If I lived my life solely to prove people wrong, I would be doing things for self-gratification and selfish reasons. My intent is to educate, unite, and grow Albuquerque Pride to its true potential.

With the decided theme, new elected Board of Directors, and new mission/vision secured and put in place, the 35th Annual Albuquerque Pride Parade and PrideFest would be scheduled June 5th to the 11th. It would be proclaimed as "The Largest GLBTQ Event in the State of New Mexico."

Sunday, June 5th, would be the 2011 Interfaith Service at 7:00 p.m. located at the Albuquerque Center for Spiritual Living. On Tuesday, June 7, would be Leather Night, Wednesday, the 8th, the Pride Idol competition was held at Exhale Bar & Grille, and Thursday, June 9th, the Candlelight Vigil would be held followed by the Official Kick Off at the Albuquerque Social Club. Albuquerque Pride tried to "heal the wounds" created in 2010 by not showing up at the Albuquerque Social Club after the Candlelight Vigil of 2010 with the intent that the mistake would not occur again in the future. Friday, June 10, would be a VIP/Sponsor Gala at Downtown ABQ. There were also special events held at the bars known as Effex, Albuquerque Social Club, and Exhale Night Club. There would not be a Friday Night PrideFest because the budget could not be met if this would have occurred. On Saturday, June 12th, were the Pride Parade and PrideFest. Finally, on Saturday night the 12th there would be TRIBAL SPLASH at the Radisson Resort and Water Park with Lights, DJs, and Entertainment.

The Albuquerque Pride Parade would have its staging area at the UNM parking lot located on the northwest corner of Central and Girard. Parade entries were welcome to pick up registration packets and set up starting at 7:30 a.m. Registration would close at 10:00 a.m. The parade started promptly at 10:30 a.m. and headed to EXPO New Mexico for PrideFest (title changed) 2011. Parade entries were judged on creativity, color (Rainbow Pride Colors), use of theme ("Power, the Unity of Pride") and enthusiasm of participants. Awards were presented at PrideFest later that day on the Mainstage at EXPO New Mexico. This would be the first year that a GRAND PRIZE-People Choice Award for best float would garner a cash prize of $250. Spectators were given the opportunity to text in the number of their favorite entry. Pets were allowed in the parade; however, due to the large crowds and numbers of children present pets were not allowed at PrideFest. Owners would be asked from EXPO staff, security, and Pride Staff to have the animal(s) removed from the event.

The 2011 Grand Marshal would be "hometown boy" Jason Carter (Sedillo). He returned to the Land of Enchantment to be part of PrideFest. As a native New Mexican, he would perform for productions with the local theater groups in Albuquerque. He then received a guest VJ (Video Jockey) spot on the City of Albuquerque's hottest teen show called "Dance, Dance, A Teen Thing." He would perform hip hop with other dancers at local events specifically designed for teenagers to attend at a safe environment. The dance events were videotaped and shown later for teens to watch. This was a successful campaign because the reviewing of the taped shows was highlighted Saturday nights. Many youths would stay home instead of going out late evenings to see if they were on television. Notably, Jesse Lopez would be part of this experience as a "Teen VJ."

Jason Carter's fame and nationwide recognition would be when he received the opportunity to be part of the Pit Crew on the highly successful RuPaul's Drag Race. He also worked as a Host and On-Camera Talent for various networks, even though dance has been his first love. He would state in the *Pride and Equality* magazine, "Coming home will be a victory for all who have supported me throughout the years, and to those who have not. The haters are just as important as the people who support you. They drive you to succeed and prove them wrong. All in all, I'm blessed to be part of such an amazing time for the community."

The 2011 PrideFest gates would open at 11:30 a.m. There were over 140 vendors, Art Show, Dance Tent (Foam Party- Sponsored by Tribal Pride) and Live entertainment all day, Vodka Lounge, Car Show, and larger and bigger Children's Area. New this year would be the Albuquerque Pride Poetry Slam competition. The year also marked the first year that Albuquerque Pride held open auditions for the community for the PrideFest entertainment schedule. The auditions were held in the beginning of April and ran for a little over a week and a half. The 2011 Comcast Main Stage Line Up would be as follows:

Christian Raphael
Blame it on Rebekkah Band
Brice and Catherine Belly Dancers
Kimberlee Ann Lopez
E11 Dance Group
Laticia Lovato
Off Broadway Dance Group
Trixie Con Queso
J'Adore Dance Crew
Aleah Rico
D.J. and William Acoustical Guitar Players
Burlesque Noir
Brian, Teri, and Susan Belly Dance Group
Throb Dance Crew
LaRyha Daniels
Severo y Grupo Fuego
UNM's Lady Gaga and the QSA Little Monsters
Rocco Steele
Taffy Shalamar
Tiffany DiMarco
Pride Idol Finalists
Albuquerque Pride Title Holders Group Performances

Also, performing at 6:30 p.m. on Saturday, June 11th, would be Albuquerque Pride's 2011 Headliners Kristine W, Erika Jayne, Dario and Shangela from RuPaul's Drag Race. They would be described as performers who would, "serve it to you with full force on the Comcast Main Stage!" Problems would arise for the 2011 Pride Board because Shangela would be a no show, and logistics for limo services would not be considered. The 2011 Albuquerque Pride Board would not take any legal actions against Shangela's non-performance because contractual agreements could not be located or produced. Despite these fiascos that occurred on the Main Stage the event would still produce a show that would have the crowd (at the edge of the stage) full of pride and excitement.

Albuquerque Pride had for many years provided a space or children's area at PrideFest. In 2011 under the direction of Miranda Hanes the children's area was expanded and titled the Family Park at PrideFest. There was a Family Entrance that opened at 11:30 a.m. There were water misters and an area for children to use chalk to decorate the sidewalks which were surrounded by carnival games where children could win some great prizes. There was also an arts and crafts area. Finally, there were a multitude of inflatables which included an enormous obstacle course, a slide, "Kiddie Corral," and two jumpers-one for children under five and one for children five and older. The scheduled events at the Family Park area were as follows:

12:00 p.m. Story Time- Christee Meleski and Meg Freestone
1:00 p.m. Pinata
1:30 p.m. Three-Legged Race
2:00 p.m. Crazy Hair Spray-Miranda Haynes and Volunteer(s)
3:00 p.m. Pinata

3:30 p.m.	Belly Dance Lessons
4:30 p.m.	Water Balloon competition/Fight
5:15 p.m.	Pinata
5:45 p.m.	Origami-Miranda Haynes
7:00 p.m.	Pinata- Area Closes
8:00 p.m.	Open for all Ages to Jump/Play Carnival Games

Neil Champion Macernie, Vice President of Albuquerque Pride, would spearhead a new area known as Weddings at PrideFest. There would be commitment ceremonies conducted by MCCA which had an outdoor chapel complete with 40 seats, runway aisle, and decorations the way only Pride knows how to do. The event would be stated as, "Ready to make that next step with your Boyfriend or Girlfriend? Albuquerque Pride has a whole New Area just for you!"

Also, new to PrideFest 2011 was an area designated as the OUTSpoken Poetry Slam that had a competition Championship Slam with Celebrity Judges. The poet Lindsay Miller was highlighted at 3:00 p.m., and the winners of the contest were revealed after Lindsay Miller had performed. Lindsay Miller won the Denver Citywide Spelling Bee in seventh grade, kicking off an illustrious life of being a total word nerd. She studied creative writing at the Denver School of the Arts and the University of Arizona and was a Founding Mama of the Tucson Poetry Slam. She, also, traveled the country with Doc Luben as the Smaller Shark Poetry Tour. Since 2008, she had hosted the Queer Mic at the National Poetry Slam.

An additional attraction would be part of the usually "jammed packed" Pride Dance Tent which would be a Foam Party with go-go dancers. This would be sponsored by TRIBAL SPLASH who notably competed for the Friday and Saturday night events after the conclusion of PrideFest Albuquerque. Jesse Lopez, President of Albuquerque Pride, had negotiated with the event producers to become sponsors of the 2011 event despite the fiasco held the year before. One of the producers of TRIBAL SPLASH, Tom Rice, would be noted as a Board Member for Albuquerque Pride with the title of Dance Tent. TRIBAL SPLASH 2011 would have a full-page advertisement in the *Official Pride Program* and on top of the advertisement was stated, "One of the Largest and Most Incredible Pride Events In the Entire Country Returns for its 3rd Out Year!" On the bottom of the advertisement would be the wording, "Proud To Be The Official ABQ Pride Party."

During the 2011 PrideFest, leadership changes occurred within Albuquerque Pride following a discussion regarding organizational matters. At that time, Jesse Lopez stepped down from his role as President, concluding his service, which began after his election in August 2010. His tenure spanned approximately ten and a half months and did not extend through a full annual cycle.

Following his departure, Neil Macernie assumed the responsibilities of President on June 11, 2011. He oversaw the completion of PrideFest events and the final wrap-up activities. Although the transition occurred unexpectedly, Macernie focused on ensuring continuity and meeting the organization's immediate needs. With this leadership transition, Macernie joined a line of dedicated individuals who had previously guided Albuquerque Pride. As President, he faced the responsibility of supporting the organization's mission while addressing operational challenges and maintaining unity within the community.

Albuquerque Pride 2012

The 2012 *Pride and Equality* magazine proclaimed as *THE OFFICIAL 2012 ALBUQUERQUE PRIDE PROGRAM -Pride Linking Us Together for 36 Years* would write, "With new faces come new ideas, fresh passion and extreme motivation amongst our LGBTIQ (first time "I" used for intersex) Community. This new path would be led by the direction of five competent members of the Executive Board of Directors. Neil Macernie-President would welcome all to a whole new PrideFest event that would, "definitely show the power in unity and working together for a common goal." He would also state that Albuquerque Pride would b,e "redesigned for a new experience." Ricardo Cruz-Treasurer would state, "We have made a lot of accomplishments over the past year to become a better organization for our community—we have redefined our vision, our look, [and] made changes to our finances." Craig LaBerge-Esparza-Secretary hoped that Albuquerque Pride would not only provide a large event to celebrate our community, a huge party, but also be known as, "an organization that impacts, the entire LGBTIQ (first time that the "L" was used before the "G") Community, that assists, LGBTIQ people from day to day."

The official t-shirt for 2012 would use the International Pride theme "Pride Links Us Together" with the wording and the graphic of a simple linking of a rainbow chain also the new official corporate logo for Albuquerque Pride. The t-shirts were offered in a variety of colors. In 2012 the community would see a new branding of the official logo of Albuquerque Pride conducted years before. Over twenty submissions in many different fashions would be entered. The community was then asked to vote on their favorite logo. This would not be the first time that this process would occur throughout the 36 years of Pride history. The final decision and current logo were decided by the Board. Austin Evans, a member of the University of New Mexico's Queer Straight Alliance, would be the designer. This new logo for Albuquerque Pride visually had the wording Albuquerque on the top line and Pride located on the bottom line with rainbow stripes underlining each of the words. Underneath the word Pride was the labels of Lesbian, Gay, Bisexual, Transgender, Intersex and Queer. This would be the first year that the word Lesbian would be put forth before Gay since the inception of the corporation established in 1996.

2012

Miranda Haynes-Vice President of Public Relations would state, “This new logo shows exactly what we as a board are trying to accomplish—making Albuquerque Pride Inc. exciting, fresh, fun and professional.” Similar verbiage could have described logos previously approved by Albuquerque Pride. J.R. LaBerge-Esparza-Vice President of Operations would be the one to move forward to honoring Albuquerque Pride’s past. He would state, “Although Albuquerque Pride Inc. speaks highly of their new and diverse ideas, recognition to past leaders and advocates is referred to frequently.” Furthermore, he would state, “The past community advocates, the past Board Members and the past executive Board Members made us who we are today. Without what they have done in the past and what they brought to our community; we would not be what we are today.”

1996

2012

This statement from the J.R. LaBerge Esparza would become an 'olive branch' that PJ Sedillo, past President would be honored to receive. He would join the Board in a small capacity as the archivist and historian of Albuquerque Pride and would write a three-page article summarizing Pride in Albuquerque from 1976 to 2012 that would be printed in the *Pride & Equality Official 2012 Albuquerque Pride Program.* Despite the Vice President's reaching out to past advocates, Presidents, Board Members and participants of past Prides in Albuquerque, 2012 would become a year of many different changes, resurrections, and revisions within the culture, management, and leadership of Pride in Albuquerque.

Albuquerque's 35 years of producing a Pride event would be led yearly by either one person, a committee of individuals, different organizations working together (or not), and an elected Board of Directors. There would be 5 Executive Board of Directors for Albuquerque Pride in 2012 and a total of fifteen Board Members who would become the largest collective Board in the history of Albuquerque Pride's existence. They were as follows: Graham Thomas-Director of Development, Tony Carson-Coordinator of Candlelight Vigil and Pride Parade, Anneke Blair-Coordinator of Social Networking, Ana-Lisa Montoya-Torres-Coordinator of OUTstanding Awards, Christopher Joshua Garcia-Coordinator of Sponsored Events, Gwen CK-Director of Titleholders, Gerald McLean-Co-Director of Volunteers, Brandon Jensen-Coordinator of Media Relations, Marcos Jay-Director of Special Events, Jon Martinez-Co-Director of Volunteers, Reverend Judith Maynard-Coordinator of Spiritual Relations, Gary Peterson-Director of Education and finally James Reese-Office Manager.

In 2012, James Reese was no longer known as the administrative assistant for Albuquerque Pride but noted as an office manager. Since the Albuquerque Pride office had been moved to Effex Night Club, James Reese would also be handed duties from the owner of Effex, thus making him an office manager. This would become an issue for Albuquerque Pride because his duties were specifically needed to produce Pride.

Another issue and controversy that Albuquerque Pride would encounter was left over from Jesse Lopez's time as President. It had been announced that Albuquerque Pride would be providing counseling services. The Board of Directors of Albuquerque Pride would have a meeting with James Reese, who was not a licensed counselor about answering the phones from those who called about counseling services. It was noted by the Board of Directors that James may have provided advice to some of the individuals who called for counseling services. Upon finding this out, the Board asked for him to immediately stop providing any advice to those who called Albuquerque Pride needing counseling services. The issue of providing counseling services would have to be delt with this year.

The Gay Pride New Mexico Pageant began in 1996 under the direction of the Royal Imperial Sovereign Court of the Land of Enchantment Empire and selected Miss Gay Pride New Mexico Victoria Vale and Ms. Gay Pride New Mexico Diana Johnson. The pageant would be renamed the NM Gay Pride Pageant. In 2005, the pageant was again renamed the New Mexico Pride Pageant. The final name changes assisted Albuquerque Pride to reach out to others who wanted to participate in this event. Past Pride Titleholders for Albuquerque Pride were on part of the Executive Board; however, in 2012 the titleholders became more as ambassadors and spokespersons of Albuquerque Pride even though they represented all Prides in New Mexico. This title would also be questioned by other Prides in the state. Although not part of the Board of Albuquerque Pride the titleholders selected on November 5th were Shaila Cavali-Miss New Mexico Pride, Nic 'Rocco' Sedillo-Mr. New Mexico Pride, and Shannon Hanynes-Ms. New Mexico Pride who would eventually resign. As in the past, these individuals would become influential ambassadors in the promotion of Albuquerque Pride 2012 and did not have to help Albuquerque Pride financially.

Many have heard and repeated the saying "those who do not learn from history are doomed to repeat it." The Albuquerque Pride Board of Directors would consider in 2012 many ideas and events that had already been attempted or considered previously. Some were successes, and others were failures. A few of the Board of Directors would reach out to learn from the past; however, many decisions would be made by those unaware of what had been attempted in the past. Despite what worked or did not work in the past, actions would be attempted and proclaimed as new events attempted because of a new mission and vision statement.

Despite some failures and some successes, these attempts would be the best for Albuquerque Pride. In 2012 Albuquerque Pride would experience a "rebirth" which brought forth new and fresh ideas under a new leadership. This new and exciting Board of Directors would take creative risks such as changing locations and buildings at EXPO NM, creating new venues, and creative marketing the OutStanding Awards. Albuquerque Pride would move in a positive direction. The Albuquerque Pride Executive Board would become a cohesive and responsible Board that would move Pride positively into the future providing detailed plans and directives for 2012 as well as for years to come.

In 2012, Albuquerque Pride using operational costs would hold a Charity Rummage Sale to benefit the newly created LGBTIQ Scholarship Fund. The event would be decided upon during the Annual Albuquerque Pride Corporate meeting held in August. It was decided that the Charity Rummage Sale would be held from September 21st to 23rd. Also, proposed and approved would be the introduction of the Shop ABQ Pride Booth (which also sold items like a rummage sale). The Shop ABQ Pride Booth would open in November of 2012 at The Market located at 610 Central Ave., SW. The space and all products would be donated; however, after several months it was closed because of low sales and interest.

Albuquerque Pride introduced a new fund raiser for HIV and AIDS on World AIDS Day, December 1, 2012. The Circle of Life Gala event was a great setup and had community involvement in putting the event together. However, dinner tickets sales were very poor. The Albuquerque Pride Board would hold the event; however, most of the tickets were given away to people and organizations that helped Albuquerque Pride throughout the years. Some Board Members would state that this event "was not much of a circle" and that the loss of revenue would affect producing Pride for 2012.

After introducing the Albuquerque HIV/AIDS Walk underneath the "umbrella" of Albuquerque Pride in 2011, Bunnie Cruse would make strides to provide financial support throughout New Mexico by the continuation of the event this year. The beneficiaries would be five New Mexican non-profit organizations which included N'MPower, Alianza of New Mexico, First Nations Community Health Source HIV, Navajo AIDS Network, and Albuquerque Pride, Inc. Albuquerque Pride would take the lead in assisting other organizations in 2012; however, as in the past taking on alternative community events would be detrimental to obtaining the intense budget requirements that needed to be obtained just to produce Albuquerque Pride. The AIDS walk would not be produced by Albuquerque Pride in 2013. Due to budget constraints, it would not be produced and sponsored again by Albuquerque Pride until 2016.

Other organizations who produced community events like the AIDS Walk would ask Albuquerque Pride to either assist or produce the entire event. This would be since Albuquerque Pride had consistently been the largest event in the State of New Mexico; however, the community did not realize the amount of capital that was needed to continue the event. Previous mission and vision statements for Albuquerque Pride in the 1990's to 2000's would focus primarily on the best interest of producing a Pride event in Albuquerque and nothing more. It was under the mission statements during these years that other GLBTQ organizations would be given the opportunity to promote their ideas, missions, and values at the annual Albuquerque Pride event held each June. The 2012 Albuquerque Pride Board of Directors and its members began defining the basic logistics of the whom, what, and how the organization would proceed despite what had been done in previous years. In a sense, Albuquerque Pride was under an "audit" from its current Board Members, simply dissecting the organization.

Despite taking on new events, Albuquerque Pride's focus would still be putting on the annual Parade and PrideFest. However, there were some other events that were sanctioned by Albuquerque Pride or produced by the organization itself:

June 2n	ABQ GAY DAY AT CLIFFS
June 2nd	LOS RANCHOS PRIDE 2ND ANNUAL (Abq. Pride Sponsors)
June 3rd	PAOLA BAGIGALUPI (located at Bookworks-4022 Rio Grande)
June 9th	ABQ PRIDE PRESENTS LAUGHTER LINKS US TOGETHER
June 14th	MAURICE SENDAK TRIBUTE STORYTIME (Bookworks)
June 15th	GAYCO'S SWEET SIXTEEN; SWALLOW YOUR PRIDE
June 22nd-23rd	ROCKY HORROR: GAY PRIDE EDITION (Guild Cinema)
June 24th	LOVE LINKS US TOGETHER (Pride Interfaith Worship Service)
June 28th	ALBUQUERQUE PRIDE CANDLELIGHT VIGIL
June 30th	ALBUQUERQUE PRIDE PARADE and PRIDEFEST

The sixth annual Albuquerque Gay Days kicked off the month of Pride events scheduled on June 2nd. Albuquerque Gay Day gave LGBTIQ individuals, their families, friends, and supporters a day to come together as a community for fun, sun, rides, food, water and excitement at Cliff's Amusement Park.The Pride Idol competition had become a "staple" for locating the next Albuquerque Performer to be part of the Mainstage at Pridefest. The competition started Tuesday May 8th at 9 p.m. at Sidewinders Bar. Different contestants competed every Tuesday until June 19th. On June 26th the weekly winners competed in the semi-finals for the three finalists that performed on the Mainstage at Pridefest on June 30th. They competed for over $1000 in prizes.

The "Laughter Links Us Together" Comedy Show was believed to be a first for Albuquerque Pride scheduled for Saturday, June 9, 2012. Albuquerque Pride in 2001 would sponsor a comedy night at Laff's Comedy Club, but it proved to be unsuccessful. Also, Albuquerque Pride would sponsor Funny Lesbians for Change which was held in the early 2000's. These also were limited in attendance. The 2012 event "Laughter Links Us Together" would have the comedy stylings of Dana Goldberg, Jason Dudey, and Ian Harvey, respectively, a lesbian, gay man, and a transgender man to Albuquerque's African-American Performing Art Center. Unfortunately, the event was a loss with poor attendance. The event would be noted as "Sadness Links Us Together" because of the lack of turnout. Despite these "downfalls" Albuquerque Pride would make great changes for Pridefest 2012.

Albuquerque's 36 annual Parade would be held Saturday, June 30, 2012. The biggest change for the Pride Parade would be moving the date to the end of June. For many years, the community had experienced the annual event scheduled for the second Saturday in June. The reason for establishing a consistent date was so that the community could plan. Also, InterPride would know about what events were planned throughout the year to avoid multiple Pride events on the same day. Typically, and statistically the date held in the second week in June would not yet be the hottest week in the month. Despite this change there were spectators in upwards of 20,000 on Central Avenue. Some parade entries would win awards judged on creativity, use of Rainbow Pride Colors, and the use of the theme "Pride Links Us Together."

Repeal of the Don't Ask, Don't Tell Act of 2010 (H.R. 2965, S. 4023) was a landmark United States federal statute enacted in December 2010, that established a process for ending the Don't ask, Don't tell(DADT) policy (10 U.S.C. § 654), thus allowing gays, lesbians, and bisexuals to serve openly in the United States Armed Forces. It ended the policy in place since 1993 that allowed them to serve only if they kept their sexual orientation secret and the military did not learn of their sexual orientation. The Act did not ban discrimination on the basis of sexual orientation in the military, as provided for in the proposed Military Readiness Enhancement Act. President Barack Obama, Defense Secretary Leon Panetta, and Chairman of the Joint Chiefs of Staff Admiral Mike Mullen provided the certification required by the Act to Congress on July 22, 2011. Implementation of repeal was completed 60 days later, so that DADT was no longer policy as of September 20, 2011. Albuquerque Pride would celebrate the milestone by having the American Veterans for Equal Rights (AVER) as the Grand Marshall for the 2012 Pride Parade.

The other 2012 Pride Parade Grand Marshal was actress and activist Linda Blair. From the age of five, Linda Blair had to get used to the spotlight, first as a child model and then as an actress, when out of 600 applicants she was picked for the role of Regan, the possessed child, in *The Exorcist* (1973). Linda quickly rose to international fame and won the Golden Globe. More recently, she had become an animal rights activist and humanitarian, working with PETA, Feed the Children, Variety-the Children's Charity, and other organizations. She had continued her activism working with local lesbian, gay, bisexual, transgender, intersex, and queer/questioning community.

There were also many changes made for PrideFest. The Mainstage was moved to the renovated and remodeled Villa Hispaña (also known as the Spanish Village). PrideFest took place here until 2000 when the event outgrew the space. In 2012 the space would be dedicated only to the Mainstage. There was local entertainment and headlining acts in the new professional outdoor performance stage with a covered seating area for 600 people. Villa Hispaña's renovations also included new landscaping and site lighting. The lineup for the Mainstage as follows:

11:00 a.m. Local Entertainment

1:30 p.m.	Manila Luzon
1:40 p.m.	Local Entertainment
2:00 p.m.	Manila Luzon
2:10 p.m.	JVigil
2:30 p.m.	Local Entertainment
2:50 p.m.	Manila Luzon
3:00 p.m.	Jojo

On the Mainstage would be touted as, "Hot Couture Realness Direct from NYC Headlines 2012 Albuquerque PrideFest Main Stage – Manila Luzon." She was an internationally acclaimed drag superstar known for her outrageous creations such as kimonos made of Ramen Noodle wrappers and other fierce sequined gowns. Celebrating her Filipino background, Manila was named after the capital of the Philippines, and her last name came from the Philippine island, Luzon. Manila was the first runner-up on the third season of RuPaul's Drag Race and had performed as a Drag Professor on RuPaul's Drag U on LOGO. She released her debut single "Hot Couture" which was co-written and produced by Grammy Award winning producers of KNS Productions which included Britney Spears and Lady Gaga.

JVigil was noted as an extraordinary local vocalist who joined the other headliners on the Mainstage. JVigil, a contemporary pop and R&B vocalist, began singing at the age of three. At the age of 17 he recorded a Spanish demo album as a tribute to his father, family and Hispanic heritage. He would perform to an audience who would immediately become his fans. In the future he aspires to record and release a Spanish track with Spanish lyrics infused with his English projects.

Award Winning Pop Sensation and Albuquerque PrideFest Headliner would be JoJo. She was an American singer, songwriter and actress. She performed in various singing competitions as a child. After competing on the television show *America's Most Talented Kids* in 2003, she was noticed by producers and received a recording deal with *Blackground Records*. JoJo released her debut album in June 2004. "*Leave (Get Out)*"; her debut single, reached number one on the *Billboard* Pop songs chart, which made her the youngest solo artist to have a number-one single in the United States at the age of thirteen. The song peaked at 12 on the Billboard Hot 100 and was certified gold. The album to date has since sold over four million copies worldwide.

JoJo released her second album *The High Road* which debuted at number 3 on the Billboard Top 200 and spawned the hit single *Too Little Too Late*. In 2010, she released her first ever mixtape *Can't Take That Away From Me* which saw over 185,000 downloads the first week of the release. In addition to her music career, JoJo also launched a career in acting. She made guest appearances on several television series, beginning with the 2002 American sitcom *The Bernie Mac Show* and later in *American Dreams* in 2004 and *Romeo!* in 2006. That same year, JoJo made her feature film debut in two major Hollywood films *Aquamarine* and *RV*. She starred in the Lifetime Television film *True Confessions of a Hollywood Starlet* in 2008. She would perform live and in-person, headlining on the 2012 PrideFest Mainstage, telling her story through music.

There would also be new venues located at PrideFest 2012. "Unleash" was a new attraction for adults to learn and experiment with ideas for enhancing their sexuality. It was a safe air-conditioned area that had vendors who sold merchandise and shared information. This attraction was for adults only and required a valid photo ID for entry. The guest speaker for Unleash was Patrick Mulcahey who presented on Master/slave, leather, and SM topics. Here was the schedule for the attraction:

11:00 a.m.	Shopping
12:30 p.m.	NM Leather League Presentation
1:30 p.m.	TNG Presentation
2:30 p.m.	"How to Play Kinky with a Cupcake" Class
3:30 p.m.	Patrick's Class
4:30 p.m.	Moonlight Creations Talk/Demo on Making Floggers
4:40 p.m.	Daniel's Demo
4:55 p.m.	Kevin's Demo

As in the past, pets were not allowed at Pridefest; however, in 2011 a Pet Park provided a space for pet owners and their pets to enjoy PrideFest. This ever-popular attraction would be continued in 2012. There were vendors, educational pieces, some pet services, contests and pet "babysitting" by the hour provided by New Mexico Pet Sitters Alliance. The VIP Area was relocated to an outdoor retreat which gave VIP's and guests the opportunity to relax and enjoy live music and entertainment. Courtesy drinks and complimentary food were provided by the Cooperage for their Sponsorship.

There were also a Band and Drag Stage that had local performers throughout the day where spectators could hear live music and watch the pageantry and spectacle of Albuquerque's greatest drag queen/king performers. The Wedding Area would be a continued event from 2011's Pridefest which offered that each couple would receive a certificate, sparkling cider punch, and a wedding cupcake. Reverend Judith Maynard performed the marriage rites from 12:00 p.m. to 4:00 p.m. Weeks before PrideFest occurred, registration was offered online that provided sample vows.

A new NMGRA Corral would provide a designated space for the New Mexico Gay Rodeo Association to showcase their horses and share their rodeo experiences. It was also a way for the organization to promote their local rodeo and membership. The Kids' Park offered a safe place with games and more provided by A Ton of Fun. The ever-popular Dance Tent was always a "big hit" with music, movement, and mayhem. Effex Night Club sponsored the Dance Tent and provided great DJ's throughout the day. Also, continuing from 2011 was the OUTspoken Poetry Slam. Theresa Davis was the featured artist known as an educator, activist, poet, artist, and pirate. She was also known as one of Atlanta's best performance poets.

The ever-popular Pride Art Show was sponsored by *albuquerqueARTS Magazine*. Artists of all ages, sexual orientations, and gender identities displayed their work at the 2012 PrideFest. The event was a juried exhibition of both professional and amateur artists. There was also a non-juried exhibition area for artists just wanting to display at PrideFest. The event was in the Fine Arts Building at EXPO New Mexico. A special Art Show Preview VIP Party for the artists, their families, and friends was hosted by Albuquerque Pride and *albuquerqueARTS Magazine* on Friday, June 29th from 5:30 p.m. to 7:00 p.m. Stephanie Hainsfurther was the coordinator.

A PrideFilm Festival that invited filmmakers to create their own 5-minute film for competition would be showcased at the 2012 PrideFest. The festival was created by multi-award-winning filmmaker, Brandon Scott Jensen, along with Roxanne Youngblood. Filmmakers had the month of May to create their film, which was then judged by a panel for prizes donated by local and national businesses. Each filmmaker was given his or her own off-beat genre. The filmmaker also needed to include a GLBTIQ character in the film using the theme "Pride Links Us Together." Filmmakers, guests, and attendees had the opportunity for film viewings at 1 a.m. and prizes were awarded at 3 pm.

Main Street & Vendor Square was a smoke-free place to meet and greet, find and make friends, do some fabulous shopping, and get something wonderful to eat. Fierce Pride would sponsor the "Queer the Air" at Main Street. Fierce Pride, a community LGBTIQ health advocacy group in New Mexico supports health providers in caring for the well-being of the communities and fires up LGBTIQ people to embrace their health by realizing that the gay community has been targeted by tobacco companies. At the time, statistics would reveal that the gay community smoked at twice the rate as straight people in New Mexico. Also, located on Main Street was a Classic Car Show brought to the attendees by the members of the Rainbow Roadrunners Car Club.

Finally, The Albuquerque Pride Archives would be reintroduced for 2012. The Board had asked PJ Sedillo, past President of Albuquerque, to spearhead this attraction which would reveal Pride's history in a collection of over 150 panels or memorabilia. It was stated, "this is your opportunity to remember and to learn about our Pride journey." The year 2012 had become a decisive year with change, transition, and growth. Despite this, the Albuquerque Pride Executive Board and extensive Board of Directors had "pulled off" one of the most successful Pride events experienced in its 36 years of existence. The entire event would be produced with a budget close to $200,000. Most outstandingly the event would be in the "black" and not in the "red." There would be "colored rainbows of success" on the horizon as well as some "black clouds" full of different challenges as preparation began to reach 40 years of Pride.

Chapter 13

Albuquerque Pride 2013, 2014, 2015 - Highlights of Pride - Growth and Controversy

Albuquerque Pride would encounter a 360-degree change of heart for Dr. PJ Sedillo and Tony Ross starting in 2013. The Albuquerque Pride Board in 2014 would honor Dr. PJ Sedillo with a Lifetime Achievement Award at the OUTstanding Awards which in 2014 was the most important fundraiser for Albuquerque Pride. Over 200 attendees at the awards would be part of and would experience all the pomp and circumstance like the *Oscars*. Jesse Lopez had discontinued Albuquerque Pride's membership with the Consolidated Association of Pride, Inc. (CAPI) organization in 2010. Albuquerque Pride would rejoin the organization in February 2015 realizing the importance of being a member of CAPI. This would be led by the effort of the Vice-President of Operations, J.R. LaBerge-Esparza to rebuild bridges.

In the years following these leadership transitions, Albuquerque Pride began a period of reflection and renewal. By 2013, individuals who had played key roles in the organization's early development were invited to participate in efforts to strengthen and rebuild Pride in Albuquerque. This marked a renewed recognition of the organization's history and the contributions of past leaders and community partners.

Honoring these positive contributions—from early organizations and advocates to former leaders—helped reaffirm Albuquerque Pride's foundation and values. This renewed appreciation of its history supported the organization's growth and helped prepare for the milestone 40th anniversary celebration in 2016.

Albuquerque Pride 2013

The 2013 Executive Pride Board would include a President, Vice President of Operations, Vice President of Public Relations, Treasurer, and Secretary. The framework of the organization would have the Executive Board responsible for supervising directors and other key volunteer positions.

At the helm was President Neil Macernie who would be responsible for ensuring that all responsibilities were moving smoothly forward. His Vice President of Operations, J.R. LaBerge-Esparza, would be responsible for supervising Tony Carson the Director of Pride Parade and Candlelight Vigil. The Director of Events, Gabby Gabaldon, would be responsible for supervising Bunnie Cruise Coordinator for the HIV/AIDS Walk. The

Director of Pridefest was left vacant; however, the individuals who should have been supervised under the Director of Pridefest were Amanda Coulburn Entertainment Coordinator; Erin Northern, Poetry Slam Coordinator: and Mattee Jim, Art Show Coordinator. Since this position was left vacant, it was the responsibility of J.R. LaBerge-Esparza to ensure that all of what was happening under the supervision of the Director of Pridefest would occur at Pridefest 2013.

Treasurer Raven Fox would be responsible for supervising the Director of Development, a position which was also left vacant. Craig La Berge-Esparza would be the Secretary who was responsible for the lead volunteer Kevin Binkley and the Office Manager which was now a vacant position. The Vice President of Public Relations was Miranda Haynes who supervised John Murphy, Director of Education; Andrew Harrison, Director of Marketing and Media; Shannon Massey, Director of Volunteers; and Jay Decker, Director of Titleholders. Jay Decker would be responsible for the 2013 New Mexico Pride Titleholders who were Mr. Ricardo Cruz, Miss Alea Rico, Ms. Stella Martin, and Miss Youth Hozhoni Sky. This would be the Board that would lead in producing Albuquerque Pride 2013.

Marriage Equality "same-sex marriage" would become legally recognized statewide in New Mexico through a ruling by the New Mexico Supreme Court on December 19, 2013. This required all county clerks to issue marriage licenses to qualified couples seeking marriage regardless of gender. Until then, same-sex couples could only obtain marriage licenses in certain counties of the state. Eight of 33 counties, covering 58% of the state's population, had begun issuing marriage licenses to same-sex couples in August and September of 2013. Because of this, Albuquerque Pride would celebrate the event with a marriage on Main Stage at PrideFest 2014.

This year, Antigay Protesters would also try to shut down the Albuquerque Pride Parade, which would be a first. In the past, protestors had been present, invited even so that the press would view their hatred; however, in 2013 the hatred had become even more enraged with the community. These so-called Christian protesters carried picket signs. One, who clearly had a gun strapped to his belt, would attempt a protest at the end of Albuquerque's LGBT Pride parade route in 2013 on San Mateo and Central Avenue.

The Pride crowd quickly shouted them down, resulting in a police escort that removed the hateful group from the scene. The event hit the national news with an article in the *Advocate Magazine*. This would be a first for the Albuquerque Police Department who would take and make a positive stand for the Pride spectators and participants. This decisive and unquestionable change would ensure that the Albuquerque Police Department's involvement and proclamation would safeguard that future protests would hopefully not occur in a disrespectful manner.

The police department, most who signed up for the event, had endured bullying and assumptions made that they were gay or lesbian (and not 'out'). Some officers would be LGBT while some had a family member in their life that was gay, but a declaration would not take place. This labeling as being gay or a "faggot sympathizer" would be stamped and branded upon those who would be part of this ever increasing "in your face" gay event. In the 1990's and early 2000's, most officers who would sign off to be part of the event would not "write their name on the dotted line" of the required permit prior to the day or actual day of the event. This would leave the directors, who were responsible for producing the Pride Parade, to be "on edge" as to whether the event would take place. If the specific determined number of APD officers duly noted on the City of Albuquerque Permit would not arrive for the event, the Board of Albuquerque Pride, as had occurred years previously, determined it would continue the event whether the police would be there.

Eventually, most officers would be forced to work the event. They would sign up for 'Chiefs Overtime' to participate for this event. Times in 2013 had drastically changed from the 20 years previously. The year had become extremely positive because past attitudes had been shattered a new vision of acceptance was evident and it was somewhat no longer a risk for the police to sign-up for overtime that would ultimately label them at a "homosexual sympathizer." This change of support would mean that future Prides in Albuquerque would not have to endure further physical hatred from the protestors such as what happened to the marcher in 1989 who was spat on by five protestors and hit on the head by protest sign; however, protestors in the future would still show up to use their hateful voices to protest against the Albuquerque Pride Parade and Pridefest.

The theme used for the 2013 Pride events again used the International Pride theme "PRIDE 365." The declaration of this theme showcased that Pride should occur and be honored each day of the year. The t-shirt would have the wording Pride 365 in black and underneath the wording Albuquerque Pride 2013 in a smaller font. The wording would be next to a world swirling with the rainbow colors.

The theme "Pride 365" was a proclamation that would be exercised for Albuquerque Pride in 2013. In the past, PJ Sedillo who had obtained his PhD in 2013, for over ten years attended InterPride and would be sanctioned and responsible for the workshop held at each conference to determine the selection of possible submitted themes. Every theme submitted had to be translated in every language attended at the conference. At that time many languages did not have a word for "Coming Out" or "Out."

His theme was presented and "tweaked" from the original submission "Pride 365-Reflections of Pride." It was simplified to Pride 365 which would be used for 2013. Themes had to be chosen two years in advanced based on the multitude of Prides that occurred around the globe. This theme would be chosen in Brussels in 2011 to be used for 2013. Furthermore, it would be decided to use part of the original submitted theme "Reflections of Pride" which would be voted upon and become the 2014 International Pride Theme. Dr. Sedillo had become instrumental in how the theme selection/process for InterPride would be presented and how the process would occur. His initiated procedures would be employed for the future determinations of how to select an international theme.

2013

The most controversial proclamation that the 2013 Albuquerque Pride Board had to contend with was the name change or wording of the Pride Parade. In 2013, some advertisements had noted the event as the HEWLETT PACKARD PRIDE PARADE. The community had concerns that the Gay community was "selling out" to corporate America.

The community asked questions such as, "Is the almighty dollar so important that we lose our integrity?" The majority of the GLBTQI community did not care about the wording as they understood the branding of events such as the most attended event in Albuquerque which had been noted as the Kodak International Balloon Fiesta.

A few members of the community, some of the same individuals from the past who had questioned the location and promotion of Pride in Albuquerque fifteen to twenty years earlier, would cause limited commotion; however, they would eventually produce a free event at Morningside Park for those to protest paying an entrance fee at the PrideFest grounds. On record none of these community members who had caused havoc for the past many years had ever served in the capacity as an Albuquerque Pride Board member. They would or could not understand the intricate and demanding Pride budget that would be over $200,000 to produce the events for 2013 or future events that would cost even more. Many, who did not serve on the Board, were unaware of the demands to produce this event for the past 37 years. They could not comprehend the importance of needed event sponsorship, thus the event title HEWLETT PACKARD PRIDE PARADE.

Albuquerque Pride would not be the only Pride that had been accused of "selling out to commercialism." Some other noted Prides such as those in Los Angeles and Seattle would similarly deal with this problem. During a dance party at Seattle Pride to proclaim against commercialism for Pride, a flash mob with rainbow flags created havoc in the streets smashing an America Apparel storefront and a Bank of America ATM. Most major Prides had to deal with this issue, and smaller Prides would have to deal with it in their future. This is one of the reasons why many unsanctioned Pride events hinder and do not assist in a positive promotion of Pride. These unsanctioned Pride events would plague Albuquerque Pride, and in 2013 a segment of the community would produce their own free Pride event after the parade. This "touted" free event would be located at Morningside Park.

PrideFest 2013 would have Joey Diamond as their headliner. Joey Diamond had declared himself as a celebrity who was anything and everything but ordinary. As a teenager who loved singing, sharing music in the world would become his passion. This YouTube Internet sensation would sign on for PrideFest entertainment as their Headliner; however, Joey Diamond would be a "No-Show." Despite this glitch, Albuquerque Pride was able to book Blu Cantrell as a last-minute replacement. Cantrell rose to fame in 2001 with the release of her debut single, *Hit 'Em Up Style (Oops!)*. It peaked at number two on the US *Billboard* Hot 100 and topped the US Mainstream Top 40 chart, along with charting across several countries and being included in her debut album, *So Blu*. The song earned Cantrell two Grammy Awards nominations. Later in 2003, Cantrell released her second album, *Bittersweet*, which was nominated for a Grammy Award and spawned the single "Breathe" (featuring Sean Paul); written and produced by Ivan Matias *Breathe* was a major success worldwide in 2003. It topped the European Hot 100 Singles and the

UK Singles Chart for four consecutive weeks and also reached the top ten of several other charts across the world.

Previous Pridefest attractions would be present in 2013 which included the Water and Play Park, Pet Park, Mainstage, Kids Park, Archives, Art Show, Wedding Area, Queer Poetry Slam and VIP "Fling." The VIP "Fling" would get the most complaints from sponsors because they felt that the area was not managed well and liquor lines were too long. Ultimately, this area needed to be enhanced.

There would also be new attractions for 2013. The Barn and Barrel Country Dance Area was somewhat of a success; however, it needed more promotion about the space to reach a new audience. There was also an En Fuego Dance Area. Some areas of future improvement would be for this area to have more décor and traditional music. The location was also in the sun, which made it too hot to dance in that area without shade. Also, some felt that this area also needed more promotion.

Despite these new attractions/areas that did not get positive attention, notably, an exciting and creative event for Albuquerque Pride would occur in 2013. The Board Members had decided to create an indoor dance space branded as the Rainbow Room Dance Club. This space had never been rented by Albuquerque Pride because of the massive 10,000 plus square feet space of the building known as the Manuel Lujan Building. Albuquerque Pride in the past had used the Creative Arts Building to showcase the archives but had incorporated an indoor car show, Queer Bake Off, and Poetry Slam within one building similar in dimensions.

In 2013 the Albuquerque Pride Board would take a risk to produce this new venue an indoor dance club to replace the outdoor dance tent space. The massive space would be transformed into a nightclub including go-go dancers, named DJ's spinning music, a high intensity light show, and tables for sitting and relaxing while listening to the intense-high energy music. There would be a sectioned off area for those who were over 21 who could partake in beer or liquor. Above all, this new location for dancing (previously known as the Pride Dance Tent), would be an air-conditioned place indoors full of excitement. The Albuquerque Pride Board in 2013 would "hit it out of the ballpark" for creating a new and exciting venue, one that would be recorded in this history. Because of these simple, risk-taking events, Pride in Albuquerque was ensured its existence.

Despite some negative experiences encountered in 2013 that could have resulted in its destruction, Albuquerque Pride would rise out as a "Phoenix of Pride" an organization transformed and ready to proceed forward to sustain the very original intentioned missions of all Prides in the world. Albuquerque Pride would continue to have an event each year that would generate a celebration to honor those brave "Stonewallian" individuals from 1969.

Albuquerque Pride 2014

The Albuquerque Pride Board for 2014 would be like the 2013 Board. Miranda Haynes would leave the Albuquerque Pride Board as the Vice President of Public Relations and the position would be left vacant. Patrick Rubio would be added as the new En Fuego coordinator. He would oversee the new attraction entitled the En Fuego Latin Dance Stage. However, the Director of Pridefest was still vacant and not filled from 2013. J.R. LaBerge-Esparza would be responsible for supervising this event. Under the supervision of the Secretary Craig LaBerge-Esparza a new position known as the Official Photographer would be created with Max Woltman filling the job. This would not be the first time that Albuquerque Pride would have an Official Pride Photographer as a Board position. Also, under Craig's supervision would be the Director of Marketing and Media spot which would be filled by Andrew Harrison.

Director of Titleholders for 2014, supervised under Secretary Craig LaBerge-Esparza, again would be Jay Decker. Notably in 2014, for the first time in the New Mexico Pride Pageant Miss NM Pride Bryan Andre Sears, aka Jacquêsán Taylor Stratton, would become the first African American to win the title. Also, selected as New Mexico Pride Titleholders for 2014 were Mr. Pride Damian DeLa Amor, and Miss Youth Denaili A'Dare. They would represent their titles well.

The Stonewall Riots celebrated 45 years in 2014, and Albuquerque Pride was pleased to announce the 37th Annual PrideFest celebrating the LGBTIQ community in New Mexico. The year's theme was "Reflections of Pride –Stonewall 45." The organization known as the Gay & Lesbian Alliance Against Defamation (GLADD) officially added the Q (Queer/Questioning) to the acronym in its resource guide in 2016 because younger LGBTQ+ Americans reclaimed the word as they embraced a shift toward fluidity in identity. Widespread use grew from there because GLAAD had officially added the Q to the acronym in its resource guide in 2016 and other organizations would follow as did Albuquerque Pride.

The 2014 InterPride (international) Pride Theme was "Reflections of Pride – Stonewall 45" which was intended to celebrate and honor the Stonewall Riots that occurred that hot and volatile summer evening of June 28, 1969. The t-shirt used the logo and theme from InterPride; however, it was not an overall "best" seller for merchandise. Despite the lack luster logo the Executive Board of Directors stated that this theme "gives us the opportunity to celebrate how far we have come while still reminding us how much more we still need to accomplish in our community."

2014

The event press released from Albuquerque Pride provided the following information:

Date: Saturday, May 31, 2014
Time: 10:00 – 11:30 Parade / 11:00 to 6:30 Main Festival
Place: Expo NM
Tickets: $15 at abqpride.com/tickets
Info: 505-873-8084 or info@abqpride.com

PrideFest and the Pride Parade for the first time in the 37 years existence of Pride in Albuquerque would have events held that occurred in May and not the second Saturday in June or in the month of June. The events were scheduled in May 2014. One of the main reasons for the change in date was the heat in June. This would be a drastic change because June had been considered as the "sacred" month for Pride to honor the Stonewall Riots. This commemoration of the Stonewall Riots would be the primary reason why Albuquerque Pride for many years had been held the second Saturday in June or sometime in that month. The consistency of the date was also helpful for other Prides in the State of New Mexico to plan as well as other Prides held throughout the U.S. and the world.

Due to the date change, the attendance was lower than previous years. This was attributed to the fact that many had come accustomed to Pride in Albuquerque occurring in June. Many would be furious when they heard that they had missed the date because they had not been notified that the date for Albuquerque Pride had been moved. The general negative response was that Albuquerque Pride did not keep and honor the traditions of the past of Pride by moving the event from the month of June to May. Many community members felt that having the event in June was a sacred, celebratory event that should not have "been messed with" especially when it came to moving it away from June. Others would also state vehemently that the event should have been moved especially since President Obama's Presidential Proclamation stated June 2014 as Lesbian, Gay, Bisexual, and Transgender Pride Month.

Albuquerque had tried to show the community of the date change by providing research that revealed that approximately 41% of the Pride celebrations worldwide were not celebrated in June. However, educating the masses about changes for Albuquerque Pride had always been a struggle. In 2013 social media had become a powerful force to get information out to the community. Social media was utilized to somewhat alleviate the problem of getting information about changes made for Pride; however, there were many older members of the GLBT community who did not use email, *Twitter,* or were on *Facebook*. They would not be provided information about any changes. Another problem existed because there were no longer New Mexican Gay "print" publications/magazines that existed in 2013 to help promote the event or notify people of any changes.

According to the Board Members of Albuquerque Pride another reason why the event was moved from May to June was due to the weather (extensive heat) as the biggest factor. Many Prides in the United States did not have their celebrations in June because of the heat. Albuquerque Pride felt that this was one of the major factors for moving the event to May. Also, some Prides had moved their celebration to coincide with National Coming Out Day or LGBT History Month which were both held in October.

Despite the facts about other Pride events that are not held in June, the event moving to May had not been properly vetted or evaluated. The community had not been entirely educated about why the event had been moved to May. The community was not surveyed as to whether to move the date or not. The Board, who made this decision, would have to be accountable to those who were upset. In the end, because of the dedicated, strong and courageous Executive Board of Directors led by President Neil Macernie, the Board would successfully make it out of the "muck," regroup, and plan next year's PrideFest and the Pride Parade for 2015. Despite this mistake, the Pride Board would be prepared and ready for the 2014 event.

Thursday, May 29th, at 7:30 p.m. would be the Albuquerque Pride Candlelight Vigil at Morningside Park on Lead and Morningside. This would again be a time for the community to come together to remember and show respect for one of the first gay and lesbian memorials in the United States dedicated specifically for a Pride event. Notably, the first Trans March in Albuquerque's history would take place on May 29th, as part of this year's Pride activities. Organizers of the march said that Albuquerque was the second city in the Southwest region, and only the eighth city in the United States and Canada to organize a Trans March. The marchers ended at Morningside Park where they joined those for the Albuquerque Pride Candlelight Vigil.

On Friday, May 30th, at 7:00 p.m. the Century 21 Unica Real Estate Art Show Reception took place at Expo New Mexico in the Hispanic Arts Building. On Saturday, May 31st at 10:00 a.m. would be the 38th Annual Albuquerque Pride Parade presented by T-Mobile. The Pride Parade would again start from UNM at Girard and Central going east to Expo New Mexico to Gate 3.

In 2014, Albuquerque Pride would celebrate marriage equality in the state of New Mexico by having Equality New Mexico as the Grand Marshal. Equality New Mexico had played an instrumental part in making marriage equality a reality in New Mexico. Along with Equality New Mexico many of the newly legally married same sex couples joined the parade to celebrate marriage equality. PrideFest 2014 would also showcase areas to dance, music, art, fun, and diversity. The celebration took place on May 31st from 11:00 a.m. to 6:30 p.m. at Expo NM. Tickets were $15 each. Children ten and under were also free for this family friendly event. About 10,000 people all over the Southwest attended Pridefest 2014.

In addition to Albuquerque Pride's three New Mexico Pride Titleholders there were many local and national talents performing on the Xfinity Main Stage (wording changed from *Mainstage*). Alex Newell brought his gleeful music to excite the crowd. Beverly McClellan from *The Voice* got the audience to their feet, and Colton Ford rocked the house. The following were some of the attractions located at Pridefest 2014:

- Hewlett-Packard Main Street Experience
- Xfinity Main Stage presented by 93.3 KOB-FM
- Century 21 Unica Real Estate Art Show
- Water and Play Park for Adults sponsored by 99.5 Magic FM
- OUTspoken Poetry Slam sponsored by 103.3 ED-FM
- Effex Night Club Rhinestone Roundup Country Dance Stage sponsored by 92.3 KRST

- Effex Night Club Rainbow Room Dance Club
- Effex Night Club En Fuego Latin Dance Stage presented by Severo y Grupo Fuego
- Albuquerque Pride Archives
- Lexus of Albuquerque Car Show
- Wells Fargo Kids Park sponsored by 99.5 Magic FM
- Fiat Fun Zone
- Reflections of Pride Archives

There would be no major changes for the 38th Annual PrideFest with the set-up of attractions, booths and vendors at EXPO NM except for one new attraction for PrideFest 2014. This would be the UNM Pride Village located in the EXPO NM Flower Building directly east of the Xfinity Main Stage. The UNM Pride Village would have information booths pertaining to the different groups at UNM such as the UNM Hospital, Agora Crisis Center, UNM LGBTQ Resource Center, and American Civil Liberties Union to name a few. The Truman Clinic providing free HIV testing was also located in this area.

In 2014, Mainstreet at PrideFest with over 200 exhibitors/booths would be titled as Hewlett-Packard Main Street Experience. Interesting enough the sponsorship would be only for Mainstreet because of the controversy the year before for naming the parade the 2013 HEWLETT PACKARD PRIDE PARADE.

The Pride Main Stage would still occur at the Spanish Village and be known as the Xfinity Main Stage presented by 93.3 KOB FM. The entertainment schedule for the Pride Main Stage was as follows:

11:00 a.m.	DJ Music
11:40 a.m.	Opening Session-Presentation of Colors & National Anthem
12:00 p.m.	Meg Mackey
12:30 p.m.	Alibi Weddings
12:50 p.m.	Denali A'Dare
12:55 p.m.	Ka La Kapu Polynesian Dance School
1:25 p.m.	Damian Dela Amor
1:30 p.m.	Severo y Grupo Fuego
2:30 p.m.	Throb
2:35 p.m.	Colton Ford
2:55 p.m.	Encore
3:00 p.m.	Parade Winner Announcements & Recognitions
3:30 p.m.	Jacqueson Taylor Stratton
3:25 p.m.	Alex Newell
3:55 p.m.	Royalty Hour with Phoenix Pride's Barbara Seville & Eddie Broadway

4:55 p.m. Beverly McClellan
5:40 p.m. Bella Gigante
5:50 p.m. Off Broadway Dance Studio
6:15 p.m. Christian Ticey
6:20 p.m. Anita Date
6:30 p.m. Closing Ceremony

The Headliners for the Albuquerque PrideFest Mainstage would be Colton Ford, Alex Newell, and Beverly McClellan. Colton Ford was the stage name of the former American gay pornographic actor, Glenn Soukesian, who returned to his original career path of singer and actor. Colton Ford appeared in a dozen gay adult celebrated films. Notable performances included *Conquered* that earned him 2002 Grabby Awards for "Best Group Sex Scene." His lead role in *Colton* would also garner him "Gay Performer of the Year" during the 2003 GayVN Awards. He appeared in his first mainstream film in the 2005 documentary *Naked Fame* directed by Christopher Long. The film followed Ford's transition from the world of adult films to a vocal artist for mainstream club/dance music. The movie was circulated in 2005 primarily in the United States and Canada. Ford could also be seen on the television series *The Lair* where he co-starred for three seasons playing the role of Sheriff Trout. The series was broadcast on *here! TV*.

Ford became a club/dance, house music singer-songwriter and released several singles. His first album, *Tug of War* was produced in 2008. He was then offered to open for the True Colors Tour with Cindi Lauper. His second album, *Under the Covers* was released in 2009. In 2013, he released his third album *The Way I Am*. He had several hit singles and videos, including Billboard charting, *The Way I Am, That's Me, Let Me Live Again,* and *Losing My Religion.* His cover of Stevie Wonder's *Signed, Sealed, Delivered I'm Yours* was vocally collaborated with Club/Dance singer-songwriter Pepper Mashay. The song would peak at #9 on the Hot Dance Club Play and #25 on the Hot Dance Singles Sales charts.

The second Albuquerque Pride Headliner would be Alex Newell, an American actor and singer. He was known for playing the transgender student Unique Adams on the Fox musical series *Glee.* Alex Newell was among 34,000 to submit an audition video in 2011 for the first season of Oxygen's *The Glee Project*. Producers were so impressed that they decided to bring him on *Glee* for two episodes.

Alex first appeared on *Glee* in the third season episode and was cast in the role of Wade "Unique" Adams, a male-to-female transgender teenager. Wade broke ground by being one of the most visible transgender characters on television and one of the first on a network prime time show. His character would allow him to rejoin the cast for the show's fourth and fifth season. In the final season (the sixth) he had become an integral part of the regular cast. His highlighted song was during the sixth season when he performed "*I*

Know Where I've Been" from *Hairspray*. Over the years, Alex Newell has sung at numerous events, such as the Coachella Festival, but also at many LGBT events and Gay Pride festivals. He announced in October 2013 that he had been signed by *Big Beat Records* where he would release his debut album. His debut single "Nobody to Love" was released on June 3, 2014.

The final headliner for the 2014 PrideFest Main Stage was Beverly McClellan. Beverly McClellan was an American singer and a contestant on the first season of the American TV series *The Voice* where she reached the final four. She first played with Tammy Gorden in a duo called Uncommon Ground and later formed her own band called DJ's Daughter. She was able to record with that band and began playing for many gigs. It is then that she decided to begin to perform as a solo act.

While Beverly McClellan was recording in the studio, her producer invited her to try out for the first season of *The Voice*. Prior to auditioning for the show, McClellan had already recorded five independent albums without having been signed by any record label. She was coached by Christina Aguilera and finished in 3rd/4th place in the competition. McClellan also was an openly Lesbian artist. In June 2011, she appeared on the cover of *SHE* magazine, a South Florida lesbian magazine.

As stated previously, the 2014 year's theme "Reflections of Pride – Stonewall 45" would provide the LGBTQI community the opportunity to celebrate how far they had come while still reminding them how much more they still needed to accomplish in the Gay community. Despite problems that occurred in 2014, lessons learned would help the Board of Directors produce a successful 2015 event.

Albuquerque Pride 2015

The amount of Board Members for Albuquerque Pride had fluctuated in the past 39 years between having a massive Board to having only a few key participants. Many would debate that the more Board members an organization has, including directors, the more the work is spread out and the individual workload is less. However, on the other side with a smaller Board of Directors and members, there is less bureaucracy. Decisions, thus, can be made easily and not questioned and questioned and questioned. In 2012, 2013, and 2014 there would be over 25 Board Members and Directors each year. In 2015 there would be a total of five Executive Board Members, five Coordinators, an Official Photographer, and a position for an Office Manager that would still be vacant.

The Executive Board for 2015 would consist of President Neil Macernie who would supervise the Office Manager position that would be vacant. In 2016, there would be no mention of procuring an Office Manager. The next Executive Board Member was Vice President of Operations J.R. LaBerge-Esparza who would supervise the HIV/AIDS Walk Coordinator Bunnie Cruse; Entertainment Coordinator, Amanda Colburn; Poetry Slam

Coordinator, Erin Northern; En Fuego Coordinator, Patrick Rubi; and the Art Show Coordinator Mattee Jim. The Director of Pride Parade and Candlelight Vigil would be Tony Carson noted as an Executive Board Member but under the supervision of J.R. LaBerge-Esparza.

Craig LaBerge-Esparza would be elected to serve as the Vice President of Public Relations, and the Treasurer was Raven Fox. The position was still open for Director of Development. Finally, Gabby Gabaldon would be Albuquerque Pride's Secretary for 2015. Gabby would be responsible for supervising the Official Pride Photographer, Max Woltman. The 2015 New Mexico Pride Titleholders would be Miss NM Pride Lady Hawk, Miss NM Pride Youth Serket Vane and Mr. NM PrideTyrese T. Stratton.

There would be major changes made for Albuquerque Pride in 2015 because of the backlash of having the event in May which resulted in lower attendance. The Board would move the Pride Parade and Pridefest back to the original date which was the second Saturday in June. Also, because of the expanded uses of space at EXPO NM, the event looked and felt as if it had even more of a lower "turnout." Therefore, the Mainstage would be moved back to its 2012 "big tent" original location. This new Board finally realized that "aha moment" when they needed to look at the past so that fumbles in the future would not take place.

Thursday, June 11, at 7:30 p.m. would be the annual Candlelight Vigil at Lead Ave. and Morningside Drive. Friday, at 7:00 p.m.at Expo New Mexico would be the Art Show and Reception sponsored by Century 21 Unica Relators. This was a free event on the state Fairgrounds and was in the Hispanic Arts Building.

Saturday, June 13, 2015, would be the 39th Annual Albuquerque Pride Parade presented by T Mobile. The theme chosen for Albuquerque Pride would also be the international theme "Color Our World with Pride." The t-shirt image is printed on an orange shirt. This would be the color designated for only the volunteers to wear. Providing a t-shirt to volunteers became a "badge of honor" and sometimes past t-shirts would be exchanged for new ones. The t-shirt sold to the public would be only offered in white to be sold. Also, not shown is the back of the t-shirt for volunteers, staff, board of directors etc. who would have all the sponsors and their logos on the back who partnered with Albuquerque Pride that year. This was a benefit that would be offered and became a staple and request from sponsors.

2015

June 2015 marked the first year that there were no protesters on the parade route for the Albuquerque Pride Parade. All attractions for the PrideFest would be located on the Hewlett-Packard Main Street Experience. The UNM Pride Village would be moved to the African Arts Pavilion. This would be a first for purchasing this building for Albuquerque Pride. Also new would-be gender-neutral bathrooms located at PrideFest.

The Pocket Pride Guide, which was now the only form of information passed out, would be used by participants to find the location of each attraction. By 2015 a Pride Program would not be produced, and most of the advertisement and information occurred on Pride's website, Facebook and Twitter Account, and in the *Alibi* newspaper. The Pocket Pride Guide for 2015 did not provide names of the vendors and times of performances on the Mainstage. Performers were broken down into categories. The following were the performers for 2015:

Titleholders
Lady Hawk- Miss NM Pride
Typrese T. Stratton Mr. NM Pride
Serket – Miss Youth NM Pride

Drag Perfomers
Kaleb T. Stratton
Felicia Minor (AZ)
Tsunami Couture
Coco Bardot
Trey C. Michaels
Christian Ticey
Jessica R. Daniels
Josephine Justice
Freddy Prinze Charming (AZ)
Raven Fox

Live Music
Severo y Grupo Fuego
Tanya Griego
Taralynn & AJ Martinez
Ernestine Romero
Underground Cadence

Dance Groups
Throb
Déjà vu Dance Crew
Off Broadway Dance Studio
Enchantment Dance Studio
NM Ballet Company
Ritmo Dancers

Track Performers
Prince Julian Wolf
Marissa Sandoval
G. Precious

By 2015 one of the most loved and celebrated TV shows in the Gay community was *RuPaul's Drag Race* which was an American reality competition television series produced by World of Wonder for Logo TV. The show documents RuPaul in the search for "America's next drag superstar." RuPaul played the roles of host, mentor, and source of inspiration for this series. Contestants were given different challenges each week. *RuPaul's Drag Race* employed a panel of judges, including RuPaul, Michelle Visage and a host of other guest judges, who critiqued contestants' progress throughout the competition. The headliners for the PrideFest Mainstage would be from *RuPaul's Drag Race.* They were Jaidyn Diore, Jasmine Masters, Kennedy Davenport, Tempest Dujour, and Mrs. Kasha Davis.

Chapter 14

Albuquerque Pride 2016 - 40 Years "Solidarity Through Pride"

Neil Macernie as President wanted to ensure that all voices would be heard concerning the new direction of Pride in Albuquerque; therefore, from 2011 to 2015 he would start off with about ten Board members that would eventually swell to over 25 individuals on the Board. All Board members would be required to attend sanctioned Board meetings. Because of the size number of attendees at the meetings, they would last for three hours or more.

Neil Macernie, and past presidents of Pride would come to the realization that having a smaller Executive Board and Directors would ensure that actions and authorizations for the event could be discussed and voted on which would lead to easier and less time-consuming Board meetings. Pride Boards experienced many time constraints, and as a business these constraints were encountered on a weekly basis. Neil had experienced how a larger Board "bogged" down the procedures for Pride with numerous viewpoints being repeated repeatedly. Therefore, the Albuquerque Pride Board in 2016 would become extremely "streamlined."

The Albuquerque Pride website would state, "The Pride Board consists of the Executive Committee and the Planning Committee. These Board members work all year long to produce the New Mexico Pride Pageant, OUTstanding Awards, the New Mexico HIV/AIDS Walk, the Pride Parade and PrideFest." The Executive Board consisted of Neil Macernie-President, Craig LaBerge-Esparza-Vice President of Public Relations, J.R. LaBerge-Esparza-Vice President of Operations, Miranda Sedillo-Secretary (who had returned to the Board), and Raven Foxx-Treasurer who would resign from the position in May of 2016 one month before the events scheduled in June. The position would be left vacant, and the collective Board would assume the duties of the treasurer. The Albuquerque Pride Board would be responsible for procuring and securing the overwhelmingly demands of obtaining the 2016 proposed budget which was $183,000. As a reminder, the Gay & Lesbian Pride Week '88 was budgeted for $1,475.00. Twenty-eight years had seen a great increase in the proposed budget.

The Albuquerque Pride Board of Directors consisted of Tony Carson, Thomas Higgs, Jonathan Martinez, Patrick Rubi and Marcos Sedillo. The 2016 New Mexico Pride Titleholders were Miss NM Pride-Lady Shug, Mr. NM Pride-Tre Brewbaker, and Miss Youth NM Pride-Cherri Heartattack who became the youngest individual who would ever win the title of Miss New Mexico Pride Youth. She was fourteen years of age in 2016, and she would have the support of her entire family who attended the event to see her crowned.

The Albuquerque Pride Board began to plan the events for 2016; however, this "streamlined" new Board would come face to face with individuals in the past who had questioned the "materialism" of Pride and selling out commercially. These individuals also began to produce a Pride event at Morningside Park to occur after the Pride Parade during the same time as the Albuquerque Pridefest.

PJ Sedillo would be asked to attend a Board meeting in March of 2016 to present past historical events that had been conducted within the 39 years of Pride in Albuquerque. The Pride Board would be exploring, studying, and considering similar events that could be presented to the community for a "40 days to Pride" which was similarly done in 2006 for the 30th Anniversary.

Dr. PJ Sedillo was honored to support the 2016 Pride Board as he had been denoted as the official archivist/historian for Pride. In 2014, he had decided to produce a book to showcase and highlight the struggles, experiences, and historical accounts of Pride in Albuquerque. This came to fruition in 2016 where he introduces Solidarity Through Pride which one best book in NM/Arizona in 2018. This book is a sequel from that original text which is now out of print. Dr. Sedillo would state that Pride started from the few, leading to the many. In essence "Albuquerque's Stonewall" would embody the reverse declaration of "E Pluribus Unum" referring to "out of many, one," Pride in Albuquerque would become "out of few, to become many, to become one."

Notably, for 2015 and the year before, there were a few volunteers who would assist with ensuring the events would happen. In 2016, most individuals who would assist in the massive "move in" to Expo New Mexico that usually occurred on Thursday would be hired employees. This would be one of the most important decisions that the Albuquerque Pride Board would make. Since the office manager had never been replaced, it would be easy to use that budgeted salary allotment to hire individuals for the dreaded set-up and tear-down of the event. No longer would the Executive Board of Directors have to "break their backs" to set-up, put on the event, tear-down and take placards, computers, tables, chairs, and clipboards back to the Pride office to await another Albuquerque Pride. There would be assistance from these hired individuals.

Some of the events prior to the annual Pride Parade and Pridefest produced from the 2016 Albuquerque Pride Board would be the LGBTIQ Prom Night which would be reintroduced to the community after many years of not occurring. The event would be followed by the OUTstanding Awards on March 26, 2016, at Sandia Resort and Casino.

Also, in 2016, the Albuquerque Public Schools would adopt a gender identity policy into the Student Handbook that addressed transgender inclusion on March 16th. Albuquerque Pride Board members showed their support for this policy at the meeting with the President of ABQ Pride and other advocates who addressed the Board on the issue. As in the past, since Albuquerque Pride was the largest and most influential organization in the State, it would be of utmost importance for the President of Albuquerque Pride to speak out about the importance of this issue.

2016 Front

In 2016, this would be the first year that there would not be a conclusive declarative theme chosen for the 40th Annual Parade and PrideFest; the closest would be "40 Years of Pride" and "40 Years Proud." The InterPride Theme for 2016 was "Solidarity Through Pride," and some Board members did not want to use the theme because they had felt that it was too harsh and depressing for a 40-year celebration. There would be no official theme that could be properly used for branding purposes. Time would be limited to ask the community to summit a possible logo design to be considered for 2016, 40 years of Pride.

2016 Back

Eventually, the Board would declare the 2016 event as ALBUQUERQUE PRIDEFEST for branding purposes. This wording would be "flashingly" highlighted with a sanctioned event using the Albuquerque Pride Logo which was proceeded by the wording PRIDEFEST. The emblem for 2016 was "retro" looking and shaped as an eight-pointed asterisk with each spoke a different color. The same color of dots within the spoke, from large to small, would descend into the middle to the end of the asterisk. The 2016 logo was strikingly beautiful and very marketable.

The wording 40 years would be added to the back of the t-shirts and on Pride hats (first time introduced). This would be the first t-shirt that had a logo on the front and wording on the back (normally used for sponsors). Problematic for Albuquerque Pride they would not be able to include the celebratory 40 years in most of the advertising, placards, and the official Albuquerque Pride Pocket Pride Guide. Subsequently, even on the homepage of the Albuquerque Pride website did not mention the 40 years Pride in Albuquerque. This would be fixed closer to the date of Pride.

In due course, the International Pride Theme that was not utilized in 2016 would be revealed and revered and integrated into Pride on Sunday. On Sunday morning after the completion of an awesome Pride Parade and PrideFest, horrific events in Orlando, Florida would, "shock the Gay community to its core" and the significance of "Solidarity Through Pride" would ring throughout Albuquerque, New Mexico, the U.S and the world. Explanation of the importance of introducing this theme will be presented in the coming pages.

Thursday, June 10th, would be the tenth annual celebration of the Candlelight Vigil. Past celebrations had titled the event as the "Candle-Light Vigil," "candlelight vigil," and the "Candle-light of Remembrance." Although there have been different words to brand this event in the last ten years, the Candlelight Vigil would become a sacred, introduction to the Pride events that would follow. Tony Ross, a past Pride President, treasurer, and Board member for over seventeen years, would recount overwhelmingly that, "Pride did not start until after the Candlelight Vigil took place." As a past protector/Board member of Albuquerque Pride, he would further assert that, "it was a time for him to stop and reflect about who he was and where he had come from." In essence the Candlelight Vigil for Tony Ross and others who had been part of the 40 years celebration and those who were brand new to the event would experience a connectedness that brought all together as a family.

The event would be powerful. The schedule would start off with the national anthem and the AVER presenting the colors. PJ Sedillo would speak about the history of Pride; Reverend Judith Maynard would give the invocation; the Encantada Band (comprised of GLBTQI musicians) and NM Gay Men's Choir all would perform under the chance of thunderstorms and rain. The goal was to have all candles lit before a downpour would occur. PJ Sedillo, past president of Albuquerque Pride and historian, would solemnly deliver at the Candlelight Vigil the following history of Pride in Albuquerque:

> So here we are 40 years later honoring those brave 25 individuals who started at the MCC located on Copper and Central after getting free donuts at Kapps and some who would march from Foxes and proceed on the South

sidewalk of Central Avenue to UNM to meet with Juniper...a gay organization in New Mexico in 1976. After the meeting some would proceed back to MCC and come upon others who did not know the event had occurred but still wanted to participate. This year's International Pride Theme is 'Solidarity Through Pride.' The definition of solidarity means unity or agreement of feelings or action, especially among individuals with a common interest where there is mutual support within a group. Yet, throughout our 40-year history we sometimes did not show solidarity, and it is amazing how Pride in Albuquerque has continued.

Whether it was the infighting to incorporate in the 1970's, the lack or harmony and cooperation between the gays and lesbians in the 1980's especially with the condescending wording of Galesbian to try to force unification, and in the mid 1980's AIDS had reared its ugly head in NM. That was a time when we as a community came together and showed true solidarity. It sometimes takes difficult times to smack us in the head and unify.

In 1996, Pride left Common Bond to incorporate and become Albuquerque Pride. The community again would fail to come together and attack the Pride Committee; however, the event survived and grew more prosperous. I can truly state that Pat Baillie and I became co-presidents for six years where we would bring that solidarity and needed healing between the gay and lesbian community. Pride would make the biggest decision in 2000 to move from the Spanish Village to Main Street at Expo New Mexico. In that year the parade was noted as the 3rd Largest Parade in the State of New Mexico with over 10,000 spectators and over 150 entries.

So here we are celebrating 10 years of the Candlelight Vigil and 40 years of Pride here in Albuquerque. We should honor the fact that there are only 6 other Prides older that our event and that there are only two other known Memorials for the Gay Movement and one of those is here in Morningside Park we have been truly blessed as a community and for that I state that we all embody the true meaning of Solidarity Through Pride. See you in 2056 when we celebrate 40 more years of Pride."

After PJ Sedillo recited the history of Pride, President Neil Macernie introduced the Board, NM Pride Titleholders and Dignitaries. During this section of the event, it started to lightly rain, and thunder could be heard in the background. By the time the candles were all lit the rain stopped, and in a magical cue a rainbow appeared in the sky to the west. It is at that moment that the NM Gay Men's Chorus began to sing "Somewhere Over The Rainbow."

In 2016, the Albuquerque Pride Board would plan from Friday, June 10th to Sunday, June 12th, a three-day PrideFest in commemoration of 40 years of Pride. Friday's events would include exhibitor booths, an art reception, movie in the park, a pet parade, and carnival rides. All events would be free except for the carnival rides. Saturday was to be the main event for $15 at the gate. The main event presented a Mainstage, En Fuego Stage, car show, family fun zone, carnival rides, Pride archives, water/play park, UNM Pride Village, Main Street exhibitors, and art show. Sunday would be a free bandstand concert at the En Fuego stage, also known as the Box Car Stage which was the original Mainstage in 2001 when Albuquerque Pride decided to move from the Spanish Village to Main Street of Expo New Mexico.

Friday, June 10th, was a free event with most of the booths being open for people to view. The Art Show Preview would open with free food and drinks for the public provided by the sponsorship of the Cooperage (restaurant); The Pride Archives would be open for review, and for the second time in Pride history, carnival rides would be available for those in attendance; however, those who would partake would need to pay for their ride. The event would end with a movie night held at the "Boxcar Stage" were *Jurassic III*, an American Science Fiction adventure primarily about dinosaurs would be shown. Some would question why this movie was chosen over the many gay iconic movies from which to choose.

The 40th Annual Albuquerque Pride Parade was scheduled for Saturday, June 11th. Set-up time, line-up, and route would be the same as what was conducted in 2015. The Grand Marshals for 2016 were past Presidents of Albuquerque Pride. Tony Ross, pat baillie (with lower case letters to honor how she originally preferred her name to be written), and PJ Sedillo would ride together in a convertible provided by the Rainbow Roadrunners Car Club. Their names along with other Presidents' names covered the car. PJ, Tony, and pat would all wear rainbow pride capes with the wording "Albuquerque Pride-President Emeritus." They all would be honored as they rode down Central Avenue and reminisced about how the parade used to be and how it had amazingly and powerfully grown. They would reflect about their many years of service when they were in charge; and because they were responsible to ensure that the event ran smoothly, they could not take time to enjoy the event. Now in 2016, as Grand Marshals, all three would be able to savor the Parade while sitting on top of the back of a convertible decorated with rainbow boas and flowers. PJ Sedillo, pat baillie, and Tony Ross had bubbles in hand to blow at the spectators. PJ Sedillo would state, "Riding with pat baillie his co-president for ten years and his devoted husband Tony would be surreal." These Grand Marshals for the 40th anniversary would encounter a dreamlike experience that brought to light the past, present and future; all coming together at once.

Interesting enough, Neil Macernie was to ride in front of the Grand Marshals in his own car. As has happened in the past, there were not enough cars to go around, and he gave up his car so that Lady Shug-Miss NM Pride 2016 could ride in the parade. Neil would hop into the Grand Marshal car and sit in the passenger seat. With bullhorn in hand, he would tout witty sayings heading east on Central. Within the car were three Past Albuquerque Pride Presidents and the current one Neil Macernie, whose years of service added together came to be over 40 years of making sure the Pride event occurred each year in Albuquerque.

The Parade followed the same route as that of 2003 and entered gate three for the annual PrideFest at the New Mexico State Fair Grounds-EXPO NM. The ticket price was $15, and the set up was very similar to how it was set up when the Albuquerque Pride Board made that scary decision to move to Main Street in 2000, for year 2016 would mark sixteen years at this location. Similarly, the Pride Archives would be in the Indian Arts Building which was the original location in 2000 when the archives were first unveiled to the community. Upon walking into this venue, one could see in the back of the room the massive Gay Pride Flag that was given to Albuquerque Pride from InterPride with Gilbert Baker's signature. In one of the cases t-shirts were displayed from 1980 to 2016 that were official Gay Pride, Pride in Albuquerque, and Albuquerque Pride T-shirts (Albuquerque Pride did not incorporate until 1996). The other case revealed the Pride Pageant Archives that had not been entirely shown since 2009. PJ Sedillo, pat baillie, and Tony Ross would speak throughout the day about the history of Pride in Albuquerque from 1976 to present day. Also, the Art Show would be moved back to the Fine Arts Building, the original location in 2000 when the Albuquerque Pride Art Show was revealed to the community for their participation and celebration of the GLBTQI community.

PJ Sedillo envisioned the event becoming as large as the annual New Mexico State Fair. Most of the attractions were created and patterned after this event, such as the art show, archives/history, car show, mainstage, food court, and beer gardens to name a few. Also, the New Mexico State Fair showcased one of the largest areas for carnival rides in the State, and it had been a dream for PJ Sedillo to have carnival rides at PrideFest. In 2009, he was able to obtain five carnival rides including a Ferris wheel. Despite this new attraction, the carnival rides were placed far away from Main Street and those in attendance did not realize that the rides were part of PrideFest. Similarly, in 2016 the Albuquerque Pride Board would put in their budget 15,000 for carnival rides.

The En Fuego Stage located at the Box Car Stage (the original Mainstage in 2001) highlighted live music. The En Fuego Stage had grown as an attraction in its own right. The bands that performed live needed time for the sound system company to "strike the stage" and for the bands to transition their equipment, microphones, and instruments. The schedule of performers was as follows: (Those italicized in the schedule were performers using track music who were incorporated in the schedule so that transitions could be made easier with no down time and an empty performance stage with only the crew left on the En Fuego Stage.).

11:45 Underground Cadence
12:50 Tre Brewbaker (Mr. NM Pride 2016)
1:00 Tanya Greigo
2:05 Off Broadway Dance Studio
2:15 Severo Y Grupo Fuego
3:20 Lady Shug (Miss. NM Pride 2016)
3:30 Las Florecitas
4:35 Cherri Heartattack (Miss NM Pride Youth 2016)
4:45 Felix Y Los Gatos

The Mainstage Entertainment would be the largest undertaking than previous Prides. The schedule would get on and off the stage forty-seven acts from 11:40 a.m. to 6:00 p.m. The acts that were on the Main Stage Entertainment Schedule were as follows: (Those who were capitalized were the Headliners for 2016)

11:40 Opening Session-Presentation of Colors/AVER & Anthem-Marissa Sandoval
12:00 KBENALLY/LETSJUSB (Rap)
12:06 Missy Venure (Burlesque)
12:10 Kaleb T. Stratton
12:16 J'Adore Dance Crew
12:26 LAZARO
12:55 Narcisca Vanity (Drag)
1:00 GIA GUNN
1:05 LAGANJA ESTRANJA
1:10 Cherrie Heartattack (Miss NM Pride Youth)
1:15 Coco Bardot (Drag from AZ)
1:20 Marissa Sandoval (Pop)
1:30 COLBY O'DONIS
1:50 #TEAMTOOMUCH (GIA GUNN & LAGANJA ESTRANJA)
2:00 Lady Shug (Miss NM Pride)
2:05 PABLO HERNANDEZ (Andrew Christian Model)
2:10 Trey Charming Michaels
2:15 Throb Dance Crew
2:20 ViLette T. Stratton (Drag)
2:25 Khloe Layla Malone (Drag)
2:30 DANNY DASH ANDREWS (Michael Jackson Impersonator)
3:00 GIA GUNN
3:05 LAGANJA ESTRANJA
3:10 Tre Brewbaker (Mr. NM Pride)
3:15 TWERKING CONTEST (hosted by:JULIAN SERRANO & PABLO HERNANDEZ)
3:30 Tsunami Couture/Boy Couture

3:35 BRIAandCHRISSY (YOUTUBE'S MOS POPULAR SINGING LESBIAN DUO)
4:10 Victoria Vale (First Miss NM Pride-Drag)
4:15 Cruz Carter (AZ)
4:20 Perla Foxxx (Burlesque)
4:25 Kaleb T. Stratton
4:30 Off Broadway Dance Crew
4:45 Christian Ticey
4:50 Kissmetta Kyng (Drag)
4:55 Venus de Folie (Burlesque)
5:00 The Dolls
5:10 Narcisca Vanity and Those Guuurls
5:15 Cruz Carter (AZ)
5:20 ViLette T. Stratton (Drag)
5:25 Trey Charming Michaels
5:30 Coco Bardot (AZ)
5:35 DoubleTrouble (TX)
5:45 Cherri Heartattack (Miss NM Pride Youth)
5:50 Tre Brewbaker (Mr. NM Pride)
5:55 Lady Shug (Miss NM Pride)
6:00 Closing Remarks- SEE YOU IN 2017!!!

Albuquerque Pride Inc. and Pride in Albuquerque (produced by different organizations) for the past 40 years of its existence would try to secure important and influential advocates and entertainers on the national level who would be honored as a speaker, headliner, grand marshal, or noted figurehead that would represent and present what was deemed as the most important current issues facing the community in terms of politics, music, and the Gay culture. Following this practice, notably in 2002, Albuquerque Pride would contractually secure Thelma Houston who would become the first ever Headliner and Honorary Grand Marshal. Albuquerque Pride would state on all branding and to the media, "Come hear the woman who got us through the 70's and continues to call to us to grow, learn and fly into 2002."

Social media, which utilizes websites and applications, would be instrumental in changing Albuquerque Pride and Prides throughout the world especially in 2016. Social media enabled those on a computer to create, share, and produce any content for others to participate in social networking. Event pages, twittering, blogging, could reach millions with the brief writings of happenings in "real time." Headliners for 2016 would be attained primarily from individuals who were social media "stars." They would be revered and celebrated in 2016.

Lazaro would perform at 12:26 p.m. He was a Cuban-born American singer from Naples, Florida, who finished in sixth place on Season 12 of *American Idol*. He would become an International YouTube Favorite and be contracted to perform on the Main Stage for Pridefest 2016. He would be well received, and the audience would go wild when he performed. Due to his limited time on the stage the crowd would shout for an encore; however, due to time constraints this would not occur.

Notably, *RuPaul's Drag Race* had changed the course of many Prides in the United States for procuring the winners and losers of this reality TV show to perform. Albuquerque Pride as well as other Prides would yearly ensure that some of the losers and or winners of RuPaul's Drag Race would grace the stages at their Pride events. Gia Gunn and Laganja Estranja who were on Season 6 would be noted headliners. The name Gia came from the supermodel Gia Carangi and the movie *Gia* starring Angelina Jolie. The last name came from her drag mother Alyssa Gunnwhich whose name originated from *Project Runway*'s Tim Gunn.

Laganja's talents as noted from her web page included, "splits, twirling, contortion, dancer trained in ballet, contemporary, musical theatre, nailography, jazz and hip hop, jive, foxtrot, death drops, toe touch, finger pop, rapper, actor, bator, professional chain smoker, bedazzler, model, spokesperson, makeup artist, styling, cinematographer, music editor, redditor, filmer, choreographer, and social mediator."

Pablo Hernandez (Andrew Christian Model) would perform on the Mainstage for Albuquerque Pride. Andrew Christian was an American men's underwear, swimwear, and sportswear manufacturer named after its founder and head-fashion designer Andrew Christian. His brand was known for its underwear, where the company heavily targeted the Gay community using Social Media to sell their merchandise. Notably, their underwear would be highlighted in many gay clubs throughout the U.S sometimes known as being very provocative. In 2013 the company began to promote safer-sex events in conjunction with National Condom Day.

Julian Serrano had become an internet favorite for twerking in 2015. Twerking is a dance to popular music in a sexually provocative manner involving thrusting hip movements and a low, squatting stance. His twerking caught the attention of the web in June when he released a video of twerking all around his apartment. GIFs (Graphic Interchange Format are image files compressed to reduce transfer time) of his underwear-clad body immediately made their way around *Tumblr* (a microblogging and social networking website that allows users to post multimedia and other content to a short-form blog). Soon, he was twerking on stage with Ciara during LA Pride, and later he appeared in Kevin Mikal's music video for "Candy Yum Yum." Eventually, Julian Serrano's "ass" was shaking all over the internet. At 3:20 p.m. there would be a Twerking Contest which promoted the underwear line on the Mainstage hosted by Julian Serrano and Pablo Hernandez. An interesting Pride fact for 1993 was that Rush Industries Inc. wanted exclusivity with their product (line of underwear) for the parade. Needless to say, Common Bond and the Board of Directors would turn them down because they did not want "Padded Briefs" to have sole sponsorship of the event. Times had sure changed over twenty-three years of sponsorship and entertainment for Pride in Albuquerque.

BRIA AND CHRISSY would be noted as YouTube's most popular singing Lesbian "Duo." Their website would state from the Huffington Post that, "Bria and Chrissy have shown the power that musicians can have on the queer community. The couple have raised the bar where outreach is concerned using their YouTube channel and music." Furthermore, it was stated, "With over 250amillion views and 800 thousand combined subscribers, the performing duo known as Bria and Chrissy had quickly become YouTube's most popular singing lesbian couple. They are known for their catchy songs with inspiring lyrics the two performers who use music and comedy to promote equality." The couple notable celebrities from YouTube would do comedy sketches, sing, advocate and provide advice for the lesbian community based on their own personal daily experience with love and life.

The final Headliner to be noted for 2016 was Danny Dash Andrews known as the world's #1 Michael Jackson Impersonator. His website would state, "Since the tragic death of Michael Jackson, Andrews has resurrected the spirit of the legend, traveling throughout the world performing live as the late King." He had been interviewed by the media, been seen on television and was on *America's Got Talent Season 8.* He would perform on the Mainstage for PrideFest and would captivate the audience with an energy that would "blow the tent off." He would give to all the Michael Jackson experience which was "one to remember forever."

Albuquerque PrideFest 2016 would successfully produce one of the best Pride celebrations in the Southwest and would rival Prides nearby such as Phoenix and Denver. It could be considered as a "large" Pride that had the "corner market" on attractions that made the event feel more like a State Fair. It would be a niche that Albuquerque Pride could capitalize for future events. Even though populations in Phoenix and Denver are larger than Albuquerque's population, it was evident that the numbers in Albuquerque's attendance would match closely with those events.

Many previous Boards of Albuquerque Pride considered having an event on Sunday after the Pride Parade and PrideFest (occurring on a Saturday). Past Board Members of Albuquerque Pride had suggested and tried to attempt an event; however, it never came to fruition. In 2016, the first ever attempt would occur Sunday, June 12th.

The 2016 Board of Directors took on this idea and prepared for a new Sunday event. It was deemed the "PRIDEFEST MUSIC FESTIVAL." It was an event for those to experience "MUSIC IS WHAT FEELINGS SOUND LIKE" and would be free. The gates would open at 10:00 a.m. with the event scheduled to end at 3:00 p.m. or after all bands had performed. Vendor and information booths were also given the opportunity to open on Sunday. Drag acts were scheduled in between the bands so that sets, sound equipment, and instruments could be moved and transitioned for the next act. The Drag performers entertaining were Miss NM Pride 2016-Lady Shug and Miss Youth NM Pride 2016-Cherri Heartattack. They would entertain at the PRIDEFEST MUSIC FESTIVAL between the following bands:

11:00 a.m.	Dawn Luz Padilla
11:55 a.m.	Severo Y Grupo Fuego
12:55 p.m.	Fun Adixx
1:50 p.m.	Sorela
2:45 p.m.	Wildflowers of the Mojave

Despite the fantastic line-up and attempt to have a Pride Music Festival that could have become a new reoccurring tradition for Albuquerque Pride on a Sunday after the annual Pride Parade and PrideFest, the Sunday event and the world would encounter and be forced to deal with one of the most horrific and gruesome incidents that "shook the Gay community to its core!" This next revelation of what occurred is a retrospective account of what took place on Saturday, June 11, which led to the unspeakable, dreadful events on Sunday, June 12, 2016. On Saturday, June 11th, PJ Sedillo, Tony Ross, and pat baillie were honored as Past Presidents of Albuquerque Pride-Grand Marshals. They would head home on Saturday evening after riding together with their "pride capes blazed with the wording President Emeritus." They would ride in the Pride Parade like giggling six-year-olds.

They would recount that Saturday evening after experiencing PrideFest 2016 that they were overly thrilled and overjoyed. After they arrived at EXPO, they entered gate 3 and would be greeted by a longtime friend Johnny Q. Mr. NM Pride 2009. Johnny Q. had been instrumental in moving the pageants forward to the success that they had become in 2016. After Johnny Q. had met all three, these three Grand Marshals would head to the Pride Archives to lecture to the masses about the 40-year history of Albuquerque Pride. On their way from the parking lot after exiting their Grand Marshal car, provided from the Rainbow Roadrunners Car Club, they would be extremely thankful for the car club and for those who would ensure that a car would be available for the threesome because of their devoted past and connectedness of working together. Also, employees from EXPO NM located at gate 3, would for a brief moment remember the three past individuals who put on Pride. They would encounter many of individuals who worked for EXPO NM and would remember, be thankful, and then hug in a manner of respectful reminiscing of how it used to be.

This team of PJ Sedillo, Tony Ross, and pat baillie had moved Albuquerque Pride into the future and had worked tirelessly for many years with the employees at EXPO NM. Ticket takers, gardeners, security, facility coordinators would come to have the upmost respect for these individuals. Some of these individuals had come face to face with the first gay person that they had met in their life. They would be educated and become advocates for other GLBT individuals. Forty years of history would pour out for those who had encountered Pride in Albuquerque.

PJ and pat together as co-presidents would reflect on an experience, they had both encountered during earlier PrideFests. They were remembering a time when there was an individual who while celebrating PrideFest had their breasts exposed. The State Police, EXPO Staff and the assigned Facility Coordinator had secured this individual and had "her" removed to an enclosed location in the business building. Both Co-presidents would have to explain and educate the staff that it was perfectly legal for the individual to have revealed breasts because the individual at hand was a male and had a legal driver's license proclaiming his identity. Future changes, according to state law for breasts in public would both become an educational process for Pride and EXPO. This is only one encounter that PJ Sedillo and pat baillie would have to take on for educating the New Mexico State Fairground's employees. They would then spend hours at PrideFest within the building that secured the Pride Archives that recounted the Gay Pride historical past, celebrating 40 years of "blood, sweat, and tears." They would head home together as pat baillie would spend the evening with PJ and Tony and go back to California on Monday. Sunday was supposed to be a day of rest where the three could reconnect and reminisce about the past and celebrate their "joy ride" as Grand Marshals.

Sunday, June 12, 2016

Tony Ross, pat baillie, and PJ Sedillo, had planned to go to the PRIDEFEST MUSIC FESTIVAL to then take down the archives and then return them back to the Pride Office. They could then relish in the fact that 40 years had been successfully completed. They could put and tuck away another year and prepare for 2017, forty-one years of Pride in Albuquerque. Their job would be done. Yet, their job was not done. Solidarity Through Pride would become the true essence and meaning for Pride 2016.

Sunday morning PJ Sedillo, as was his ritual, would wake up at 6:30 a.m. and turn on the TV to check out the morning news. He awoke, groggy eyed, and dry-mouthed listening to an event that had occurred in Orlando, Florida. PJ Sedillo tried to decipher the events at hand and soon realized that his gay brother and sisters in Orlando had been massacred. He jumped out of bed and awoke pat baillie to have her watch what was occurring on television. Tony Ross was outside working on the yard. PJ in a loud voice called and then screamed for him to come in the house to see what had happened. All three would be glassy eyed in front of the TV, shocked and in awe, and not sure how to move forward from the devastation that was being revealed. An analysis-paralysis would become their fate for a few fleeting moments, but they would all come to realize that action needed to occur on Sunday, June 12, for the sake of the Albuquerque community.

News reports early Sunday morning confirmed that a mass shooting had occurred at the Pulse nightclub in Orlando, resulting in the deaths of 49 individuals and injuries to 53 others. The attack was later identified as both a terrorist act and a hate crime. The perpetrator, Omar Mateen, was killed by Orlando police following a three-hour standoff. Amid the tragedy, patrons and staff inside the nightclub demonstrated courage and selflessness, helping others escape and providing aid under extreme circumstances. Their actions saved lives and reflected the strength and resilience of the Pulse community, a venue widely recognized for its significance within the Latino LGBTQ+ community.

This act would be recognized as one of the deadliest incidents of violence against the GLBTQI community in America. Autopsies of all 49 deceased victims would be completed by the Orange County Medical Examiner's Office by June 14. The names and ages of the victims killed were confirmed by the City of Orlando after their next of kin had been notified. They were as follows:

- Stanley Almodovar III, 23
- Amanda Alvear, 25
- Oscar A. Aracena-Montero, 26
- Rodolfo Ayala-Ayala, 33
- Alejandro Barrios Martinez, 21
- Martin Benitez Torres, 33
- Antonio D. Brown, 30
- Darryl R. Burt II, 29
- Jonathan A. Camuy Vega, 24
- Angel L. Candelario-Padro, 28
- Simon A. Carrillo Fernandez, 31
- Juan Chevez-Martinez, 25
- Luis D. Conde, 39
- Cory J. Connell, 21
- Tevin E. Crosby, 25
- Franky J. Dejesus Velazquez, 50
- Deonka D. Drayton, 32
- Mercedez M. Flores, 26
- Juan R. Guerrero, 22
- Peter O. Gonzalez-Cruz, 22
- Paul T. Henry, 41
- Frank Hernandez, 27
- Miguel A. Honorato, 30
- Javier Jorge-Reyes, 40
- Jason B. Josaphat, 19
- Eddie J. Justice, 30
- Anthony L. Laureano Disla, 25
- Christopher A. Leinonen, 32
- Brenda L. Marquez McCool, 49
- Jean C. Mendez Perez, 35
- Akyra Monet Murray, 18
- Kimberly Morris, 37
- Jean C. Nives Rodriguez, 27
- Luis O. Ocasio-Capo, 20
- Geraldo A. Ortiz-Jimenez, 25
- Eric I. Ortiz-Rivera, 36
- Joel Rayon Paniagua, 32
- Enrique L. Rios Jr., 25
- Juan P. Rivera Velazquez, 37
- Yilmary Rodriguez Solivan, 24
- Christopher J. Sanfeliz, 24
- Xavier E. Serrano Rosado, 35

- Gilberto R. Silva Menendez, 25
- Edward Sotomayor Jr., 34
- Shane E. Tomlinson, 33
- Leroy Valentin Fernandez, 25
- Luis S. Vielma, 22
- Luis D. Wilson-Leon, 37
- Jerald A. Wright, 31

Many people were left unsure, shaken, distressed, and disturbed by what had happened. Some created a "makeshift" memorial outside the Pulse Nightclub where flowers, letters, balloons and other items were left behind to signify some way to understand what had happened. Hearts were shattered, scared, scarred, and broken. The GLBT Community Center of Central Florida would provide grief counseling for family, friends, lovers, and spouses of the deceased. Orlando would come together to support one another. How would Albuquerqueans come together to support one another? Many in Albuquerqueans were also left unsure, shaken, distressed and disturbed by what had occurred. What could they do?

Historically, Gay bars had been noted as instrumentally providing one of the first "safe havens" for the Gay community to come together to be who they are, and to just have a place to celebrate and dance. It is that sacred space that was violated at the Stonewall Inn in 1969 where the gay community had said "no more!" In other words, gay bars have been, and still are today, a sanctuary. In the simplest of terms, they are the Gay community's church, its temple. In 2016 this honored area would be desecrated by a terrorist who possibly was gay himself. This event would move the GLBTQI community to come together.

PJ Sedillo, as he had done in the past as a leader in the community, would begin to put on his "thinking cap" and find a way to make sure that all those who were hurting would have a time, space, place, and location to begin the healing process. He felt that a candlelight vigil needed to occur that Sunday evening. He realized that something needed to be done. Pat baillie was there as his reassuring "left hand." Tony Ross, his conscience, also would assist him with an event to happen that evening. PJ contacted Neil Macernie who was preparing for the Sunday event at EXPO NM and stated what he would like to attempt. Neil, the President of Albuquerque Pride, agreed that an event needed to take place. PJ Sedillo would craft an events page on Facebook. Because of the rapid response that Social Media presents, he was able to put out immediately that a Candlelight Vigil for the victims of Orlando would take place at Morningside Park, the location that honored Pride in Albuquerque.

Unbeknownst to PJ, Alma Rosa Silva-Banuelos, the LGBTQ Resource Center Program Coordinator for the University of New Mexico, had sent out a similar event page for a Candlelight Vigil at Morningside Park. PJ immediately contacted Alma Rosa so that they could work together to produce this event. Notably, PJ Sedillo's strong points for leadership have been organizing and obtaining what is needed logistically to produce an event. They both would agree on what needed to be done while keeping Neil Macernie and the Albuquerque Pride Board in the loop.

PJ Sedillo began to work on what was needed to produce the event which included a sound system, decorations, podium, candles, tables, and other items necessary to make the event happen. Alma Rosa would begin to work on the line-up of speakers, entertainers, and others who would help make this event occur. By 11:00 a.m. PJ had secured the sound company that was working for the Sunday event for Albuquerque Pride; however, he needed to acquire a generator. Tony Ross would purchase one at the Home Depot Sunday morning. The sound company would eventually donate their services and equipment to ensure that the event would take place. PJ would also realize the difficulty in obtaining over 2000 candles for the vigil that evening. He would be able to contact past resources and get in touch with Paul Garson who worked and owned a local Catholic Religious store. By chance there were candles available that would be brought to the event by 6:00 p.m.

By 12:00 p.m. a meeting would be scheduled at the Pride Office located at EXPO New Mexico with key leaders from the GLBTQI community in attendance. Neil Macernie-President of Albuquerque Pride along with the Board of Directors, PJ Sedillo-Past President, pat baillie-Past President/Current Director of Out and Equal, Reverend Judith Maynard-MCC Church, Arron Howe-Director of the NM Gay Men's Chorus, Mauro Montoya-NM Pride Guide/Gay and Lesbian Chamber of Commerce and Alma Rosa would attend via teleconference. Jobs would be designated, and the event would move forward to occur that evening.

Sunday evening, June 12, 2016, at 5:30 p.m. people began to arrive at Morningside Park and by 6:00 over 2000 community members from Albuquerque had gathered to honor the Orlando attack victims. A makeshift memorial was set up next to the podium where individuals brought forth candles, rainbow flags, flowers and other items to be placed on this memorial. There were prayers and spiritual blessings with a cleansing of the park conducted at the beginning of the event to make space for speeches and lots of tears. The crowd made it clear that Orlando may be hundreds of miles away, but their pain was felt here in Albuquerque. Speakers not only remembered the Orlando victims, but they called for the U.S. to speak out against any anti-Muslim rhetoric that could arise from this shooting. Many people in the crowd said that they shared that message and were dedicated to spreading love, not hate.

After a period of silence, LGBTQ community leaders, political activists, local politicians and religious leaders including individuals from the Muslim faith addressed the crowd about the mass shooting. Speakers included PJ Sedillo, Alma Rosa, Neil Macernie, Mauro Montoya, Senator Jacob Candelaria of Albuquerque, and City Councilor Pat Davis. U.S. Representative Michelle Grisham, APD, Chief Gordon Eden, and Mayor Richard Berry were in the audience. Local officials would state that homophobic actions of the individual who committed the atrocities did not and would not be a reflection of the general Muslim community. Participants at the vigil were encouraged to communicate political opinions pertaining to how this tragedy reflects the lack of gun control laws in our nation. Reverend Paul Anway would lead the participants in lighting their candles. The crowd began to sing in unification "This Little Light of Mine." Next, a Native American drummer played in solace and reverence. Mauro Montoya asked the participants to bow their heads in a moment of silence, and a member of the Gay Men's Chorus began to sing "Amazing Grace."

Representatives from the Muslim community spoke next. After they spoke, sadly enough the NM Gay Men's Chorus would sing the same song "belted out" three days before in remembrance and celebration of the 2016 Albuquerque Pride Candlelight Vigil. This time the song would be louder and clearer and would provide a guided assurance for all so that hopefully all would be ok for that brief period. The Gay Men's Choir, would again sing "Somewhere Over the Rainbow." Those in the audience became silent, and those present could hear many crying. These tears and cries throughout the crowd helped all present to gather strength to support one another.

The Gay community had come together to grieve to start the healing process. Amazingly enough, the city of Albuquerque would be one of the first cities in the United States to have a candlelight vigil to assist with the grieving process. Past Board Members of Pride working closely with the 2016 Albuquerque Pride Board, along with other GLBTQI leaders in Albuquerque would come to embody the International Pride Theme for 2016 "Solidarity Through Pride." Together the future of Pride in Albuquerque would be able to withstand 40 more years.

Chapter 15

Albuquerque Pride 2017 and 2018

Each year the LGBTIQ+ Community of New Mexico has come together to celebrate diversity. The annual events from 2017-2019 included a parade down the streets of Albuquerque as well as Pridefest's main event at EXPO New Mexico. The event highlighted Dance, Music, Friendship, Expression, Art, Fun, and Diversity. There would be some exciting and difficult changes made in these years with the most devastating event that hit the world in 2020 that would cancel Albuquerque Pride altogether.... or would it?

Albuquerque Pride 2017

The Albuquerque Pride Board would consist of a newly elected President Craig Laberge-Esparza. The other board members would be J.R. Laberge-Esparza/Vice President of Operations, Neil Macernie/ Vice President of Public Relations, Miranda Sedillo/Treasurer, and Suzanne Alexander/Secretary. The 2017 Albuquerque Pride titleholders included several prominent figures in the LGBTQ+ community who were recognized for their contributions to advocacy, community service, and representation. The key titleholders from that year were:

Mr. Youth NM Pride: TJ Martinez (resigned)
Mr. NM Pride: Armani Daniels
Miss Youth NM Pride: Narcisca Vanity
Miss NM Pride: Seliah DeLeon

This year the Pride Board was ready to provide a safe space for the LGBTIQ+ community to come together to raise awareness of issues concerning the community such as inequality, discrimination, and bigotry. Albuquerque Pride kicked off its celebration with a free event scheduled on Wednesday, June 7th from 5:00-9:00 pm with the Albuquerque Pride Annual Art Show entitled "Figuratively Speaking" located at the Fine Arts Building at EXPO New Mexico State Fairgrounds. This was a joint art show for David Zaintz and Max Woltman. The exhibition, in association with Albuquerque Pride, included original paintings and photographs as well as collaborations by the artists. It was promoted as a rare opportunity to see the one-of-a-kind special commissioned pieces.

On June 8th at 7:30om at Morningside Park – Morningside Dr SE & Lead Ave was the Albuquerque Pride Candlelight Vigil that would be a reflection and remembrance in solidarity through pride and a celebration of our diversity - creating a future in unity and love. It is an evening of community, sharing and music. This free event had over 500 people who gathered at the park. As in years past, the Candlelight Vigil was held on the Thursday before Pridefest. The candlelight vigil has been since its inception held every year to honor in memoriam those members of our community who we had lost, victims of hate crimes, or those who were never able to come out and be their authentic self. This year's vigil focused on the victims in the Orlando 2016 mass shooting at the Pulse, an LGBT-friendly nightclub where a gunman killed 49 people the previous summer.

Also, the Pro-Transgender Rights March took place which has been a part of the candlelight vigil for the better part of a decade. Albuquerque Pride itself had been around for 41 years now. An attendee a Trans-activist at the march and vigil was Janice Devereaux, who came out as a transgender woman 15 years before. She stated the event "reminds me that I'm very lucky," and "As tough as life can be for trans people at times, I'm still lucky to be here, and that is very important for me to hold on to."

Organizers of the vigil read the names of each victim as others released balloons in the air in remembrance. Pictures of each of the Orlando victims dotted the fence at Morningside Park. Afterwards the attendees lit candles in memory of those who have passed away. "They have tried to erase us from history, from society, and yet we are still here," Devereaux said as she spoke to the crowd. "Your very existence today is an act of resistance, so I want all of you to keep resisting." Neil Macernie, Vice- President of Public Relations from Albuquerque Pride, talked about how the first Pride after the Stonewall Riots in New York City came long before LGBT people were recognized in the mainstream. "There was a time when lesbian, gay, bisexual, transgender, intersex, queer, and questioning had to live completely in secret," Macernie said. "Hiding in the shadows in the underworld, yet many continue to live without sharing their experience because of fear, anguish and denial. Tonight, is our opportunity to be present for each other," he said.

Israel Chavez, a University of New Mexico law student who formerly worked with Equality New Mexico, said that "while things may seem bad for LGBT people on the national level, we are not going back in time. We are not going back to Jim Crow, we are not going back in the closet, we are not going back to past injustices, and we do not need division or hatred to divide us." Chavez also told the supportive crowd. "What we need is love, wisdom and compassion to one another, and that's what we have here."

On Friday, June 9th the day started with an official Pride Flag raising ceremony at Civic Plaza. Daniel Romero an Albuquerque Pride Board member spoke at the event. He stated, "Pride is not a merely a parade, a rainbow flag, a month of festivities. It is a testament to resilience, courage, and an enduring fight for equality and acceptance. Every step taken in the name of Pride is a step towards a world where love knows no boundaries"

Continuing that day was the PrideFest Free Friday at the State Fairgrounds Expo NM. The event had become a family-friendly, FREE Friday, pre-Pride celebration which included the annual Art Show, and a Music Festival with the MLC Band, Encantada-The Band of Enchantment, and featured Severo y Grupo Fuego. The event would end with the movie, Moana. The highlight of the evening was the Severo y Grupo Fuego which included Severo Martinez- Lead Vocals, Adrian Medina-Keyboards/Vocals, Albert Tafoya-Guitar, Thomas Mares- Drums, Cameron Bourg- Bass. The group was noted as the Latin superstar Severo Martinez who brought forth cumbia flavor with a touch of tropical rhythm to the Latin music genre. His style was very versatile, with a band that has embraced musicians from all over the United States. Severo and the band were described as not only musicians but are also all-around entertainers who had everyone dancing.

The Annual Albuquerque Pride Parade was on June 10th at 10:00 am (gay-standard time). This was the first year in its 41-year history that the Albuquerque Pride Parade took place on Lomas Boulevard due to ART (Albuquerque Rapid Transit) construction on Central, so the parade did not take place on its normal route. Dr. PJ Sedillo who has been passionate about having the Pride Parade continuously on Central felt that something needed to be done to solve this problem. Therefore, the Albuquerque Parade would be noted again as the oldest Parade/March held continuously on Central Avenue.

With the approval of the Board of Directors, PJ located 25 various leaders from different organizations who would symbolize the first 25 individuals who bravely marched on Central in 1976. There were three flag bearers. They were Robert Toane, holding the Pride Flag a Canadian who had supported Albuquerque Pride for years, Dr. Sedillo bearing the NM State flag, and Tony Ross a United States Veteran holding the American flag. The march was put on Facebook as a live stream. The 25 individuals met at the Albuquerque Social Club and were provided coffee and donuts, just like what had happened at the first march. The marchers were given the "okay" to proceed at the exact time that the parade would start on Lomas which would eventually join the rest of the parade and walk together into the NM State Fair Grounds. This official sanctioned march on Central would be able to tout and claim that Albuquerque Pride had continued with an annual march for 41 years.

Thousands of people would gather along the sides of Lomas Boulevard on Saturday morning to celebrate the 41st annual Pride Parade as well as a lesser crowd along the traditional route on Central. The parade was a celebration of the lesbian, gay, bisexual, transgender, intersex, and queer community. The parade route would start on Washington and Lomas and head East to San Pedro. Many local businesses participated in the parade such as Sandia National Laboratories and Albuquerque Public Schools. Nationally recognized businesses Planned Parenthood, and T-Mobile also participated. The Grand Marshal of the parade was Axel Andrews, an entertainer from Pulse Nightclub in Orlando Florida. Pulse Nightclub was the location of a deadly mass shooting that took place in June 2016, in which the shooter specifically targeted members of the LGBTIQ community. Pride Parades around the world are meant to build unity and strength in the LGBTIQ+ community as well as send a message to others that they will not tolerate hate.

2017

This year's theme was "Solidarity through Pride" which was intended to give the community the opportunity to reflect on the history of the LGBTIQ community in New Mexico. This was last year's InterPride Theme; however, the Pride Board decided to utilize this empowering theme for 2017. The t-shirt design had the official Albuquerque Pride logo with the year 2017. Underneath the logo were the words Solidarity Through Pride.

The Pride Parade included floats, classic cars, motorcycles, horses, and dancers. It is the second largest parade in New Mexico. New to the Pride Parade is Park N' Ride Service. There was a free shuttle service that run every 10 minutes from Expo New Mexico – Gate 4 (on San Pedro) to one of 3 parade route locations on Roma Ave. The shuttle service ran from 7:30am until 11:30am, as stated on the Albuquerque PrideFest website and Facebook page. After the Pride Parade, the celebration continued with PrideFest 2017 at Expo New Mexico from 10:00 am to 6:30 pm. The event included music, dance, art, local performers, radio. The event cost $15.00 and Children 10 and under were free.

The 2017 Grand Marshal would be AKA Alex Andrews whose drag mother was Roxxy Andrews from Season 5 of RuPaul's Drag Race. Michael Belvedere had been working for nearly seven years at the LGBT club known as the Pulse in Orlando. He began developing the drag queen persona Axel Andrews before joining the staff as a bartender and cast member. At two am on Sunday, a heavily armed gunman named Omar Mateen opened fire and began takin hostages. A SWAT team shot and killed Mateen, but not before the gunman declared his allegiance to ISIS (**Islamic State – an Islamic militant organization**) and killed 49 people in what is now known as the deadliest mass shooting in American history. Alex Andrew would get a wonderful welcome from all the spectators who stood on the sidelines watching his bravery go down historic Route 66. He would also receive a standing ovation when he performed on the Albuquerque Pridefest Stage.

Finally, on June 11th at 12:30-2:00 pm there was an event titled NM Resist Rally for the Equality March. The free event was located at Robinson Park-810 Copper Avenue. The event was intended to mobilize New Mexico LGBTQ+ communities, loved ones and allies. The particular focus is on those who have been actively silenced and neglected. This was a fight to affirm and protect LGBTQ+ rights, safety, and full humanity. This was a call to action, standing together for change. The event touted "Our resistance is our existence."

Albuquerque Pride 2018

The Albuquerque Pride Board would consist of President Craig Laberge-Esparza, J.R. Laberge-Esparza/Vice President of Operations, Neil Macernie/ Vice President of Public Relations, Miranda Sedillo/Treasurer, and Suzanne Alexander/Secretary, Tony Carson/Director, Caroline Monie/Director, Allen Buice/Director, and Miguel Ulloa/Director. The 2018 Albuquerque Pride titleholders included several prominent figures in the LGBTQ+ community who were recognized for their contributions to advocacy, community service, and representation. The key titleholders from that year were: Mister and Ms. Only took top two winners.

2018 Mr. NM Pride Topher Daniels
2018 Miss NM Pride Youth CeCe Knight Jones
2018 Miss NM Pride Felicia Roxx Starr Faraday

The 2018 theme for Albuquerque Pride was Viva la Vida (Live Life) which was also the International Pride Theme. The shirt had the official Pride Logo with the Pride Theme. Featured performers from *American Idol*, Jurnee and Effie Passero whose signatures are located on the t-shirt. Albuquerque Pride mounted their 42nd annual PrideFest celebrating the LGBTIQ community in New Mexico with a three-day celebration designed to bring our diverse LGBTIQ and allied communities together for a weekend of camaraderie and celebration of our past, present and future while raising funds for Albuquerque Pride's Community Programs geared towards educating the public about the historic and continued civil rights battle facing our community.

2018

Kicking off the events was a candlelight vigil on June 7 honoring the people who started this great Pride movement in Albuquerque for the lesbian, gay, bisexual, transgender, intersex and queer/questioning (LGBTIQ) community. The Candlelight Vigil was a free event where 500+ people gathered. This year's Albuquerque PrideFest continued Friday, June 8 starting at 6:00 pm with a FREE Night PrideFest & Art Reception, and movie night featuring *Peter Rabbit*. The parade this year included floats, classic cars, motorcycles, horses, dancers, and lots of excitement in the second largest parade in New Mexico. The celebration continued with the main event, PrideFest 2018 at Expo NM. This annual event had about 14,000 people who came from all over the Southwest. Headlining the main stage: From *American Idol*, Jurnee. Featured artists were Effie Passero from *American Idol*, and Alondra Garibay as Lady Gaga. PrideFest also featured:

- Live entertainment on 2 stages with locally and nationally known talent
- KiDz PaRk for family friendly activities
- Indoor Dance Club featuring the best DJs in town
- Wet & Play Area featuring over-sized water slides and water sports
- Art Show featuring local artists with varied medias
- Car Show showcasing remodeled classics
- Health Fair with free STD testing and screening
- Pride History and Archives
- Exhibitors with an extraordinary variety of shopping opportunities and community resources
- Food Vendors offering great deals for yummy treats
- Beer and Liquor Gardens for those 21+

Children under 10 received free admission, and parking was available for $5 at the gate of EXPO, NM. Admission was $15; however, the Pride Board had always realized that the admission price could be economically taxing. Therefore, FREE ADMISSION to the festival could be arranged by becoming a PRIDE VOLUNTEER and volunteering a minimum of 4 hours to receive free entrance and be provided with an official T-shirt.

Other events not produced or sanctioned by Albuquerque Pride that occurred in 2018 were the Pride Glow Party at the Library on June 9, Effex Nightclub with DJ FlightPhonic, and Tractor Brewing Wells Park on June 8 with Drag Queen Bingo: Pride Edition. Also, there was the Annual Pride Concert of the NM Gay Men's Chorus led under the artistic direction of Aaron Howe. The event was entitled *This Is Me – There is Harmony in Diversity* which was scheduled for June 16 at 7:30 pm at the Highland Theater. This would be another year that would be a huge success. The Board of Directors, volunteers, and community could take a breath and be content that this year there were no significant problems with putting on the event. There would be surplus of money for next year and the Albuquerque Pride Board was ready to "push up their sleeves" and start meeting as soon as possible begin to produce Albuquerque Pridefest 2019. Unfortunately, there would be unforeseen circumstances that would "shake the organization to the core" and possibly the future existence of Albuquerque Pride.

Chapter 16

Albuquerque Pride 2019 – Disenchantment & Dissolution of Pride?

On June 7, 2019, Mayor Tim Keller, City Councilor Pat Davis, The City of Albuquerque Office of Equity and Inclusion and others cut the ribbon on new rainbow crosswalks in Nob Hill. The new crosswalks were installed just in time for ABQ PrideFest 2019 and were along the ABQ Pride Parade route just before the 43rd Annual Albuquerque Pride Parade scheduled on Saturday, June 8th at 9 a.m. on Central Avenue in Nob Hill. "This is more than just a crosswalk, it is a piece of public art, and a fun visual acknowledgement, a celebration of our commitment to inclusion and the LGBTQ+ community," said Mayor Tim Keller. "Regardless of the recent hate and desecration that unfortunately remains, we are a community that welcomes and values people from all walks of life. As One Albuquerque, we will always stand up for our people, regardless of how they choose to identify." Albuquerque is one of many cities across the country to put in rainbow crosswalks in a demonstration of support for the LGBTQ+ community and the crosswalks represent the latest development in a series of efforts that were led by the City aimed at showing support for its LGBTQ+ community members since Mayor Keller had taken office. Some of his positive actions brough fourth for his tenure were:

- The formation of the Office of Equity and Inclusion.
- The City of Albuquerque created several policies in place for LGBTQ+ employees, including domestic partner benefits, employer-based health coverage for transition-related care, procedures that honored employee's needs and wishes when employees change their name and gender on employee records. As well, the city prohibiting discrimination in city employment.
- Finally, the City worked with Equality New Mexico, the Transgender Resource Center of New Mexico and the UNM LGBTQ Resource Center to bring Safe Zone training and Transgender 101 Training to all City employees.

Sadly, the Rainbow Crosswalks were vandalized on June 8, 2019. At least a dozen bikers vandalized the recently unveiled crosswalk that had been painted in rainbow colors to celebrate LGBTQ+ Pride week. They later bragged about it on social media. Gilbert Gallegos, a spokesman for the Albuquerque Police, said that the department received several videos of the incident. One of them, which had been posted online, showed the bikers riding along Route 66 before a couple of them take turns burning rubber over the crosswalk, the Albuquerque Journal reported.

"The facts will determine the appropriate charges, including whether damages amount to misdemeanor or felony charges," Gallegos said. Craig LaBerge-Esparza, the president of Albuquerque Pride, saw the vandalism as a possible anti-LGBTQ attack. He stated, "We don't know the motivations behind what happened. It's hard to see the videos and not take that as a personal attack against our community." The $30,000 rainbow crosswalks were installed just a few days before the incident. It must be noted that the price tag was roughly three times the price of a traditional crosswalk and had raised some eyebrows within the Albuquerque community. However, a spokesman for the city's Department of Municipal Development, Johnny Chandler, explained that they can be cost-effective: while white crosswalks have a lifespan of around three years, the rainbow-colored surfacing should last for about ten years.

After the vandalism occurred, Mayor Tim Keller was defiant and stated, "Hate will not deter us!" he tweeted and reinforced his support for the community. "We installed his crosswalk because we are a city that stands for equity and inclusion and we are city that supports our LGBTQ+ community." He also invited the community to take part in city's pride parade, which took place Saturday. Sen. Jacob Candelaria, the only openly gay member of the New Mexico Legislature, also reacted to the vandalism. "Little boys like that, who defaced that sidewalk, they're never going to take our Pride away," he said. "To the vandals, I hope you got something out of it. But my message to you is, grow up." Despite this hatred this event would assist in a larger number of spectators to support the LGBTQ+ community have a successful event.

The 2019 board of directors were Craig Laberge-Esparza/President, JR Laberge-Esparza/VP-operations, Neil Macernie/VP-Public Relations, Miranda Sedillo/Treasurer, Suzi Alexander/Secretary, Maryanne Miceli-Mendoza/Director, Justin Vigil/Director, Tony Carson/Director, Michelle Miceli-Mendoza/Director, Ray Sierra-Lopez/Director, Miguel Ulloa/Director, Chris Homan/Director, Angela Redman/Director, Logan Wells/Director, Augustina Joanna Montoya/Director, and Michael Benavidez/Director.

In 2019, there would be a change made by the Board of Directors concerning the Pride Pageant. Instead of the previous titles established by the past Board they would move to have only two titleholders (despite gender/gender identity/sexual orientation) who garnered the top scores during the competition. The Board would also decide to eliminate the youth and adult categories and lump them together. The two individuals who won the title were 2019 MX NM Pride Frieda Steel Roxxx who would be first to use the MX title prefix to denote individuals who identify as non-binary or gender-neutral which served as an alternative to the traditional titles like Mr. Miss, or Miss which are gender-specific. This title was used to promote inclusivity for those who do not conform to the binary gender system. The 2019 Mr. New Mexico Pride 2019 was Roman Phallistine D. Cox whose title was relinquished. He gave up his title because he was under 21 and could not meet the financial requirements.

2019 the Albuquerque PrideFest would continue to be a three day celebration which touted [we are] "designed to bring our diverse LGBTIQ and allied communities together for a weekend of camaraderie and celebration of our past, present and future while raising funds for Albuquerque Pride's Community Programs geared towards educating the public about the historic and continued civil rights battle facing our community." The Candlelight Vigil would be June 6 at 7:30 pm at Morningside Park, Friday, June 7 at 6:00 would be the FREE Pridefest and Pride Art Reception culminating on Saturday, June 8 the Parade and Pridefest.

Albuquerque Pride utilized the International Pride Theme for 2019 which was Remember the Past, Create the Future*.* The official T-shirt was simple which were in white and had a square on the top part of the shirt with a pink background that had the Albuquerque Pride logo and the words REMEMBER THE PAST CREATE THE FUTURE.

2019

For the past 42 years it has been a challenge to put on a Pride Event every year. This is similar across the nation. It is a miracle that Albuquerque Pride could exist, would exist, and should exist. Problematic was locating the number of volunteers to produce such an event every year. The amount of time that it took to put on a Pride each year would be exhausting and as for many Pride volunteers they would experience "burn out" which would have them leave the organization and a whole new core of volunteers would have to be located, obtained, and be trained.

However, the most difficult and arduous item to obtain for all Prides has been the amount of money that is needed to secure a yearly budget to yield an event. Dr. PJ Sedillo had produced the event in 1992 with a budget of $1,500 and as now, in 2019, that budget surpassed $150,000. Obtaining monies from sponsors was importantly crucial to the stainability of the organization but would sometimes become a controversy from segments of the community would always ensue and demand that no corporate sponsorship should be allowed believing that we were "selling out."

There have always been two sides to ensuring that a Pride event occurs which are LGBTQ+ Pride Marches vs. LGBTQ+ Corporate Parades. The Pride March signifies an event like the first march after Stonewall, and the Corporate Parade typically has transitioned into an event that has support and sponsorship from organizations and/or businesses. Each differ significantly in purpose, participation, and atmosphere. It is within these two different segments of our community where sometimes the event and Albuquerque Pride has been "ripped to shreds." This "in-fighting" occurred in 2019 and lead to the possibility of not having any future Pride Events.

The following are some of the differences between these two "camps:"

Purpose and Focus

- Pride March: Celebrates LGBTQ+ identity, rights, and visibility. It often advocates for social justice and equality.
- Corporate Parade: Typically promotes a brand or company, focusing on marketing and public relations. It may include sponsorship of pride events but often centers on corporate interests. The result reaches a larger audience to get the "word" out to the multitude about the positivity of LGBTQ+ Pride.

Participation

- Pride March: Involves individuals, LGBTQ+ organizations, and allies. It emphasizes community and activism.
- Corporate Parade: Features employees and representatives from various companies, often showcasing corporate sponsorships and partnerships. This awareness highlights that LGBTQ+ individuals are a powerful workforce.

Atmosphere

- Pride March: Generally, has a festive, inclusive atmosphere, with a focus on solidarity and activism.
- Corporate Parade: May feel more commercialized, with a focus on branding and promotional activities. However, with this commercialization the event can grow and become a "powerhouse" with a stronger voice in the community and state.

Criticism and Discussion

- Some argue that corporate involvement in pride events can dilute the original message of LGBTQ+ rights and activism.
- Others see corporate sponsorship as a means of increasing visibility and support for LGBTQ+ issues.

Both types of events can coexist, but their motivations and impacts can vary widely and if you have a board member that is extremely vocal it can be a detriment to the dissolution of any organization. This has been a "balancing act" to make everyone happy each year since Albuquerque Pride was incorporated and received their non-profit status solely depending on sponsorships to exist.

Albuquerque Pride's Past Presidents and Board of Directors would come to consensus to ensure that the budget would be obtained, and an event would occur by securing sponsorships. The most important reason this belief took place is that each member would ultimately be responsible for the event if it failed, that included obtaining the finances to put on the yearly event. The community at large tends to forget that the organization is run by volunteers (except in the past where briefly there was a paid office manager) and the extensive amount of money needed to produce such an event.

Many large non-LGBTQ+ events in Albuquerque as in other cities offer sponsorship benefits that have their name be associated as the primary presenter of the event. One was the naming of the Albuquerque International Balloon Fiesta which was known as the ExxonMobil Albuquerque International Balloon Fiesta and previously the Kodak Albuquerque International Balloon Fiesta.

In 2019, the Albuquerque Pride Board voted to title the event the Hewett Packard Albuquerque Pride Parade. There would be immediate backlash from certain segments of our community. A group of college students and other members of our community would attend an Albuquerque Pride Board Meeting to protest. The group had felt that the board had "sold their souls" of the community to corporate America and the true honoring of the Stonewall Riots had been desecrated.

Hundreds of people were expected to gather for the 43rd Annual Candlelight Vigil entitled an evening for *Reflections, Remembrance, and Celebration* of the LGBTQ+ community. The free event was held at 7:30 pm at Morningside Park, off Lead Avenue. However, the United States was experiencing a movement of protesting against corporate America, the police, and anything seen as establishment. The same group that had confronted the Albuquerque Pride Board at a previous monthly meeting would "hijack" the honored Trans March and try to overtake the sacred Candlelight Vigil event.

As the protestors entered Morningside Park with the National Anthem getting ready to start from the NM Gay Men's Chorus, flag bearers from AVERs (American Veterans for Equal Rights), the Pride Board, volunteers, and spectators were taken aback by the intense anger from the marchers who wanted to literally end this event. For a moment in time, it was "surreal" to experience the intense anger from members of our own LGBTQ+ community wanting to cause harm to those at the event and end the event.

It is then that the Pride Board, volunteers, and individual spectators from our community, would join in hands encircling the flags (US, NM, Rainbow, Transgender) as well as AVERs as the protestor's intent was to end the event and have their voices heard. Tony Ross a past Albuquerque Pride Board Member, hand in hand, and on his right side the current President of Albuquerque Pride and President Emeritus Dr. PJ Sedillo on his left were being pushed by members of their own community who were set on destroying the American, State, and Pride flag.

All involved were shocked, in awe, and distraught. It is then that the individual who conducted the Candlelight Vigil Blessing at the beginning of the event, Mattee Jim of the Zuni People Clan, an active individual in the HIV Prevention field for the past 20+ years, and who had been engaged in transgender advocacy since the late 1990s at local, state, and national levels began to speak. She was instrumental as one of our elders in the community who had started the Trans March and was equally horrified by the individuals who possessed so much hatred and anger. It was then that she went to the middle of the circle and spoke in a tone that everyone would stop "dead in their tracks" to what was happening to listen to her calming words of wisdom all without the use of a microphone.

Mattee was able to calm everyone down and then peacefully ask the protestors to leave the event and from the sacred ground. The protestors left in silence and the event was able to proceed. Shaken, enlightened, and experiencing a lack of hopelessness and despair permeated the air of this event which was originally intended to *Remember the Past * Create our Future* which was the 2019 Pride theme.

All those who were there did not know about the future existence of Albuquerque Pride, one being the acting President Craig LeBerge-Esparza, but the Friday Night Event, the Parade and Pridefest still needed occur and this event needed to be put in the past, forgotten for now and hopefully have the strength to analyze later. On Friday the festivities continue with live local music, drag performances, the annual art reception, food and street vendors, historical archives, and a movie in the park. This event is also free to the public starting at 6 p.m. and held at Expo New Mexico.

The streets of Albuquerque were filled Saturday June 8th, in honor of the Albuquerque Pridefest. The celebration kicked off with the annual parade that encouraged New Mexicans to embrace both individuality and unity. Albuquerque's Mayor Tim Keller spoke at the parade, giving a speech through a megaphone calling for unity among attendees. He passionately stated to an excited crowd, "We're all in this together; no matter where we came from, no matter what kind of lifestyle we choose to live, we are One Albuquerque. Keller sported a rainbow lei and his One Albuquerque shirt while shaking hands and sharing a smile with everyone who approached him. Groups and pairs posed for pictures and children wore pride flags as capes. The celebration rang through the streets as bubbles floated through the blue, cloudless sky.

The parade started at the intersection of Central and Tulane with a performance of the National Anthem, followed by Keller cutting the ceremonial ribbon. As the marching continued, floats adjourned the streets with balloons and streamers. Many onlookers joined marchers blending the two crowds to create a kaleidoscopic celebration. Every few feet walked provided a new flavor of music, welcoming a variety of people with long hair, shaved heads, and synthetic wigs of all colors that glowed in the sunlight. Despite the diversity of the crowd, the message of unity rang clear throughout the event, as the attendees welcomed new marchers with every step. The parade welcomed all, whether they were marching or simply watching everyone pass by.

From the sidelines, onlookers pushed closer into the street, melding with the parade. The occasional onlooker often ran up to hug a stranger walking in the parade before they continued down the streets, side by side, seamlessly and naturally. The parade welcomed adults and children alike with candy being tossed out to children as marchers passed by. With a tightly packed crowd of over 10,000 attendees, everyone contributed to a welcoming atmosphere sharing stories, smiles, and tears, transferred through hugs and laughter.

The PrideFest main event took place Saturday, June 8. It incorporating dancers, great music, food, art, and so much more at Expo New Mexico from 10:00 am to 6:30 pm. Designed to bring our diverse LGBTIQ and allied communities together, it was a weekend of camaraderie and celebration of our past, present, and future while raising funds for Albuquerque Pride's Community Programs geared towards educating the public about the historic and continued civil rights battle facing our community. Features at the event were:

- Live entertainment on 2 stages with locally and nationally known talent
- KiDz PaRk for family friendly activities (Children under 10 receive Free Admission)
- Indoor Dance Club featuring the best DJs in town
- Wet & Play Area featuring over-sized water slides and water sports
- Art Show featuring local artists with varied medias
- Car Show showcasing remodeled classics
- Health Fair with free STD testing and screening
- Pride History and Archives
- Exhibitors with an extraordinary variety of shopping opportunities and community resources
- Food Vendors offering great deals for yummy treats
- Beer and Liquor Gardens for those 21+

Other than celebrating Pride in Albuquerque in 2019, the business known as *PRIDE & Equality* celebrated another year of Models of Hope. The Vincent R. Johnson Models of Hope Award honors individuals and organizations making a difference, being seen as role models in the community. This award has created a roster of quality honorees over the past twelve years and where the 2019 role models were honored at a special brunch on August 25th. The Community Honoree was given to Neil Macernie. Pride and Equality would proclaim:

> If you haven't heard the name Neil Macernie in the LGBTQ community, you are in for a treat. Neil is the epitome of volunteerism. Macernie has been a major asset for Albuquerque Pride for years holding many titles including President and now Vice-President of Public Relations. His introduction into the community is pretty much what you would expect. He "started by getting a group of friends together to create a pride float." When it came to his childhood, Neil found it difficult. "It was very challenging as a youth," shared Macernie. "Because you were expected to express yourself a certain way as a boy and people were very mean if you did not." When it comes to his advice for LGBTQ youth, it's simple, "Don't be afraid to express yourself," says Macernie. "I know it feels like the people in your school life are important, but that's less than a quarter of your life, you have only just begun. Find friends that will stand by you and advocate for you.

This well-deserved award came at a needed time for celebrating and acknowledging those who worked tirelessly throughout the year to put on our event. However, in 2020 extremely difficult times would ensue and any "normality" for our community would not completely be reached until 2025. Would Albuquerque Pride be able to celebrate 50 years of existence?

Chapter 17

Albuquerque Pride 2020 - Tumultuous Times
Albuquerque PrideFest (CANCELED)...but Pride Still Happened

What will Americans know about the COVID-19 pandemic fifty years from now? The year will be 2076 and Albuquerque Pride would be celebrating 100 years of Pride. How will our great-grandchildren understand what Americans experienced during the pandemic? How did people's experiences with COVID-19 differ based on where they lived, their work, and/or their identities?

In late 2019, a mysterious illness began appearing in Wuhan, a city in central China. At first, it seemed like a cluster of pneumonia cases, perhaps something seasonal or a localized outbreak. Within weeks, however, the world began to realize that something far more dangerous was unfolding. By early 2020, countries across the globe were scrambling to shut borders, cancel flights, and lock down cities. Hospitals overflowed. Streets fell eerily silent. Economies halted. A virus had emerged that would not only claim millions of lives but also challenge our modern civilization. Its name was COVID-19.

COVID-19, caused by the novel coronavirus SARS-CoV-2, became the defining global crisis of the 21st century. It was more than just a disease; it was a test of public health systems, scientific progress, political leadership, and global solidarity (a theme used often by our LGBTQ+ community). This pandemic forever reshaped the future of medicine, society, and human behavior and what began as a local outbreak in China rapidly evolved into a global catastrophe. By January 2020, cases were appearing in Thailand, Japan, South Korea, and the United States. On March 11, 2020, the World Health Organization (WHO) officially declared COVID-19 a pandemic. Despite lockdowns, border controls, and social distancing, the virus moved with breathtaking speed. Europe became the epicenter in early 2020, followed by devastating waves in the United States, Latin America, India, and Africa. Hospitals were overwhelmed, and morgues ran out of space. Health systems strained under the pressure of treating thousands of patients simultaneously.

Starting with the first cases of COVID-19 in the New Mexico, the four cases were all believed to be travel related involving one couple that traveled to Egypt and two others that had traveled to New York. Governor Michelle Lujan Grisham would then issue a state of emergency which would ensure the cancellation of Albuquerque Pride, at the time possibly the future existence for any Pride event began with the first declaration banning mass gatherings. Below is what occurred in New Mexico during this pandemic.

March 12, 2020: Mass gatherings banned-In an attempt to slow the spread of COVID, the state announces that mass gatherings that bring 100 or more people are banned. The Archdiocese of Santa Fe halts in person church services.

- March 13, 2020: Schools announce 3-week closure
- March 14, 2020: Drive-up testing
- March 16, 2020: NM Governor orders businesses to limit capacity to 50%
- March 19, 2020: Businesses ordered to close
- March 24, 2020: Stay-at-home order issued for five or more people
- March 25, 2020: First COVID-19 related death
- March 27, 2020: Schools closed and moved to remote learning
- March 27, 2020: The state issues travel quarantine directing all visitors or New Mexicans returning to the state to self-quarantine for 14 days.
- March, 28, 2020: New Mexico liquor stores are ordered to close and grocery stores are ordered to limit the number of customers they have in the store at one time
- **April, 2020: Albuquerque Pride Parade-postponed / PrideFest-canceled**
- May 11, 2020: State opens testing to all New Mexicans
- May 16, 2020: Masks-up as we enter Phase 1 of reopening New Mexicans
- June 1, 2020: More businesses allowed to open
- **June 22, 2020: Balloon Fiesta 2020 postponed**
- **June 26, 2020: NM State Fair canceled**
- July 1, 2020: $100 fine violation for not wearing a mass in public spaces
- July 13, 2020: Indoor dining closed
- August 29, 2020: Another reopening of indoor dining at 255 capacity
- September 8, 2020: Some schools move into hybrid model
- October 20, 2020: Many businesses ordered to close
- November 16, 2020: 2-week lockdown begins
- December 14, 2020: COVID-19 Vaccine arrives
- December 16, 2020: Restrictions loosened
- December 27, 2020: Vaccine distribution widens
- January 8, 2021: Phase 1B of Vaccine distribution begins
- January 26, 2021: Schools given green-light to start hybrid model
- February 11, 2021: More states move out of the red
- **February 15, 2021: Gathering of Nations will be online only**
- February 17, 2021: Albuquerque Public Schools stays virtual
- March 3, 2021: APS kids can play sports
- March 7, 2021: Back to school, full time
- **March 11, 2021: One-year later: A year after the first cases of COVID-19 were diagnosed in New Mexico, the state has seen 187,720 total cases and 3,846 COVID related deaths.**

It must also be noted that COVID-19 has significantly impacted the LGBTQ+ community in various ways, affecting health, mental well-being, and social dynamics. The following list is what has become detrimental to our community and has continued to have a negative rippling effects on our community and the future of Pride events. However, there have also been some positive effects from this horrific time.

NEGATIVE EFFECTS

- LGBTQ+ individuals often face higher rates of certain health issues, which can complicate COVID-19 outcomes.
- Access to healthcare services was disrupted, leading to delays in routine care and preventive services.
- Increased isolation due to lockdowns and social distancing measures has heightened feelings of loneliness and anxiety within the community.
- Many LGBTQ+ individuals rely on social networks for support, which were limited during the pandemic.
- Job losses and economic instability disproportionately affected LGBTQ+ workers, particularly those in-service industries.
- Many LGBTQ+ organizations faced funding cuts, impacting their ability to provide essential services.

POSITIVE EFFECTS

- The pandemic spurred increased activism and mutual aid efforts within the community.
- Virtual events and online support groups emerged as alternatives to in-person gatherings, helping to maintain connections.
- Targeted outreach efforts were implemented to ensure equitable access to vaccines and health resources for LGBTQ+ individuals.
- Public health campaigns aimed to address specific concerns within the community regarding vaccine hesitancy.
- Overall, the pandemic has highlighted existing inequalities while also fostering resilience and solidarity within the LGBTQ+ community.

The 2019 board of directors were Craig Laberge-Esparza/President, JR Laberge-Esparza/VP-operations, Neil Macernie/VP-Public Relations, Miranda Sedillo/Treasurer, Suzi Alexander/Secretary, Maryanne Miceli-Mendoza/Director, Justin Vigil/Director, Tony Carson/Director, Michelle Miceli-Mendoza/Director, Ray Sierra-Lopez/Director, Miguel Ulloa/Director, Chris Homan/Director, Angela Redman/Director, Logan Wells/Director, Augustina Joanna Montoya/Director, and Michael Benavidez/Director.

This must be noted because Albuquerque Pride's Official Annual General Meeting did not occur until August and the newly appointed/voted Board of Directors had not been yet selected. Therefore, the board in 2019 had to make the decision to postpone the parade and Pridefest. Despite the heaviness that we as a community, state, nation, and the world would experience collectively humanity did not know how to deal. Mauro Walden-Montoya a treasured and honored leader in the GLBTQ+ movement in Albuquerque and the United States would write the following statement:

> For the first time in 46 years, Albuquerque Pride would be canceled. Not because of protesters or a hostile government, but an invisible enemy in the air that can strike anyone, leaving devastating effects. If you lived through the AIDS crisis in the 1980s and 1990s, you might be having flashbacks to that horrible time. Everyone was afraid. There were calls for quarantine for gay men. Flash forward to 2020, and we're ALL in quarantine. Albuquerque Pride wasn't canceled during the AIDS epidemic, but as we learned more about HIV, we learned how it is - and is NOT - transmitted. COVID-19 is a new (to humans anyway) disease that is mostly airborne. And therein lies its danger. No one knows who has it and who doesn't unless they become sick. They could be contagious long before they exhibit symptoms. And if you have underlying medical conditions, such as HIV or cancer, as well as being over 60, your chance of death is much higher. Even healthy people have died from this disease. It strikes everyone differently. And that's part of the problem. So, the leaders of ABQ Pride made a wise choice to cancel this year's Pride events. Hopefully, thanks to actions by Governor Michelle Lujan Grisham and local officials, we have hit the peak and cases, and deaths, will start to taper off. But that is unknown at this point. Hence the cancellation.
>
> The cancellation has caused great disappointment in the LGBTQ+ community, but most understand why. For those that are upset about the cancellation, and for those that are disappointed, but get the reasoning, let's examine what we call "Gay Pride." Pride events can be traced back to 1970, the year following the Stonewall Riots in New York City. Stonewall was the turning point for the homosexual community. We collectively said, "We won't take second class status anymore!" The following year, celebrations were held in various cities to show our pride. We began using our language rather than the clinical word homosexual. We chose "gay" because we each believe our lives are something to be celebrated, not something shameful. Something happy and cheerful. But our lives before Stonewall were not that way, and remain that way, in many places. Yet, we still celebrate Pride every year. We won't be marching down Central Avenue or having a festival at the Santa Fe Plaza, but we can continue to carry our PRIDE in ourselves, what our community has accomplished, and how much work we still have to do. We can get married in all 50 states. But in over half the States, you can still be fired for being LGBTQ or denied housing or employment. Our

pride carries us through these difficult situations. We know when we work together, we can make things better. We're working on getting a federal, non-discrimination law passed so States won't deny protections, and LGBTQ citizens will be protected under federal law. We're working on acceptance of gender identity for our transgender brothers and sisters. We work to protect our kids in schools from bullying. We should be proud of our victories. We should celebrate them while forging ahead to become full citizens in this country.

A big parade, festival, and related events aren't all there is to Pride. Pride means being YOU every day. It means becoming who you are supposed to be. It's about taking pride in the steps getting there, as well as having a newfound respect for yourself living your own life. Pride is being held virtually by many organizations worldwide. You can join in with friends and families. You can celebrate along with the community. Hopefully, by the end of June, we'll be hosting parties, dinners, or other events to celebrate. You can be proud of yourself, your community, and the ability to live as you choose. Pride is about loving and respecting yourself and your community. It's about helping others come out of the closet and getting legislation passed to protect our community. It's about meeting with your elected officials and pushing them! There are so many ways to celebrate Pride outside of just a few days a year. Let's make PRIDE every day of the year!

P&E - Mauro Walden-Montoya

On top of the Pandemic another horrific newsworthy event would occur on May 25, 2020, when police were called by a Cup Foods grocery store employee, who suspected that Floyd had used a counterfeit $20 bill. Floyd was sitting in a car with two other passengers. Police officers forcibly removed him from the car and detained him. Police alleged that Floyd struggled with the officers, and "began saying repeatedly that he could not breathe" even before being pinned to the ground. Floyd would be murdered by Derek Chauvin, a white Minneapolis police officer, who pressed his knee to Floyd's neck for 9 minutes and 29 seconds while Floyd was handcuffed face down in the street. As seen in a witness's cellphone video, two other officers further restrained Floyd, and a fourth prevented onlookers from intervening as Floyd repeatedly stated that he could not breathe. During the final two minutes, Floyd was motionless and had no pulse, but Chauvin kept his knee on Floyd's neck and back even as emergency medical technicians arrived to treat Floyd.

The medical examiner found that Floyd's heart stopped while he was being restrained and that his death was a homicide caused by "cardiopulmonary arrest complicating law enforcement subdual, restraint, and neck compression," though fentanyl intoxication and recent methamphetamine use may have increased the likelihood of death. A second autopsy commissioned by Floyd's family, also found his death to be a homicide, specifically citing asphyxia due to neck and back compression; it ruled out the possibility that underlying medical problems contributed to Floyd's death and said that Floyd being able to speak while under Chauvin's knee did not mean he could breathe. The killing of George Floyd by a police officer in Minneapolis leads to a massive resurgence of the movement, resulting in global protests and increased awareness of racial injustice. The impact of this movement would influence public discourse, policy discussions, which would lead to the call for police reform and social justice initiatives. It would further reinvigorate The Black Lives Matter movement which began in 2013 in response to the acquittal of George Zimmerman, who fatally shot Trayvon Martin, an unarmed Black teenager. The George Floyd murder would also inspire various organizations and coalitions to focus on racial equality including Black Lives Matter. On June 1st, after a planned peaceful protest that began at 7:00 p.m. at University and Central that lasted several hours, another group came out to downtown Albuquerque after midnight and began vandalizing businesses and damaging property.

The first wave of protesters was organized peacefully, with APD's traffic officers helping block traffic for the large group. There were some acts of graffiti, but most people marched in peace. When they reached UNM and splintered into smaller groups, the protest eventually ended. Later, after midnight, there were reports of a gathering that started vandalizing businesses and damaging property. Some started small fires in dumpsters and eventually in the middle of some intersections. APD deployed its Emergency Response Teams to a large portion of Downtown to keep people from vandalizing property and causing violence. Roving crowds moved up and down Central Avenue between 1st and 8th Streets. They also moved north and south, between Copper and Silver.

Some people threw bottles and other items at officers. Some climbed on building rooftops and threw things down to the street. After a few hours, shots were fired at police on Central, in front of the KiMo Theater with no injuries. Shortly after that, several individuals started breaking windows at the KiMo and entered the historic building with some making it to the rooftop. There was a fear they might start a fire inside the historic building. Fortunately, several police units moved in quickly to stop the action and save the building from further damage. Several businesses owned by residents also sustained damage, including Humble Coffee, Filling Philly, Standard Diner. EFFEX Nightclub one of our gay clubs would also be vandalized. As vehicle traffic slowed on Central and additional police units were called into the area, the Emergency Response Teams were able to gain control and eventually end the violence. Since EFFEX was vandalized Albuquerque Pride Board would not make a statement; however, Mayor Tim Keller would make a response:

> What we saw overnight downtown was not a protest, and it was not Albuquerque. Protesting is our constitutional right as Americans. We are strongest when we use it to come together as one and use our voices to express outrage and call for change, rather than using our hands to tear each other down. As your Mayor, I want to acknowledge the pain, anger, sorrow and frustration we are feeling in these times. Here in Albuquerque, we stand with those grieving these incidents around the nation. We stand with those calling for justice. I believe that Black Lives Matter, and so does the City of Albuquerque. We stand in solidarity with the African American community who are grieving the recurring violence against their community. What we saw last night was separate violence that must stop now.

Albuquerque Pride would be thwarted into this movement which would cause tension between individual board members and the community. They were not prepared for the backlash since the Albuquerque Pride Board took such a long time to make a statement according to Seliah DeLeon, and when Albuquerque Pride did make a video to distribute to the community, members felt it was a little too late. Many vocal community members spoke passionately about the dissolution of Albuquerque Pride and because of the tensions that arose some board members would resign effective immediately. Statements were also made from board of directors that maybe this should be the end of Pride in Albuquerque.

At an Albuquerque Pride Board Meeting on June 15th, there was a discussion about the dissolution of ABQ Pride because of the attacks against several board members, the resignation of the VP of operations, and the retiring of many of the executive board members. It was stated that there was a possibility that the current directors would not return for another term because of the negativity, blaming, and lack of unity in the community. Suzi Alexander (Secretary) would make the following statement:

> I was hysterical. I was crying and I was taking the minutes. I was the secretary at the time, and I was saying, we can't end this. There's so much more we have to do. There's so much more that I have to do, I will do whatever I have to. We will keep it open. I will find board members. I will step up and lead the organization as best that I can and I'm not going anywhere. I have a lot more to do on the board.

When the pandemic hit, along with the hurdles that were going in the country. Alexander would state:

> You know, Trans rights, very important thing that we deal with still, Black Lives Matter. I wouldn't say attacks, but there was concern and there was a disconnect with the community and everything that was going on, the seasoned board members who has been with Pride for eight, nine years, ten years plus, were all retiring. So, there wasn't a lot of interest because of what was going on in the community. We struggled trying to find board members because it's hard work. It's hard work getting people to stay on. So, there was concern, I remember the meeting we had, and it was just a discussion that the president at the time brought up because of the retiring of so many of the board members— maybe we need to, you know dissolve Albuquerque Pride.

Despite this controversy, on June 13th, hundreds of people and dozens of cars lined Central in downtown Saturday afternoon to support the LGBTQ community and the Black Lives Matter movement. Vehicles decorated with pride flags and balloons made their way up and down Central between Fifth and Nob Hill while people on sidewalks held signs urging people to support transgender rights and demanding justice for George Floyd. An Albuquerque Pride board member says he is not surprised to see the big turnout in Albuquerque. "As a black man, black trans-man in this community, it's important for me to be here representing with the board of Albuquerque Pride and they've been supportive 100 percent," Maxwell McIntyre said. This parade was not organized by any specific group.

Also, on the same day there were 25 marchers that met at the Albuquerque Social Club (SOCH) with an American, New Mexican, and Pride flags and would proceed east on Central and end at the NM State Fairgrounds. This contingency was led under the direction of Dr. PJ Sedillo and Tony Ross. They were given the blessing from the Pride Board who sanctioned this as the official Pride Parade for 2020 to honor the 25 brave individuals in 1976. This act would continue the history of being the continued and longest running parade/march on historic Route 66, Central Avenue.

Albuquerque Pride would make it somewhat intact to the August, Annual Meeting. Only Suzi Alexander would be qualified to run for an officer position according to the bylaws because of the number of board members who refused to serve anymore terms or had resigned. She decided to put her hat for the presidency and won. The newly elected Albuquerque Pride Board for 2020 consisted of Suzi Alexander-President, Neil Macernie-Vice President, Matthew Maturino-King-Treasurer, Michael Benavidez-Secretary, Alanna Phillips-Director, Damian Ortiz Hernandez-Director, Joshua Lucero-Martinez-Director, Ryan Perrigo-Director, Sean Winthrop-Director, Christopher Garcia-Director, Tommy Sloan-Director, Richard Brethour-Bell-Director, Nic Sedillo-Director, and the 2020 Titleholders Mr. NM Pride Goliath Steel and Miss Seliah Deleon. Goliath Steel would move to Denver and was allowed to keep his title because of problems of being able to participate due to the pandemic. Albuquerque Pride would experience a first in 2020.

Suzy Alexander would be elected president and although not the first female who had served such as co-president pat ballie and other females in a similar role before the incorporation of Albuquerque Pride, Suzi Alexander would become the first lesbian president elected solely and would be thrown into the job of ensuring the existence of Albuquerque Pride. This team and collective board of directors would face numerous problems under the leadership of Alexander one being how to produce an event during Corvid's destruction or consider if Albuquerque Pride would even exist.

2020

The International Pride theme for 2020 was *Exist Persist Resist* which was not utilized that year. Although there would be no parade or Pridefest, due to the restrictions due to Covid. the Albuquerque Pride Board's would decide to purchase official T-shirts to honor the event by having a physical historical record for the Albuquerque Pride Archives. They purchased only 50 shirts.

Even though these were tumultuous times the Albuquerque Pride Board added a little humor to the design of the T-shirt. The design has the earth with animated eyes, wearing a Pride Flag mask. There are different germs surrounding the Earth with the wording located underneath the Earth which was Albuquerque Pridefest. The word fest was crossed out and in written in script was the word pandemic. The overall humorous presentation was needed during a time of uncertainty. Albuquerque Pride would survive another year and prepare for the 2021; however, there was another issue that was pressing the Albuquerque LGBTQ+ community. The historic club known as the SOCH (Albuquerque Social Club-longest-running LGBTQ+ bar in New Mexico's) has always played an iatrical part of the existence of Albuquerque Pride and would launch a campaign to avoid closing its doors because of the pandemic. Mydnyte (past board member of Albuquerque Pride) would state:

> The LGBTQ club on the corner of Central Ave. and Montclaire Dr. in Nob Hill had been the members-only Albuquerque Social Club since the early 80s. But for about a decade before that, it was a gay bar known as The Heights, who was there at the beginning. It was like Saturday Night Fever because we had the same dance floors with the lights under the plexiglass, but we had an after-hours club in the back bar, Last Chance Disco. They could have sodas and juice and dance for another two hours. Also, the back-parking lot was like the cruise. I mean, everybody went there.

The SOCH board of directors would reverse the decision to close permanently after their secretary, Gail Starr stated that, "*the building's landlord reached out with a generous offer.*" This would change the dynamics of how much the SOCH would have to raise to stay afloat. The Albuquerque Social Club Board would let the community know that they needed to raise at least $60,000. This is what the business owed from several years of back taxes. However, the progress of the campaign was halted when the pandemic shut the SOCH in March.

The SOCH and its members have started fundraising on multiple platforms online, including GoFundMe, Facebook and PayPal and with the support of the community coming together Albuquerque's longest running LGBTQ+ bar in New Mexico's would survive. Located in Chapter 2 is about the importance of bars for our community. We must remember that gay bars have played a pivotal role in LGBTQ+ history, emerging as safe havens when societal acceptance was minimal, if not entirely absent. Beginning in the mid-20th century, these bars provided one of the few public spaces where LGBTQ+ individuals could freely express their identities...**and it is where Pride began at the little bar known as the Stonewall Inn.**

Chapter 18

Albuquerque Pride 2021, 2022, 2023, 2024 -TRANSITION
Albuquerque Pride 2021

To explain any confusion about the process on how decisions are made, there is an election process for Albuquerque Pride that would begin at each Annual General Meeting held in August. This official board meeting has been open to the public since being incorporated it is a requirement for all businesses/organizations in New Mexico who are needed to follow with specific regulations.

Pride in Albuquerque occurred in June since 1976 and board members were elected every August (since incorporating), where the new approved annual budget and elected team of board members would be responsible to produce Pride for the upcoming year. In the past, the election of the new board members and review of the proposed budget was usually an easy transition of leadership and monetary review. That said, after the tumultuous year in 2020, it became more difficult to sustain funds, qualifying board of directors due to by-law requirements, and the attempt to fix the "brokenness" of the community.

To reiterate, the 2020 Albuquerque Pride Board consisted of Suzi Alexander-President, Neil Macernie-Vice President, Matthew Maturino-King-Treasurer, Michael Benavidez-Secretary, Alanna Phillips-Director, Damian Ortiz Hernandez-Director, Joshua Lucero-Martinez-Director, Ryan Perrigo-Director, Sean Winthrop-Director, Christopher Garcia-Director, Tommy Sloan-Director, Richard Brethour-Bell-Director, Nic Sedillo-Director, and the 2020 Titleholders Mr. NM Pride Goliath Steel and Miss Seliah Deleon. They would be responsible for recommendation for the events in 2021 while working on the tarnished image of Albuquerque Pride.

Most of these board members would end their terms in August and choose not to continue volunteering in 2021. After canceling 2020's LGBTQ Pride celebrations due to the pandemic, Albuquerque Pride pushed forward with mostly online events for 2021. Pride would have tentative plans for an in-person celebration later in the summer, if the State would allow.

Under the new leadership for 2021, Suzi Alexander, President of Albuquerque Pride would credit her new team of board members who helped her pave the way for success as Albuquerque Pride's first-ever female President. The other 2021 board consisted of Vice President-Bia Romero, Secretary-Pete Garcia, Treasurer-Matthew Maturino, Entertainment Coordinator-Steph Romero, Director-Jaden Montoya, Director-Michael Noker, and Director- Amanda Sanchez. Usually in March there would be a pageant, but in 2021, there was no pageant that took place and the Pride Board decided to honor Seliah DeLeon as Miss NM Pride who became the only triple crowned Miss NM Pride. She recommended that Trey C. Michaels be also honored as the 2021 Mister NM Pride. He had been supporting the organization for years and as the board had done in the past, they had the ability to declare a title if it was well deserved.

2021

Albuquerque Pride would be calling its June event series the "Coming Out of Pandemic Edition." The InterPride theme for 2020 was #YouAreIncluded which was not utilized, but along with the chosen title "Coming Out of Pandemic Edition"; the official 2021 Albuquerque Pride Theme would be *Coming Out Together*. The T-shirts would be available in pink with the logo at the top of the graphic which had two diverse hands clasped together with the theme circling the two hands.

Neil Macernie past Vice President of Public Relations would not run for office again but would support the board with his expertise in technology. He stated, "We had a lot of outcries from last year that people just wanted something and that something includes virtual events every weekend the month of June, including Sunday educational discussions and Friday night DJ sets for at-home dance parties." This year's Albuquerque PrideFest 2021 would be virtual. Throughout the month the official Albuquerque Pride organization is sponsoring Zoom-based dance parties, starting with DJ Stitch on June 2 from 8pm to 9:30pm. Groove to the sounds of DJ Stitch and celebrate your Pride! Join in for free on ZOOM. This was the schedule of events that took place:

- **Friday, June 4**
  Celebration Theatre Company, Metropolitan Community Church of Albuquerque, and NM Black Cat Cultural Enterprises present the original stage play *Through a Window* on June 4 at 7pm. *Through A Window*, written by Maury Evans, "silhouettes the struggles, anxieties and complexities brought about by a worldwide pandemic." Tickets are $20 general admission and available at onthestage.com/show/celebration-theatre-company/through-a-window-63785. Other performances take place on June 5, 11 and 12 at Black Cat Community Center (3013 Monte Vista Blvd NE) *Only if approved by the State of NM regulations due to COVID.*
- **Saturday, June 5**
  PrideFest and Black Cat Community Center host Forever Young on June 5 at 8pm. This special, online event is a talent showcase featuring Albuquerque's LGBTQIA+ youth. Join in for free at us02web.zoom.us/j/87379888250.
- **Sunday, June 6**
  "Implicit bias" is the unconscious attitudes, reactions, stereotypes, and categories that affect behavior and understanding. Implicit bias often refers to unconscious racial or socioeconomic bias toward people of our community. The key to combating racism is awareness. Richard Brethour-Bell speaks on the topic of Implicit Bias Awareness on June 6 at 2pm. Join in for free via Zoom (us02web.zoom.us/j/87215450391).
- **Saturday, June 12**
  A celebration of sexual orientation and gender identity hits the virtual stage with Can't Hide My Pride, a cabaret event streaming live from the stage at Sidewinders Bar and Grill. It fires up June 12 at 8pm. Live in your liberation, relish your pride and share your love (for free) at us02web.zoom.us/j/84444786570.

- **Saturday, June 12**
  It's still too early to gather for an in-person pride parade. But you can join the "unofficial" Bernalillo County Pride Drive 2021: Vaccinate Against Hate event on June 12. Starting at 10am, drivers are encouraged to gather at the parking lot at Sidewinders (4200 Central Ave. SE). The car parade will head down Central Ave. West, through Old Town, then back to Sidewinders. For more information or to register for the event, go to bit.ly/3uBGrQO.
- **Sunday, June 13**
  On June 13 at 2pm, Adrien Lawyer, co-founder and executive director of the Transgender Resource Center NM, hosts In the Life, a roundtable discussion on the transgender experience. See it
  for free on Zoom (us02web.zoom.us/j/84499693351).
- **Saturday, June 19**
  A showcase of New Mexico's culturally diverse entertainment hits the virtual stage with New Mexico Collage. On June 19, starting 8pm, experience some of the countless customs, traditions and experiences that create our LGBTQ+ tapestry. To check out this free showcase, go
  to us02web.zoom.us/j/83698233739.
- **Saturday, June 19**
  From the creator of *I Am Harvey Milk*, comes the first fully-virtual production of Andrew Lippa's *Unbreakable*. The New Mexico Gay Men's Chorus presents this "musical chronology of the Gay Experience in America spanning 120 years of history too long unsung." Aaron Howe conducts the NMGMC and full orchestra. Featuring guest soloists Bill Brooks, Dianna Hughes, Lina Ramos and Brian Seals. It's available for viewing on June 19 at 7:30pm. Tickets ($20 to $50) are available at eventbrite.com/e/unbreakable-tickets-156190155961.
- **Friday, June 25**
  Santa Fe Pride kicks off with a movie night featuring the 2019 Elton John biopic, *Rocketman*. Doors open at Railyard Park in Santa Fe (740 Cerillos Rd.) at 6:30pm. The films start around 8pm. This outdoor event is free. To guarantee a spot, reserve your ticket at holdmyticket.com/event/373501-rocketman.
- **Saturday, June 26**
  Santa Fe Pride returns with Pride Drive 2021, a virtual event broadcast "live" from the Plaza in Santa Fe on June 26 from 11:30am to 3:30pm. Join the parade in a vehicle—preferably decorated to show your Pride for a Pride Drive around Santa Fe through Downtown and around the Plaza. Organizers are asking for a $25 donation per large, motorized vehicle or a $15 donation per smaller vehicle. Drivers will be provided a full-size Pride flag for their large vehicle and a small Pride flag for their small vehicle—in addition to some other Pride favors. Register online at hrasantafe.org/pride-events-2021.

- **Sunday, June 27**
  Experience of the past, present and future of Pride. New Mexico Highlands professor and author of *Solidarity Through Pride: LGBT Pride in Albuquerque 1976–2016. Dr. PJ* Sedillo presents Pride Alive. Listen to this free, historical lecture, June 27 at 2pm on Zoom (us02web.zoom.us/j/87225735658).

The Pride Board had made a statement to the news and community that a parade would be off the table this year because the city still was not issuing event permits for the streets. It did not want negative reactions from the State who had the power to fine any events not appropriately following the rules and regulations stated for social distancing and the number of individuals at an event. Neil Macernie would state that whether a colorful Nob Hill parade would be part of Pride will depend on the city's shutdown status. "We're hopeful," said Macernie and "We're constantly checking with the city asking, 'OK, where are we at? Can we go ahead and start planning for this?'" Statements from the board would be released weekly to keep the community informed. However, as June approached the board would release a statement, "if you are looking for a parade during Pride Month aren't totally out of luck, though there is an unaffiliated pride (P not capitalized) parade which is not associated with Albuquerque Pride which is Vaccinate Against Hate." The event was COVID-safe.

This pride car parade was scheduled to roll down Central Avenue on Saturday, June 12, beginning at 10:00 a.m. As mentioned above on the list of events on Saturday, June 12 there was an in-person pride parade noted as the "unofficial" Bernalillo County Pride Drive. Also, on the same day, as was done in previous years, there were 25 marchers that met at the Albuquerque Social Club (SOCH) with an American, New Mexican, and Pride flags and would proceed east on Central and end at the NM State Fairgrounds. This contingency was again led under the direction of Dr. PJ Sedillo and Tony Ross. They were given the blessing from the Albuquerque Pride Board who sanctioned this as the official Pride Parade for 2020 to honor the 25 brave individuals in 1976. By doing this they were able to have the historical event by bypassing the COVID restrictions from the State of New Mexico. This act would continue the history of the event being the longest, continued running parade/march on historic Route 66, Central Avenue.

Albuquerque Pride/PrideFest held in August of 2021

Even though Pride Month was in June, Albuquerque locals celebrated on Aug. 20th and 21st. PrideFest was located at Expo New Mexico and had several events throughout the two days for the community to participate in. Albuquerque Pride would occur as new regulations imposed from New Mexico's Department of Health would proclaim that larger events could occur. The Pride Board moved swiftly and voted upon having a slightly scaled-down "In-Person Edition" of PrideFest with entertainment and vendors at the state-run Expo New Mexico on August 20th and 21st. Channel 13 News (KRQE) would state, "Even though Pride Month was in June, Albuquerque locals celebrated on August 20 and 21 and would have a number of events throughout the two days for the community to participate in." The Candlelight Vigil at Morningside Park would be on August 20th, and City Council President Cynthia Borrego would attend and show her support. She would state that, "the vigil offered reflection, remembrance, and celebration of living life and creating a future of unity and love." Council President Borrego was honored to join and support the Pride movement and our lesbian, gay, bisexual, transgender, intersex and queer/questioning (LGBTIQ) community and further state, "It was great to see so many amazing people, to gather again with friends, and share a smile, a memory, and a hug."

Others would come together to hear the voices of our diverse community and remember loved ones. Mattee Jim, Antonio José, James Brethour, and Suzanne Alexander shared their stories. The hosts of the event were New Mexico Titleholders, Seliah DeLeon and Trey C. Michaels. Members of the community were also asked to bring a photo of a lost loved one and use their mobile phone for a virtual candlelight.

Printed in the Albuquerque Journal Newspaper they would have the headline, "**PRIDE PARADE RETURNS TO ALBUQUERQUE, ATTENDEES CELEBRATE 'BEING ABLE TO BE WHO YOU ARE FINALLY'**." The second day of Albuquerque's PrideFest kicked off with the Pride Parade in Nob Hill. The parade traveled east and led participants to the state fairgrounds, where the final day of the festival was located. Saturday morning's parade drew a large crowd down Central Avenue. For many of the onlookers, attending Pride Parade has become an annual tradition. "We have probably been coming for at least 15 years. We came to celebrate ourselves and our community," said an Albuquerque resident. Another Albuquerque resident said he participates in the parade with his church. "To be present here is sending a message out that people aren't going to send me back into the closet and no pandemic will also force us there. It's like I tell people who don't understand, build a rainbow and fly over it," he said. Saturday morning's parade drew a large crowd down Central Avenue. For many of the onlookers, attending Pride Parade had become an annual tradition which had been missed by many because of the pandemic.

PrideFest would be located at Expo New Mexico and would be held for the first time in two locations in the fairgrounds which was the Spanish Village and the Indian Village two side by side venues. The experience of diversity would include live music from local musicians, amazing drag performances, an art reception, food and street vendors, historical archives, and more.

The Spanish Village would be called the FIERCE ZONE that had alcohol sales, and the main entertainment stage was called the Unicorn Stage which had local entertainment. There were also booths, food sales, and a beer garden. The Indian Village would be called the FABULOUS ZONE which was designated as family friendly and substance free. There was also a smaller stage called the Rainbow Stage which had covered seating and a dance area. In addition, there was a Kids Zone which had inflatable jumps and activities specifically designed for children, and vendors and food booths were also available.

Albuquerque Pride had completed 44 years of celebration for the lesbian, gay, bisexual, transgender, intersex and queer community and it would be a brief opportunity to "breath" and plan for next year. The struggles that the organization had been through would only make Albuquerque Pride stronger, but on the horizon, there would be more difficulties that could finally end the dissolution and existence of Albuquerque Pride.

Albuquerque Pride 2022

Albuquerque Pride Parade and PrideFest had made it through some difficult years and was ready to continue presenting this annual event celebrating lesbian, gay, bisexual, transgender, intersex, and queer (LGBTIQ) culture and pride. The Board started early with promotion by sending out social media posts stating:

> The upcoming Albuquerque Pride Parade is our unabashed celebration; a living, breathing manifestation of the out-and-proud mantra, putting the LGBTIQ community on full display. The two-mile parade is an opportunity for everyone to show their support and express this year's theme of pride, **"From Silence to Solidarity**."

The official T-shirt was offered in different colors and had the official logo at the top with the wording of the theme. Underneath them were raised fists in the each in a color of the rainbow.

2022

There was a second shirt available for sales in 2022. It was available in blue which had the Albuquerque skyline with balloons in the air. The wording Albuquerque Pride was in the black cityscape. The Pride Board had decided to market a shirt with no theme or dates that could be sold at future Prides if there were left over shirts to be sold in 2023 or could be sold throughout the year online.

2022

The elected board for 2022 was Suzi Alexander-President, Bia Romero-Vice President, Pete Garcia-Secretary, Matthew Maturino-Treasurer, Steph Romero-Entertainment Coordinator, Jaden Montoya-Director, Michael Noker-Director, Amanda Sanchez-Director. In 2022 the pageant returned with the requirements of the title be what the individual wanted to compete in. The following were the 2022 Titleholders:

- 2022 Mr. NM Pride Seph Michele Alan (Relinquished)
- 2022 MX NM Pride Lola La Bruja
- 2022 Miss NM Pride Tomahawk Martini

The Albuquerque Pride Board elected in August, at the general meeting, would begin to plan the event for June of 2022. Unfortunately, the board would experience even more controversies this year that would highlight growing rifts in the community.

In April, two months before Pride would occur, The Albuquerque Pride Board of Directors voted to ban the Albuquerque Police Department (APD) from this year's events, citing the 1969 Stonewall riots as their reason. All but one Albuquerque Pride Board member voted during a meeting to ban the police from having a float in the parade, according to KOB 4 a local television news station. The board also banned the police from having a booth at the PrideFest. Board member Frankie Flores, New Mexico Pride 2022 titleholder, said during the meeting that having police at the event would be, "disrespectful to our community, but also to our ancestors," KOB 4 reported. "You know, people forget that Stonewall wasn't, 'Hey, let's get together and play 'I will survive." It was a riot! It was an intersectional riot that lasted three days," Flores said.

Bia Romero, Vice-President would make the motion to ban the police, "I (Bia Romero) motion to not allow APD in the Pride parade or in PrideFest 2022, with the possibility to revisit for 2023 at the Annual General Meeting if lines of communication have been opened and the community feedback has been positive." The motion would be seconded and voted upon even though some board members thought the police should be included, as they have been at past Pride events. One such person was Mathew Maturio who said, "I think we should, in some sense, have them at Pride this year just to build that relationship to show the community we are with them, and they are with us."

The APD was part of the Pride Parade in 2019 and 2021; officers rode down the parade route with the floats. The APD had a booth at Pride Fest in 2021 on the Expo New Mexico grounds and being banned in 2022 was unexpected. APD Community Ambassador Chase Jewell was surprised with Sunday's vote to ban the Albuquerque Police Department from Pride. He said this was not the outcome he was expecting. "I would say it is more of a surprise, but it is something that we are willing to work with the Pride board moving forward."

Chase Jewell further would state, "It's not something that we are going to force ourselves to be a part of. If they are not ready for us to be in the events or in Pride, then that's OK, and that is a relationship we will continue to work on." It must be mentioned that no representatives from the APD were present at the board meeting, despite being invited to attend. Vice-President Bia Romero would state, "the news is here, where is APD? This is not a private thing where they didn't know it was going on; they had the opportunity to be here today or send a representative today."

On a positive note, both the APD and the Albuquerque Pride Board vowed to work together so the police can be invited to future Pride events. "Moving forward, I will take this on myself to work with Officer Chase, the community ambassador with APD, because we do want to heal this," Josh Martinez, secretary of the ABQ Pride Board, said. "We are an organization that has the power to impact our community, and we do want to have that relationship, moving forward." Despite the controversy and the rift between community members and the organization, Pride events would continue for the 46th annual event. The following is the schedule of events for 2022:

June 6-11 Albuquerque Pride:

- June 6th 1-5 pm Silver Pride: Senior Social Orpheum Community Hub, 500 2nd Street NW
- June 7th 4-8 pm Kids of Pride Orpheum Community Hub, 500 2nd Street NW
- June 8th 4-8 pm She+ Fest Orpheum Community Theater, 500 2nd Street NW
- June 9th 6:30 pm From Silence to Solidarity Candlelight Vigil, Morningside Park [Reception following at 4021 Central NE]
- June 10th 5-9 pm ***Prefest*** (**description first time ever used**) 2022, Expo NM
- June 11th 10 am Albuquerque Pride Parade (starting at Girard Ave)
- June 11th 12 pm Albuquerque PrideFest (Expo NM – Indian Village/Spanish Village)

The Pride Parade returned bigger and better in Albuquerque since the pandemic began. Pride would be able to provide the mandatory and "stable" organizational practices that are needed to produce an event that is considered to be one of the largest events that occur each year in New Mexico. The following requirements were taken from an online form for those interested in having an entry to participate.

IMPORTANT DATES AND TIMES:

- **Seminar (MANDATORY):** We will send out notifications for seminars available both in person and on Zoom.
- **Ticket+Pass Distribution (MANDATORY):** Tuesday, May 31 to Thursday, June 2, 2022, from 8:30 AM to 5 PM at Kesselman Jones, Inc. on 6100 Indian School Rd NE, Ste 115 and Friday, June 10th from 11:00 AM to 5:00 PM at Expo New Mexico.
- **Check-in:** time is 7:30 a.m. to 9:00 a.m. on Saturday, June 11th. Entry time will be dependent on your type of entry and will be included in your parade packet. **New entries are not allowed to register on the day of the event!**
- **Step-off:** The start of parade will step-off at 10:00 AM.
- **Tear-down:** time is approximately 11:00 a.m. All groups enter Gate 2 of EXPO NM. **PENDING**
- **Sunrise:** Saturday at 5:10 AM (MST)
- **Sunset:** Saturday at 7:54 PM (MST)

After a pause from the pandemic, not even the sun could scorch the excitement of a full-fledged Pride Parade! Albuquerqueans felt it was finally safe to be us in public. The event drew an enthusiastic crowd, according to Ariana Carabeajal, who attended her first Pride event, celebrating openly stated, "this event is special just for freedom, for the most part, being able to be who you are. I'm very happy to be able to be out here with everybody and just be happy." The outbreak of COVID-19 caused the parade's cancelation in 2020 and 2021 in the traditional celebratory month of June. This year offered a chance for new Pride goers and others who have participated for years to meet in a spirit of togetherness and freedom. Old attendees afraid of being out in public were happy and that new attendees would enjoy the festival and believe the new excitement made the parade more enjoyable than in years past.

One Pride was excited that the parade resumed with approved safety protocols and said, "I'm very, very excited because it's been a while since I've been to Pride, I was still unsure about coming out to support in 2021 at the August event, especially during quarantine, that is why I feel like so many people came out today, and I was anticipating that there was going to be a very large crowd today and there is, and I'm so excited and I'm very, very, happy." Starting in 2022 the parade would have KOAT Channel 7 news lead weatherman Byron Morton and anchorwoman Sasha Lenniger emcee along with Dr. PJ Sedillo. Music would be blaring from the DJ before the Parade would start to get the crowd going. The emcees would give free tickets to spectators to attend PrideFest by having them show their best dance moves, strutting their Pride outfit, or just for being there for the first time. When the parade started the emcees were able to introduce each entry. Byron and Sasha would also be the official judges to choose the best entry in the parade. In 2022, there were over 40,000 spectators.

The Albuquerque PrideFest annual event was held at the state fairgrounds of Expo New Mexico. The public will be entering the event at Gate 3, which is located at the corner of San Pedro Dr. NE and Copper Ave. NE in Albuquerque, New Mexico. PrideFest would become a safe space for expression, support, and unity of the LGBTIQ community from Albuquerque to all of New Mexico. Over 20,000 people attended PrideFest in 2022, showing the fullness of New Mexico's diverse community.

The location would be similar as in 2021 at the Spanish Village and Indian Village at Expo NM. The Pride Board ensured that the event was safe for all ages, orientations, gender identifications, and cultures! Some of the attractions at PrideFest were two entertainment stages, a child-friendly area, enclosed drinking areas, exhibitors, and food stands. The Headliner for PrideFest was the singer and songwriter known as Tinashe. She is an American singer, songwriter, dancer, and actress. After an early career in acting and as a member of a girl group, she launched a successful solo music career in the 2010s. Tinashe is known for her versatility and hands-on approach to her music. She is often credited with combining immediate pop hooks with intimate R&B textures, drawing from genres like trap, dancehall, and electronic music. In addition to her music, she is a multi-talented artist who also produces, mixes, and creative directs her work.

Albuquerque Pride wanted to ensure a positive identity because of the APD controversy that they would market statements that the priority of Albuquerque Pride was to, "Continually work for inclusivity, equality, community connections, and awareness of LGBTIQ issues with leadership development, education, support programs, and community events throughout the year." KOAT an official sponsor would also make a statement of support:

> In celebration of LGBTQ+ Pride Month, KOAT honors the dignity, equality and self-affirmation of lesbian, gay, bisexual, and transgender people. We shine light on challenges individuals have faced but overcame as they graciously power through their journey. Many who have helped paved the way unapologetically and continue to serve as a beacon of light within the LGBTQ+ community and beyond.

Suzi Alexander, a New Mexico native, and Albuquerque Pride's first-ever female stand-alone president elected in August of 2020 wanted to take her team and the organization to new heights. However, Alexander said the journey to become president of the organization wasn't easy. She would state:

> Albuquerque Pride is a board of passionate individuals who all have the same goal for Albuquerque to provide a safe space. We want to educate. We want to share our stories and have people share their stories. We want to make a difference. We want to honor you. We're an organization that wants to educate and provide a safe space for our LGBTQ youth.

Again, it must be mentioned that Suzi Alexander had stepped up to be the leader, the only one qualified according to the bylaws when Albuquerque Pride was on the brink of closing its doors. Suzi Alexander would explain to the community that:

> My term is coming up in August. We have our annual general meeting where we install new board members. So, I know there's more that I can do. So, I plan on running again for president. I want to continue this female power drive that we started. We're not going to proceed more powerful and prideful than ever.

Albuquerque Pride 2023

Finally, in 2023 there would at last be no difficult controversies that Albuquerque Pride or the community would have to face. The Albuquerque Pride Board consisted of Suzi Alexander-President, Bia Romero-Vice President, Amanda Sanchez-Secretary, Jaden Montoya-Director, Stephanie Romero-Director, and Michael Noker-Director. The NM Pride Titleholders were,

2023 Mr. NM Pride Leonidas Rico Steel
2023 MX NM Pride Katie K. Bouvier
2023 Miss NM Pride Sativa Rico Stratton

More than 400 anti-LGBTQ bills have been filed in state legislatures across the country in 2023 and Saturday's Pride Parade would be the first since New Mexico's state lawmakers passed new protections for the LGBTQ community. Most notably the Reproductive and Gender-Affirming Health Care Freedom Act. Equality New Mexico would state, *"We've worked very hard for our rights, and we're very, we feel very strong about that. Right now, we're under attack.* There was an extra show of support from political leaders like Albuquerque Mayor Tim Keller, state Rep. Pameyla Herndon, and U.S. Sen. Martin Heinrich.

Pride would start of by celebrating Pride Month with The City of Albuquerque unveiling of a Bus Wrap and Flag Raising ceremony at Civic Plaza. Albuquerque Mayor Tim Keller, leaders from the City of Albuquerque, and Albuquerque Pride would come together to kick off a month of love and to show support for our LGBTQ+ community. A press conference was held in front of the Albuquerque Convention Center with an ABQ RIDE bus wrapped in a Pride wrap, which was curated by an in-house graphic designer who incorporated photos of local Albuquerque residents from previous Pride marches held in the city. After the press event, the group shuffled a few feet over to three flagpoles located at the Albuquerque Convention Center, and Mayor Tim Keller raised a Pride flag on one of the poles. Pride events for the 47th Annual Event would take place throughout the month of June in the City of Albuquerque.

In 2023, the International Association of Pride (InterPride) would no longer issue an international theme primarily due to the pandemic. Therefore, the Albuquerque Pride Board would choose/crate the theme "Your Pride is Showing." The shirt had the Albuquerque Pride logo at the top with the theme underneath. In the year 2023 there was an image of a balloon that replaced the zero in the year. The shirts were only available in the color white.

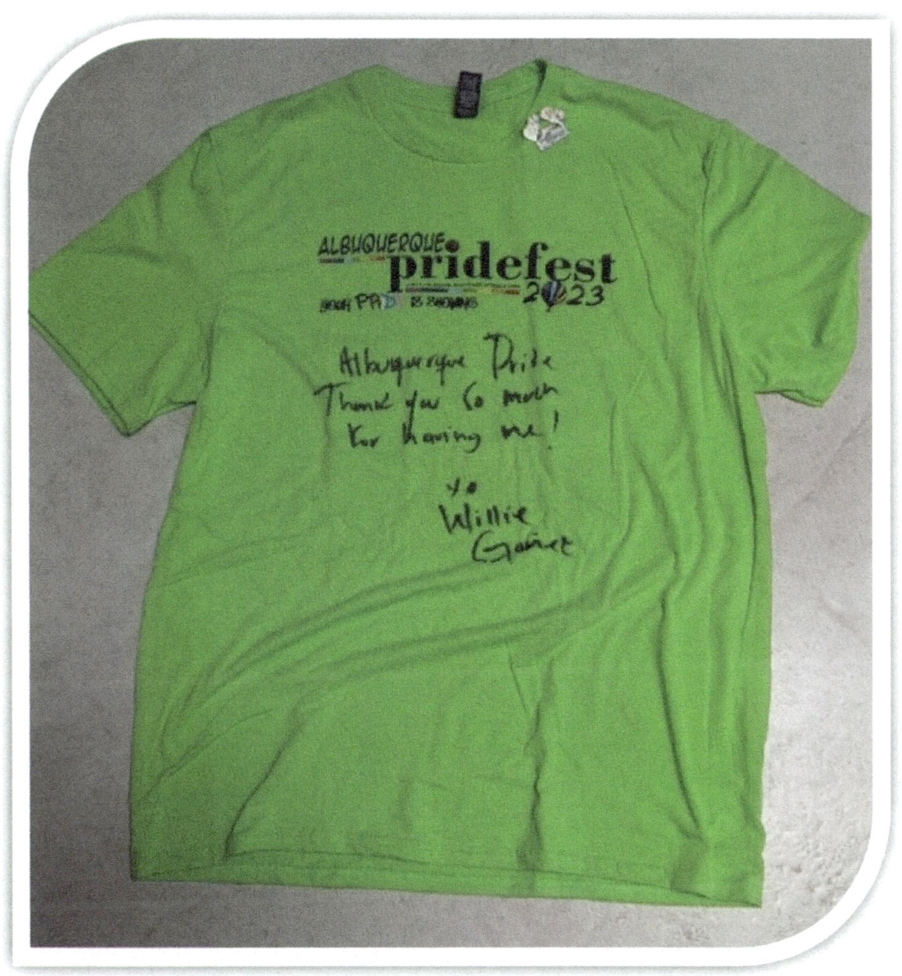

2023 Front

The image of the back of the T-shirt highlights the official Albuquerque Pride Sponsors. All volunteers would receive a free shirt for working the event(s) and these shirts were the only ones that had the sponsors on the back. Also, they were in a different color (this year green) so the volunteer could be identified easily during the event. These volunteer shirts in a different color were not available for sale to the public and throughout the years participants who did not volunteer would try to get a volunteer shirt as memorabilia.

2023 Back

The Albuquerque Pride Board would send out a statement to the community:

> We have experienced many challenges due to the COVID-19 pandemic since March 2020. Thanks to sponsors like you 2022 was a huge success! Although we were still at a smaller footprint at Expo NM, the attendance was phenomenal. Albuquerque Pride is very excited that we will be celebrating Pridefest 2023 at Balloon Fiesta Park.

The following is a list of the scheduled events:

- Monday June 5th with our SilverFest
- Tuesday June 6th is our KidsFest
- Wednesday June 7th SheFest
- Thursday, June 8th, we will honor those no longer with us at the Candlelight Vigil at Morningside Park.
- Friday, June 9th, PrideFest kicks off at Balloon Fiesta Park with a no charge event PreFest is from 5-9pm.
- Saturday, June 10th starts off with the Pride Parade still on Central Ave beginning at 10 am.
- Pridefest 2023 will begin at 3pm at Balloon Fuesta Park.

The ABQ LGBTQ+ Aids Pride 2023 Candlelight Vigil Thursday, June 8th. 630-830pm held again at Morningside Park on 3901 Lead Ave. SE 87108. That year the Albuquerque Pride board at the Candlelight Vigil wanted to honor all those we have lost to AIDS and those who are gone now for their work and advocacy for Gay Rights.

For the first time ever, a PreFest to the weekend festivities would begin for free on Friday Night Event at Balloon Fiesta Park. From 5-9 pm. Attendees would be able to witness a balloon glow after an open mic event. Bryce Risley, a seasoned balloonist would be the Pride Balloon Glow organizer for the Friday Night Spectacular. Not since 2009 would an Official Pride Pin be part of the merchandising of the event and an official Pride Balloon Pin would be available for purchase. The Balloon Glow was free on Friday starting with 7 pm glow to 8:00 pm. There were over 15 balloons present; however, due to the high winds, thunder, lightning, and rain they could not inflate which was a disappointment for the attendees. Many vendors and participants would leave the event grounds, and many would not show up because of the weather.

Saturday marked the City of Albuquerque's Pride celebration, one of the oldest in the country and is the second largest parade in New Mexico. UNM Truman Health Services lead with a float, followed by classic cars, motorcycles, horses, dancers and supporters as they marched through the Uptown neighborhood. The event had become a time-honored tradition in Albuquerque was back again with a wave of color. Dr. PJ Sedillo was interviewed by Channel 7 news and stated:

> We are here to honor those individuals of the past but also to honor those of the future of those here in Albuquerque, especially those in the LGBTQ+ community. We are all humans. We just want to be treated with respect. That's why this day is so important.

For the 47th Annual Albuquerque Pride the board had selected The University of New Mexico Truman Health Services as Grand Marshal. As New Mexico's premier health provider for the Lesbian, Gay, Bisexual, Transgender, Queer/Questioning, Intersex and Asexual (LGBTQIA+) community, their families, and other allies, UNM Truman Health Services had provided a safe medical home with highest level of care and latest treatment options for New Mexicans living with HIV, requiring gender services, seeking Hepatitis C testing and treatment and HIV post-exposure prophylaxis (PrEP). Craig LaBerge-Esparza, community health resources manager at UNM Truman Health Services, would state:

> For many years, Truman had been a part of the Albuquerque Pride tradition by marching, testing and uplifting the community year-after-year. Pride and Truman have been partners, making a difference in our community. Being the Grand Marshal for the 2023 Pride Parade is an honor our entire team is so proud of. We are excited to help lead the parade down Central Avenue for its 47th year.

According to Celina Herrera, health education coordinator for UNM Truman Health Services, PrideFest is one of the most anticipated events of the year for the clinic's staff and their patients. "*I can't imagine a Pride celebration without Truman*," Herrera said. "*Every June, I look forward to picking out a wig, slapping on some glitter and getting ready to march. It's become a tradition.*"

PrideFest 2023, celebrating the LGBTQ+ community in New Mexico had many activities, booths, the Pride Archives, a beer garden, and entertainment. The event was a success, but some people had to wait nearly an hour to get in, and said that waiting wasn't going to stop them. However, there were some people who left and said it was too much waiting in line in the 100-degree weather and decided to seek other events celebrating Pride in the city. In addition to the New Mexico Pride Titleholders hosting the event, Albuquerque Pride brought in local and national talents to the Unicorn and Rainbow stages. Pride Row celebrates all things Pride, and the Art Show showcased our amazing local artists. The KiDz Zone also had inflatables and an obstacle course for kids of all ages

The Headliner was Willie Gomez from the competition known as "The Voice." He was a Queer Latinx, dancer, singer, songwriter, actor and legend who had danced for

Britney Spears. Born in the Dominican Republic and raised in the city of Miami at the age of 13, became inspired by the greatest Pop artists of our generation. He immediately began taking dance and vocal training at MDA Studios. By the age of 17, he had already appeared with Latin artists such as: Thalia, Paulina Rubio, India and David Bisbal. Willie went on to perform on some of the biggest Latin award shows such as: "The Latin Billboards," "Latin Grammys," "Premios Juventud," and "Premios Lo Nuestro." Willie made the move to Los Angeles with high hopes of making it big in the pop music industry. He and his talents were quickly noticed and a whirlwind of success followed. He danced/toured the world with artists such as Britney Spears, Christina Aguilera, Katy Perry, Kesha, Kylie Minogue, Chayanne, Little Mix, and Mary J Blige. Along with his amazing vocal and dance skills, he has become an important performing artist and has recorded original songs with top writers and producers.

In 2020, in the midst of the quarantine and social distancing, he focused on his health, spending time with his family, and staying creative with his first-ever Global "Mojados" Virtual tour, by LiveNation. Reaching over 800 thousand fans in 35 different countries globally. In 2021, Willie released the single, "Salvaje", and "Borracho de tus Besos" alongside reggaeton heavyweight, Randy. But in 2022, he released his very first full album featuring all his greatest singles. Finally, Willie kicked off in 2023 strong with being selected to participate in season 24 of THE VOICE. Albuquerque Pride was thrilled to have him grace his entertainment savvy on the PrideFest Mainstage.

It should be reiterated that the Albuquerque Pride events bring in a flood of money to the City of Albuquerque businesses because hundreds of businesses and people gather for the Parade, PreFest, and the PrideFest in 2023. Turnout spoke for itself. Patrons and businesses alike gathered to enjoy Pridefest 2023 Saturday as it was the first time to take place at Balloon Fiesta Park.

The number of people showing up to enjoy themselves was a surprise for everybody. "This is the most amount of people that I have seen in years past," Daisy Rocero said. From vendors and businesses to everyday people, everyone enjoyed the turnout. Isabella Apodaca said, "I'm really excited. I love the support I love seeing the queer-owned businesses." LGBTQ+ businesses like Wiggle Wreaths and Crafts participated in Pridefest. Kimberly Jennings says it's great for business and good to get involved with the community. "It's a very inclusive opportunity every year and it's a very inclusive event to be a part of," Jennings said. Dozens of businesses showed up to display their work and services. Many said it's to get exposure and get involved, but it's also personal to them for families who identify as LGBTQ+, like his mother (Suzi Alexander), who is also president of ABQ Pride. "She's the best mom in the universe and I support a million percent. I support all her decisions, all her pride," Dusty Dibenedetti said, who also works at Dank Smoke & Grocery.

From basic wears to booths of every choice, businesses took advantage of the festival. Owners specified the importance of the event not only for their own businesses, but for the message the event is about showing your Pride.

Albuquerque Pride 2024

Albuquerque Pride would have a successful event in 2023, especially with daunting move of the PrideFest to Balloon Fiesta Park and the event out of Expo New Mexico (NM State Fair Grounds) where it had been produced there successfully for many years. The event had new logistics and a new team, but success was obtainable.

At the Annual General Meeting held in August 2023, would be the opportunity to select the official board officers to lead the 2024 Pride events. Suzi Alexander would be voted in as President, Jayden Montoya-Vice President of Operations, Sativa Rico Stratton (Raymond Sierra Lopez), Juan Rosales-Treasurer, Amanda Sanchez-Secretary, Leonidas Rico Steel (Robert Sierra Lopez), Daniel Romero-Director, and Savanna Martinez-Director. The 2024 NM Pride Titleholders were: Matthew Maturino-Mr. NM Pride, Rori the Rebel- MX NM Pride, and Miss Venture Faraday.

Riding on the success of the 2023 events, President Suzi Alexander would send out a letter to the community.

> Hello all, It's been a while since I've talked to you. I have been going through some personal family issues. I realize we all are going through issues in one way or the other, whether it's with the family we are born into, our chosen family, or with the issues that are happening in this world we live in. We are going through hardships and loss that affects us all deep within our soul. I know whatever is happening we are **stronger together**. In this world we live in, where we struggle but still, we honor and celebrate our existence. One thing is certain: we have a chance to make an indelible mark on history. If we don't vote we don't exist.
>
> We have to make our voices heard; we have to stand up to all who don't agree that "Equal rights for all doesn't mean fewer rights for you. It's not pie" And, to be clear, these are not new fights. The echoes of past discrimination against the LGBTQIA+ community are unmistakable. Similar tactics that were once wielded against gay men and lesbians are now being repurposed to target trans and nonbinary individuals. Records for the number of anti-trans bills introduced in state legislatures have been

shattered year after year, with 2024 poised to continue this troubling trend. Albuquerque Pride stands with Black Lives Matter, and Trans Lives Matter. May is around the corner, and you know what that means?

Pride month is nearly here. Albuquerque Pride is extremely excited to present this year's Pridefest, our theme is "Gather Dream & Amplify" More in 2024! We have a full week of events starting June 3rd. As an organization we want to give back to the community all year long, so we celebrate Pride 365 every second Saturday of the month at S4200 [Sidewinders Bar & Grill]. You are my brothers and sisters, and siblings! As president of this organization, I will continue to lead with honor with dignity which to me means recognizing the inherent worth of people and treating them in a way that shows them they matter. I still believe that a safer and freer world is possible.

Thank you for your support,
See you at Pridefest!

If you have any questions or concerns, you can come to our board meetings the 3rd Sunday of every month at one o'clock at MCCA church located on Lomas and Texas. You can also email me directly suzi.alexander@abqpride.com.

Have a prideful day,
Suzi Alexander

The following list of Pride Event is what happened around the City of Albuquerque in 2024:

Monday June 3

- Silverfest: An event celebrating the 55+ community. This is an all-ages event with food, fun, games, karaoke, and entertainment.
    - Location: The Orpheum Community Hub 500 2nd St. Albuquerque, NM 87102
    - Event information: https://www.abqpride.com/

Tuesday June 4

- Kids Fest: A celebration for the youth. This is an all-ages event with food, fun, games, story time, and entertainment.
    - Location: The Orpheum Community Hub 500 2nd St. Albuquerque, NM 87102
    - Event information: https://www.abqpride.com/

Wednesday, June 5

- She + Fest: A celebration of femininity. This is a 21+-only event. With performances, poetry, food, fun, music, and education.
    - Location: The Orpheum Community Hub 500 2nd St. Albuquerque, NM 87102
    - Event Information: https://www.abqpride.com/

Thursday, June 6

- Pride Memorial Candlelight Vigil: A yearly tradition remembering lost loved ones. With speeches from community members and titleholders.
    - Location: Morningside Park - 3901 Lead Ave SE Albuquerque NM 87108
    - Event information: https://www.abqpride.com/

Friday, June 7

- Raising Pride on Civic Plaza: Mayor Tim Keller commemorates Pride Month by raising the flag at Civic Plaza.
    - Time: 10 - 10:30 AM
    - Location: Civic Plaza - 1 Civic Plz, Albuquerque, NM 87102
- Prefest: A free event for all ages. Music, exhibitions, food, open mic, outdoor art show, dancing, and educational events.
    - Location: Balloon Fiesta Park 5500 Balloon Fiesta PKWY Albuquerque NM 87113
    - Event Information: https://www.abqpride.com/

Saturday, June 8

- Albuquerque Pride Parade: Starts on Central and Gerard and then moves east to Central and San Mateo.
    - Time: 10 AM
    - Location: Historic Route 66
    - Event Information: https://www.abqpride.com/
- Family Pride Celebration
    - Summary: Head over after the Pride Parade for a carnival-themed celebration. There will be games, live music, resources, and more!
    - Time: 11 AM - 2 PM
    - Location: Morningside Park - 3901 Lead Ave SE Albuquerque NM 87108
- Pride Afterparty
    - Summary: Join us after the Pride Parade for music, games, and activities at the Newday Drop-In Center. Open to all ages, and it is a dry event. Musical performances by Annestasia and Spencer Rick.

- Time: 11:30 AM - 3 PM
  - Location: 142 Truman NE 87108
  - Event Information: https://www.facebook.com/photo?fbid=847122270779519&set=a.452781906880226
- New Mexico PrideFest: Gather, Dream, Amplify. There will be music, exhibitors, food, entertainment, a drag show, dancing, and educational events. A nighttime balloon glow will end the event.
  - Time: 2 - 8 PM
  - Location: Balloon Fiesta Park 5500 Balloon Fiesta PKWY Albuquerque, NM 87113
  - Event Information: https://www.abqpride.com/

Sunday, June 9

- BIPOC Brunch: An event celebrating Black, Indigenous, and People of Color.
  - Event Information: https://www.abqpride.com/

Wednesday, June 12

- Navigating Intersectional Challenges: Supporting Two-Spirit Survivors Amidst COVID-19 & Housing Insecurity
  - Summary: A webinar that explores the challenges faced by Two-Spirit survivors of gender-based violence at the intersection of the COVID-19 pandemic and housing insecurity. In this session, our speaker will delve into the multifaced impacts of these overlapping crises and discuss strategies for supporting and advocating for the Two-Spirit community. They will offer practical insights and shared lived experiences and explore culturally responsive solutions to address systemic barriers.
  - Time: 1 - 2:30 PM
  - Location: https://us06web.zoom.us/webinar/register/WN_IiGYHATUSTW5x7VJOry4mg#/registration
  - Event Information: https://www.niwrc.org/events/navigating-intersectional-challenges-supporting-two-spirit-survivors-amidst-covid-19-and

Saturday/Sunday, June 22-23

- Orgullo: A Latinx Pride Celebration
  - Summary: Showcases the culture and passion of the Latinx community. Join the New Mexico Gay Men's Choir and special guests for a Pride performance sure to be muy caliente!
  - Time: 7:30 PM
  - Location: National Hispanic Cultural Center, 1701 4th St SW, Albuquerque, NM 87102
  - Tickets & Event Information: https://www.nmgmc.org/orgullo.html

Saturday, June 29

- Imperial Sovereign Court of New Mexico: PR Picnic
    - Summary: Have a hamburger or hotdog and help kick off the back-to-school drive.
    - Time: 10 AM - 3 PM
    - Location: Morningside Park
    - Event Information: https://www.iscnm.org/

In 2024, the was no longer an International Pride Theme that was selected for various countries to utilize. Despite this, the Albuquerque Pride Board would select the theme as *Gather Dream, Amplify Doing More in '24*. The T-shirt was offered in gray with the words in the rainbow colors.

2024

2024

There was also a second T-shirt available for purchase which was offered only in blue and had five various hot air balloons. Each balloon had either the Albuquerque Pride Corporate logo, PrideFest logo, Zia symbol and the Albuquerque Pride symbol. There was also an official pin that was sold that year that had PrideFest logo with three hot air balloons in front of a Pride Flag.

As mentioned previously in President Alexander's letter to the community she was experiencing several medical issues with her family. She had to depart in October of 2023 to another state to assist her families' medical needs and would attend official board meeting online.

Stativa (Raymond) would take up the local leadership role to ensure that the meetings were ran smoothly along with all the logistics that needed to take place with in-person contacts in Albuquerque. The process set in place would hopefully work with the acting leader of Pride trying to produce and event from a distant state. It was at that moment when some directors felt that the event was doomed to fail; however, they all knew that they needed to work as a team to move on with passion and dedication to ensure that there would be a Pride in 2024. It is at this same time that the Albuquerque Pride Treasure stopped answering calls or emails according to the board of directors. What else could endanger the production of this important event? President Suzi Alexander stepped up and would be available in person for the events planned in June.

On Monday, June 3rd would be the SilverFest which is an event celebrating the 55+ community would be a successful event located at the Orpheum Community Hub. At the same location on Tuesday, June 4th would be the annual celebration known as Kids Fest, and free event with food, fun, games, Drag Queen story time, and entertainment. Wednesday, June 5th the She + Fest which was noted as a celebration of femininity and deemed a 21+ only event which highlighted poetry, food, fun, music, and education. Thursday, June 6th would be the official Pride Memorial Candlelight Vigil which had become a yearly tradition remembering lost loved ones with speeches from local community members and titleholders, again held at Morningside Park. President Suzi Alexander would be present to give her address, but tension was in the air from the board of directors who had worked so hard to put on the event without her physical presence for the past 8 months or preparation.

On June 7, 2024, Mayor Tim Keller and the Office of Equity and Inclusion, along with leaders from the Albuquerque Pride Board, the Albuquerque Gay Men's Choir, and Marshall Martinez of Equality New Mexico, would raise the Pride flag on Civic Plaza and celebrate the City's expanded Human Rights Ordinance.

In May, the City would update its Human Rights Ordinance to include protection against discrimination on gender, identity, sexual orientation, and pregnancy, or childbirth. The amendment passed City Council unanimously, sending a clear message that Albuquerque celebrates and will protect diversity. For the second year in a row, Albuquerque would score a 100 on a report card issued by the National Human Rights Campaign for LGBTQIA+ inclusivity. The mayor would state:

> Pride is a month of celebration, and it is also an important reminder that the LGBTQIA2S+ community is still fighting against systemic violence and injustice across the country, here in Albuquerque, the City is doing more than ever to ensure our community enjoys access to opportunities and protection from discrimination, like updating our City Human Rights Ordinance to include gender identity, sexual orientation, disability, and pregnancy.

Marshall Martinez, Executive Director of Equality NM, would also state:

> Equality NM is honored to be invited to this momentous kickoff of Pride weekend! We are grateful to the Mayor's Office for their ongoing commitment to the values of Pride, inclusion, and affirmation of the LGBTQ community. We will use Pride to recommit to our work to make Albuquerque and New Mexico a beacon of safety for queer and Trans people everywhere!

The flag, located on the Northeast corner of Civic Plaza, would be a symbol of both the struggles and oppression that people in the LGBTQIA2S+ community have faced and continue to face and the hope they hold for the true liberation of everyone in the community. The City would raise the updated Pride Progress Flag, which includes a yellow triangle with a purple circle to acknowledge the intersex community. The Progress Pride Flag debuted in 2018 with the white, pink, baby blue, black, and brown stripes in a triangle shape with the original six color stripes stacked next to them. The black and brown colors would represent marginalized LGBTQIA2S+ people of color and those living with AIDS/HIV and the light blue, pink, and white represented the transgender community. "Raising the flag is important," said Dawn Begay, Acting Director of the Office of Equity and Inclusion. It shows our LGBTQIA2S+ family that as a city, we stand with them."

Most people could or would not comprehend the amount of dedication that it takes to produce the many Pride events for our community. ALL VOLUNTEERS are dedicated to their hard work, giving "blood, sweat and tears," and working for free to ensure that Pride happens. Our community needs to realize that every year the event was produced, no one got paid, but only briefly in the past when an administrative assistant was hired for one year. As you have been reading this book you can now realize the extreme hardships for the past years that the volunteers had experienced all for just volunteering to put on Pride in Albuquerque.

The official theme was *Gather Dream, Amplify Doing More in '24* and in 2024 this would not be more evident to what would occur, a situation that could again be the end of Pride in Albuquerque. The business did able to rest in 2023 with success, but another difficult transition would be on the horizon expanding amongst the hot air balloon glow.

As mentioned previously, the set-up for all the events has been thought out extensively, months of preparation in advance. President Suzi was unable to be present physically and many decisions had to be made on the "spot." During the crucial staging and lay-out process on the field at Balloon Fiesta Park, which had been approved by the Albuquerque Fire Department, President Alexander would arrive and start making some changes. Time was crucial and changes at this late moment could affect the progress. Tensions were high, but the Friday PreFest would go off well with the set-up for the booths, food sales, entertainment stages, Pride Office, Pride Archives, kids' area, etc., without any problems.

As a whole, the different areas on the grounds were spread out too far from each other and the participants felt disconnected. Some felt they were walking miles upon miles to get to each location. This was done despite the tension in the air between the board and the lay-out of PrideFest. Complaints from attendees started to be brought to the board and volunteers' attention and many were afraid that the event would become disastrous. The board would re-group together when the event was done, without their leader, and have a late-night meeting to discuss the logistics of the parade that would happen in the morning and PrideFest that started at 2:00 pm.

Saturday, June 8th the entire Board would at the Parade to assist with what was needed as Albuquerque held the 2024 LGBTQ+ Pride parade. The event celebrated diversity of sexuality and identity through a caravan of parade floats with signs displaying messages of love and acceptance. Including music and dancers, many attendees waved Pride flags and dressed in rainbow, while some – including several people on top of floats – dressed in drag.

The parade began at the intersection of Central Avenue and Girard Boulevard and progressed east to the intersection of Central Avenue and San Mateo Boulevard. It was organized by the non-profit organization Albuquerque Pride. Cora Reyes, a Pride attendee, brought both her little brother and someone who had never attended a Pride parade before. Reyes enjoyed the parade and her brother had fun playing with bubbles, she said:

> I think it's cool to see the whole community come out together and just support everybody. You can be yourself, even if you're not gay. It's such a supportive atmosphere and I like that.

Many organizations, businesses, and other entities participated in the parade, including the Albuquerque Teachers Federation, American Veterans for Equal Rights Bataan Chapter, the American Civil Liberties Union (ACLU) of New Mexico, New Mexico United, and the University of New Mexico a student-led group participated. The United Grad Workers sang and chanted messages about workers' rights, and individuals from the UNM Palestine solidarity encampment had banners and a float, chanting "No Pride in genocide."

The ACLU's float featured posters that read "No more solitary confinement" and "End mass incarceration." Lena Weber-Salazar, a reproductive rights policy advocate at the ACLU of New Mexico, was on the float and said, "LGBTQ+ youth, are stopped, searched, detained and arrested by police at disproportionate rates." She stated further, "this Pride month we really wanted to highlight the intersections with Queer justice, ending mass incarceration and reimagining public safety, because public safety means safety for everybody."

New Mexico United – Albuquerque's professional soccer team – appeared with a float during the parade. United provides a safe place for the LGBTQ+ community, unlike some other sports teams, Jules Myers, facilitator of United's participation in the parade, said, "There were so many people out. I think every year it gets bigger, which is wonderful." Myers was accompanied by her colleague, David Wiese-Carl, who said he enjoyed handing out stickers, magnets and flags to children who attended the parade. She further stated, "Kids who might be in a place where they're either confused about how they're going to be accepted in their lives, or question whether they're going to be accepted, will know that they've got a place with (United)."

PrideFest: *Gather, Dream, Amplify*, would occur with more options to enter the grounds which had been an issue in 2023. Starting at 2:00 pm entering the grounds at Balloon Fiesta Park was a "flawless" experience, but attendees still would express that the event was too far spaced out and since the layout was so expansive it looked like the number of attendees would be small. The event would highlight music, exhibitors, food, entertainment, a drag show, dancing, and educational events, and a nighttime balloon glow that would end the event. The main headliners for the PrideFest Mainstage were none other than Gia Gunn.

Gia Gunn is an American drag performer from Carpentersville, Illinois where she is best known for being a contestant on Season 6 of *RuPaul's Drag Race*, where she placed 10th, and on All Stars 4 where she placed 8th. Gia also competed on the second season of The Switch Drag Race; the Chilean spin-off of RuPaul's Drag Race, where she placed as Runner-Up. Gia Ichikawa was born on May 10, 1990, into a Japanese American family. She grew up in a small diverse town in the Northwest Suburbs of Chicago in Carpentersville, Illinois. At the age of five years old, Ichikawa had made her stage debut. After completing her high school education, she enrolled in a cosmetology school, where Ichikawa had received her cosmetology license. Soon after moving to Chicago, she had observed numerous drag shows. Possibly being influenced by the observation of the numerous drag shows, Ichikawa had decided to perform herself and became a headlining drag performer. She auditioned for Logo TV's reality television series *RuPaul's Drag Race* whilst Ichikawa was working in the hair industry full-time and performed as Gia Gunn by evening. Additionally, Gia is the sixth contestant to come out as transgender.

The next headliner on the PrideFest's Mainstage was Inaya Day who is an American singer best known for her vocal work on house music tracks such as "Horny '98" by Mousse T, and her cover version of "Nasty Girl" by Prince protégées Vanity 6.

Another notable headliner, Evah Destruction, started doing drag in Atlanta at age 18 after seeing Phoenix and her drag mother Jasmine Antoinette perform. Her first performance was at Le Buzz in Marietta, Georgia, to Lady Gaga's "Bad Romance." Her lesbian friend gave her the name Evah Destruction. She also went with Genevieve and won Best of Atlanta in 2016. Evah Destruction appeared on season 3 of *The Boulet Brothers' Dragula*, where she placed fifth overall. She placed 4th/5th on *Titans*, and she returned for the second Season of *Titans*.

The final headliner was Jeremy Brian Griffis. Known professionally as Dahli, an American musician, drag performer, and entertainer who competed on season 2 and season 4 of *The Boulet Brothers' Dragula*, the latter of which they won and was crowned the "World's Next Drag Supermonster."

Unfortunately, the Board President would go missing that night. She was not answering calls or email during the events as several board member tried contacting her. Over time different Board members heard different stories as what may have happened with the Board President. Some related to her health and others to the health of a familiarly members out of state. The mentally and physically drained Pride Board had multiple concerns, but the event had to continue for the safety and conclusion of the event.

Many emotions were experienced by the Board as there was still a celebratory atmosphere from those assisting and those participating, even though there was an underlying turmoil that existed amongst the board of directors, the "missing" president, the tensions felt by others, including the multitude of willing volunteers. The hot air balloons would inflate at 7:00 pm and would showcase the first ever balloon glow in Albuquerque Pride history, but as they deflated so would be the enthusiasm and satisfaction of a job well done be experienced by the board of directors.

It is then that, Dr. PJ Sedillo, as a President Emeritus, and the rest of the Board would come together. Whatever had happened, happened and he immediately felt it was his duty to make sure that the board members, who put on the event, needed some encouragement and words of wisdom. With the event closing, Dr. Sedillo met up with Sativa (Raymond) who was now forced to take on the leadership role. Her face looked bright and happy, but underneath there was fear and exhaustion. They contact all the board members and key volunteers on the multitude of headsets to show up by the mainstage for a brief meeting.

The many golf carts from multiple directions would arrive at the mainstage and slowly the on-the-ground, key volunteers would arrive like a slow-moving bunch of Pride zombies all exhausted and hungry with the mission, still instilled, of supporting Pride within their soul. Dr. PJ Sedillo knew those similar emotions and has always held them deep within his inner being and knew that those volunteering and all the other volunteers from the past 48 years were still cheering on together from the past, present, all for the future, with one focus PRIDE!

When all had arrived, he asked for all to hold hands and would bless the grounds and all who were present. He wanted to empower the volunteers and proceeded to let them know about his first Pride experience. His goal was to leave them with the reason why he had sacrificed his entire life to producing and assisting with this event. In the simplest of explanations, President Emeritus Dr. PJ would proclaim the reason for having a Pride event by telling them a story about:

> One kid who, hiding behind the walls in 1989, listening to the Albuquerque advocates use a loudspeaker to proclaim the Gay is good. The boy listened with his entire being but was afraid of being found out as being gay by having his picture on the 6:00 news. Thoughts entered his mind with the numerous possibilities of losing his home, job, and dignity, who had in the past had even contemplated suicide because he was Gay and that little boy was me."

Dr. Sedillo's voice cracked and continued by proclaiming:

> What this event does is it gives hope to that one kid to believe that I am good and okay and that I have the inner strength and comfort that there are others exactly like him/her/they. It is all of you, hardworking, dedicated, and exhausted volunteers who must understand that what you accomplished might have only reached one kid hiding behind a building, but that one kid is alive today because you gave him strength to survive another day.

The event was done, all was being packed, put away for hopefully a Pride event in 2024. The next day there was an onslaught of resignations from members of the board of directors. Dr. PJ and Sativa would chat, and she was willing accept the role as Interim-President, and an emergency executive session for Albuquerque Pride was to be scheduled. President Suzi Alexander and Juan- Treasurer were invited to state their case. At 1:00 pm when the meeting had come to order, the board of directors would receive and an email with the resignation of Suzi Alexander. It was accepted.

The next step was to vote Sativa-Raymond Sierra Lopez as Interim-President who would graciously accept. All-in-all the legacy of Suzi Alexander should not be tarnished as she contributed a great deal of positive change for the organization. She stepped up when no one else could for the presidency, and became Albuquerque Pride's first-ever, serving alone, female President. We all can comprehend how daunting it is to take on a leadership role, and we must realize that the leaders of today face challenges for sometimes which they are utterly unprepared.

Chapter 19

49 Years of Pride in Albuquerque
(Should We, Could We, Would We, Make it to 50)
Albuquerque Pride 2025

Albuquerque Pride would survive its existence for another year, but difficult decisions needed to be made about the future of the event. Should, could, would the organization make it to 50 years to be seen in 2026? That was the least of the concern of the Albuquerque Pride, but to even attempt to have another event in 2025 would be a huge undertaking. Raymond Sierra Lopez (AKA Sativa Rico Stratton) would share his story of what occurred in 2024 and the 2025 event that would revisit a past location for Pridefest.

Raymond Sierra Lopez, President, Albuquerque Pride:

> In the months leading up to PrideFest 2024, I was serving as Vice President of Marketing and Public Relations for Albuquerque Pride. While my primary responsibilities included overseeing marketing, communications, and supporting our titleholders, I also assumed the duties of Acting President due to the extended absence of our then-President, Suzi Alexander. My previous experience as a titleholder and my work with several nonprofit boards helped prepare me for the unexpected challenges our organization faced throughout the year. Although Suzi remained partially engaged through virtual meetings, her physical absence placed considerable pressure on the board, which was already operating with limited capacity.
>
> As PrideFest approached, our executive board—reduced to just three active members—was stretched to its limit. Organizing a festival of this size is a demanding undertaking, especially for a team with many first-time members. Despite the stress and obstacles, we pushed forward with determination and resilience, often at the expense of our own well-being.
>
> The week of Pride brought tensions to the surface. Suzi returned briefly to assist with preparations, but frustration among board members was already high. A particularly difficult moment occurred while assembling VIP packs, when negativity and conflict overshadowed an already strenuous task. Still, we came together to ensure the candlelight vigil was executed with dignity and care—because that event, above all, is about honoring those who paved the way for us.

PrideFest 2024 ultimately became our final year at Balloon Fiesta Park. With only a handful of active board members and volunteers, we accomplished what many doubted was possible. We welcomed extraordinary talent—including Inaya Day, Eva Destruction, Dahli, and Gia Gunn—and successfully delivered the long-awaited balloon glow. When the festival concluded, I found myself in tears, overwhelmed with pride and relief. We had achieved something remarkable against the odds.

During the event, Suzi was assigned a task off-site and did not return. The remainder of the board and volunteers continued without hesitation, working tirelessly to ensure the success of the festival. That night, several executive team members expressed their desire to resign. Their exhaustion was palpable. I pleaded with them to stay, knowing that without them, our organization would not survive.

In that moment of uncertainty, I received a phone call from former Board President Dr. PJ Sedillo, joined by two additional past presidents. PJ thanked us for our dedication, reminding us that our work may have saved someone's life that very day—that someone may have found hope, safety, or belonging because Pride exists. His words brought us all to tears, and I firmly believe that call helped convince my team to remain.

At our July board meeting, we formally addressed concerns involving Suzi and scheduled an executive session with appropriate notice. On the day of that meeting, Suzi submitted her resignation. The board then asked me to assume the presidency. I agreed to continue as Interim President until our Annual General Meeting, where I requested open nominations to ensure fairness. At the August meeting, I was officially nominated and elected to complete the remainder of the presidential term per our bylaws.

Stepping into this role, I knew I wanted to lead differently. We restored our task-based structure, ensuring each executive member had directors to support their work. I invited new, dedicated individuals to join the board, and I am grateful they accepted. We listened closely to community feedback, which overwhelmingly requested a more central, accessible location. As a result, we moved PrideFest to Civic Plaza—a space that proved to be an exceptional partner and host.

Despite national sponsorship challenges, we found unwavering support from local community organizations and long-time partners such as Truman Health Services, KOAT 7, Cumulus Media, and the Civic Plaza team. Their generosity, paired with community contributions, allowed us to produce one of our most successful festivals yet, featuring Landon Cider, Victoria "Porkchop" Parker, and Frenchie Davis.

Serving as President of Albuquerque Pride is a profound honor—and, at times, a deeply humbling responsibility. I am constantly aware of the legacy I am stepping into. During this year's festival, a volunteer in his seventies pulled me aside. Expecting an urgent issue, I was surprised when he simply asked me to stop, breathe, and look out at the crowd. He told me that when he was younger, gatherings like this were filled with fear. "Look out there," he said. "Not one scared face. Everyone is free. Everyone is happy." His words reminded me why this work matters.

I do this for those who came before us, who fought for the right to exist. I do this for those who are still fighting. And I do this for those who will come after us—those who may sneak away from home just to feel safe for one day, those who may see someone like themselves for the first time, and those who may find hope in the celebration of authenticity.

True equality remains a shared journey, and I am committed to walking it with courage, compassion, and unwavering dedication. Our board works tirelessly, often unseen, to bring Pride to life. They are the reason these events succeed, and their commitment deserves recognition.

Pride is more than a festival. It is a lifeline, a celebration, a statement, and a promise. And as long as I have the privilege to serve, I will fight to ensure that our community always has a place to feel seen, safe, and celebrated.

Raymond Sierra Lopez (He/Him/His)
Aka Sativa Rico Stratton Miss NM Pride 2023
Board President
Albuquerque Pride Inc.

The mandatory Annual Albuquerque Pride Board meeting held in August, and opened to the public, would have a new set of directors voted in. The Albuquerque Pride Board consisted of the Executive Committee and the Planning Committee. The board members as in the past would work all year long to produce a myriad of quality events, seminars, and educational events. The new board elected would be President-Raymond Sierra Lopez, Vice President of Operation- Robert Sierra Lopez. This would be the third gay couple that would hold the positions together on the Albuquerque Pride Board. First starting with Dr. PJ Sedillo and Tony Ross, next Craig Labarge Esparza and JR Labarge Esparza, and finally Raymond Sierra Lopez and Robert Sierra Lopez.

The next group of elected officials would be Vice President of Marketing and Public Relations-Danielle Medina, Tami Whitlow-Secretary, Matthew Maturino-Treasurer, Andrew Salazar-Director, Tim Osborn-Director, Elizabeth Hewit-Director, Jeffery Olson-Director, Jonathan Juarez-Director, Savannah Martinez-Director, Damian Dominguez-Director, Aurora Garcia-Director, Michael Benavidez Director, and Titleholders Mr. Cairo Jones Steel and MX Jimmy Lee Lucero.

This powerful, youthful team would successfully put on 2024 Pride in Albuquerque. They would start their tenure announcing to the community *Why Pride Matters?* by stating:

> Pride is more than a party — it is a powerful declaration of visibility, resilience, and love. For marginalized LGBTQ+ individuals, especially those navigating racism, ableism, transphobia, and economic injustice, Pride is a space to be seen, be safe, and be celebrated. We come together to empower each other, unite across our differences, fight for our rights, and thrive in our truth. Pride is a protest. Pride is a homecoming. Pride is a reminder: we belong. Whether you are marching, dancing, or showing up in support — come make this year unforgettable.

The organization known as the International Associations of Pride would no longer present an international Pride Theme. Therefore, the 2025 theme for Albuquerque Pride would be *EMPOWER, UNITE, FIGHT, THRIVE*.

The T-shirt would showcase a desert scene with a rainbow road. There would be a raised fist with the theme over the fist and below the fist the wording *WE STAND TOGETHER*. Notably in 2024 and the in 2025 there had been a slew of executive orders targeting the trans community, and in the month of June the federal government had declined to issue a Pride Month Proclamation. Despite these negative proclamations, and no federal support, Albuquerque would hold its 49th Annual March/Parade down Route 66. The most difficult decision made by the Pride Board would be to move the PrideFest to Civic Plaza which had been a controversy in the past and sometimes viewed as a location that could end in a disaster. However, this new and enthusiastic Pride Board was intent on proving everyone wrong and they did!

The T-shirt would showcase a desert scene with a rainbow road. There would be a raised fist with the theme over the fist and below the fist the wording *WE STAND TOGETHER*. Notably in 2024 and the in 2025 there had been a slew of executive orders targeting the trans community, and in the month of June the federal government had declined to issue a Pride Month Proclamation. Despite these negative proclamations, and no federal support, Albuquerque would hold its 49th Annual March/Parade down Route 66. The most difficult decision made by the Pride Board would be to move the PrideFest to Civic Plaza which had been a controversy in the past and sometimes viewed as a location that could end in a disaster. However, this new and enthusiastic Pride Board was intent on proving everyone wrong and they did!

Along with the parade, Albuquerque Pride hosted three events during the first week of Pride Month. On Thursday, dozens gathered for the annual Candlelight Vigil in Morningside Park, the site of Albuquerque's first pride event, to remember those loved ones who have been lost. For its 49th anniversary, Albuquerque Pride switched PrideFest venues from the Balloon Fiesta Park to Civic Plaza. The move was partially to open the event to more attendees with a bigger venue, more shading and access to public transportation, but also to celebrate on the steps of City Hall. "It's amazing that we are right here in the city center, where our community is supporting all of us for existing today and every day," said drag performer Miss Vanessa Patricks during opening remarks.

2025

In 2025, for Pride Month the Trump administration would take action to target the LGBTQ+ community, like including executive orders that ban transgender people from joining the military and competing in college sports as well as an effort to expel diversity, equity, and inclusion from the federal government. The American Civil Liberties Union had tracked almost 600 anti-LGBTQ+ bills across the nation that year, including several in New Mexico. However, none of the seven proposed bills, in New Mexico, passed before the end of the legislative session that March of that year. Raymond Sierra-Lopez, Albuquerque Pride board president, said during a speech at the event:

> We must return to our roots, of grassroots activism, of direct action, of taking our future into our own hands. We cannot wait for institutions or politicians to save us. We must save ourselves, and that starts with building community.

Following the parade, Pridefest would take place at Civic Plaza, and the event would feature 125 vendors, various activities, and musical performances. Headlining the main stage was three national artists: Victoria "Porkchop" Parker, Frenchie Davis and Landon Cider. Pridefest has previously been held at Morning Side Park, Expo New Mexico, and Balloon Fiesta Park. This year's move to Civic Plaza aimed to make the event more accessible and central.

Albuquerque Pride 2026-50 Years

The 2025 Albuquerque Pride Board would relish in their huge success and plans would begin immediately with no rest to start producing the 50th Anniversary. The once "little Pride in the desert" is now one of the premier and larger Prides in all the Southwest. They would continue to build on the momentum for 2026 by improving the venue at Civic Plaza with their newfound leadership skills. In 2026, the Albuquerque PrideFest would be planned as a festival that would feature live music stages, drag performances, food trucks, and vendor booths spread across Civic Plaza, with a central focus on visibility and solidarity. The celebration's highlight would be the Albuquerque Pride Parade, which usually steps off in the afternoon, marching proudly along historic Route 66 through Nob Hill. Thousands of people, from families to activists, would gather for the 50th Anniversary to celebrate in the city's revitalized downtown, where the glow of Pride decorations would light up Civic Plaza and downtown streets into the evening.

There will be a new and improved designated Pride Village at the Civic Plaza. Festivities begin with a family-friendly daytime festival. Civic Plaza will be transformed into a Pride Village, with multiple stages for live bands, DJ sets, and drag shows, plus community booths and an art installation. Organizers promise local and national acts headlining the lineup, plus cultural performances. Vendors, including 100+ local businesses and nonprofits, will line the plaza with crafts, local art, and rainbow merchandise. Food trucks and drink stands will provide Southwest cuisine and festive treats. Young attendees will be able to experience a KidZone with games and face-painting, ensuring that families are welcome.

Beyond the Pride Weekend Albuquerque Pride will organize several lead-up events. In the weeks before PrideFest, local organizations, and gay-friendly bars host fundraisers, film screenings, and discussions to build momentum. On Pride weekend itself, there is a community volunteer drive ("Pride Makes a Difference") where attendees can contribute to food banks or youth shelters. On Friday night before PrideFest, some bars will host drag brunches and dance under official Pride banners. After the parade, the celebration continues with music performances at local clubs and bars throughout Nob Hill and downtown, often featuring headliners drag queens and performers from RuPaul's Drag Race or local talent showcases.

Metropolitan Community Church of Albuquerque (MCCA)-50 Years

Notably, in 2025 there was another milestone celebration. MCCA would celebrate 50 years. Arguably, MCC-ABQ's most important contribution to the gay and lesbian community was its cooperation in organizing Albuquerque's first Gay Pride March in 1976. Juniper, the gay and lesbian organization that formed in the wake of the Gay People's Union's demise, would work with MCC-ABQ to coordinate the march. Twenty-five pioneers marched in the parade that launched New Mexico's entrance into national pride celebrations.

Chapter 20

Synopsis of Albuquerque Pride - 49 years

The 1970's, with the formation of Pride in Albuquerque, the organization would experience turmoil surrounding which organization should lead this community event. The 1980's brought forth some stability for the community which was centered from the formation of The Common Bond Community Center; however, the community would be shaken to the core from AIDS rearing its ugly head of destruction. AIDS could have decimated Pride in Albuquerque, but it did the opposite. The community became stronger and more determined to support one another. Gays and Lesbians who were on "rival camps" in the 1970's would come together to support one another in the 80's.

The 1990's, Pride in Albuquerque experienced a transformation when it decided to become its own entity defined by its identity. A certain segment of the community did not want Pride to become a business that needed to incorporate with next steps to becoming a not-for-profit. This idea would be the demise of previous organizations in the past who tried to do this. Individuals from the community would spew unwarranted and vile rhetoric about the Board members of AG&LPaP (Albuquerque Gay & Lesbian Parade and Pridefest) which would be "flamed" by the local GLBT newspaper towards the Board. The Board members in 1996 and 1997, which become an organization that was for profit would bet touted by the group Lesbians for Change as, "the ruination of Gay Pride in Albuquerque." Pride in Albuquerque would survive the horrible accusations that their intent was to "line their pocket" by producing Pride. However, because of the incorporation process that took forth became a metamorphosis that would blossom Albuquerque Pride Inc. to produce one of the most successful, consistent Prides in the Southwest.

The twenty-first century brought forth new challenges. Albuquerque Pride would make the ultimate decision to move from the safe and secure location of the Spanish Village to Main Street in the New Mexico State Fair Grounds. The budget would also be doubled. This risky move would be a success that would move Albuquerque Pride from being noted as a small Pride in American to a force to be reckoned with for GLBTQI organizations in the State of New Mexico. The organization would now be able to compete with other Prides like Denver and Phoenix (even with the extreme difference in population). In 2000 there would be a new direction in leadership. PJ Sedillo and pat baillie would become co-presidents for eight years and would transform Pride in Albuquerque. One of the most important contributions during their tenure would be assisting in the unification between the gays and lesbians of the Albuquerque population. The division between the groups had existed and festered for over 30 years. Most of the elder community members would have old wounds healed; however, many of the younger generation did not know what the fuss was all about because most were unaware of the GLBT history in Albuquerque.

PJ Sedillo, after serving as a volunteer for Pride in Albuquerque for over 15 years, in 2000 would realize that he had boxes upon boxes of notes, memos, pictures, programs, proclamations, t-shirts and other historical artifacts lying around. It was at that moment in January of 2000 that the Pride Archives would be created to be showcased in June. The archives would serve as a jumpstart for this book. Pat Baillie would move out of state to work with *Out and Equal* in 2008, and PJ Sedillo would assume the singular role as President of Albuquerque Pride. In 2010, PJ Sedillo would step down after 21 years of service and Tony Ross after 17 years. Both would be honored by Albuquerque Pride, and there would be ups and downs that followed.

By 2013, a new mission statement had been procured, and the philosophy would be to produce other events than the yearly Pride Parade and Pridefest. This would be a different belief system than that established by Boards before 2010. Despite these visionary differences, the newly formed Albuquerque Pride Board was able to resurrect the defunct AIDs Walk and make it new and successful. Also, the Board would move the OUTstanding Awards to an event that rivaled the "*Oscars.*" They had also revamped the Pride Pageant, and through a few struggling years were able to produce a successful event that was profitable. All in all, this newly defined and refined Board under the direction and leadership of Neil Macernie would present an event 40 years after those brave individuals walked down the sidewalks on Central to honor Stonewall an awesome and incomprehensible feat of "Solidarity Through Pride.

The Stonewall Riots celebrated 45 years in 2014, and Albuquerque Pride was pleased to announce the 37th Annual PrideFest celebrating the LGBTIQ community in New Mexico. The year's theme was "Reflections of Pride –Stonewall 45." The organization known as the Gay & Lesbian Alliance Against Defamation (GLADD) officially added the Q (Queer/Questioning) to the acronym in its resource guide in 2016 because younger LGBTQ+ Americans reclaimed the word as they embrace a shift toward fluidity in identity. Widespread use grew from there because GLAAD had officially added the Q to the acronym in its resource guide in 2016 and other organizations would follow as did Albuquerque Pride. PrideFest and the Pride Parade for the first time in the 37 years existence of Pride in Albuquerque would have events held that occurred in May and not the second Saturday in June or in the month of June. The events were scheduled in May 2014. In 2014, Mainstreet at PrideFest with over 200 exhibitors/booths would be titled as Hewlett-Packard Main Street Experience. Interesting enough the sponsorship would be only for Mainstreet because of the controversy the year before for naming the parade the 2013 HEWLETT PACKARD PRIDE PARADE.

There would be major changes made for Albuquerque Pride in 2015 because of the backlash of having the event in May which resulted in lower attendance. The Board would move the Pride Parade and Pridefest back to the original date which was the second Saturday in June. June 2015 marked the first year that there were no protesters on the parade route for the Albuquerque Pride Parade.

In 2016, the Albuquerque Pride Board would be responsible for procuring and securing the overwhelmingly demands of obtaining the 2016 proposed budget which was $183,000. As a reminder, the Gay & Lesbian Pride Week '88 was budgeted for $1,475. Twenty-eight years had seen a great increase in the proposed budget. In 2016, this would be the first year that there would not be a conclusive declarative theme chosen for the 40th Annual Parade and PrideFest; the closest would be "40 Years of Pride" and "40 Years Proud." Sadly enough, amongst the celebratory events, on Sunday, June 12, 2016, the news being broadcasted stated that Omar Mateen had killed 49 individuals inside the gay nightclub known as the Pulse, and he had wounded 53 individuals. This event would be noted as a terrorist attack and hate crime. Mateen was eventually shot and killed by the Orlando police department after a three-hour standoff. Those in the nightclub performed acts of heroism and helped ensure that many would escape the violence within the walls of this celebrated Latino nightclub. This occurrence, this vehement act would be titled as one of the deadliest incidents of violence against the GLBTQI community in America.

By Sunday evening, June 12, 2016, at 5:30 p.m. the entire LGBTQ+ community under the leadership of Albuquerque Pride would have people arrive at Morningside Park and by 6:00 over 2000 community members from Albuquerque had gathered to honor the Orlando attack victims. A makeshift memorial was set up next to the podium where individuals brought forth candles, rainbow flags, flowers and other items to be placed on this memorial. There were prayers and spiritual blessings with a cleansing of the park conducted at the beginning of the event to make space for speeches and lots of tears. The crowd made it clear that Orlando may be hundreds of miles away, but their pain was felt here in Albuquerque. Speakers not only remembered the Orlando victims, but they called for the U.S. to speak out against any anti-Muslim rhetoric that could arise from this shooting. Many people in the crowd said that they shared that message and were dedicated to spreading love, not hate.

leaders in Albuquerque would come to embody the International Pride Theme for 2016 "Solidarity Through Pride." Together the future of Pride in Albuquerque would be able to withstand 40 more years. 2017 and 2018 would experience new leadership under the direction of Craig Laberge-Esparza with no major controversies and smooth transitions. However, in 2019 as the chapter was titled it was a time of disenchantment and dissolution of Pride. This is the year when the rainbow painted crosswalks on Central and Morningside would be destroyed by a group of bikers. This was also the year that the board experienced backlash from some in the community who were upset with the corporate sponsorship and the adding of their corporate names before the wording Albuquerque Pride. This was also the year the extreme division between the community would occur at the Candlelight Vigil by protestors who were against the police and the military. This event would lead to some resignations from the board.

2020 would be the most disastrous experience felt by our LGBTQ+ community, state, and the world. By early 2020, countries across the globe were scrambling to shut borders, cancel flights, and lock down cities. Hospitals overflowed. Streets fell eerily silent. Economies halted. A virus had emerged that would not only claim millions of lives but also challenge the very fabric of modern civilization. Its name was COVID-19.

On top of the Pandemic, another horrific newsworthy event would occur. On May 25, 2020, was the death of George Floyd, caused by the police, which would move forward The Black Lives Matter movement which began in 2013 in response to the acquittal of George Zimmerman, who fatally shot Trayvon Martin, an unarmed Black teenager. Albuquerque Pride Board would not make a timely statement, which would cause tension between individual board members and the community. The board was not prepared for the backlash that came. Attacks against several board members would lead to the resignation and retiring of many of the executive board members.

After canceling 2020's LGBTQ Pride celebrations due to the pandemic, Albuquerque Pride pushed forward with mostly online events for 2021. Pride would have tentative plans for an in-person celebration later in the summer, if the State would allow under all current restrictions for events. There would be a car parade not sanctioned by Albuquerque Pride but would participate; however, Albuquerque Pride would sanction an official march with 25 individuals to start at the Social Club and march to the NM State Fair grounds for historical participation.

In 2021, Pride, instead of June, would be held on August 20th and 21st with a Parade and PrideFest at Expo New Mexico. It was titled as a slightly scaled-down "In-Person Edition" of PrideFest with entertainment and vendors. In 2022, Albuquerque Pride Parade and PrideFest had made it through some difficult years and was ready to continue presenting this annual event celebrating lesbian, gay, bisexual, transgender, intersex, and queer (LGBTIQ) culture and pride. Consequently, the board would experience even more controversies that would tear the community apart by the Directors of Albuquerque Pride voting to ban the Albuquerque Police Department from events, citing the 1969 Stonewall riots as their reason.

In 2023 there would be no difficult controversies that Albuquerque Pride or the community would have to face; however, 2024 would be challenging. There would be problematic leadership issues with the president of Pride having to take leave to take care of family and would end with an executive session where Albuquerque Pride would vote Sativa-Raymond Sierra Lopez as Interim-President. She would graciously accept and lead a new, excited, and youthful board of directors to begin producing the 50th Anniversary of Albuquerque Pride.

Chapter 21

Albuquerque Pride 2076 – 50 Years Later

So, what does the future hold for Albuquerque Pride 50 years from now? The year would be 2076. Hopefully human beings will undergo a transformation that will infuse technology that assists all to become more unified. No longer will there be a separation between heterosexuals, cisgenders, and anyone who is different via sexual orientation or gender identity.

The acronym GLBTQI+ will no longer be in existence, as all humans are now labeled "transformative heterosexuals." Albuquerque Pride 80 years later will become a cultural event like Hispanic Heritage Days or African American History Month remembering those GLBTQI+ brave individuals who were trailblazers. Their struggles and perseverance will become a part of a social studies and civic lesson for most curriculums in the public-school system in New Mexico.

In the month of June, all Albuquerqueans will have the day off the second Saturday in June to celebrate the "Albuquerque Stonewallian Day of Remembrance." The 2076's Albuquerque Pride Theme would look back to 2016 and do something similar but will have 80 days of Pride events. Albuquerque Pride will also take on similar wording that was selected by the InterPride Theme in 2016 "Solidarity Through Pride." The theme would be transformed and proclaimed as "We Have Solidified Through Pride." One can only hope.

New Mexico LGBTQ+ Organizations and Resources

These organizations offer a range of services, including advocacy, education, support groups, and resources for LGBTQ+ individuals and their families in New Mexico.

- **Albuquerque Pride:** Offers a comprehensive resource director and support groups for LGBTQ+ individuals and their families. https://www.abqpride.com/
- **Equality New Mexico**: A statewide LGBT advocacy and civil rights organization that focuses on equity, full access, and sustainable wellness for LGBTQ New Mexicans. https://www.eqnm.org/
- **Transgender Resource Center of New Mexico**: Provides support, education, and advocacy for transgender, nonbinary, and gender nonconforming communities. https://tgrcnm.org/
- **HEAL Plus NM:** The Health Equity Alliance for LGBTQ+ New Mexicans, which works to build health resources and increase queer power through creative collaboration. https://www.healplusnm.org/
- 988NM: New Mexico's 24/7 free and confidential lifeline for emotional, mental, or alcohol and substance use support, available to all New Mexicans. https://988nm.org/
- **The Arcoíris Center**: Located at the University of New Mexico was founded in 2010 by students, staff, faculty, and community members to create a space where our LGBTQQIA community can not only survive but thrive. https://arcoiris.unm.edu/
- **Common Bond New Mexico:** Empowers LGBTQ+ individuals through outreach, personal support, and education. Their goal is to keep a directory of the most comprehensive and up-to-date reference for Albuquerque's LGBTQ+ Community. https://www.commonbondnm.org/community-resources.html
- **U-21 Youth Program:** For more than thirty years, our U-21 program has provided one of the few places for Albuquerque's LGBTQ+ youth to socialize in a safe, welcoming, and affirming environment. Every Friday night, participants under the age of 21, come together to hang out with friends and take part in events. https://www.commonbondnm.org/u-21.html

- **Casa Q:** Providing a safe living through housing, services and advocacy. We are family and friends, supporting and strengthening our community through love and acceptance.
  We are celebrating and welcoming BIPOC and LGBTQ+ youth and allies. At Casa Q we are thinking long-term to build resiliency, self-determination and self-efficacy for every young person that needs us. https://www.casaq.org/
- **ORCA (Older Rainbow Community Albuquerque):** The Older Rainbow Community of Albuquerque (ORCA) is a volunteer-run organization that provides social support and advocacy for LGBTQ+ older adults in the Albuquerque metro area and neighboring communities. https://orcaabq.org/
- **NMOBA (New Mexico Out Business Alliance):** This organization serves as a welcoming hub for LGBTQ+ owned and allied businesses across New Mexico, fostering economic inclusion and equity within organizations of all sizes and industries. Our extensive membership includes non-profits, small businesses, public entities, and corporate members, provides access to a multitude of valuable benefits and opportunities. https://www.nmoba.org/

About the Author

Dr. PJ “Paul James” Sedillo, Associate Professor for the Special/Gifted Education Department at New Mexico Highlands University teaches the Gifted Endorsement coursework. Published in *Gifted Child Today*, *Journal of Education & Social Policy*, *Parents of High Potential,* and *ABQ Press* where his book *Solidarity through Pride* won best book in Arizona/ NM 2018 and won in 2024 a children's book *Embraced or Excluded? Fact & Fiction of Famous LGBTQ+ Persons*. His book chapter *Identifying and Serving Diverse Gifted Learners* introduces Stages of Identity for LGBT-Gifted persons.

As a Suicidologist, he has created an assessment for suicide/suicidal ideation for the gifted in the *International Journal of Arts, Humanities, and Social Sciences* (2025). He served as President for the NM Association for the Gifted, Communication Member & Chair-Elect for the NAGC-GLBTQ Network, NAGC State Affiliate Leadership and Advocacy member, Co-Chair for the 2019 NAGC Conference in Albuquerque, and as an At-Large Board Member for NAGC.

Contact information

Dr. PJ "Paul James" Sedillo
505-362-2237
pjsedillo@nmhu.edu
4119 Dietz Loop NW
Los Ranchos de Albuquerque, NM 87107

About the Editor

Adam C. Laningham brings more than two decades of experience in public education and a deep passion for supporting gifted and twice-exceptional learners. Recognized as *Arizona Gifted Teacher of the Year*, Adam has taught across multiple grade levels, developed and led innovative gifted programs, and managed district-wide initiatives serving over 6,000 gifted students. In 2023, he established The Gifted Collective, a thriving learning center that supports gifted and neurodivergent children and their families in Arizona.

As founder of Bright Child Books, Adam is the author of several works dedicated to nurturing the potential of advanced & unique learners. He also partners with authors from all over to bring stories and history to a greater audience.

Adam's leadership extends nationally and internationally. He served six years on the board of Supporting the Emotional Needs of the Gifted (SENG), including serving as President, and contributes his expertise as a member of the Arizona Association for Gifted and Talented (AAGT) Advisory Council, a founding member of Callisto (supporting gifted foster youth), and an advisor for CogAT Riverside Insights. Most recently, he founded the nonprofit Growing Intellect & Fostering Talent.

Recognized as an engaging speaker and trusted consultant, Adam is committed to creating opportunities, resources, and communities that empower people to thrive—academically, socially, and emotionally.

adam@brightchildbooks.com

Thank you for purchasing one of our resources!
We are continuously working on improving our titles, so we would love your input. If you see anything that needs to be adjusted or have any recommendations, please email us.

adam@BrightChildBooks.com

Also, we would love it if you could take a minute and leave us a positive review on Amazon. Every little bit helps small publishers and authors get their work out there!

Made in the USA
Coppell, TX
04 March 2026